Economics and Marijuana

Do marijuana users cut back on consumption when the price rises? To what degree is marijuana consumption related to drinking and tobacco usage? What would happen if marijuana were legalised and taxed in the same way as alcohol and tobacco? Is marijuana priced in a similar way to other goods?

Economics and Marijuana deals with these and other questions by drawing on a rich set of data concerning the consumption and pricing of marijuana in Australia, a country where the drug has been decriminalised in some, but not all, states. The book applies the economic approach to drugs to analyse consumption, pricing and the economics of legalising the use of marijuana. The result is a fascinating analysis of this widely used, but little understood, illicit drug that provides much needed information and policy advice for a wide range of readers, including economists, policy makers and health professionals.

KENNETH W. CLEMENTS is Winthrop Professor of Economics at the University of Western Australia Business School, Perth.

XUEYAN ZHAO is Associate Professor of Econometrics in the Department of Econometrics and Business Statistics at Monash University, Melbourne.

Economics and Marijuana

Consumption, Pricing and Legalisation

KENNETH W. CLEMENTS
Business School
The University of Western Australia

XUEYAN ZHAO
Department of Econometrics and Business Statistics
and Centre for Health Economics
Faculty of Business and Economics
Monash University

CAMBRIDGE
UNIVERSITY PRESS

Shaftesbury Road, Cambridge CB2 8EA, United Kingdom

One Liberty Plaza, 20th Floor, New York, NY 10006, USA

477 Williamstown Road, Port Melbourne, VIC 3207, Australia

314–321, 3rd Floor, Plot 3, Splendor Forum, Jasola District Centre, New Delhi – 110025, India

103 Penang Road, #05–06/07, Visioncrest Commercial, Singapore 238467

Cambridge University Press is part of Cambridge University Press & Assessment, a department of the University of Cambridge.

We share the University's mission to contribute to society through the pursuit of education, learning and research at the highest international levels of excellence.

www.cambridge.org
Information on this title: www.cambridge.org/9780521884952

First published 2009
First paperback edition 2014

A catalogue record for this publication is available from the British Library

Library of Congress Cataloging-in-Publication data
Clements, Kenneth W., 1950–
    Economics and marijuana : consumption, pricing and legalisation /
    Kenneth W. Clements, Xueyan Zhao.
        p.   cm.
    ISBN 978-0-521-88495-2 (hardback)
    1. Marijuana industry–Australia.   2. Marijuana–Economic aspects–Australia.
    3. Marijuana industry.   4. Marijuana–Economic aspects.
    I. Zhao, Xueyan, 1971–   II. Title.
    HD9019.M382A873 2009
    338.1´33790994–dc22
    2009031394

ISBN   978-0-521-88495-2   Hardback
ISBN   978-1-107-42147-9   Paperback

To my family – KWC
To Glyn, Aiden and Liam – XZ

Contents

List of figures   *page* viii

List of tables   xi

About the authors and contributor   xv

Acknowledgements   xvi

1   Introduction   1

2   Microeconometric evidence on marijuana
    consumption   15

3   The pricing of marijuana   67

4   More on the economic determinants of consumption   145

5   Decriminalising and legalising marijuana   235

6   Are Australians unique?   350

7   Perspectives   406

Index   418

Figures

2.1 Participation rates over time: marijuana,
    tobacco and alcohol   *page* 22
2.2 Participation rates for 2004   22
2.3 Observed marijuana participation rates   25
2.4 Observed participation rates for all drugs   28
2.5 Predicted participation probabilities for
    sample means   32
2.6 Marginal effects on conditional and
    unconditional probabilities   43
2.7 Frequency of marijuana consumption   47
3.1 Regional dispersion of prices and incomes   78
3.2 Marijuana and housing prices   79
3.3 Marijuana price index   80
3.4 Relative prices of marijuana   81
3.5 Marijuana and commodity relative price
    changes   81
3.6 Thirty more relative price changes   82
3.7 Relationship between unexpected arrests
    and infringement notices   89
3.8 Ounce and gram unit prices of marijuana   91
3.9 The volumes of two cubes   92
3.10 Histogram of discount for bulk buying of
    marijuana   95
3.11 Histogram of discount elasticities for
    marijuana   98
3.12 Discount elasticities for heroin   99
3.13 Discount elasticities for illicit drugs   99
3.14 Histograms of ratios of standard deviation
    of prices to standard deviation of size   101
A3.1 Changes in marijuana prices   112
A3.2 Regional differences in marijuana prices   122

A3.3 Three measures of relative difference   129
 4.1 Quantities consumed   156
 4.2 Effects of legalisation and a price decrease
      on marijuana consumption   174
 4.3 Gross and net price elasticities of demand
      for marijuana   177
 4.4 Price elasticities of demand   184
 4.5 Actual and simulated consumption of
      alcoholic beverages and marijuana   194
 5.1 Incidence of tax   240
 5.2 Welfare effects of taxation: no externality   241
 5.3 Welfare effects of taxation: with externality   243
 5.4 Marijuana participation by state   253
 5.5 Participation, deviated from trends, by
      decriminalised state   255
 5.6 More on participation, deviated from
      trends, by decriminalised state   256
 5.7 Price elasticities of demand for marijuana
      with respect to the price of tobacco and
      the degree of complementarity   279
 5.8 Simulated demand elasticities for marijuana   286
 5.9 The marijuana market   294
 5.10 Revenue from taxing marijuana   307
 5.11 Marijuana revenue and the marijuana tax   316
 5.12 Tobacco revenue and the marijuana tax   317
 5.13 Alcohol revenue and the marijuana tax   318
 5.14 Total revenue and the marijuana tax   319
 5.15 Markups for six commodities   325
 5.16 Risk premium and price elasticity of
      demand for marijuana   329
 5.17 Distribution of the risk premium for
      marijuana: (I) Elasticity random   331
 5.18 Distribution of the risk premium of marijuana:
      (II) Elasticity and expenditure random   333
A5.1 Legalising marijuana   338
 6.1 Scatter of food budget share against income   354
 6.2 Unweighted sum of squared residuals   364
 6.3 The geometry of drinking: two journeys   378

6.4 Drinking regions   379
6.5 Drinking patterns in 44 countries   381
6.6 Alcohol entropies in 44 countries,
       average 1997–2006   385
6.7 Quantity of alcoholic beverages consumed,
       average 1997–2006   390
6.8 Changes in the quantity of alcoholic
       beverages consumed, average 1997–2006   391
6.9 Relative price change in alcoholic beverages,
       average 1997–2006   394
7.1 Decriminalisation and the marijuana market   409
7.2 The incidence of decriminalisation   409
7.3 Sellers gain more when supply is less elastic   410
7.4 Supply chain for drugs   415
7.5 Globalisation and drugs   415

Tables

2.1 Participation rates: proportion of the
population aged 14 years and over   *page* 21

2.2 Participation rates for marijuana and
other drugs   24

2.3 Coefficients and marginal effects on the participation
probability for marijuana   31

2.4 Summary sample statistics for participation
in tobacco, alcohol and marijuana   34

2.5 Estimated conditional and unconditional
participation probabilities   34

2.6 Summary sample statistics for participation
in marijuana, cocaine and heroin   35

2.7 Estimated conditional and unconditional
participation probabilities   35

2.8 Cross-drug correlation coefficients of error terms   38

2.9 Predicted probabilities for two trivariate probit
models   40

2.10 Marginal effects on selected probabilities for
marijuana   42

2.11 Price elasticity for conditional and
unconditional participation probabilities   44

2.12 Level of marijuana consumption by group   46

2.13 Results for the sequential model of
marijuana consumption   50

2.14 Estimated coefficients: OP versus ZIOPC   56

2.15 Marginal effects of OP vs. ZIOPC:
Non-participation and zero consumption   58

2.16 Marginal effects of OP vs. ZIOPC: Levels
of consumption   60

3.1 Marijuana prices: leaf   71

3.2   Marijuana prices: heads   72
3.3   Estimated regional effects for marijuana prices,
      income and house prices   75
3.4   Infringement notices for minor cannabis offences   85
3.5   Arrests and prosecutions for marijuana offences   86
3.6   Estimates of penalty model   88
3.7   Discount elasticities for groceries   98
A3.1 Marijuana prices: leaf, with holes   107
A3.2 Marijuana prices: heads, with holes   108
A3.3 Population data   109
A3.4 Marijuana prices   109
A3.5 Indexes of marijuana prices   111
A3.6 Relative prices of marijuana   113
A3.7 Marijuana price log-changes   114
A3.8 Regional differences in marijuana prices   116
A3.9 Changes in relative prices of 24 commodities   124
A3.10 Changes in relative prices over the 20th century   126
4.1   Price elasticities of demand for marijuana   148
4.2   Marijuana consumption in Australia   150
4.3   Estimated number of marijuana users and total
      population   151
4.4   Estimated marijuana consumption by frequency
      of consumption   152
4.5   Estimated marijuana consumption   153
4.6   Estimated expenditure on marijuana   154
4.7   Quantities consumed and prices of alcoholic
      beverages and marijuana   157
4.8   Expenditure on and budget shares of
      alcoholic beverages and marijuana   158
4.9   Log-changes in quantities consumed and prices
      of alcoholic beverages and marijuana   159
4.10 Divisia moments   161
4.11 Relative quantity correlation coefficients   165
4.12 Demand elasticities for alcoholic beverages   168
4.13 Income elasticities, budget shares and marginal
      shares   168
4.14 Price elasticities of demand   170
4.15 Ever used marijuana?   172

4.16 Frequency of marijuana consumption 172
4.17 Percentage change in consumption of marijuana
due to legalisation 173
4.18 Percentage change in consumption of
marijuana due to both legalisation and
a 50 per cent price decrease 175
4.19 Price elasticities of demand for marijuana 176
4.20 Price elasticities of demand for marijuana
for more frequent users 178
4.21 The effect of marijuana legalisation and
a price fall on alcohol consumption 180
4.22 Price elasticities of demand for selected products 182
4.23 More price elasticities of demand 190
4.24 Data for simulation 192
4.25 Counter-factual quantities consumed of
alcoholic beverages and marijuana 192
A4.1 Per capita alcohol consumption and price indexes 200
A4.2 Population, total consumption expenditure
and expenditure on alcoholic beverages 201
A4.3 Average weekly household expenditure on
alcoholic beverages 201
A4.4 Per capita expenditures on alcoholic beverages 202
A4.5 Prices of alcoholic beverages 202
A4.6 Summary of differential approach 221
5.1 Possible reasons for prohibition of drugs 246
5.2 Australian laws for minor cannabis offences 251
5.3 Estimated decriminalisation effects in Australia 259
5.4 Baseline data for vice demand 270
5.5 First specification of baseline price
responsiveness of demand 274
5.6 Second specification of baseline price
responsiveness of demand 278
5.7 Stochastic specification of data and demand
coefficients 281
5.8 Summary of demand elasticities 284
5.9 Taxation and consumption of vice 287
5.10 Simulations of vice consumption and taxation
revenue 288

5.11 Consumption of marijuana, tobacco and
alcohol when marijuana is legalised and taxed — 296
5.12 Revenue from legalising and taxing marijuana — 308
5.13 Summary of price changes, tax proceeds and
consumption changes — 314
5.14 Tobacco prices — 322
5.15 Marijuana and tobacco prices and the
apparent risk premium for marijuana — 323
5.16 Cost components of retail cocaine, 1990 — 328
5.17 Probability of the risk premium for marijuana — 332
A5.1 Vice expenditure and total consumption — 336
A5.2 Sensitivity of tax proceeds and consumption
changes — 339
6.1 Affluence and food in 42 countries in 2002 — 353
6.2 Matrix of differences in food budget shares
for 42 countries — 355
6.3 Consumption data for rich and poor countries — 357
6.4 Demand elasticities for rich and poor countries — 359
6.5 Squared residuals from the demand equations — 360
6.6 Sum of squared residuals from the demand
equations — 361
6.7 Sum of squared residuals with the same
coefficients for both country groups — 363
6.8 Further sums of squared residuals from the
demand equations — 366
6.9 Quality of budget share predictions in OECD
countries and Australian states — 368
6.10 Own-price elasticity of demand for alcoholic
beverages in ten countries — 372
6.11 Alcohol budget shares, average 1997–2006 — 375
6.12 Dispersion of budget shares — 377
6.13 Alcohol entropies, 1997–2006 — 382
6.14 Quantity of alcoholic beverages consumed,
average 1997–2006 — 387
6.15 Price of alcoholic beverages, average 1997–2006 — 392
A6.1 Alternative definitions of rich and poor countries — 396

About the authors and contributor

KENNETH W. CLEMENTS has been at the University of Western Australia since 1981 as Winthrop Professor of Economics. He is a generalist economist with interests in international finance, monetary economics, index numbers and the economics of drugs. His research has been supported by a series of grants from the Australian Research Council and he has published recently in journals such as the *Journal of Business, Journal of International Money and Finance, Economics Letters* and *International Statistical Review*. He is a fellow of the Academy of Social Sciences in Australia and in 2008 received a UWA Award for Excellence in Teaching (Postgraduate Supervision).

XUEYAN ZHAO is Associate Professor of Econometrics with the Department of Econometrics and Business Statistics at Monash University in Melbourne, Australia. Her current research interests are in the area of discrete and limited dependent variable models and the analysis of micro-unit data, with research projects in health, recreational drugs, labour and agricultural economics funded by the Australian Research Council. She has published in journals such as the *Journal of Econometrics, Journal of Business and Economic Statistics, American Journal of Agricultural Economics* and *Journal of Health Economics*.

YIHUI LAN is Assistant Professor of Finance at the University of Western Australia. She has published in journals such as *Applied Economics, Resources Policy* and *Journal of Agricultural and Applied Economics*. Her current research interests are exchange rate economics, capital markets research, value-at-risk modelling, futures hedge ratios and the application of wavelet analysis to economics and finance. She has also researched in the areas of stochastic index numbers, resource economics and applied demand analysis.

Acknowledgements

In carrying out our research on economics and marijuana over the course of several years, we have been fortunate in receiving helpful comments, advice and data from a large number of individuals. We would like to acknowledge the help we have received from Kym Anderson, Jon Caulkins, Mert Daryal, James Fogarty, Effie Giaros, Robert Greig, Mark Harris, Mark Hazell, Carol Howard, Yihui Lan, Jean-Baptiste Lesourd, Bill Malcolm, Bob Marks, Keith McLaren, Paul Miller, Gordon Mills, Rosalie Pacula, Don Poskitt, Alan Powell, Ye Qiang, Preety Ramful, Tom Rohling, David Sapsford, Steven Schilizzi, Michael Schneider, Antony Selvanathan, Saroja Selvanathan, Raymond da Silva Rosa, Larry Sjaastad, Jan Smith, Greg Swensen, MoonJoong Tcha, Gerard Tellis, Lester Telser, Darrell Turkington, George Verikios, Don Weatherburn, Glyn Wittwer, David Wesney, Jenny Williams and Paul Williams. Almost needless to say, these individuals do not necessarily agree with our analysis and they should not be held responsible for any errors.

We have also enjoyed working on this project with a number of excellent research assistants: Andrew Ainsworth, Renae Bothe, Germaine Chin, Joan Coffey, Mei Han, Zhao Hao, Ze Min Hu, Callum Jones, Emily Liang, Maxwell Maesepp, Vitaly Pershin, Jiawei Si, Lisa Soh, Kate Stephanou, Katherine Taylor, Clare Yu, Patricia Wang, Lukas Weber and Robin Wong. Earlier versions of this research were presented at the Australian Conference of Economists, La Trobe University, 1999; the Annual Conference of the Australian Agricultural and Resource Economics Society, Fremantle, 2003; the Australian Conference of Economists, University of Sydney, 2004; the Workshop on the Economics of Alcohol, Tobacco and Illicit Drugs, organised by Turning Point Alcohol and Drug Centre, Melbourne, and the Melbourne University Centre for Microeconometrics, 2005; the ANU/UWA PhD Conference in Economics and Business, The University of Western Australia, 2005; The Econometric Society European

Meeting, Budapest, 2007; the CESifo Venice Summer Institute 2008 on "Illicit Trade and Globalisation", Venice International University, 2008; and seminars and lectures at Curtin University of Technology, La Trobe University, The University of Western Australia and Sung Kyun Kwan University. While we have been unable to agree with everyone at these presentations, we thank participants for their valuable encouragement, feedback and comments.

We have also benefited from the helpful guidance and suggestions from Chris Harrison, Publishing Director (Social Sciences), Cambridge University Press and anonymous readers who commented on earlier versions of this material. We also acknowledge the editorial services of International Science Editing, as well as the support of the Cambridge University Press team, Sarah Coakley, Aya Kelly, Helen Reidy and Eleni Stephanou of the Business School, The University of Western Australia.

Chapter 2 of this book has drawn material from two previously published papers: X. Zhao and M. Harris (2004), "Demand for marijuana, alcohol and tobacco: participation levels of consumption, and cross-equation correlations", *Economic Record* **80**, 394–410 and P. Ramful and X. Zhao (2009), "Demand for marijuana, cocaine and heroin in Australia: a multivariate probit approach", *Applied Economics* **41**, 481–96. Chapters 3 and 4 of this book draw in part on two previously published papers: K. W. Clements (2004), "Three faces about marijuana prices", *Australian Journal of Agricultural and Resource Economics* **48**, 271–300 and K. W. Clements (2006), "Pricing and packaging: the case of marijuana", *Journal of Business* **79**, 2019–44. Part of Chapter 4 is also based on K. W. Clements (2008), "Price elasticities of demand are minus one-half", *Economics Letters* **99**, 490–93 and K. W. Clements and M. Daryal (2005), "The economics of marijuana consumption", Chapter 10 in *The demand for alcohol, tobacco and marijuana: international evidence*, S. Selvanathan and E. A. Selvanathan (eds), Aldershot: Ashgate, pp. 243–67. Chapter 6 in part draws on K. W. Clements and Y. Qiang (2003), "The economics of global consumption patterns", *Journal of Agricultural and Applied Economics Supplement* **35**, 21–37. We acknowledge the willingness of these journals and the publisher of the above book to let us use that material and thank referees and editors for helpful comments on earlier versions. The front cover picture is copyright of *Newspix/Matt Nettheim*.

This research was financed in part by the Business School, The University of Western Australia, and the Australian Research

Council. Kenneth Clements would additionally like to acknowledge the productive research environment provided by the Business School that greatly facilitated this research. Xueyan Zhao would also wish to thank her colleagues at the Department of Econometrics and Business Statistics, Monash University for stimulating conversations and friendly support.

1 | *Introduction*

KENNETH W. CLEMENTS

Anecdotally, marijuana is a popular product. But it is not a product that is well understood from an economic perspective. What is the size of the marijuana industry? Is it a substitute or a complement for other drugs such as alcohol and tobacco? How sensitive is consumption to changes in its price? By how much would marijuana prices and consumption change if it were decriminalised further and/or legalised? How much tax revenue could be raised from marijuana? These are some of the major issues in the economic analysis of marijuana. In this book we consider in detail these and other economic dimensions of the marijuana industry, including:

- The nature of consumers of the product and how the consumption of marijuana and other drugs are interrelated.
- Intriguing patterns in prices, including quantity discounts, regional disparities in prices and the extent to which marijuana prices have fallen over time.
- The likely size of the industry.
- The price sensitivity of consumption of marijuana, cocaine, heroin, beer, wine, spirits and tobacco.
- The possible implications of decriminalising or legalising marijuana, including the amount of revenue that the government could raise by subjecting it to taxation in a manner similar to that for tobacco and alcohol.

1.1 Economic dimensions of marijuana

The marijuana industry is of interest to economists for several reasons. First, although official data are lacking, available estimates indicate that the industry is of substantial size. For example, approximately one-third of all Australians admit to having tried marijuana and a much larger proportion of young people have done so (see National

Drug Strategy Household Survey, 2005, for details). In addition, expenditure on marijuana in Australia is estimated to be about three-quarters of that on beer and twice wine sales, as discussed in Chapter 4. Although these estimates are subject to considerable uncertainties, the indications are that the marijuana sector is of sufficient size to merit careful investigation.

A second reason why marijuana is of economic interest is that it forms the basis of appealing teaching material, possibly because young people tend to be more intensive users, and because its illicit nature endows marijuana with some form of edgy mystique that captures the imagination of students. Marijuana provides good examples for lively classroom discussions of demand analysis (what are the substitutes for marijuana and what is its price elasticity of demand?), the demand and supply model (the effects of marijuana legalisation on the price and quantity transacted), the role of technological change in lowering the price to consumers (the switch to hydroponic techniques for growing marijuana in the 1990s) and the economics of packaging (why are there substantial discounts for bulk purchases of marijuana?).

A third reason for interest in marijuana relates to public finance issues. As its production and consumption are illegal, marijuana escapes the tax net. Can producers of alcoholic beverages – likely substitutes for marijuana – legitimately argue that on the basis of competitive neutrality, marijuana should be legalised and taxed in a similar manner? Would such a policy be a more effective way to control marijuana consumption than the current prohibition approach? If so, exactly how should marijuana be taxed? The possibilities include a uniform rate applied to marijuana and alcohol, Ramsey optimal taxes that balance revenue requirements with deadweight losses and the use of taxes to correct for externalities in consumption. There are also public policy issues associated with marijuana. Exactly what are the health consequences of marijuana use and to what extent are these genuine external effects that justify policy intervention? What is the case for regulating consumption and what are the least-cost policy instruments?

Finally, the illicit nature of marijuana presents both intriguing challenges and opportunities for research into underground markets. As producers and consumers have incentives to conceal their activities, information on the marijuana industry is not readily available and has to be compiled using unconventional and indirect methods and sources. The criminal aspect of marijuana opens up research possibilities regarding the impact of expected penalties on consumption, issues of asymmetric information about product quality, risk-return tradeoffs, etc. If conventional microeconomic analysis can be applied to marijuana, a good that is not only illicit but also has mind-altering effects on users, then the economic analysis of marijuana can be viewed as a form of stress-testing of theory.

Research on the workings of drug markets is also of professional interest to groups other than economists. These groups include researchers in public policy (who may be interested in questions such as whether drugs should be legalised and taxed like tobacco and alcohol), law enforcement agencies (how should scarce enforcement resources be allocated?), health professionals (which type of individual is most at risk of abusing drugs?) and government organisations (who are the most vulnerable socioeconomic groups and what are the implications for effective public health campaigns of the relationships between marijuana consumption and other legal and illegal drugs?). Another reason for interest is that there seems to be a distinct change in society's attitudes towards illicit drugs in a number of countries. A more tolerant approach to the use of some drugs is now being reflected in the workings of the police, the courts and parliament in a number of jurisdictions. For example, in the Australian context Wodak and Cooney (2004) argue that:

[T]he community has gradually come to accept that some form of regulation is the least worst arrangement for unreducible appetites the majority disdain, but a substantial minority desire, such as gambling and prostitution. It is time to seriously consider the hitherto unthinkable: the least worst arrangement for cannabis is taxation and regulation.

This book provides an economic perspective on the marijuana industry and in a number of ways compares and contrasts economic characteristics of marijuana with those of other products. This comparison involves the following elements:

- The identification of individual socioeconomic and demographic characteristics of marijuana users and a comparison with those of users of other legal and illegal drugs.
- A comparison of consumption patterns of marijuana with those of alcohol, tobacco and other drugs to reveal interesting similarities and differences. For example, it is likely that marijuana and alcohol are substitutes in consumption, so that policies that serve to reduce

marijuana use by increasing its price (such as a police crackdown on production) would be likely to encourage drinking. A further example is that, to a first approximation at least, the price sensitivity of the demand for marijuana is the same as that for beer, wine and spirits – each of these products has a price elasticity of approximately minus one-half.

- An analysis of marijuana prices in different regions of Australia reveals a surprising degree of dispersion that is much greater than that of regional incomes, but of the same order as the dispersion of house prices. This finding points to the importance of local processing and distribution costs, in addition to the cost of the raw product, in determining marijuana prices.

- Over time, the relative price of marijuana has decreased substantially, much faster than the prices of many other primary products, which tend to fall at approximately 1–2 per cent per annum on average. We argue that this decrease in prices is likely to be due to productivity improvements in growing marijuana (associated with the adoption of hydroponic techniques) and/or a softening of community attitudes to marijuana use that has led to lower risk of incurring substantial criminal penalties.

- The unit price of marijuana is as much as 50 per cent lower when purchased in the form of an ounce rather than a gram. We show that once this discount is formulated in a manner that is comparable across widely different types of products, it is more or less the same as that available for grocery products, as well as for other illicit drugs. This leads to the elegantly simple pricing rule that a 10 per cent increase in the package size of a product is associated with a 2.5 per cent decrease in the unit price. The fact that such a pricing rule applies to a number of products in addition to marijuana seems to reflect the same basic economic forces at work in a variety of situations.

Thus, although marijuana does have some unique characteristics associated with its illicit status, these do not seem to be sufficient to put the product in a special category for the purposes of economic analysis.

1.2 The economic approach to drugs

The approach to marijuana described above is part of a wider body of research dealing with the operation of drug markets and how economics contributes to an understanding of their workings. In broad outline, such research starts with the idea that many of the conventional tools of economic analysis can be applied to drugs, so that the commodity does not constitute a special case, notwithstanding that they can have mind-altering effects on consumers and be addictive. As an example, the study by Clements and Johnson (1983) was one of the first to apply the theory of the utility-maximising consumer to the demand for beer, wine and spirits. They tested the three key predictions of consumption theory. First, that the demand for each beverage is negatively related to its price, which is known as the law of demand, or that demand curves slope down. Second, that an equiproportional change in all nominal prices and total expenditure has no impact on the demand for each of the beverages, a condition known as demand homogeneity. Third, that the effect of a one-dollar increase in the price of beverage A on the consumption of beverage B is exactly the same as an identical increase in the price of B on consumption of A, under the condition that real total expenditure on alcohol remains unchanged. This proposition is known as Slutsky symmetry and represents consistency in beverage choice, or rationality associated with utility maximisation. Clements and Johnson find that data from Australia are not inconsistent with these three tenets of consumption theory, a finding that has largely been confirmed for a number of other countries by Selvanathan and Selvanathan (2007), among others.

The papers by Stigler and Becker (1977) and Becker and Murphy (1988) provided a major stimulus to research on the economics of drugs by introducing the concept of rational addiction. According to the search engine Google Scholar, each of these papers has been cited well over 1,000 times. Although imperfect, these citation counts provide some measure of the scholarly influence of this research. Under the Becker–Murphy–Stigler approach, consumption of an addictive good is associated with a stock of consumption capital that enters the utility function to reflect a "learning by doing" process. This stock increases with consumption and depreciates with time, so that current utility depends on past consumption. In Becker and Murphy (1988), the individual's problem is then to choose the consumption path to maximise the present value of utility, appropriately discounted, subject to a resources constraint. Part of the resources constraint involves labour earnings, which are affected by the stock of consumption capital. This formulation operationalises the idea of rational addiction, with the consumer exhibiting forward-looking behaviour and consciously trading off current benefits from using the addictive good today against its future costs. For addictive goods that are harmful, such as tobacco, current consumption decreases future utility and future labour earnings, whereas the opposite is true for beneficial goods such as going to the gym. This intertemporal utility-maximisation problem leads to a rich set of implications, including that consumption of an addictive good responds less to a temporary change in its price, more to a permanent change and can be subject to abrupt cessation (going "cold turkey") and bingeing behaviour, all results of consistent rational choice. In broad terms, Becker and Murphy establish that addictive goods are not incompatible with rational consumer choice.

Over the last decade and a half, as better data on the consumption of illicit drugs and their prices have become available, a number of econometric studies have been conducted on the demand for drugs. These studies typically use large cross-sectional databases that provide information at the individual level on whether or not drugs are used. Among other issues, this body of research is concerned with measuring the price sensitivity of consumption and the effects of decriminalisation of drugs. A useful survey of this literature was carried out by Pacula *et al.* (2001, Section 6.2), while more recently Pacula (2005) reviewed this type of research as it applies to marijuana. Australian research along these lines that deals with marijuana has been conducted in recent years by Cameron and Williams (2001), Ramful (2008), van Ours and Williams (2006), Williams (2004), Williams and Mahmoudi (2004) and Williams and Skeels (2006).

An important concern in the economics of drugs is whether the current approach of declaring certain drugs to be illegal is the most efficient way to control consumption (assuming it needs to be controlled). Simply passing a law is no guarantee that consumption will cease; indeed, the evidence is that underground markets flourish if demand for drugs is sufficiently high. Major issues are the unintended consequences of prohibition such as the criminality, corruption, violence, disrespect for the law and uncertain product quality associated with underground drug markets. Why not simply legalise, say, marijuana and then control its consumption by taxing it in the same way as alcoholic beverages and tobacco are taxed? This would have the effect of transferring to the government substantial resources that would otherwise be captured by criminals and the government could then either lower other taxes and/or carry out valuable public expenditure programmes.

One of the first major economists to support the legalisation of drugs was Friedman (1972), who wrote:

> On ethical grounds, do we have the right to use the machinery of government to prevent an individual from becoming an alcoholic or a drug addict? For children, almost everyone would answer at least a qualified yes. But for responsible adults, I, for one, would answer no. Reason with the potential addict, yes. Tell him the consequences, yes. Pray for and with him, yes. But I believe we have no right to use force, directly or indirectly, to prevent a fellow man from committing suicide, let alone from drinking alcohol or taking drugs. I readily grant that the ethical issue is difficult and that men of goodwill may well disagree. Fortunately, we need not resolve the ethical issue to agree on policy. *Prohibition is an attempted cure that makes matters worse – for both the addict and the rest of us.* Hence, even if you regard present policy towards drugs as ethically justified, considerations of expediency make that policy most unwise. [Friedman's emphasis.]

In a similar vein, Becker (2005) argues that:

> the legalisation of drugs combined with an excise tax on consumption would be a far cheaper and more effective way to reduce drug use. Instead of a war [on drugs], one could have, for example, a 200 per cent tax on the legal use of drugs by all adults – consumption by, say, persons under age 18 would still be illegal. That would reduce consumption in the same way as the present war . . .

In a recent paper, Becker *et al.* (2006) analyse ways to reduce the consumption of a particular good, and compare the effects of a ban that makes it illegal with an excise tax. Their comparison emphasises the role of enforcement costs when the good is illegal; greater enforcement leads to higher costs incurred by producers of the illegal good, which, if the market is competitive, are passed onto consumers in the form of higher prices. Thus, greater enforcement activities by the government lead to an increase in prices and a decrease in the quantity consumed but an increase in total outlay on the good if demand is inelastic, as is likely to be the case for drugs. If drug production is a competitive industry and takes place under conditions of constant costs, producers earn no rents and the total outlay by consumers also represents the value of resources devoted to the production of drugs. This means that a crackdown on drugs resulting from greater enforcement would lead to the surprising result of an increase in the resources devoted to supplying drugs, even though consumption decreases. These additional resources flow into the drugs industry as producers incur costs to avoid detection and punishment. If drugs were legalised and taxed, the government would receive taxation revenue, most of which is not a net cost to the economy but a transfer from drug users to the government. However, under prohibition, what would have been tax proceeds become a real resource cost to the economy as a whole in the form of the higher costs incurred by drug producers. Becker *et al.* thus establish that prohibition is an expensive policy compared with the tax option, a result that holds under fairly general conditions.

This work has profound implications for understanding the workings of drug markets and public policy, which Becker *et al.* (2006) describe in the following terms:

> This analysis in particular helps us understand why the war on drugs has been so difficult to win, why international drug traffickers command resources to corrupt some governments and thwart extensive efforts to stamp out production by the most powerful nation, and why efforts to reduce the supply of drugs lead to violence and greater power to street gangs and drug cartels. To a large extent, the answer lies in the basic theory of enforcement developed in this paper and the great increase in costs of production from punishing suppliers to fight this war. Suppliers who avoid detection make huge profits, which provides them with resources to corrupt officials and gives them incentives even to kill law enforcement officers and competitors.

Calls for decriminalisation/legalisation of drugs have also come from a number of others, such as Buiter (2007), *The Economist* magazine (2001), Miron and Zwiebel (1995), Nadelmann (1988) and Wodak and Cooney (2004), to mention just a few. It still has to be acknowledged that drug legalisation would entail its own costs. As consumption would likely increase following legalisation, there would be higher health costs to users and costs inflicted on third parties caused by driving while under the influence of drugs and other anti-social behaviour. The case for legalisation relies on these costs being less than those of the unintended consequences of prohibition mentioned above.

1.3 Overview of the book

The book contains seven chapters and below we briefly describe the contents of the subsequent chapters.

Chapter 2: Microeconometric evidence on marijuana consumption. This chapter presents an extensive discussion of factors relating to individuals' consumption of marijuana and other drugs (both legal and illegal), using the rich unit-record data from the Australian National Drug Strategy Household Surveys. It highlights recent trends in consumption, the socioeconomic and demographic characteristics of users, the effects of own and related-drug prices, and the inter-relationships between marijuana and other drugs via observable and unobservable factors. As individual-level survey data provide information on consumption in the form of binary participation status or discrete levels, the typical econometric strategy involves the use of models with discrete dependent variables. This leads to a discussion of a collection of modern econometric models for the analysis of marijuana consumption. The chapter covers the following issues:

- A probit model with a binary dependent variable is used to study the probability of marijuana participation, in particular its relationship with individual characteristics, own and cross-drug prices, and whether or not marijuana has been decriminalised.
- Anecdotal evidence indicates that users of one drug tend to simultaneously consume other drugs. We thus use multivariate probit models to study marijuana and other legal and illegal drugs. Cross-drug correlations via unobservable factors are important pieces of information that can be used in investigating drug policies in a multi-drug framework and in contributing to discussion of the "gateway" hypothesis, whereby users move from softer to harder drugs.
- A two-part sequential model with an ordered probit is used to study the factors affecting the probability of different levels of consumption. This allows for differentiation of occasional and heavy users and identification of policy implications.
- Other econometric issues can be particularly important for drug data. One special feature of representative surveys of the whole population is that the majority of people are not current drug users. In other words, these databases contain a large number of zeros corresponding to the response "no, I do not use drugs". We use a zero-inflated ordered probit model to separate two types of zero

observations: those corresponding to genuine non-participants for health or legal concerns and those representing zero-consumption participants who respond to economic factors such as price and income. We show that ignoring this difference in the nature of the zeros could result in erroneous policy implications.

Chapter 3: The pricing of marijuana. This chapter first documents the unique data on marijuana prices obtained from the Australian Bureau of Criminal Intelligence. These data are used as a basis to construct index numbers of marijuana prices over time, regions and major product types. Analysis of the prices reveals: (i) a large decrease in prices over the last decade, which we argue is likely to be due to the adoption of hydroponic production techniques and/or more relaxed community attitudes towards marijuana; (ii) an intriguing pattern of regional prices, whereby Australia can be conveniently divided into three regions according to the cost of marijuana; and (iii) marijuana seems to be subject to pricing principles that are very similar to those observed for legal products such as groceries. Using new methods, we apply the economic theory of packaging to understand the existence of substantial quantity discounts that are available when marijuana is purchased in large quantities.

Chapter 4: More on the economic determinants of consumption. This chapter deals with measurement of the price sensitivity of drug consumption as summarised by the price elasticity. It draws a distinction between what is known as participation elasticity, a concept that features prominently in the literature (and used in Chapter 2) when there are only binary consumption data available, and conventional elasticity, which pertains to the price sensitivity of the actual volume of consumption. We present time-series estimates of the volume of marijuana consumption in Australia and use a system-wide approach to estimate demand functions for marijuana and the closely related products beer, wine and spirits. This leads to a matrix of own- and cross-price demand elasticities for these four commodities. Other material in this chapter includes index numbers of consumption and the identification of a useful rule of thumb according to which own-price elasticities are equal to minus one-half. The underlying technical material on the economic theory of the utility-maximising consumer is presented in an appendix, which means that the chapter is self-contained.

Chapter 5: Decriminalising and legalising marijuana. From an economic perspective, the banning of marijuana is equivalent to the imposition of a prohibitive tax. This chapter thus starts with a discussion of the economics of taxation and the experience with prohibition. This is followed by an analysis of the impact of the decriminalisation of marijuana on its consumption. This material includes details of the Australian decriminalisation experience and provides a survey of previous studies of the effects of decriminalisation on consumption in the US and Australia. The chapter also considers the radical policy of legalising marijuana and then taxing it in the same way as alcohol and tobacco. We investigate the likely government revenue that could be raised by taxing marijuana, making proper allowance for the indirect effects stemming from the pre-existing taxes on alcohol and tobacco. A key feature of this chapter is the introduction of new measures of uncertainty of the findings. This uncertainty reflects open questions about the quality of the data and the precise values of key parameters (such as the price elasticities) that underlie the results.

Chapter 6: Are Australians unique? As much of the analysis of the book deals with the situation in Australia, in Chapter 6 we discuss the extent to which the results are likely to be transferable to other countries. We use cross-country evidence to establish that consumer tastes are more similar than different. Although no guarantees are possible, this finding provides some basis for believing that the earlier chapters identify certain economic laws that have wide applicability and implications for other countries.

Chapter 7: Perspectives. This chapter provides some broader perspectives by discussing two prospective areas of future research in the economics of drugs.

Before concluding this chapter, a word on the scope of the book. The study of marijuana is multidisciplinary, involving law, medicine, psychiatry, public health and social policy, as well as economics. To keep things manageable, and applying the principle of comparative advantage, we restrict our attention to economic dimensions of marijuana. There are four recent books dealing with some of the broader issues of marijuana and drugs in general. First, Chaloupka *et al.* (1999) present econometric approaches and behavioural research methods involving experiments to understand the use of alcohol, tobacco and illicit drugs, and some related topics. Second, MacCoun and Reuter (2001) use an interdisciplinary, public policy approach to the question of drug control. The book discusses the philosophical basis for the regulation of behaviour/products and deals mostly with drugs in the US. The experience with drugs in Europe, as well as other vices such as gambling, prostitution, alcohol and tobacco consumption, is also discussed by MacCoun and Reuter, as is the uncertainty of the consequences of alternative regulatory regimes. Third, the volume edited by Gruber (2001) contains economic perspectives on a wide range of risky activities, including smoking, drinking, driving, sex and crime, in addition to drug-taking. It contains a substantial chapter by Pacula et al. (2001) on "Marijuana and youth" which focuses on the determinants of marijuana demand. Fourth, a valuable reference book devoted to cannabis is by Hall and Pacula (2003), which is an extensive review of the existing literature relating to health policy, public health and legal issues. The health and behavioural effects of cannabis use receive particular emphasis, and economic issues are discussed in chapters on "The benefits of cannabis use", "The impact of prohibition on cannabis use" and "The monetary cost of enforcing prohibition", which includes material on tax revenue that is foregone when cannabis escapes the tax net.

Other major publications in this area that have appeared recently include the special issue of De Economist on the Economics of illicit drugs (van Ours and Pudney, 2006), the parliamentary inquiries in both New Zealand and the UK (New Zealand House of Representatives Health Committee, 2003, United Kingdom House of Commons Science and Technology Committee, 2006) and the Statutory Review of the Cannabis Control Act in Western Australia (Western Australian Drug and Alcohol Office, 2007).

References

Becker, G. S. (2005). "The failure of the war on drugs." The Becker-Posner Blog, March 20. Available at www.becker-posner-blog.com/archives/2005/03/.

Becker, G. S. and Murphy, K. M. (1988). "A theory of rational addiction." Journal of Political Economy 96, 675–700.

Becker, G. S., Murphy, K. M. and Grossman, M. (2006). "The market for illegal goods: the case of drugs." Journal of Political Economy 114, 38–60.

Buiter, W. (2007). "Legalise drugs to beat terrorists." Financial Times, August 7.

Cameron, L. and Williams, J. (2001). "Cannabis, alcohol and cigarettes: substitutes or complements?" *Economic Record* 77, 19–34.

Chaloupka, F. J., Grossman, M., Bickel, W. K. and Saffer, H., eds. (1999). *The economic analysis of substance use and abuse: an integration of econometric and behavioural economic research*. Chicago, IL: The University of Chicago Press.

Clements, K. W. and Johnson, L. W. (1983). "The demand for beer, wine and spirits: a system-wide analysis." *Journal of Business* 56, 273–304.

Friedman, M. (1972). "Prohibition and drugs." *Newsweek*, May 1, p. 104. Reprinted in M. Friedman, *There's no such thing as a free lunch*. LaSalle, IL: Open Court, 1975, pp. 227–9.

Gruber, J., ed. (2001). *Risky behaviour among youths: an economic analysis*. Chicago, IL: The University of Chicago Press.

Hall, W. and Pacula, R. L. (2003). *Cannabis use and dependence: public health and public policy*. Cambridge, UK: Cambridge University Press.

MacCoun, R. J. and Reuter, P. (2001). *Drug war heresies: learning from other vices, times and places*. Cambridge, UK: Cambridge University Press.

Miron, J. A. and Zwiebel, J. (1995). "The economic case against drug prohibition." *Journal of Economic Perspectives* 9, 175–92.

Nadelmann, E. (1988). "The case for legalisation." *The Public Interest* 92, 3–31.

National Drug Strategy Household Survey (2005). Canberra: Social Data Archives, The Australian National University.

New Zealand House of Representatives Health Committee (2003). *Inquiry into the public health strategies related to cannabis use and the most appropriate legal status*. Wellington: New Zealand House of Representatives.

Pacula, R. L. (2005). "Marijuana use and policy: what we know and have yet to learn." *NBER Reporter*, Winter, 22–4.

Pacula, R. L., Grossman, M., Chaloupka, F. J., O'Malley, P. M., Johnston, L. D. and Farrelly, M. C. (2001). "Marijuana and youth." In J. Gruber, ed., *Risky behaviour among youths: an economic analysis*. Chicago, IL: The University of Chicago Press, pp. 271–326.

Ramful, P. (2008). *Recreational drug consumption in Australia: an econometric analysis*. PhD thesis, Department of Econometrics and Business Statistics, Monash University, Australia.

Selvanathan, S. and Selvanathan, E. A. (2007). "Another look at the identical tastes hypothesis on the analysis of cross-country alcohol data." *Empirical Economics* 32, 185–215. .

Stigler, G. J. and Becker, G. S. (1977). "De gustibus non est disputandum." *American Economic Review* 67, 79–90.

The Economist (2001). "The case for legalisation." July 28, 12–13.

United Kingdom House of Commons Science and Technology Committee (2006). *Drug classification: Making a hash of it?* London: United Kingdom House of Commons.

van Ours, J. C. and Pudney, S. (2006). "On the economics of illicit drugs." *De Economist* 154, 483–90.

van Ours, J. C. and Williams, J. (2006). "Why parents worry: initiation into cannabis use by youth and their educational attainment." Unpublished paper, Department of Economics, The University of Melbourne.

Western Australian Drug and Alcohol Office (2007). *Statutory review of Cannabis Control Act 2003. Report to the Minister for Health: Technical report.* Perth, Western Australia: Drug and Alcohol Office.

Williams, J. (2004). "The effects of price and policy on marijuana use: what can be learned from the Australian experience?" *Health Economics* 13, 123–37.

Williams, J. and Mahmoudi, P. (2004). "Economic relationship between alcohol and cannabis revisited." *The Economic Record* 80, 36–48.

Williams, J. and Skeels, C. (2006). "The impact of cannabis use on health." *De Economist* 154, 517–46.

Wodak, A. and Cooney, A. (2004). "Editorial: Should cannabis be taxed and regulated?" *Drug and Alcohol Review* 23, 139–41.

2 | Microeconometric evidence on marijuana consumption

2.1 Introduction

Unlike data on the consumption of legal commodities, those on marijuana consumption are scarce at both micro and macro levels for empirical investigation of consumer behaviour. According to an Australian study (Collins and Lapsley, 2002), illicit drug-related illnesses, deaths and crimes cost approximately AU$6.1 billion in 1998–9 in Australia. As in many developed countries, significant amounts of public funds have been spent by the Australian government on dealing with the consequences of illicit drug abuse and on educational programmes. Much debate has surrounded the use of governmental coercive power in influencing drug consumption through education and legislation.

Crucial to any effective marijuana policy are empirical studies that afford a better understanding of consumer behaviour. For example, who and where are the marijuana users? What proportion of the population is using the drug regularly? What are the socioeconomic and demographic factors that affect an individual's decision to participate in the consumption of marijuana? How does an individual's consumption of marijuana relate to his/her consumption of other legal (such as tobacco and alcohol) and illegal (such as heroin and cocaine) drugs? How do consumers respond to changes in the prices of marijuana and other related drugs? What is the impact on consumption of decriminalisation? And how has Australian consumption of marijuana changed over time? The popularity of marijuana, the size of its underground market, ongoing debate surrounding government policies regarding decriminalisation or legalisation, and the notion of gateway effects of marijuana leading to consumption of harder drugs for the young have all made micro-level research on marijuana consumption worthwhile. Answers to the above questions are invaluable in designing and evaluating marijuana policies and education campaigns within a multiple drug framework.

Nationally representative survey data on Australian individuals' marijuana consumption have been available since 1985 via the Australian National Drug Strategy Household Surveys (NDSHS, 2005). The surveys collect information from the non-institutionalised civilian population aged 14 years and over on drug awareness, attitudes and behaviour. The questions involve alcohol, tobacco, marijuana, heroin, cocaine, speed and other prescription or illegal drugs. The NDSHS is conducted every two to three years and there have been nine surveys since 1985.[2] Australia also has in place reporting systems for illicit drug prices. Two notable sources are the Australian Crime Commission (ACC) and the Illicit Drug Reporting System (IDRS). These systems collect information on illicit drug prices via covert police officers, injecting drug users and other informants, including health professionals, who have regular contacts with illicit drug users. The availability of these data has allowed empirical examination of a range of questions concerning marijuana consumption at the individual consumer level.

There is a body of economic literature that investigates the determinants of illicit drug consumption. Demand for drugs has been considered the result of consumer utility maximisation under budget constraint and is related empirically to drug prices, income and personal socioeconomic and demographic characteristics to account for taste heterogeneity (e.g. Sickles and Taubman, 1991, Grossman and Chaloupka, 1998, Saffer and Chaloupka, 1999). A theory of rational addiction has also been proposed that formulates consumer behaviour in relation to addictive good consumption (Becker and Murphy, 1988), but a scarcity of inter-temporal consumption data often restricts empirical application of the model.

The availability of micro-level data has allowed some econometric studies on marijuana consumption in developed countries such as the US, the UK and Australia. These studies have found significant correlation between observable socioeconomic and demographic characteristics and marijuana use. The lack of price data often hinders empirical estimation of price responsiveness. Where price data are available, they are often not individually specific and estimated price effects vary widely across studies (see, e.g., Saffer and Chaloupka, 1999, Cameron and Williams, 2001, Farrelly *et al.*, 2001, Zhao and Harris, 2004, Ramful and Zhao, 2009). Price elasticities are often reported in terms of participation probability owing to a lack of data on quantities consumed from survey data. The effects of some related drug policies on marijuana consumption have also been investigated (Pacula, 1998a, DiNardo and Lemieux, 2001, Pacula *et al.*, 2003).

In Australia, using data from the NDSHS, several studies have investigated the consumption of marijuana (Cameron and Williams, 2001, Williams, 2004, Zhao and Harris, 2004, Ramful and Zhao, 2009, Ramful, 2008). The demographic characteristics of marijuana users, correlation with the consumption of other recreational drugs, and the effects of decriminalisation policy have been investigated. These studies provide important empirical evidence for Australian marijuana policies and a valuable comparison with similar micro-level studies in the US and the UK. In addition, owing to the absence of published aggregated quantity and price data that are usually available for legal goods, traditional demand analysis at a national level for marijuana becomes difficult. Clements and Daryal (2005) use some inferred data based in part on the NDSHS data to study aggregated demand using a demand-system approach.

Another strand of the literature on marijuana consumption relates to the so-called gateway theory. Anecdotal observations suggest that marijuana is closely related to other legal drugs such as tobacco and alcohol, as well as to illegal drugs such as heroin and cocaine. For example, marijuana is frequently mixed with tobacco to smoke. Other drugs may also serve similar needs as marijuana does in consumers' minds. As a result, consumption of marijuana needs to be studied in conjunction with that of other drugs to allow for the effects of both observable and unobservable individual characteristics in the study of joint consumption. The economic relationships across different drugs have been studied in terms of cross-price responses (Cameron and Williams, 2001, Zhao and Harris, 2004). In addition, much discussion has focused on the gateway effect between soft and hard drugs (e.g. Pacula, 1998b). It has been postulated that the use of softer drugs may provide a gateway to the use of harder drugs because of psychological or physiological needs, exposure to harder drug dealers or misinformation on the dangers of harder drugs (Pudney, 2003). Empirical evidence has unambiguously pointed out that an individual using one illicit drug is more likely to use other illicit drugs. However, it is very difficult to disentangle this empirically observed correlation into the effects of observable and unobservable individual characteristics and the causality of the gateway effect while controlling for individual heterogeneity. The gateway effect is particularly difficult to estimate without longitudinal dynamic data on the onset and progression of the consumption of various drugs. When such information is available, there is evidence that the apparently strong gateway effects are mostly due to joint effects of unobservable personal characteristics on the use of all illicit drugs rather than to causality (Pudney, 2003, van Ours, 2003).

This chapter reports empirical findings on marijuana consumption by Australian individuals using modern econometric techniques and unit-record data from the Australian NDSHS (2005). Although we cover the Australian empirical literature on marijuana by summarising other published studies, detailed accounts in this chapter relate predominantly to studies in which the author is directly involved. As we concentrate on micro-unit data from the NDSHS, our dependent variables of interest in this chapter are discrete variables and relate to participation status for marijuana consumption or discrete levels of consumption. Demand analysis using a traditional demand-system approach and aggregated level data, with aggregated quantities of consumption as dependent variables, is discussed in Chapter 4. Australia represents a unique situation in terms of marijuana decriminalisation policies at individual state level. A detailed empirical evaluation of this decriminalisation experience in relation to marijuana consumption and a comparison with the US experience is provided in Chapter 5.

The NDSHS data set is described and consumption trends over time for marijuana and related drugs are presented in the next section. The socioeconomic and demographic characteristics of marijuana users and related drug users are presented in Section 2.3, and the marginal effects (MEs) of each of these personal characteristics and drug prices on the probability of marijuana participation are estimated using a probit model. In Section 2.4, the relationships between participation in marijuana use and the consumption of legal (tobacco and alcohol) and illegal (cocaine and heroin) drugs are analysed using two sets of trivariate probit models, allowing both observable and significant unobservable individual characteristics to be accounted for in the joint analysis of multiple drug consumption. Conditional probabilities relating to multiple drugs are analysed, which shed light on some gateway hypotheses relating to marijuana and other drugs. In Section

2.5, we focus on differentiating heavy and occasional users, considering factors related to the probabilities of different levels of marijuana consumption. Finally, the large concentration of zero observations in the data (related to individuals with zero reported marijuana consumption) is the focus of Section 2.6. We model the decision on marijuana consumption as the result of two decisions of participation and levels of consumption. Furthermore, we aim to separate two types of zero observations, corresponding to non-participation and zero consumption, in an analysis of marijuana consumption using a zero-inflated ordered probit model. A summary and some conclusions are presented in the final section.

2.2 Data description and consumption trends

NDSHS data

The econometric analyses reported in this chapter are based on data from the NDSHS (2005). The National Drug Strategy was initiated in 1985 with strong support from the major political parties to confront the impact of licit and illicit drugs on Australian society. The aims are to prevent and reduce the uptake of harmful drug use and minimise the harmful effects of licit and illicit drugs in Australia. It brings together the Australian federal and state governments to ensure that Australia has a nationally coordinated and integrated approach to reducing the substantial harm associated with drug use (AIHW, 2005b).

The NDSHS are nationally representative surveys of the non-institutionalised civilian population aged 14 years and above in Australian households. The surveys collect information on individuals' knowledge, attitudes and behaviour in relation to licit and illicit drugs in Australia. The surveys have been carried out nine times since 1985, with the latest survey being in 2007.[3] Whereas the 1991 survey covered only approximately 3,000 individuals and the 1998 survey involved about 10,000, almost 30,000 people provided information in the 2004 survey. For the first time, the 2004 survey also included respondents of 12 and 13 years of age (AIHW, 2005b).

Households were selected using a multi-stage, stratified area sample design to provide a random sample of households within each geographical stratum. Once a household was contacted, the respondent selected was the person with the next birthday. More rigorous measures have also been put in place in the more recent surveys to ensure confidentiality and to reduce misreporting. In the 2004 surveys, a self-completed drop-and-collect method and a computer-assisted telephone interview method were utilised. The questionnaire has become increasingly comprehensive over the years, with many more questions added to more recent surveys.

Trends for consumption of marijuana and other drugs

According to the NDSHS conducted in 2004 (AIHW, 2005a), 11.3 per cent of the respondents had used marijuana at least once in the previous 12 months. The average age at which Australians first used marijuana was 18.7 years. Approximately one-fifth (20.6 per cent) of the population reported that they were offered or had the opportunity to use marijuana in the 12 months preceding the survey. This availability measure is lower than the 24.2 per cent reported for the 2001 survey. Support for the legalisation of marijuana decreased to 27.0 per cent of the population (30 per cent of males and 24 per cent of females) in 2004 from 29.1 per cent in 2001. Interestingly, support for tougher penalties for the sale or supply of marijuana also decreased slightly from 61.1 per cent in 2001 to 58.2 per cent in 2004.

Table 2.1 lists the participation rates for marijuana use for the five surveys between 1993 and 2004 in comparison with the rates for several other legal and illegal drugs for the same period. The first row of Table 2.1 reveals that approximately one-third of the population reported that they had tried or used marijuana at some time in their lives, and this percentage fluctuated only slightly in the 10 years considered. The results in the second row indicate the prevalence of recent/current use of marijuana. The percentage of Australians who had used marijuana in the preceding 12 months decreased to below 12 per cent of the population for the first time in 2004.

Frequently considered a soft drug, marijuana is the most commonly used substance among illicit drugs. It is evident from Table 2.1 that user participation rates for other illicit drugs are much lower. Non-medical use of speed (methamphetamines/amphetamines) and ecstasy (designer drugs) is next in popularity, with recent participation rates

Table 2.1: *Participation rates: proportion of the population aged 14 years and over*

	1993	1995	1998	2001	2004
Marijuana					
Ever used	34.7	31.1	39.1	33.1	33.6
Recently used[a]	12.7	13.1	17.9	12.9	11.3
Recent use of other drugs					
Meth/amphetamine (speed)[a,b]	2.0	2.1	3.7	3.4	3.2
Ecstasy (designer drugs)[a]	1.2	0.9	2.4	2.9	3.4
Cocaine[a]	0.5	1.0	1.4	1.3	1.0
Heroin[a]	0.2	0.4	0.8	0.2	0.2
Tobacco[a]	n.a.	n.a.	24.9	23.2	20.7
Alcohol[a]	73.0	78.3	80.7	82.4	83.6

[a] Results relate to use in the last 12 months. For tobacco and alcohol, recent use means daily, weekly and less-than-weekly smokers and drinkers, excluding once or twice a year.
[b] For non-medical purposes.
Source: AIHW (2005a).

increasing during the decade considered. Over 3 per cent of Australians aged 14 years or older had used either speed or ecstasy in the previous 12 months according to the 2004 survey. The rates of heroin and cocaine use decreased after the 1998 survey. This may be due in part to the heroin drought experienced in Australia since late 2000, resulting from a shortage in world supply related to opium production in Afghanistan and the crackdown on several major trafficking groups supplying Australia.

Being legal, tobacco and alcohol are the most commonly used recreational drugs. Time trends for participation rates for tobacco and alcohol use are plotted in Figure 2.1 and compared with marijuana use. One in five Australians smoked cigarettes in 2004, and the proportion of tobacco users decreased by a significant 4 percentage points from 1998. However, more Australians reported that they drink alcohol; the proportion of alcohol use has increased considerably over the decade, by 10 percentage points. These trends are in contrast to the slight decreasing trend for marijuana use. Participation rates for all drugs for 2004 are depicted in Figure 2.2.

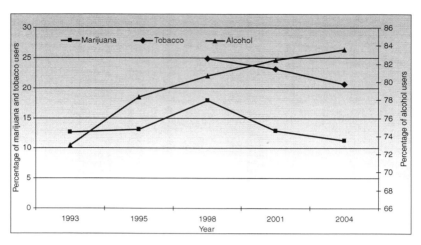

Figure 2.1. Participation rates over time: marijuana, tobacco and alcohol
Source: Table 2.1.

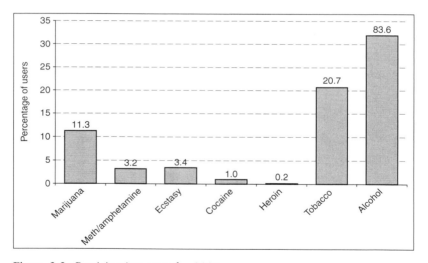

Figure 2.2. Participation rates for 2004
Note: The bar for alcohol is not drawn to scale.
Source: Table 2.1.

all drugs except alcohol. People in capital cities are more likely to use all three illicit drugs and alcohol, but non-capital city residents are slightly more likely to smoke tobacco.

It is also interesting to compare the relationship to income for the five drugs. Whereas marijuana and tobacco are clearly more likely to be associated with low income and alcohol participation is associated with higher income, the observations for cocaine and heroin are less straightforward. For the combined data from 1998 and 2001, participation in heroin use is highest among people with an annual personal income between $40,000 and $49,999 and those with less than $10,000. Cocaine, meanwhile, is associated with people with very high income of more than $60,000 and those on a lower middle income of $20,000–$39,999.

Associations between drug use and work status, education and age are illustrated in Figure 2.4A–C. In terms of work status or main activity, unemployed individuals exhibit the highest participation rate compared with the other three groups for marijuana, tobacco and heroin. Interestingly, the student group has the highest participation rate for cocaine, whereas those who work or are unemployed are similarly ranked (second highest). Different from all other drugs, alcohol use is highest among people who are employed, with the unemployed having the second-highest participation rate.

For education, alcohol use again shows a different pattern to the other drugs in that it is positively related to educational attainment. For all other four drugs, those with year-12 education have the highest participation rates compared with all other groups. Marijuana broadly shows a closer pattern to that of tobacco. Results for cocaine are again interesting in that the highest participation rates are observed among those with year-12 education and tertiary degrees.

Finally, we consider the participation rates by age for all five drugs, as shown in Figure 2.4C. For marijuana and cocaine, participation rates are highest among young people: marijuana use peaks around the late teens to early twenties before steadily decreasing, whereas cocaine peaks over an older and wider age range (early to late twenties). For heroin, age is less important than for the other illegal drugs; the participation rate does not start to decrease until the age of 35 or 40 years. For the legal drugs, participation in alcohol use is steady after the age of 20 and starts to decrease slowly only after the age of 45 years. For tobacco, the highest participation

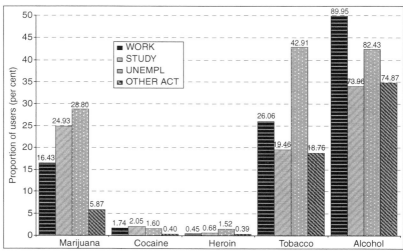

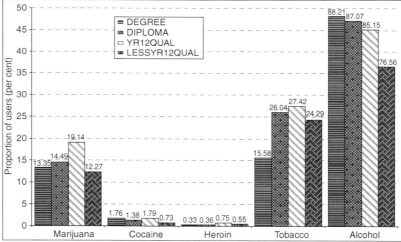

Figure 2.4. Observed participation rates for all drugs
Note: The bars for alcohol are not drawn to scale.
Source: Table 2.2.

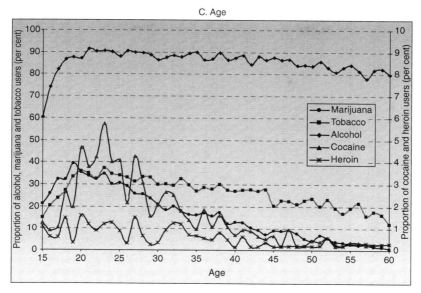

Figure 2.4. (*continued*)

rate is for those aged 20–30 years, with a slight decrease for those aged 30–40 years before a more significant decrease at approximately 45 years.

A probit model for participation in marijuana use

In the above, we have considered some *observed* sample descriptive statistics regarding correlations between marijuana consumption and socioeconomic and demographic factors. However, as personal characteristics are often correlated, descriptive statistics such as those presented in Table 2.2 cannot isolate the effects of individual factors on drug-taking behaviour and can sometimes even be misleading. For example, although we observe significantly higher marijuana use among the unemployed population, it is often the case that such individuals also have a low level of education and lower income, are single and perhaps are of ATSI background. Thus, the significantly higher prevalence observed for the unemployed compared with the rest of the population may be partly due to the effects of these other factors rather than the factor of unemployment alone. Econometric models allow us to attribute the observed difference in participation to individual characteristics.

We use a probit model to study the probability of marijuana use. Consider a probit model in which the latent propensity for marijuana consumption is given by:

$$y^* = x'\beta + e, \qquad (2.1)$$

where x is a vector of explanatory variables with unknown coefficients β and e is an error term representing unobservable factors and following a standard normal distribution. The latent variable y^* is mapped to observable binary variable y via:

$$y = \begin{cases} 1 & \text{if} \quad y^* > 0 (\text{for participation}), \\ 0 & \text{if} \quad y^* \leq 0 (\text{for non-participation}). \end{cases} \qquad (2.2)$$

A probit model is estimated in Ramful and Zhao (2009) that relates the probability of marijuana use to individual socioeconomic and demographic characteristics and drug prices, using pooled data from the two surveys of 1998 and 2001. Table 2.3 summarises the estimated coefficients of the probit model and the marginal effects (MEs) on participation probabilities for marijuana for individual covariates. In the case of a continuous explanatory variable, the ME relates to the actual change in participation probability in response to a unit change in the explanatory variable, whereas in the case of a dummy variable it is the change in participation probability when the dummy variable changes from 0 to 1, all evaluated for the sample means for all explanatory variables.[4]

The MEs of individual explanatory variables in Table 2.3 reveal that, holding all other explanatory variables fixed at the sample means, Australian males are 4.7 per cent more likely to have recently used marijuana than females. All other factors being equal, married or *de facto* partnered individuals have a 6.9 per cent lower probability of using marijuana relative to individuals without a partner. It is interesting to compare this ME of the variable MARRIED with the observed sample statistics in Table 2.2; the *observed* frequency of marijuana use in Table 2.2 for married or partnered individuals is almost 20 per cent lower than for non-partnered individuals when other factors are not controlled.

Comparison of MEs of other explanatory variables in Table 2.3 with the observed sample frequencies by personal attributes in Table 2.2 further illustrates how an econometric model allows isolation of the

Table 2.3: *Coefficients and marginal effects on the participation probability for marijuana*

Variable	Coefficient	Marginal effect
CONSTANT	−16.966 (1.088)**	−2.862 (0.153)**
PRH	0.162 (0.045)**	0.027 (0.009)**
PRC	0.233 (0.051)**	0.039 (0.013)**
PRM	−0.121 (0.079)	−0.020 (0.013)
INCOME	0.038 (0.016)**	0.006 (0.001)**
CAPITAL	0.020 (0.025)	0.003 (0.002)*
YR01	−0.065 (0.032)**	−0.011 (0.006)*
AGE	9.563 (0.555)**	1.614 (0.045)**
AGESQ	−1.550 (0.079)**	−0.261 (0.006)**
MALE	0.279 (0.022)**	0.047 (0.002)**
MARRIED	−0.410 (0.025)**	−0.069 (0.004)**
WORK	−0.047 (0.037)	−0.008 (0.005)*
STUDY	−0.051 (0.046)	−0.009 (0.009)
UNEMP	0.290 (0.058)**	0.049 (0.004)**
YOUNGKIDS	−0.106 (0.031)**	−0.018 (0.005)**
ATSI	0.208 (0.072)**	0.035 (0.018)*
DEGREE	−0.080 (0.034)**	−0.013 (0.005)**
DIPLOMA	0.033 (0.031)	0.006 (0.004)
YR12	0.008 (0.032)	0.001 (0.004)
SIN-PARENT	0.133 (0.038)**	0.023 (0.010)**

Notes: Standard errors in parentheses. Significance is indicated at the *10% and **5% levels. For each continuous explanatory variable, the marginal effect relates to the actual change in participation probability in response to a unit change in the explanatory variable, whereas for a dummy variable it represents the change in probability when the dummy variable changes from 0 to 1, all evaluated for sample means for all explanatory variables.
Source: Ramful and Zhao (2009).

partial effects of individual factors while holding other factors fixed. ATSI background has an ME of 3.5 per cent higher participation probability than non-ATSI, and single parents are 2.3 per cent more likely to use marijuana than others. These MEs are significantly lower than the observed differences in the sample statistics in Table 2.2. In terms of main occupation, only unemployment has a significantly non-zero ME (4.9 per cent lower probability) relative to the base group of retired people and homemakers, whereas the sample statistics reveal

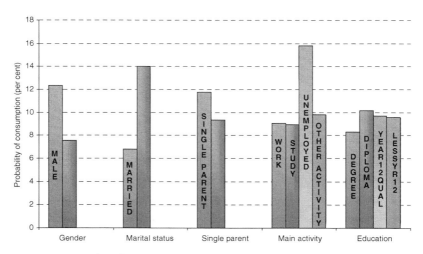

Figure 2.5. Predicted participation probabilities for sample means
Source: Ramful and Zhao (2009).

that the employed, students and unemployed have at least 10 per cent higher observed probability than the base group. Similarly for educational attainment, once other factors are held equal, only a tertiary degree has a significant effect on decreasing the participation probability (1.3 per cent lower) compared with the base group (less than year-12 education), whereas the observed probabilities reveal that the middle two groups (year-12 and diploma education) exhibit the highest disparities from the base group. In fact, we observed a 1 per cent higher participation rate for degree holders compared with the base group, but the econometric model reveals that the ME of tertiary education is significant and negative once other factors are controlled.

To further illustrate the partial effects of individual explanatory variables, the predicted probability results by various attributes when all other factors are controlled at the sample means are presented in Figure 2.5. Comparison of the bars in Figure 2.5 with those in Figure 2.1 for the observed sample frequencies reveals clear differences. Finally, the MEs of drug prices indicate that marijuana use negatively responds to its own price and that the other two illicit drugs act as substitutes. Although it is not statistically significant at the 5 per cent level, at a 7 per cent significance level there is evidence that a 10 per cent increase in marijuana price will result in a 0.20 per cent (or 0.002) decrease in the participation probability.

2.4 Relationship to other drugs: multi-drug participation analysis

Observed cross-drug correlation

Anecdotal evidence indicates that consumption of marijuana is closely related to the consumption of other drugs. In this section we quantify the intrinsic relationships between marijuana consumption and that of other legal and illegal recreational drugs as a function of both observable and unobservable factors. We first consider some raw sample statistics from the NDSHS data on cross-drug relationships. Tables 2.4 and 2.5 present observed sample frequencies and estimated conditional and unconditional probabilities in terms of joint consumption of tobacco, alcohol and marijuana using NDSHS data for 1995, 1998 and 2001.

Table 2.4 shows that whereas an estimated 14.2 per cent of the total population participated in marijuana consumption during the three surveys, 14.0 per cent used marijuana in conjunction with at least one of the other two legal drugs (tobacco and alcohol) and only 0.2 per cent used marijuana only. The estimated conditional and unconditional probabilities in Table 2.5 based on the sample statistics in Table 2.4 highlight correlations across the three drugs. Table 2.5 shows that the probability of an individual participating in marijuana consumption is much higher if he/she is known to participate in using one of the other two drugs. The participation probability for marijuana is 14.2 per cent for the general Australian population, but this probability increases to 16.5 per cent among alcohol drinkers and to 33.8 per cent among the subpopulation of tobacco smokers. Meanwhile, whereas 23.7 per cent of the general population smoke tobacco, the percentage of tobacco smokers among marijuana users is much higher at 56.3 per cent. These empirical statistics confirm the anecdotal observation that marijuana is closely related to tobacco and alcohol in consumption.

Similarly, the NDSHS data also indicate a close relationship between marijuana consumption and that of other illegal drugs. Tables 2.6 and 2.7 show an even stronger correlation between the consumption of marijuana and that of cocaine and heroin. For example, whereas 14.6 per cent of all respondents used marijuana in the two surveys of 1998 and 2001, 86.2 per cent of cocaine users and 90.0 per cent of heroin users consumed marijuana. If an individual is known to use both cocaine and heroin, he/she is almost certainly a

Table 2.4: *Summary sample statistics for participation in tobacco, alcohol and marijuana*

% participating in	Joint	Tobacco	Alcohol	Marijuana
T only	1.9	1.9		
A only	55.4		55.4	
M only	0.2			0.2
T and A only	13.8	13.8	13.8	
T and M only	0.3	0.3		0.3
A and M only	6.0		6.0	6.0
T and A and M	7.7	7.7	7.7	7.7
None	14.7			
Total	100	23.7	82.9	14.2

Notes: T, tobacco; A, alcohol; and M, marijuana.
Source: Zhao and Harris (2004) based on pooled data from NDSHS for 1995, 1998 and 2001.

Table 2.5: *Estimated conditional and unconditional participation probabilities*

	$i =$		
Probability	Marijuana	Alcohol	Tobacco
$P(Y_i = 1)$	14.2	82.9	23.7
$P(Y_i = 1 \mid Y_M = 1)$	100	96.5	56.3
$P(Y_i = 1 \mid Y_A = 1)$	16.5	100	25.9
$P(Y_i = 1 \mid Y_T = 1)$	33.8	90.7	100

Notes: Probabilities are multiplied by 100. Y_i is a binary variable representing the participation status for drug i ($i = $ M, A and T).
Source: Zhao and Harris (2004) based on pooled NDSHS data for 1995, 1998 and 2001.

marijuana user, with a probability of 94.8 per cent, which is much higher than the unconditional probability of 14.6 per cent. Similarly, whereas only 1.4 per cent of the general population is expected to use cocaine, the probability of cocaine use increases to 8.0 per cent for marijuana users and to 66.9 per cent among those who use both marijuana and heroin.

Table 2.6: *Summary sample statistics for participation in marijuana, cocaine and heroin*

% participating in	Joint	Marijuana	Cocaine	Heroin
M only	13.23	13.23		
C only	0.17		0.17	
H only	0.03			0.03
M and C only	0.87	0.87	0.87	
M and H only	0.15	0.15		0.15
C and H only	0.02		0.02	0.02
M and C and H	0.30	0.30	0.30	0.30
None	85.23			
Total	100	14.55	1.35	0.50

Notes: M, marijuana; C, cocaine; and H, heroin.
Source: Ramful and Zhao (2009) based on NDSHS data for 1998 and 2001.

Table 2.7: *Estimated conditional and unconditional participation probabilities*

	$i=$		
Probability	Marijuana	Cocaine	Tobacco
$P(Y_i = 1)$	14.55	1.35	0.50
$P(Y_i = 1 | Y_M = 1)$	100.00	8.03	3.07
$P(Y_i = 1 | Y_C = 1)$	86.23	100.00	23.28
$P(Y_i = 1 | Y_H = 1)$	90.06	63.54	100.00
$P(Y_i = 1 | Y_C = 1, Y_H = 1)$	94.78	100.00	100.00
$P(Y_i = 1 | Y_M = 1, Y_H = 1)$	100.00	66.87	100.00
$P(Y_i = 1 | Y_M = 1, Y_C = 1)$	100.00	100.00	25.59

Notes: Probabilities are multiplied by 100. Y_i is a binary variable representing the participation status for drug i ($i = $ M, C and H).
Source: Ramful and Zhao (2009) based on NDSHS data for 1998 and 2001.

Multivariate probit models for multi-drug consumption

Although there are strong correlations across participation in marijuana use and that of other drugs as indicated by the observed conditional and unconditional frequencies in Tables 2.5 and 2.7, some of these cross-drug correlations may be explained by their joint relationships with observable personal characteristics (such as education level) or price variations, and some are due to unobservable personal characteristics such as those related to an addictive personality or family upbringing. These unobserved factors are difficult to quantify, but can play a major role in an individual's decision to use various drugs. For example, if we know that an individual is a 20-year-old single male who is unemployed, we would expect his probability of using marijuana when and where its price is low to be higher than for an average Australian at a time and place where the marijuana price is high. However, if we also know that he is using both cocaine and heroin, we may predict an even higher probability for his use of marijuana. As indicated below, a multivariate-systems econometric model allows us to examine observed cross-drug correlations due to both observed personal characteristics and unobservable factors after controlling for differences in observable socioeconomic and demographic characteristics.

Although it is well accepted that marijuana is closely related to other drugs in consumption, studies explicitly addressing this relationship have mostly examined cross-drug price or policy responses (Chaloupka and Laixuthai, 1997, Pacula, 1998a, DiNardo and Lemieux, 2001, Cameron and Williams, 2001, Farrelly *et al.*, 2001, DeSimone and Farrelly, 2003). Moreover, although the responsiveness of marijuana use to changes in other drug prices or policies has been investigated, the correlation across decisions on the use of different drugs for the same individual through unobservable characteristics has been ignored. In the following, we present results from two multivariate probit models that separately examine the relationship between marijuana consumption and that of (i) the legal drugs tobacco and alcohol and (ii) the illicit drugs cocaine and heroin, allowing for cross-drug correlations via unobservable factors.

Assume that Y_j^* is a latent variable proportional to the unobserved propensity for participating in the consumption of drug j $(-\infty < Y_j^* < +\infty, j = 1, \ldots, K)$. The latent demand variables are linearly related to a set of observed characteristics X_j as follows:

$$Y_j^* = X_j' \beta_j + \varepsilon_j \quad (j = 1, \ldots, K) \tag{2.3}$$

where β_j is a vector of parameters to be estimated and ε_j is a stochastic component that represents unobserved characteristics. The latent variable Y_j^* is related to the observed binary variable Y_j via:

$$Y_j = \begin{cases} 1 & \text{if} \quad Y_j^* > 0 \\ 0 & \text{if} \quad Y_j^* \leq 0 \end{cases} \quad (j = 1, \ldots, K) \tag{2.4}$$

where $Y_j = 1$ if the individual consumes drug j and $Y_j = 0$ otherwise.

Assume that the error terms in the K latent equations in (2.3) jointly follow a multivariate normal distribution; that is, $(\varepsilon_1, \ldots, \varepsilon_K)' \sim MVN(0, \Sigma)$, where the variance-covariance matrix Σ is given by

$$\Sigma = \begin{pmatrix} 1 & \rho_{12} & \cdots & \rho_{1K} \\ \vdots & \vdots & \ddots & \vdots \\ \rho_{K1} & \rho_{K2} & \cdots & 1 \end{pmatrix} \tag{2.5}$$

and ρ_{ij} are the correlation coefficients of ε_i and ε_j $(i, j = 1, \ldots, K; i \neq j)$. Under this assumption, equations (2.3)–(2.5) define a multivariate probit (MVP) model that jointly models the participation decisions on using the K drugs. The potentially non-zero off-diagonal elements in Σ allow for correlations across the K error terms in the latent equations, which represent unobserved characteristics for the same individual. This allows knowledge on an individual's use of one drug to be used to predict his/her probability of participating in the use of another drug. Unit variances are assumed for the error terms for identification purposes. Note that when $\rho_{ij} \equiv 0$, the MVP model defined above becomes K univariate probit (UVP) models in which the K equations are estimated independently. For mathematical expressions for various multivariate probabilities for the MVP model for the case of $K=3$, see Ramful and Zhao (2009).

Ramful and Zhao (2009) estimate a trivariate probit model for the joint decision on participation in relation to three illicit drugs (marijuana, cocaine and heroin) using pooled data from the 1998 and 2001 surveys. The left panel in Table 2.8 shows the estimated correlation coefficients across the error terms of the three illicit drug equations, together with the standard errors. These indicate that after accounting for observable covariates in the model, the correlations among the three drugs are still very high: 0.835 between cocaine and heroin, 0.651 between marijuana and cocaine and 0.59 between marijuana and heroin.

In a similar model for marijuana, tobacco and alcohol using combined data from the three NDSHS surveys of 1995, 1998 and 2001, Zhao and Harris (2004) estimate the three correlation coefficients after controlling for observed covariates. These are summarised in the right panel of Table 2.8. The results show that after accounting for observed personal characteristics and prices, there is significant

Table 2.8: *Cross-drug correlation coefficients of error terms*

	Marijuana	Cocaine	Heroin
Marijuana	1	0.651 (28.3)**	0.590 (13.4)**
Cocaine	0.651 (28.3)**	1	0.835 (32.1)**
Heroin	0.590 (13.4)**	0.835 (32.1)**	1

	Marijuana	Tobacco	Alcohol
Marijuana	1	0.50 (45.8)**	0.37 (21.2)**
Tobacco	0.50 (45.8)**	1	0.20 (14.7)**
Alcohol	0.37 (21.2)**	0.20 (14.7)**	1

Notes: Statistical significance is indicated at the **5% level. Values in parentheses are *t*-statistics.

Sources: Results for correlation coefficients for marijuana, cocaine and heroin are for error terms of a trivariate probit model from Ramful and Zhao (2009), and results for marijuana, tobacco and alcohol are from Zhao and Harris (2004).

correlation between marijuana and the two legal drugs via unobserved factors, with the correlation between marijuana and tobacco being as high as 0.5.[5]

Knowledge of these correlation coefficients can help greatly in predicting an individual's participation probability for marijuana when knowledge of his/her use of other drugs is available. Similarly, information on marijuana use will also help in predicting the participation probability for the use of other drugs. Table 2.9 presents some predicted unconditional, conditional and joint probabilities using both UVP and MVP models. The UVP models ignore the cross-drug correlations via unobserved error terms, whereas the MVP models account for such correlations.

For example, using univariate models in which cross-drug correlations via the error terms are restricted to zero, for an individual with personal characteristics controlled at the sample means, the probability of marijuana use is predicted to be 9.5 per cent with or without knowledge of his/her use of other drugs. However, when such correlations are accounted for using a multivariate model, the predicted probability of marijuana use increases to 79 per cent if the person is known to be a cocaine user and to 87 per cent if he/she is known to use both cocaine and heroin. Similarly, with the trivariate probit model for marijuana, alcohol and tobacco, the participation probability for marijuana predicted for an average Australian changes from 10.7 per cent to 27 per cent if it is known that the person uses both alcohol and tobacco. This predicted probability decreases to 1.5 per cent if the person is known to abstain from both of the legal drugs.

The predicted joint probabilities are also different. Accounting for the cross-equation error correlations, the joint probability for an average individual with mean values for personal characteristics for use of marijuana, alcohol and tobacco is predicted to be 5.2 per cent, whereas the univariate model predicts 2.2 per cent. This compares to an observed frequency of 7.7 per cent in Table 2.4 when personal characteristics are not controlled for.

Note that the predicted marginal probabilities from the two models are rather different, as they used data from 1998–2001 and 1995–2001, respectively. There are also slight differences in the predicted marginal probabilities from the univariate probit and trivariate probit approaches for two reasons. There are slight differences in the sample observations included, as there are more missing observations for the

Table 2.9: *Predicted probabilities for two trivariate probit models*

Marijuana, cocaine and heroin			*Marijuana, alcohol and tobacco*		
Probability	*Univariate*	*Trivariate*	*Probability*	*Univariate*	*Trivariate*
$P(Y_M = 1)$	0.0950	0.0948	$P(Y_M = 1)$	0.1071	0.1066
$P(Y_M = 1\|Y_C = 1)$	0.0950	0.7943	$P(Y_M = 1\|Y_A = 1, Y_T = 1)$	0.1071	0.2687
$P(Y_M = 1\|Y_C = 1, Y_H = 1)$	0.0950	0.8697	$P(Y_M = 1\|Y_A = 0, Y_T = 0)$	0.1071	0.0145
$P(Y_C = 1\|Y_M = 1, Y_H = 1)$	0.0043	0.5692	$P(Y_T = 1\|Y_M = 1, Y_A = 1)$	0.2312	0.5564
$P(Y_H = 1\|Y_M = 1, Y_C = 1)$	0.0016	0.2308	$P(Y_A = 1\|Y_M = 1, Y_T = 1)$	0.8750	0.9732
$P(Y_M = 0, Y_C = 0, Y_H = 0)$	0.8997	0.9043	$P(Y_M = 0, Y_A = 0, Y_T = 0)$	0.0858	0.1064
$P(Y_M = 0, Y_C = 1, Y_H = 0)$	0.0039	0.0007	$P(Y_M = 1, Y_A = 1, Y_T = 1)$	0.0217	0.0516

Notes: All predicted probabilities are evaluated for sample means for the whole population. Standard errors are not presented and can be found in the original papers.

Sources: Results for marijuana, cocaine and heroin are from Ramful and Zhao (2009) and results for marijuana, tobacco and alcohol are from Zhao and Harris (2004).

trivariate model than for a univariate probit model for marijuana alone. Second, even though both models give consistent estimations for the true marginal probability, small differences in different estimations are possible. The differences are small in magnitude in any case.

The MEs of individual explanatory factors on unconditional and associated conditional probabilities can also be different. To further illustrate the extra insight afforded by the multivariate approach, MEs of personal characteristics and prices on the unconditional and some conditional participation probabilities for marijuana using a trivariate probit for marijuana, cocaine and heroin are presented in Table 2.10. The magnitude and sometimes even the sign can differ for the MEs on unconditional versus various conditional probabilities when the population is reduced to subgroups according to the status of other drug use. MEs in all columns are the same when univariate models are used.

Taking the unemployment dummy and marriage dummy for example, differences in the MEs of these two explanatory variables on unconditional and various conditional probabilities for marijuana use are illustrated in Figure 2.6. When other factors are equal at the sample mean, an unemployed person is approximately 5 per cent more likely to participate in marijuana consumption than the base group of retirees, pensioners and homemakers among the general Australian population. However, among heroin users or cocaine users, the effect of unemployment on the probability of marijuana use is 10 per cent higher relative to the base group. Interestingly, in the subgroup of individuals who use both heroin and cocaine, the ME of unemployment on participation probability is slightly lower at 7 per cent. Note that the predicted base probabilities for marijuana use among other illicit drug users are also much higher than the unconditional probability, as indicated in Table 2.10. Another example is marriage status. Married or *de facto* partnered people generally have a 6.9 per cent lower probability of using marijuana, but for those who are already using both heroin and cocaine, the ME of being married is only 3.6 per cent lower. This seems to suggest that although married people are much more unlikely to use marijuana in general, among serious drug users who use both heroin and cocaine, being married or living with a *de facto* partner does not reduce the probability of marijuana use as much. Note that, unlike the case of unemployment, the ME of marriage status has an opposite relationship with the magnitude of the predicted probabilities.

Table 2.10: *Marginal effects on selected probabilities for marijuana*

Variable	P(M = 1)	P(M = 1|C = 0, H = 0)	P(M = 1|C = 1, H = 1)	P(M = 1|C = 1)	P(M = 1|H = 1)
Constant	−2.862**	−2.667**	−0.713	−1.096	−1.604
PRH	0.027**	0.028**	0.064**	0.109**	0.049
PRC	0.039**	0.039**	0.055**	0.078**	0.068*
PRM	−0.020	−0.024*	−0.126**	−0.131**	−0.198*
INCOME	0.006**	0.006**	−0.002	−0.020*	0.023*
CAPITAL	0.003*	0.001	−0.038**	−0.069**	−0.019
YR01	−0.011*	−0.011**	−0.013	−0.052**	0.028
AGE	1.614**	1.517**	0.743**	0.934**	1.477**
AGESQ	−0.261**	−0.246**	−0.134**	−0.165**	−0.259**
MALE	0.047**	0.046**	0.049**	0.077**	0.056**
MARRIED	−0.069**	−0.065**	−0.036**	−0.049**	−0.064**
WORK	−0.008*	−0.008	0.002	−0.020	0.031
STUDY	−0.009	−0.009	−0.009	−0.048*	0.036
UNEMP	0.049**	0.048**	0.071**	0.094**	0.098**
YOUNGKIDS	−0.018**	−0.017**	−0.024*	−0.012	−0.061**
ATSI	0.035*	0.034**	0.053*	0.052	0.096
DEGREE	−0.013**	−0.013**	0.004	−0.034*	0.053**
DIPLOMA	0.006	0.006	0.024*	0.001	0.070**
YR12	0.001	0.002	0.019	0.003	0.051**
SIN-PARENT	0.023**	0.022**	0.027*	0.055**	0.012

Notes: Significance is indicated at the *10% and **5% level. Standard errors are not presented, but can be found in the original paper.
Source: Ramful and Zhao (2009).

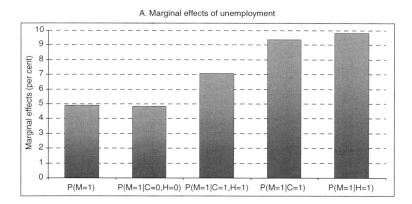

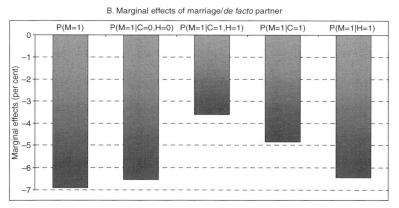

Figure 2.6. Marginal effects on conditional and unconditional probabilities

Finally, it is also interesting to note the differences in price effects on unconditional versus conditional probabilities. Whereas an increase in the price of marijuana appears to have a less significant effect on the unconditional probability of marijuana use, it has more significant effects in reducing the conditional probabilities for marijuana use for the subpopulations which consume other drugs. Table 2.11 depicts the price elasticities of marijuana use estimated from the price MEs in Table 2.10. These elasticities show percentage changes rather than absolute changes in the probabilities in response to a 1 per cent change in the relevant price. For example, a marijuana price elasticity of − 0.132 (third column) indicates that a 1 per cent increase in the price of marijuana will result in a 0.132 per cent reduction in the probability

Table 2.11: *Price elasticity for conditional and unconditional participation probabilities*

| Price | $P(M=1)$ | | $P(M=1|C=0, H=0)$ | | $P(M=1|C=1, H=1)$ | | $P(M=1|C=1)$ | | $P(M=1|H=1)$ | |
	ME	SE	ME	SE	ME	SE	ME	SE	ME	SE
PH	0.188	(0.064)**	0.212	(0.062)**	0.067	(0.021)**	0.126	(0.031)**	0.055	(0.043)
PC	0.270	(0.093)**	0.288	(0.072)**	0.058	(0.025)**	0.091	(0.041)**	0.076	(0.042)*
PM	−0.140	(0.087)	−0.178	(0.102)*	−0.132	(0.049)**	−0.152	(0.056)**	−0.220	(0.116)*

Note: Significance is indicated at the *10% and **5% levels.
Source: Ramful and Zhao (2009).

of marijuana consumption in the subpopulation which also jointly consumes cocaine and heroin. More importantly, Table 2.11 shows that whereas the own-price elasticity for marijuana for the general population is statistically non-significant, in a subpopulation of cocaine and heroin users, marijuana users respond significantly to its price, with a participation elasticity of −0.132. The participation elasticities are even higher at −0.152 and −0.220 in subpopulations of cocaine users and heroin users respectively. Among those who do not consume cocaine and heroin, the own-price participation elasticity for marijuana is estimated at −0.180. Similarly, there are some important differences in the cross-price elasticities of participation in subpopulation groups compared with the general population. These results emphasise the importance of the MVP model over the UVP approach.

2.5 Levels of marijuana consumption

Who are heavy users? Observed user characteristics by consumption levels

For respondents who used marijuana in the preceding 12 months, the surveys also ask for information on the frequency of consumption. This information is important, as individuals who use marijuana once or twice a year are very different from those who use it every day in terms of both health consequences and targeted drug education programmes. Table 2.12 presents the observed percentages for 5 different levels of marijuana consumption for the whole sample and for individual socioeconomic and demographic groups, using combined data from 1998 and 2001. Percentages for different levels of participation by gender, marriage status, main activity, education, income and age are also illustrated in Figure 2.7.

As indicated in Table 2.12, of the 14.4 per cent of the general population who used marijuana in the preceding 12 months, 2.3 per cent of the population used it every day, 3.4 per cent used less than daily but at least once a week, 1.9 per cent used less frequently than every week but at least once a month, and 6.9 per cent used less frequently than monthly but at least once in the preceding 12 months. Men are more likely to be represented in all consumption levels than women, particularly for the heavy-use categories. Non-partnered individuals have higher proportions for all non-zero consumption

Table 2.12:   *Level of marijuana consumption by group (unit: per cent)*

Variable	Frequency				
	Abstainers	*Infrequent*	*Monthly*	*Weekly*	*Daily*
Overall	85.6	6.89	1.91	3.41	2.32
MALE	82.86	7.01	2.25	4.70	3.18
FEMALE	87.58	6.79	1.63	2.36	1.64
MARRIED	91.39	4.12	1.01	2.02	1.47
NON-PARTNERED	77.93	10.43	3.04	5.18	3.41
WORK	83.57	7.83	2.03	3.94	2.63
STUDY	75.07	14.10	3.88	5.01	1.93
UNEMPLOYED	71.20	8.51	4.41	8.21	7.67
OTHER ACT (RETIREE/ HOME DUTY)	94.13	2.46	0.71	1.39	1.32
DEGREE	86.65	7.89	1.78	2.82	0.85
DIPLOMA	85.51	6.27	1.74	3.65	2.84
YR12	80.86	9.16	2.59	4.44	2.95
LESSYR12	87.73	5.30	1.65	2.92	2.41
YOUNG KIDS	87.02	6.13	1.67	3.04	2.14
NO YOUNG KIDS	85.25	7.03	1.94	3.45	2.33
ATSI	73.55	9.86	3.29	6.26	7.04
NON-ATSI	85.70	6.82	1.88	3.36	2.24
CAPITAL CITY	84.43	7.65	2.05	3.56	2.31
NON-CAPITAL CITY	87.91	5.11	1.57	3.05	2.37
SINGLE-PARENT	74.58	11.20	3.51	6.37	4.34
NON-SINGLE PARENT	86.28	6.58	1.81	3.17	2.16
Income					
$0–$9,999	85.22	7.11	2.15	3.17	2.34
$10,000–$19,999	83.40	6.82	2.01	4.47	3.31
$20,000–$29,999	82.44	8.03	2.14	4.27	3.10
$30,000–$39,999	85.60	7.47	1.91	3.29	1.73
$40,000–$49,999	85.79	7.87	1.52	3.30	1.52
$50,000–$59,999	87.66	7.16	1.47	2.48	1.22
$60,000 or more	88.51	7.22	1.24	2.41	0.62

Notes: *Abstainers*: no marijuana use in the past 12 months; *Infrequent*: used less frequently than monthly, but at least once in the past 12 months; *Monthly*: used at least once a month, but less frequently than weekly; *Weekly*: used less than daily, but at least once a week; and *Daily*: used every day.

Sources: Zhao and Harris (2004). Results relate to the percentage of the relevant population group for different levels of consumption, based on pooled samples from 1998 and 2001 surveys (NDSHS, 2005).

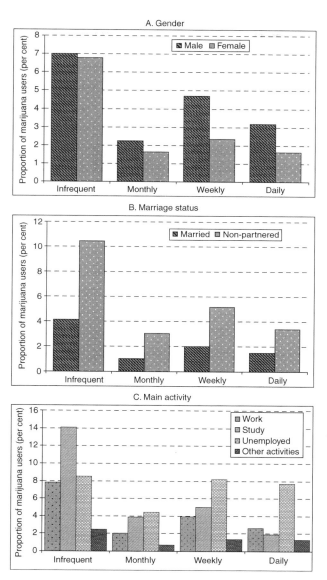

Figure 2.7. Frequency of marijuana consumption
Source: Table 2.12.

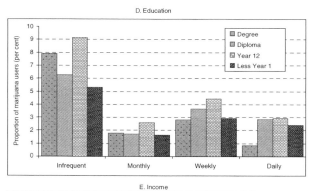

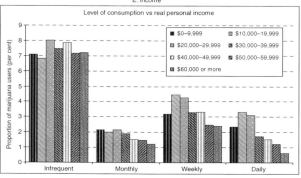

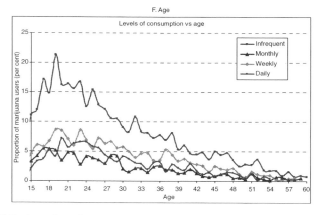

Figure 2.7. (*continued*)
Source: Table 2.12.

levels compared with those who are married or *de facto* partnered. In terms of main activity, unemployed individuals are significantly more likely to be in all four non-zero consumption levels, especially the heavy-use levels. It is also interesting that although students have a much higher participation rate than the employed, a higher proportion of the latter report daily consumption compared with students.

In terms of the highest education level achieved, individuals with year-12 education are more likely to be represented in all non-zero marijuana consumption levels than those with a higher or lower level of education. Individuals with a diploma or trade certificate have the second highest proportions for the heavy consumption levels (weekly and daily). The results for those with a tertiary education are interesting. Whereas those with tertiary degrees have higher participation rates for marijuana use than those with less than year-12 education, degree holders are mostly infrequent users and have significantly lower probability for daily use than all other education groups.

Panel E of Figure 2.7 illustrates the relationship between levels of marijuana use and income. The proportion of infrequent users does not vary greatly by income levels, with those earning $20,000–$49,999 a year having a slightly higher prevalence. However, there seems to be a clear pattern for the weekly and daily categories whereby the proportion of users decreases with increasing income above a certain income level. Those with low income of $10,000–$29,999 a year have the highest probability of being daily users. The expected probability of frequent use decreases as income increases beyond $20,000 a year.

Finally, the relationship between consumption level and age (panel F of Figure 2.7) reveals a sharp peak at approximately 19 years of age for the probability of infrequent use that then decreases consistently with increasing age. However, for the frequent-use categories, the peaks seem to span the whole range of late teens to mid-late twenties.

A sequential model for levels of marijuana consumption

We now consider the relationship between individual characteristics and levels of marijuana consumption. Results in Table 2.12 reveal how the observed sample frequencies for various levels of marijuana consumption differ by socioeconomic and demographic groups. However, an econometric model is required to isolate the partial effects of individual explanatory factors when other factors are controlled.

Table 2.13: **Results for the sequential model of marijuana consumption**

Variable	Participation		Level of consumption (Conditional on participation)					
					Marginal effect			
	Coefficient	Marginal effect	Coefficient	Infrequent	Monthly	Weekly	Daily
Constant	8.77*		4.77				
YR98	0.34*	0.07*	0.26*	−0.11*	0.00	0.04	0.06*
YR01	0.42*	0.07*	0.39*	−0.16*	0.01	0.06	0.09*
LNAGE	−14.35*	−2.63*	−0.37*	0.15*	−0.01	−0.06	−0.08*
MALE	0.28*	0.05*	0.31*	−0.13*	0.00	0.05	0.07*
MARRIED	−0.35*	−0.07*	0.03	−0.01*	0.00	0.00	0.01
DECRIM	0.13*	0.02*	0.16*	−0.06*	0.00	0.02	0.04
WORK	0.18*	0.03*	−0.11*	0.05*	0.00	−0.02	−0.03
STUD	−0.11*	−0.02*	−0.37*	0.15*	−0.01	−0.06	−0.07
UNEMP	0.39*	0.09*	0.05	−0.02*	0.00	0.01	0.01
CAPITAL	0.07*	0.01*	−0.09*	0.04*	0.00	−0.01	−0.02
ATSI	0.15*	0.03*	−0.04	0.01*	0.00	−0.01	−0.01
ENGLISHS	0.58*	0.08*	0.03*	−0.01*	0.00	0.01	0.01
SCHOOL	−0.77*	−0.09*	−0.34*	0.14*	−0.01	−0.06	−0.07
DEGREE	0.04	0.01	−0.35*	0.14*	−0.01	−0.06	−0.07

DIPLOMA	0.08*	0.01*	−0.08*	0.03*	0.00	−0.01	−0.02
YR12	−0.01	0.00	−0.16*	0.07*	0.00	−0.03	−0.04
DEPCHILD	−0.01	0.00	−0.02	0.01	0.00	0.00	0.00
LNPA	1.13	0.21	6.55	−2.61	0.10	1.02*	1.49
LNPM	−1.64*	−0.30*	−0.51	0.21	−0.01	−0.08	−0.12
LNPT	−8.8*	−1.61*	−7.78	3.10	−0.11	−1.21	−1.77*
LNINC	−0.57*	−0.10*	−1.68*	0.67*	−0.02	−0.26	−0.38*

Notes: Marginal effect results indicate changes in probability for the relevant consumption level. Significance is indicated at the *5% level.
Standard errors are available in the original paper.

Source: Results compiled from Zhao and Harris (2004).

Participation studies such as that reported in Sections 2.3 and 2.4 make no distinction between those who use marijuana only a couple of times a year and those who smoke every day. Zhao and Harris (2004) further study the determinants for different levels of marijuana consumption. They assume that observed marijuana data on consumption levels are the result of sequential decisions involving a decision on whether to participate in consuming the illicit drug and then a decision on how much to consume once the decision on participation is made. They use a two-part model with a probit model for the first decision on participation and an ordered probit model for the conditional probabilities for the second decision. It is not unreasonable to expect that the two decisions may relate to different factors or that the same explanatory variable may have different effects on the two decisions.

Results for coefficients and MEs for both parts of the sequential model for marijuana consumption are presented in Table 2.13. For social and demographic effects, factors such as age, income and gender have similar effects on both decisions. For example, males are more likely to participate and, conditional on participation, are more likely to consume marijuana more frequently than females. However, for some other explanatory variables, the effects on the two decisions are different or even have opposite directions. Being single, unemployed, of ATSI background or speaking English at home significantly increases the probability of participating in marijuana use, but among marijuana users these factors no longer have a significant effect on the frequency of consumption. In terms of educational attainment, those with a higher level of education do not significantly differ in participation from those with less than year-12 education, or are even more likely to participate, but among users, all the groups with higher levels of education are less likely to engage in frequent consumption than those with less than year-12 education. Finally, whereas being employed increases the probability of participation, the employed are less likely to smoke heavily compared with the base group (retirees, pensioners and those carrying out home duties). The dummy variables for residence in a capital city are significant and have opposite signs in the two equations; individuals in capital cities are more likely to participate, but among users, heavier smokers are more likely to reside in non-capital cities.

2.6 Modelling non-participation

Two types of zero observations

As shown in Table 2.1, more than 80 per cent of the NDSHS respondents had not used marijuana in the 12 months prior to the survey. It is often the case in empirical economic research that data are characterised by excessive observations of zero consumption. For the discrete ordered dependent variable here for levels of marijuana consumption from NDSHS data, traditional ordered probit models (OP) have limited capacity in modelling such a preponderance of zero observations, especially when these may relate to two distinct sources.

In the case of self-reported marijuana consumption, zero is recorded for genuine non-participants who abstain because of, for example, health or legal concerns and who pay no attention to drug prices or what they can afford in their decision making. However, zero observations may also correspond to those who are the corner solution of a standard consumer demand problem and who may become consumers if the price decreases or their income increases. This may include infrequent users who are not *currently* smoking and potential users who might smoke when the price decreases. It could also be argued that some zero observations may also correspond to misreporting respondents who prefer to identify themselves as non-smokers. Thus, it is likely that these different types of zero observations are driven by different systems of consumer behaviour. Here, zero-consumption potential users are likely to possess characteristics similar to those of users and are likely to be responsive to standard consumer demand factors such as prices and income. Genuine non-participants, meanwhile, are likely to have perfectly inelastic price- and income-demand schedules and are driven by a separate process relating to sociological, health and ethical considerations. If such underlying processes are modelled incorrectly, this could invalidate any subsequent policy implications. In addition, even the same explanatory variable could have different effects on the two decisions. One example is the effect of income on drug consumption. Higher income, acting as an indicator of social class and health awareness, may increase the probability of genuine non-participation. However, for participants, higher income will be associated with a lower probability of zero consumption and a higher probability of heavier consumption. An OP model generated by a single latent equation cannot allow for differentiation between the two opposing effects.

In a manner analogous to the zero-inflated/augmented Poisson (ZIP/ZAP) models for count data and double hurdle models for limited dependent variables, Harris and Zhao (2007) propose a zero-inflated ordered probit (ZIOP) model to take account of the possibility that zeros can arise from two different aspects of individual behaviour. The model involves a system of a probit 'splitting' model and an OP model, with correlated error terms for the two latent equations that relate to potentially differing sets of covariates. In this section, the ZIOP model is used to model the ordered levels of marijuana consumption allowing for zero observations from two different sources.

A zero-inflated ordered probit model for marijuana consumption

Let the ordered levels of marijuana consumption be represented by an observable variable y that assumes the discrete ordered values of $0, 1, \ldots$ and J. Suppose y is generated by a ZIOP model that involves two latent equations: a probit participation equation that determines whether an individual participates in marijuana use and an ordered probit equation conditional on participation for the levels of consumption that also include zero consumption. The participation switching probit is given by:

$$r^* = x'\beta + \varepsilon \tag{2.6}$$

where r^* represents the propensity for participation that is mapped to a binary indicator variable r via $r = 1$ for $r^* > 0$ for participants and $r = 0$ for $r^* \leq 0$ for non-participants. x is a vector of covariates that determine the choice between the two regimes, β is a vector of unknown coefficients and ε is an error term following a standard normal distribution.

Conditional on $r = 1$, consumption levels under the participation regime are represented by a discrete variable $\tilde{y}$ ($\tilde{y} = 0, 1, \ldots, J$) that is generated by an OP model via a second underlying latent $\tilde{y}^*$:

$$\tilde{y}^* = z'\gamma + u \tag{2.7}$$

where z is a vector of explanatory variables with unknown weights γ and u is an error term following a standard normal distribution. The mapping between $\tilde{y}^*$ and $\tilde{y}$ is given by:

$$\tilde{y} = \begin{cases} 0 & \text{if} \quad \tilde{y}^* \leq 0 \\ j & \text{if} \quad \mu_{j-1} < \tilde{y}^* \leq \mu_j \quad (j = 1, ..., J-1), \\ J & \text{if} \quad \mu_{J-1} \leq \tilde{y}^* \end{cases} \tag{2.8}$$

where μ_j ($j = 1, \ldots, J-1$) are boundary parameters and we define $\mu_0 = 0$. Although r and $\tilde{y}$ are not individually observable in terms of zeros, they are observed via the criterion $y = r\tilde{y}$. Note importantly that, unlike the two-part sequential model reported in the second subsection of Section 2.5, the participation regime here also allows for zero consumption and the two error terms are assumed correlated.

Further assuming that the two error terms ε and u jointly follow a bivariate standard normal distribution with correlation coefficient ρ, the above give a ZIOP with correlated errors. For details of the model, see Harris and Zhao (2007).

We use the pooled data from the 1998, 2001 and 2004 sweeps of the NDSHS to estimate a correlated ZIOP model for levels of marijuana consumption. Removal of missing observations in any variables used in the analysis yields approximately 45,000 observations for the estimation. We consider 4 levels of observed marijuana consumption, with $y = 0$ for no use, $y = 1$ for use once every few months or less, $y = 2$ for use once a month, and $y = 3$ for use once a week or more, all in the previous 12 months. The sample proportions for these four levels are 87 per cent, 6 per cent, 2 per cent and 5 per cent, respectively. Note that, compared with the 2001 survey, there was an almost 2 per cent increase in 12-month abstainers in 2004, as shown in Table 2.1.

The participation decision in equation (2.6) is likely to be driven by factors relating to an individual's attitude towards smoking and health concerns. Thus, r^* is likely to be related to an individual's education level and other standard variables such as income, marital status, age, gender, work status and ethnic background that capture socio-economic status. In terms of the decision on the consumption level conditional on participation in equation (2.7), in addition to standard socioeconomic and demographic variables for consumer taste heterogeneity, we include standard demand-schedule variables such as income and own- and cross-drug prices. We include drug prices for cocaine, heroin, speed and tobacco. The evidence in Section 2.4 indicates that marijuana is closely related to these legal and illegal drugs. Illicit drug prices are obtained for individual years and states/

Table 2.14:   *Estimated coefficients: OP versus ZIOPC*

| Variable | OP | ZIOPC | |
		Participation equation	Consumption equation
CON	0.203 (1.048)	12.000 (0.555)**	−5.61 (1.391)**
LNAGE	−1.108 (0.027)**	−3.159 (0.111)**	0.749 (0.137)**
MALE	0.235 (0.017)**	0.328 (0.0413)**	0.215 (0.029)**
MARRIED	−0.342 (0.018)**	−0.519 (0.0446)**	−0.144 (0.043)**
PRESKOOL	0.028 (0.024)	−0.192 (0.064)**	−0.081 (0.052)*
SINCHIL	0.146 (0.027)**	0.095 (0.062)*	0.010 (0.043)
CAPITAL	−0.021 (0.018)	−0.122 (0.034)**	0.073 (0.030)**
ATSI	0.210 (0.054)	−0.161 (0.125)*	0.286 (0.094)**
WORKWH	−0.005 (0.027)	0.291 (0.063)**	−0.374 (0.060)**
WORKBL	0.146 (0.030)**	0.162 (0.067)**	−0.139 (0.065)**
STUDY	0.032 (0.036)	0.534 (0.113)**	−0.305 (0.067)**
UNEMP	−0.002 (0.034)	0.726 (0.121)**	−0.329 (0.065)**
DEGREE	0.008 (0.025)	0.357 (0.059)**	−0.406 (0.051)**
YR12	0.069 (0.024)**	0.047 (0.053)	−0.097 (0.039)**
DIPLOMA	0.121 (0.022)**	0.092 (0.048)**	−0.061 (0.041)*
LRPINC	0.110 (0.012)**	−0.090 (0.028)**	0.045 (0.019)**
DECRIM	0.126 (0.021)**	0.0772 (0.042)**	0.116 (0.035)**
LRPMAR	0.083 (0.063)**		0.081 (0.081)
LRPCOC	0.170 (0.041)**		0.165 (0.054)**
LRPHER	0.236 (0.037)**		0.259 (0.048)**
LRPSPD	−0.051 (0.020)**		−0.048 (0.025)**
LRPTOB	−0.154 (0.126)		0.050 (0.159)
MU	0.256 (0.006)**		0.330 (0.009)**
MU	0.593 (0.009)**		0.741 (0.016)**
RHO		−0.268 (0.078)**	

Note: One-sided significance is indicated at the **5% and *10% levels.

territories from the IDRS (NDARC, 2004). Data on tobacco prices are obtained from the Australian Bureau of Statistics (ABS, 2006). Finally, a decriminalisation status dummy is included in both the participation and consumption equations.

The estimated coefficients and standard errors for a correlated ZIOP (ZIOPC) model are reported in Table 2.14. An OP model without the zero-inflated split mechanism is also estimated using the same data set, the coefficients of which are reported in Table 2.14 for comparison. The information criteria, the likelihood ratio test and Vuong's test favour the ZIOPC model over the OP model. For details of these tests, see Harris and Zhao (2007). The estimated correlation coefficient as reported in Table 2.14 is significantly different from zero, indicating correlation exists across the two decisions via the unobservable factors.

Although the magnitude of the coefficients in Table 2.14 is not directly meaningful in terms of their impact on the probability of consumption levels, the sign is indicative of the direction of the impact of explanatory variables on the two decisions. A most interesting example is the effect of income. The negative coefficient for the logarithm of the personal income variable LRPINC in the probit equation clearly shows that income, acting as a social class proxy in the participation decision, relates negatively to the probability of participation. However, once the decision on participation is made, income acts as an economic variable and the coefficient in the consumption level equation becomes significant and positive. If a simple OP model is estimated, these two opposing effects of income cannot be isolated and a positive coefficient in the OP results, indicating higher-income earners are both more likely to smoke and more likely to smoke more heavily, all other factors being equal.

Some other results in Table 2.14 are also worth mentioning. Male gender or residence in a decriminalised city increases the probability of both participation and smoking more heavily conditional on participation, whereas being married or having pre-school-aged children reduces the probability of both. Compared with those with less than year-12 education, an individual with a tertiary degree is more likely to participate in marijuana use but is less likely to be a heavy user. Although the consumption level is not responsive to marijuana price changes, it is related to the prices of some other illicit drugs.

The MEs on the probabilities of the four consumption levels in terms of the observable y variable are presented in Tables 2.15 and 2.16, together with the associated standard errors and the MEs and standard errors from a simple OP model. Note that for variables appearing in both x and z, we have combined the two parts of the MEs via the two decisions. For the MEs on $P(y = 0)$ from the ZIOPC model in Table 2.15, we also decompose the overall effect into two

Table 2.15: *Marginal effects of OP vs. ZIOPC: Non-participation and zero consumption*

	OP	ZIOPC decomposed		
Variable	$P(y=0)$	$P(y=0)$ (full)	$P(r=0)$ (non-participation)	$P(r=1, \tilde{y}=0)$ (zero consumption)
CON	−0.037 (0.192)	−1.418 (0.199)**	−4.467 (0.278)**	3.050 (0.323)**
LNAGE	0.203 (0.005)**	0.477 (0.013)**	1.176 (0.060)**	−0.699 (0.053)**
MALE	−0.043 (0.003)**	−0.091 (0.006)**	−0.122 (0.016)**	0.031 (0.012)**
MARRIED	0.063 (0.003)**	0.117 (0.006)**	0.193 (0.017)**	−0.077 (0.013)**
PRESKOOL	−0.005 (0.004)	0.047 (0.008)**	0.072 (0.024)**	−0.025 (0.019)*
SINCHIL	−0.027 (0.005)**	−0.019 (0.009)**	−0.036 (0.023)*	0.017 (0.016)
CAPITAL	0.004 (0.003)	0.012 (0.005)**	0.046 (0.015)**	−0.033 (0.011)**
ATSI	−0.039 (0.010)**	−0.011 (0.017)	0.060 (0.047)*	−0.071 (0.034)**
WORKWH	0.0010 (0.005)	−0.001 (0.008)	−0.108 (0.024)**	0.108 (0.020)**
WORKBL	−0.027 (0.006)**	−0.010 (0.009)	−0.060 (0.025)**	0.050 (0.020)**
STUDY	−0.006 (0.007)	−0.055 (0.017)**	−0.199 (0.043)**	0.144 (0.030)**
UNEMP	0.0003 (0.006)	−0.087 (0.018)**	−0.270 (0.047)**	0.183 (0.032)**
DEGREE	−0.001 (0.005)	−0.008 (0.008)	−0.133 (0.023)**	0.125 (0.018)**
YR12	−0.013 (0.004)**	0.005 (0.008)	−0.017 (0.020)	0.023 (0.014)*
DIPLOMA	−0.022 (0.004)**	−0.008 (0.007)	−0.034 (0.018)**	0.026 (0.013)**

LRPINC	−0.020 (0.002)**	0.010 (0.004)**	0.034 (0.011)**	−0.023 (0.008)**
DECRIM	−0.023 (0.004)**	−0.031 (0.006)**	−0.029 (0.016)**	−0.002 (0.012)
LRPMAR	−0.015 (0.012)*	−0.012 (0.012)	−0.012 (0.012)	
LRPCOC	−0.031 (0.008)**	−0.024 (0.008)**	−0.024 (0.008)**	
LRPHER	−0.043 (0.007)**	−0.037 (0.007)**	−0.037 (0.007)**	
LRPSPD	0.009 (0.004)**	0.007 (0.004)**	0.007 (0.004)**	
LRPTOB	0.028 (0.023)	−0.007 (0.023)	−0.007 (0.023)	

Notes: Standard errors are in parentheses. One-sided significance is indicated at the **5% and *10% levels.

Table 2.16: *Marginal effects of OP vs. ZIOPC: Levels of consumption*

Variable	P(y=1)		P(y=2)		P(y=3)	
	OP	ZIOPC	OP	ZIOPC	OP	ZIOPC
CON	0.0111 (0.0571)	0.5053 (0.0303)**	0.0113 (0.0582)	0.4543 (0.0496)**	0.0149 (0.0770)	0.4581 (0.1262)**
LNAGE	−0.0603 (0.0018)**	−0.1450 (0.0049)**	−0.0616 (0.0018)**	−0.1443 (0.0049)**	−0.0815 (0.0022)**	−0.1875 (0.0066)**
MALE	0.0128 (0.0010)**	0.0199 (0.0019)**	0.0131 (0.0010)**	0.0249 (0.0018)**	0.0173 (0.0013)**	0.0465 (0.0027)**
MARRIED	−0.0186 (0.0010)**	−0.0282 (0.0019)**	−0.0190 (0.0011)**	−0.0328 (0.0019)**	−0.0252 (0.0014)**	−0.0554 (0.0029)**
PRESKOOL	0.0015 (0.0013)	−0.0109 (0.0026)**	0.0016 (0.0013)	−0.0131 (0.0023)**	0.0021 (0.0018)	−0.0230 (0.0033)**
SINCHIL	0.0080 (0.0015)**	0.0049 (0.0027)**	0.0081 (0.0015)**	0.0055 (0.0027)**	0.0107 (0.0019)**	0.0086 (0.0040)**
CAPITAL	−0.0012 (0.0010)	−0.0049 (0.0016)**	−0.0012 (0.0010)	−0.0041 (0.0016)**	−0.0016 (0.0013)	−0.0032 (0.0025)*
ATSI	0.0115 (0.0030)**	−0.0033 (0.0053)	0.0117 (0.0030)**	0.0011 (0.0051)	0.0155 (0.0040)**	0.0133 (0.0078)**
WORKWH	−0.0003 (0.0015)	0.0083 (0.0025)**	−0.0003 (0.0015)	0.0029 (0.0023)	−0.0004 (0.0020)	−0.0108 (0.0040)**
WORKBL	0.0079 (0.0017)**	0.0058 (0.0027)**	0.0081 (0.0017)**	0.0040 (0.0025)*	0.0107 (0.0022)**	0.0004 (0.0043)
STUDY	0.0017 (0.0019)	0.0216 (0.0050)**	0.0018 (0.0020)	0.0183 (0.0051)**	0.0023 (0.0026)	0.0153 (0.0075)**
UNEMP	−0.0001 (0.0018)	0.0307 (0.0054)**	−0.0001 (0.0019)	0.0278 (0.0054)**	−0.0001 (0.0025)	0.0286 (0.0079)**
DEGREE	0.0004 (0.0014)	0.0111 (0.0025)**	0.0004 (0.0014)	0.0054 (0.0024)**	0.0006 (0.0019)	−0.0084 (0.0036)**
YR12	0.0038 (0.0013)**	0.0007 (0.0024)	0.0038 (0.0013)**	−0.0008 (0.0024)	0.0051 (0.0018)**	−0.0052 (0.0036)*
DIPLOMA	0.0066 (0.0012)**	0.0036 (0.0020)**	0.0067 (0.0012)**	0.0029 (0.0019)*	0.0089 (0.0016)**	0.0019 (0.0031)
LRPINC	0.0060 (0.0006)**	−0.0037 (0.0012)**	0.0061 (0.0007)**	−0.0033 (0.0012)**	0.0081 (0.0009)**	−0.0032 (0.0018)**

DECRIM	0.0069 (0.0012)**	0.0057 (0.0018)**	0.0070 (0.0012)**	0.0081 (0.0018)**	0.0093 (0.0016)**	0.0169 (0.0029)**
LRPMAR	0.0045 (0.0034)*	0.0013 (0.0014)	0.0046 (0.0035)*	0.0028 (0.0028)	0.0061 (0.0046)*	0.0075 (0.0074)
LRPCOC	0.0092 (0.0022)**	0.0027 (0.0010)**	0.0094 (0.0023)**	0.0056 (0.0019)**	0.0125 (0.0030)**	0.0152 (0.0050)**
LRPHER	0.0129 (0.0020)**	0.0043 (0.0010)**	0.0131 (0.0021)**	0.0088 (0.0017)**	0.0174 (0.0027)**	0.0238 (0.0044)**
LRPSPD	−0.0028 (0.0011)**	−0.0008 (0.0004)**	−0.0028 (0.0011)**	−0.0016 (0.0009)**	−0.0038 (0.0015)**	−0.0044 (0.0023)**
LRPTOB	−0.0084 (0.0069)	0.0008 (0.0026)	−0.0086 (0.0070)	0.0017 (0.0054)	−0.0113 (0.0093)	0.0046 (0.0146)

Notes: Standard errors are in parentheses. One-sided significance is indicated at the **5% and *10% levels.

parts: the effect on non-participation $P(r=0)$ and the effect on participation with zero consumption $P(r=1, \tilde{y}=0)$ in Table 2.15.

There are interesting effects of income in Tables 2.15 and 2.16: the results suggest that a 10 per cent increase in personal income results in a 0.0034 increase in the probability of non-participation, but a 0.0023 decrease in the probability of participation with zero consumption. Overall, there is a 0.001 net positive effect on the probability of observing zero for a 10 per cent increase in personal income. However, basing policy advice on the OP model results, we would conclude that income is positively related to both participation and higher consumption, and a 10 per cent increase in income results in a *decrease* of 0.002 in $P(y=0)$. Whereas the ME of income on the probability of weekly use is −0.0032 for a ZIOPC model, a positive ME of 0.0081 is estimated with an OP model.

We consider another example of the MEs of education on consumption via the dummy variable DEGREE. Using a simple OP model, we would conclude that individuals with a tertiary education are not significantly different from those with less than year-12 education for all categories of marijuana consumption (with none of the four effects being statistically significant). With a single latent equation in an OP model, we assume that there is a homogeneous DEGREE effect that affects an individual moving from a non-smoker to a smoker of higher levels in the same direction. However, when a ZIOPC model is used, we assume that the marijuana consumption categories observed are the result of two distinct decisions on participation and the level of consumption conditional on participation, on which DEGREE can have opposite effects. Indeed, as shown in Tables 2.14–2.16, the ZIOPC model estimates that degree holders are more likely to be participants, but less likely to be heavier users; they have a 13 per cent lower probability of being a genuine non-participant, but a 12 per cent higher chance of being a zero-consumption user, leading to a statistically insignificant total effect of observing a zero outcome $(y=0)$ because the opposing effects cancel each other out. Degree holders have a 0.84 per cent lower probability of being heavy weekly or daily users, whereas the effect for an OP model is insignificant.

Note also that the MEs on the unconditional probabilities of all three positive levels of smoking $P(y=j)$ $(j=1,2,3)$ are the combined result of effects on participation $P(r=1)$ and conditional consumption

$P(y=j|r=1)$ $(j=1, 2, 3)$. For example, the 0.0465 ME of MALE on the probability of being a heavy smoker, $P(y=3)$, in Table 2.16 is the combined result of two positive MALE effects on the two decisions. This is in contrast to the insignificant ME of 0.0006 from an OP with only one source of impact. Even the ME of 3.09 per cent higher probability of a male being a zero-consumption participant ($P(r=1, \bar{y}=0)$) is the result of the combined positive male effect on participation ($P(r=1)$) and the negative male effect on being a lower-level consumer conditional on participation ($P(y=0|r=1)$). The resulting ME on unconditional probability $P(y=0)$ from the ZIOPC model reveals that males are 9.13 per cent less likely to be observed not smoking, in contrast to only 4.32 per cent lower probability from an OP model.

The results from a ZIOP model and comparison with a simpler OP model in this section show that adding a latent zero split mechanism to the modelling strategy for marijuana consumer behaviour can potentially result in very different policy conclusions.

2.7 Conclusion

Recently available data from large-scale nationally representative surveys on drug consumption by Australians and reporting systems for drug prices have allowed empirical investigation of factors related to marijuana consumption. We presented some econometric analyses of consumption of marijuana and related drugs by Australians using unit record data from several waves of the NDSHS. We investigated the effects of individual socioeconomic and demographic factors and drug prices on marijuana use and levels of consumption, the relationship between participation in use of marijuana and other legal and illegal drugs, an alternative econometric strategy for modelling the large proportion of zero-consumption observations, and the difference such alternative assumptions on consumer decision-making behaviour can make in arriving at inferences relevant for future policy. The empirical findings provide valuable information for discussion of marijuana policies and education strategies.

A suite of econometric models was used in the studies. In particular, multivariate probit models were used to study joint participation in the use of marijuana and related licit and illicit drugs, namely tobacco, alcohol, cocaine and heroin, allowing for both observable and unobservable personal characteristics (such as taste and addictive personality) to impact on decisions on multi-drug consumption. Results indicate highly significant cross-drug correlation via the unobservables, information that is not available from a univariate approach. The multivariate probit approach allows modelling of conditional and joint probabilities and linkage to a set of explanatory factors. In addition, a ZIOP model was used to model the two separate decisions on participation and conditional levels of consumption. The specification of these two distinct data-generating processes in the model provides a better insight into the excessive zero observations in the data that can be the outcome from both regimes. Comparison with results from models without such a zero split mechanism showed that important information on opposing effects of some important explanatory variables on the two decisions may be lost and misleading policy recommendations may result. We showed that these more general econometric models generate different estimates and extra information compared with previous studies.

Notes

1. I would like to acknowledge my appreciation to Preety Srivastava (*nee* Ramful) for many helpful discussions and for her help with sorting the data set and preparing graphs. I also wish to thank Ken Clements for valuable discussions on the structure of the chapter and Mark Harris for valuable discussions regarding Section 2.6.
2. Data for the latest survey in 2007 were not available at the time of writing.
3. Data for the 2007 survey were not available at the time of writing.
4. An alternative method is to compute the average ME over all individuals. Harris *et al.* (2006) compute the MEs for a different discrete-choice model using both methods and find that differences between the two approaches are trivial.
5. Ramful (2008) estimated a five-equation MVP model including marijuana, cocaine, heroin, alcohol and tobacco using pooled NDSHS data from 1998, 2001 and 2004. The correlation coefficients range from 0.75 between cocaine and heroin to 0.32 between heroin and tobacco.

References

ABS (2006). *Consumer price index, 14th series: by region, all groups.* Canberra: Australian Bureau of Statistics (catalogue no. 640101b).

AIHW (2005a). *2004 National Drug Strategy Household Survey: first results*. Canberra: Australian Institute of Health and Welfare (catalogue no. PHE 57).

AIHW (2005b). *2004 National Drug Strategy Household Survey: detailed findings*. Canberra: Australian Institute of Health and Welfare (catalogue no. PHE 66).

Becker, G. S. and Murphy, K. M. (1988). "A theory of rational addiction." *Journal of Political Economy* 96, 675–700.

Cameron, L. and Williams, J. (2001). "Cannabis, alcohol and cigarettes: substitutes or complements?" *The Economic Record* 77, 19–34.

Chaloupka, F. J. and Laixuthai, A. (1997). "Do youths substitute alcohol and marijuana? Some econometric evidence." *Eastern Economic Journal* 23, 253–76.

Clements, K. W. and Daryal, M. (2005). "The economics of marijuana consumption." Chapter 10 in eds., S. Selvanathan and Selvanathan, E. A., *The demand for alcohol, tobacco and marijuana: international evidence*. Aldershot: Ashgate, pp. 243–67.

Collins, D. J. and Lapsley, H. M. (2002). *Counting the cost: estimates of the social costs of drug abuse in Australia in 1998–99*. National Drug Strategy Monograph Series No. 49, Commonwealth Department of Health and Ageing: Canberra.

DeSimone, J. and Farrelly, M. C. (2003). "Price and enforcement effects on cocaine and marijuana demand." Working Paper No. 0101. Department of Economics, East Carolina University.

DiNardo, J. and Lemieux, T. (2001). "Alcohol, marijuana, and American youth: the unintended consequences of government regulation." *Journal of Health Economics* 20, 991–1010.

Farrelly, M. C., Bray, J. W., Zarkin, G. A. and Wendling, B. W. (2001). "The joint demand for cigarettes and marijuana: evidence from the National Household Surveys on Drug Abuse." *Journal of Health Economics* 20, 51–68.

Grossman, M. and Chaloupka, F. J. (1998). "The demand for cocaine by young adults: a rational addiction approach." *Journal of Health Economics* 17, 427–74.

Harris, M., Ramful, P. and Zhao, X. (2006). "An ordered generalised extreme value model with application to alcohol consumption in Australia." *Journal of Health Economics* 25, 782–801.

Harris, M. and Zhao, X. (2007). "A zero-inflated ordered probit model, with an application to modelling tobacco consumption." *Journal of Econometrics* 141, 1073–99.

NDARC (2004). *Australian drug trends 2003: findings from the Illicit Drug Reporting System (IDRS)*. Monograph 50. Sydney: National

Drug and Alcohol Research Centre, University of New South Wales.

NDSHS (2005). Computer files of unit record data, National Drug Strategy Household Surveys, 2004 and previous surveys. Canberra: Social Science Data Archives, Australian National University.

Pacula, R. L. (1998a). "Does increasing the beer tax reduce marijuana consumption?" *Journal of Health Economics* 17, 557–85.

Pacula, R. L. (1998b). "Adolescent alcohol and marijuana consumption: is there really a gateway effect?" NBER Working Paper 6348. Cambridge, MA: National Bureau of Economic Research.

Pacula, R. L., Chriqui, J. F. and King, J. (2003). "Marijuana decriminalisation: what does it mean in the United States?" NBER Working Paper 9690. Cambridge, MA: National Bureau of Economic Research.

Pudney, S. (2003). "The road to ruin? Sequences of initiation to drugs and crime in Britain." *The Economic Journal* 113, C182–98.

Ramful, P. (2008). *Recreational drug consumption in Australia: an econometric analysis*. PhD thesis, Faculty of Business and Economics, Monash University, Australia.

Ramful, P. and Zhao, X. (2009). "Demand for marijuana, cocaine and heroin in Australia: a multivariate probit approach." *Applied Economics* 41, 481–96.

Saffer, H. and Chaloupka, F. J. (1999). "The demand for illicit drugs." *Economic Inquiry* 37, 401–11.

Sickles, R. and Taubman, P. (1991). "Who uses illegal drugs?" *The American Economic Review* 81, 248–51.

van Ours, J. C. (2003). "Is cannabis a stepping-stone for cocaine?" *Journal of Health Economics* 22, 539–54.

Williams, J. (2004). "The effects of price and policy on marijuana use: what can be learned from the Australian experience?" *Health Economics* 13, 123–37.

Zhao, X. and Harris, M. (2004). "Demand for marijuana, alcohol and tobacco: participation, levels of consumption, and cross-equation correlations." *Economic Record* 80, 394–410.

3 | The pricing of marijuana

KENNETH W. CLEMENTS

This chapter deals with three fascinating themes related to the pricing of marijuana:

- *The geography of marijuana prices.* We identify substantial regional differences in marijuana prices within Australia, use the cost of marijuana to conveniently divide the country into three regions, and propose reasons to explain why the price differences are not arbitraged away.
- *The economics of technical change.* Over the last decade the production of marijuana has experienced a "hydroponic revolution", whereby the crop is now predominantly grown indoors under tightly controlled conditions. We show that at the same time marijuana prices have fallen by much more than most other commodity prices. We argue that these two developments are not unrelated, as it seems likely that a large part of the benefits of this productivity improvement has been captured by consumers in the form of lower marijuana prices. However, we also recognise that part of the price decline could possibly be attributable to more tolerant community attitudes, softer laws and reduced penalties for drug offences.
- *Packaging economics.* Large price discounts are available for bulk purchases of marijuana. For example, the unit cost of marijuana purchased in the form of an ounce package is as much as 50 per cent lower than that purchased in a gram package. Using new methods, we apply the economic theory of packaging to understand the existence of these quantity discounts and show that marijuana seems to be subject to pricing principles that are similar to those observed for legal products such as groceries, as well as some other illicit drugs.

These themes are of considerable interest because they illustrate the workings of economic principles in an unusual setting.

We start the chapter with a brief discussion of issues in the collection and interpretation of illicit drug prices. A description of the rich data on marijuana prices that we have received from the Australian Bureau of Criminal Intelligence then follows. These data are used as the basis for the construction of indexes of marijuana prices over time, regions and major product types. Analysis of the prices reveals the patterns mentioned above. This chapter draws in part on Clements (2002, 2004, 2006).

3.1 Issues in drug prices

In recent years there has been considerable interest in research on the economic analysis of the prices of illicit drugs.[1] This research has identified important issues associated with the unique aspects of these prices and the working of drug markets, and in this section we discuss some of these issues.

In an early study, Caulkins (1994) notes the availability of substantial data on the prices of illicit drugs in the United States, collected by agencies such as the Drug Enforcement Administration (DEA) and the police as part of undercover operations. While it is not possible to guarantee that these prices are representative, there are reasons to believe they are likely to be satisfactory. Caulkins (1994) appeals to the self-interest of criminals in arguing:

One cannot know for certain that [the DEA and police] pay market prices, but if the price they negotiated were noticeably different from the standard price, the seller would abort the deal; momentary profits would not likely induce a criminal to wittingly engage in an illicit activity with someone suspected of being a law enforcement officer.

At the same time, the price of an illicit drug is not a well-defined concept, as prices reflect considerations such as transaction size, purity and location. Regarding transaction size, drug prices generally reflect substantial discounts for large purchases. As prices do not generally fall in proportion to drug quality, a similar phenomenon can be observed for purity. For example, two ounces of 40 per cent pure cocaine are generally worth more than one ounce of 80 per cent pure cocaine; in other words, purity does not command the expected price premium. Regarding spatial differences in drug prices, Caulkins (1994) comments on the possibilities in the context of the cost of large transactions of cocaine (kilogram transactions) in the US as follows:

It is not clear a priori whether kilogram prices are uniform across the country. One speculation is that kilograms of cocaine are so valuable and so easy to transport, an efficient market has developed that erases price differences at the kilogram level. Another view is that information flows in drug markets are so poor (e.g., because advertising is difficult) and lateral transaction costs so great, that kilogram price differences can exist.

In fact, Caulkins finds significant differences in these prices across large US cities that seem to be sustained over time.

In addition to the above points, as noted by Caulkins (2007) and Caulkins and Reuter (1998), there are three other important issues in understanding drug prices. First, the nominal prices of some drugs are more or less constant and the quantity transacted varies in response to market conditions. For example, in the US the cost of a "dime bag" of heroin remains unchanged at $10, while the corresponding quantity contained in the bag might well change over time and location. This practice is known as "conventional pricing" (Wendel and Curtis, 2000). Clearly, the nominal price has to be adjusted for by the quantity transacted to obtain the effective price of the drugs.

The second additional point is related to the lack of information in drug markets. As there can be no government regulation or advertising, in the illicit drugs industry there are few of the conventional mechanisms to assure consumers of the quality of the product being purchased. Moreover, as the turnover of drug dealers can be quite rapid, even the usual quality-control incentives associated with the maintenance of reputational capital can operate only weakly, if at all, in this business. Drugs are thus an "experience good" to consumers. As Caulkins (2007) puts it:

Economists use the term "experience good" to describe something whose quality is not known to the buyer until after the price has been negotiated and/or the purchase consummated. The classic example is a restaurant meal. Certain things about the meal are known from the menu at the time it is ordered, but not everything about how it will taste. As a result, sometimes customers end up disappointed, wishing that they had not paid so much or that they had not patronised the restaurant at all.

Likewise, drug buyers do not know the drug's quality at the time of purchase. Transactions are rushed; formal testing is time consuming and may be impractical for small quantities. Indeed, unlike the restaurant meal example, consumers still have imperfect information of purity even after consuming the drugs.

This lack of information about the product is the basis for the argument that observed prices should be adjusted by *expected*, rather than actual, purity (Caulkins, 1994).

Finally, in addition to the monetary cost of drugs, non-monetary components can be important in some cases. These include the opportunity costs of search time involved in locating a seller, and payments in kind when drugs are supplied at less than the going price.

3.2 Australian marijuana prices

This section describes the marijuana prices that are used in this chapter.

The Australian Bureau of Statistics does not collect marijuana prices, but the Australian Bureau of Criminal Intelligence (ABCI) has some "unofficial" data, which it generously provided to us. These prices were elicited by law enforcement agencies in the various states and territories during undercover buys. In general, the data are quarterly and refer to the period 1990–1999 for each state and territory. The different types of marijuana identified separately are leaf, heads, hydroponics, skunk, hash resin and hash oil. However, we focus on only the prices of leaf and heads packaged in the form of grams and ounces, as these products are the most popular. The data are described in ABCI (1996), with acknowledgement that there are some inconsistencies in the data. The prices are usually recorded in the form of ranges and the basic data are listed in Clements and Daryal (2001), who also "consolidate" and edit the data to eliminate outliers. While it is unlikely that these data constitute a random sample, a common problem when studying the prices of almost any illicit good, it is not clear whether they are biased upwards or downwards, especially when averaged over the individual prices. In summary, while these data are less than perfect, they are all we have. Further details of the marijuana prices are provided in Section A3.1 of the Appendix to this chapter.

Marijuana prices for the states and territories of Australia are listed in Tables 3.1 and 3.2. There are three important patterns in these prices:

- The substantial regional differences in prices. In 1999, for example, heads purchased in the form of a gram cost $1,224 per ounce in the state of New South Wales, while the same product cost only $560 in Western Australia.

Table 3.1: *Marijuana prices: leaf (dollars per ounce)*

Year	NSW	VIC	QLD	WA	SA	NT	TAS	ACT	Weighted mean
Purchased in the form of a gram									
1990	770	735	700	802	700	700	910	630	747
1991	1,050	770	700	770	700	700	1,050	642	852
1992	1,060	700	630	700	560	700	700	630	798
1993	583	711	683	653	630	665	613	595	645
1994	998	698	648	700	630	665	443	753	779
1995	1,085	700	560	700	630	735	560	753	797
1996	1,400	793	665	753	630	788	508	700	949
1997	1,400	490	560	653	630	718	525	613	843
1998	1,097	735	630	467	653	683	467	723	798
1999	1,155	636	700	556	630	700	642	700	816
Mean	1,060	697	648	675	639	705	642	674	802
Purchased in the form of an ounce									
1990	438	513	225	210	388	275	313	413	390
1991	475	450	215	170	400	275	350	325	381
1992	362	363	188	340	225	300	188	350	313
1993	383	409	168	200	388	281	175	250	326
1994	419	394	181	288	325	244	170	400	341
1995	319	400	400	308	347	294	163	256	350
1996	325	383	350	283	350	263	200	408	339
1997	288	285	431	263	350	288	375	386	320
1998	333	363	375	250	350	300	375	450	344
1999	275	313	444	250	350	300	262	450	322
Mean	362	387	298	256	347	282	257	369	343

Notes:

1. The means in the last column are population-weighted.

2. The grand means are the means of the corresponding rows.

- The substantial decline in prices. For example, at the national level, the average price of an ounce of heads declined from $557 per ounce in 1990 to $403 in 1999, a decline of more than 25 per cent. It should be noted that this *nominal* price declined at a time when prices in general were rising, so that the relative price decrease was greater.

Table 3.2: *Marijuana prices: heads (dollars per ounce)*

Year	NSW	VIC	QLD	WA	SA	NT	TAS	ACT	Weighted mean
			Purchased in the form of a gram						
1990	1,120	1,050	1,400	1,120	1,400	700	910	840	1,159
1991	1,120	1,120	1,400	962	1,400	700	1,120	840	1,168
1992	1,400	1,120	910	770	700	700	1,225	770	1,103
1993	863	665	858	840	1,173	700	927	747	834
1994	1,155	770	1,068	840	1,120	770	735	980	992
1995	1,190	793	843	749	1,138	793	1,155	1,033	974
1996	1,171	840	771	704	910	840	963	1,400	944
1997	1,400	858	630	700	840	863	700	793	977
1998	1,120	840	723	630	840	823	723	840	889
1999	1,224	630	589	560	840	840	630	1,006	841
Mean	1,176	869	919	788	1,036	773	909	925	988
			Purchased in the form of an ounce						
1990	600	650	413	600	400	325	525	463	557
1991	600	550	425	502	200	325	450	375	504
1992	375	450	388	390	363	450	425	500	401
1993	500	348	363	431	450	363	344	383	419
1994	550	367	328	400	425	325	363	550	432
1995	538	400	320	354	438	358	350	438	430
1996	550	400	398	325	406	283	388	525	444
1997	550	400	538	300	400	358	383	442	466
1998	488	388	550	275	340	325	367	450	437
1999	513	400	300	250	400	300	325	479	403
Mean	526	435	402	383	382	341	392	461	449

Note: See notes to Table 3.1.

- The substantial quantity discounts for bulk purchases. To illustrate, take the case of the national price of heads in 1999. When this product was purchased in the form of an ounce, the price was $403/28 = $14 per gram, but the cost when purchased in the form of a gram was more than twice as much at $841/28 = $30 per gram. As drugs pass through the supply chain and are processed further and repackaged, the value added rises, the lot size falls and unit costs increase. This rise in the unit cost as the product moves further up the supply chain, towards the ultimate consumer, represents a quantity discount to buyers of drugs and a price markup for sellers.

These price patterns are described in detail and analysed thoroughly in this chapter.

3.3 Regional disparities in prices

Relative to weight and volume, marijuana is a high-value product, so we would expect transport costs to be low relative to the price. Other things being equal, this would tend to make for a national marijuana market with regional prices more or less equalised. The tradeable nature of marijuana would also seem to be supported by the prominent role that anecdotal evidence accords to Adelaide as a major exporter. Radio National (1999) noted that:

Cannabis is by far and away the illicit drug of choice for Australians. There is a multi-billion dollar industry to supply it, and increasingly, the centre of action is the City of Churches.

The same program quoted a person called "David" as saying:

Say five, ten years ago, everyone spoke of the country towns of New South Wales and the north coast, now you never hear of it; those towns have died in this regard I'd say, because they're lost out to the indoor variety, the hydro, and everyone was just saying South Australia, Adelaide, Adelaide, Adelaide, and that's where it all seems to be coming from.

In a similar vein, the ABCI (1999, p. 18) commented on marijuana being exported from South Australia to other states as follows:

New South Wales Police reported that cannabis has been found secreted in the body parts of motor vehicles from South Australia ... It is reported that cannabis originating in South Australia is transported to neighbouring jurisdictions. South Australian Police reported that large amounts of cannabis are transported from South Australia by air, truck, hire vehicles, buses and private motor vehicles.

Queensland Police reported that South Australian cannabis is sold on the Gold Coast. New South Wales Police reported South Australian vehicles returning to that state have been found carrying large amounts of cash or amphetamines, or both. It also considers that the decrease in the amount of locally grown cannabis is the result of an increase in the quantity of South Australian cannabis in New South Wales.

The Australian Federal Police in Canberra reported that the majority of cannabis transported to the Australian Capital Territory is from the Murray Bridge area of South Australia . . .

In view of the above, it is somewhat surprising that there are significant differences in marijuana prices in the different states and territories of Australia. This is illustrated in Panel I of Table 3.3, which presents the results, for each type of marijuana, of regressing the price on dummy variables for each state and territory. In this panel, the dependent variable is $\log p_{rt}$, where p_{rt} is the price of the relevant type of marijuana in region r ($r = 1, \ldots, 8$) and year t ($t = 1990, \ldots, 1999$), and the coefficients measure the price relative to NSW, the base region. Only two of the 28 coefficients are positive, leaf ounce in Victoria and ACT, but these are both not significantly different from zero. The vast majority of the other coefficients are significantly negative, which indicates that marijuana prices are significantly lower in all regions relative to NSW. Row 4 indicates that for the product "head ounce", the most important category, NT is the cheapest region, with marijuana costing approximately 44 per cent less than that in NSW, followed by WA (35 per cent less), SA (34 per cent), Tasmania (30 per cent), Queensland (28 per cent), Victoria (20 per cent) and, finally, ACT (13 per cent). The last column of the table presents a measure of the dispersion of prices around those in NSW that is approximately the percentage standard deviation. If prices are equalised across regions, then this measure is zero. However, as can be observed, the standard deviation is substantially above zero and ranges from 24 per cent to 44 per cent.

It is clear from the significance of the regional dummies that marijuana prices are not equalised nationally. For some further results that lead to the same conclusion, see Section A3.4 of the Appendix. What could be the possible barriers to inter-regional trade that would prevent prices from being equalised? In other words, what prevents an entrepreneur buying marijuana in NT and selling in NSW to realise a (gross) profit of more than 40 per cent for a head ounce? While such a transaction is certainly not risk-free, is it plausible for the risk premium to be more than 40 per cent? Are there other substantial costs to be paid that would rule out arbitraging away the price differential? To what extent do the regional differences in marijuana prices reflect the cost of living in the location where it is sold? Panels II and III of

Table 3.3: *Estimated regional effects for marijuana prices, income and house prices* $\log y_{rt} = \alpha + \sum_{u=2}^{8} \beta_u z_{urt}$ *(t-values in parentheses)*

| Dependent variable y_{rt} | Intercept α | Coefficients of dummy variables, $\beta_u \times 100$ | | | | | | | $\bar{R}^2$ | Regional dispersion $\{(1/7)\sum_{u=1}^{7}\beta_u^2\}^{1/2}\times 100$ |
		VIC	QLD	WA	SA	NT	TAS	ACT		
I. Marijuana prices										
1. Leaf gram	6.94 (134.60)	−39.80 (−5.46)	−46.70 (−6.41)	−43.40 (−5.95)	−47.70 (−6.54)	−38.00 (−5.21)	−51.20 (−7.02)	−42.90 (−5.89)	0.44	44.45
2. Leaf ounce	5.88 (77.70)	7.00 (0.65)	−24.60 (−2.30)	−34.90 (−3.26)	−3.60 (−0.34)	−23.70 (−2.22)	−37.90 (−3.54)	1.40 (0.13)	0.28	23.56
3. Head gram	7.06 (108.30)	−31.10 (−3.37)	−28.00 (−3.04)	−40.90 (−4.44)	−14.40 (−1.56)	−41.40 (−4.49)	−27.40 (−2.97)	−24.80 (−2.69)	0.23	30.96
4. Head ounce	6.26 (106.00)	−20.10 (−2.41)	−28.20 (−3.37)	−34.50 (−4.13)	−33.50 (−4.01)	−43.60 (−5.22)	−29.80 (−3.57)	−13.40 (−1.60)	0.28	30.43
II. Income										
5. Gross household	10.11 (312.47)	−2.78 (−0.61)	−15.12 (−3.31)	−6.98 (−1.52)	−13.09 (−2.86)	−9.25 (−2.02)	−22.06 (−4.82)	28.54 (6.24)	0.68	16.23
6. Gross house disposable	9.84 (289.02)	−2.41 (−0.50)	−14.56 (−3.03)	−7.69 (−1.60)	−12.24 (−2.54)	−4.96 (−1.03)	−21.42 (−4.45)	30.34 (6.30)	0.67	16.17

Table 3.3: (continued)

Dependent variable y_{rt}	Intercept α	Coefficients of dummy variables, $\beta_u \times 100$ VIC	QLD	WA	SA	NT	TAS	ACT	$\bar{R}^2$	Regional dispersion $\{(1/7)\sum_{u=1}^{7} \beta_u^2\}^{1/2} \times 100$
				III. Housing prices						
7. Houses	5.33 (120.30)	−26.94 (−4.30)	−47.24 (−7.54)	−55.03 (−8.78)	−60.63 (−9.68)	−33.36 (−5.32)	−70.02 (−11.18)	−31.72 (−5.06)	0.68	48.82
8. Units	5.11 (115.40)	−30.80 (−4.92)	−38.95 (−6.22)	−65.50 (−10.46)	−61.85 (−9.87)	−37.39 (−5.97)	−72.48 (−11.57)	−31.42 (−5.02)	0.71	51.02

Notes:

1. The regional dummy variable $z_{urt} = 1$ if $u = r$, 0 otherwise.

2. In all cases, the data are annual for the period 1990 to 1999, pooled over the eight regions.

3. Gross household income and gross household disposable income are in terms of nominal dollars per capita.

Sources: Marijuana prices, Tables 3.1 and 3.2. Income, Australian Bureau of Statistics, *Australian National Accounts: State Accounts* (Cat. No. 5220.0, 13 November 2002), Table 27. Housing prices, David Wesney, Manager, Research and Statistics, REIA, Canberra. The housing data refer to quarterly median sale prices of established houses and units (flats, units and townhouses) in capital cities. The quarterly data are annualised by averaging.

Table 3.3 explore this issue using per capita incomes and housing prices as proxies for regional living costs.[2] In Panel II, we regress the logarithm of income on seven regional dummies. All the coefficients are negative, except those for the ACT. It is evident from the last column of Panel II that the dispersion of income regionally is considerably less than that of marijuana prices, approximately one half, which could reflect the operation of the fiscal equalisation feature of the Australian federal system. Panel III repeats the analysis with housing prices replacing incomes, and the results in the last column show that the regional dispersion of housing prices is of the same order of magnitude as that of marijuana prices. Figure 3.1 gives a graphical comparison of the regional dispersion of prices and incomes.

To compare and contrast the prices of marijuana and housing further, Figure 3.2 plots the two sets of prices relative to NSW/Sydney using the regional dummy-variable coefficients for head ounce (row 4 of Table 3.3) and those for houses (row 7 of Table 3.3). The broken ray from the origin has a 45° slope, so that as we move along the ray and travel further away from the origin, marijuana and housing prices both decrease equiproportionally relative to those in Sydney. In other words, any point on the ray represents lower prices of both goods, but the marijuana/housing relative price is the same as that in Sydney. A point above the ray, such as that for Darwin, indicates that marijuana is cheap in terms of housing in comparison to Sydney. Next, consider Perth, where marijuana is approximately 30 per cent cheaper than in Sydney, while the cost of housing is 55 per cent below that of Sydney. Relative to Sydney, although marijuana is cheap, housing is even cheaper, causing the marijuana/housing relative price to be higher in Perth than in Sydney. As all cities other than Darwin lie below the ray from the origin, we can state that relative to housing, Sydney has the country's cheapest marijuana. The solid line in Figure 3.2 is the least-squares regression line, constrained to pass through the origin. The slope of this line is the elasticity of marijuana prices with respect to housing prices, estimated to be 0.59 (SE = 0.09). Since the observation for Darwin lies substantially above the regression line, we can state that marijuana prices in that city are cheap given its housing prices, or that housing is expensive in view of the cost of marijuana. Among the seven non-Sydney cities, given its housing prices, marijuana would seem to be most overpriced, or housing most underpriced, in Hobart.

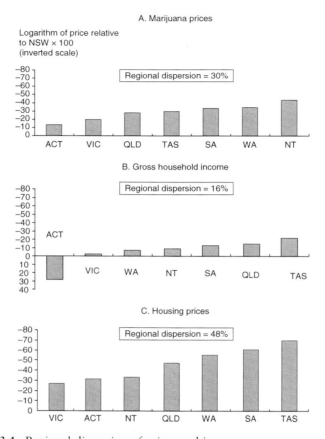

Figure 3.1. Regional dispersion of prices and incomes

The final interesting feature of Figure 3.2 relates to the geography of prices. The distance from the origin of a point in the figure can be used as a price index. On this basis, the figure can be used to naturally divide Australia into three super regions/cities: (i) NSW/Sydney, with expensive marijuana and housing; (ii) Victoria/Melbourne and ACT/Canberra, with moderately priced marijuana and housing; and (iii) the rest, with cheap marijuana and housing.

The above discussion shows that to the extent that housing costs are a good proxy for living costs, marijuana prices are at least partially related to costs in general. As a substantial part of the overall price of marijuana is likely to reflect local distribution activities, which differ

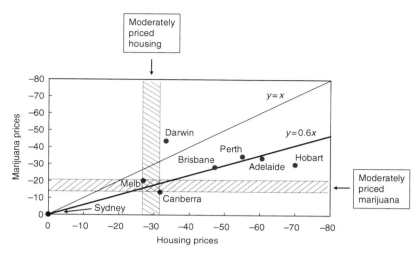

Figure 3.2. Marijuana and housing prices
(logarithmic ratios to Sydney × 100; inverted scales)

significantly across different regions, this could explain the finding
that the market is not a national one but a series of regional markets
that are not closely linked. Understanding the pricing of marijuana is
enhanced if we split the product into: (i) a (nationally) traded component comprising mainly the "raw" product, whose price is likely to
be approximately equalised in different regions; and (ii) a non-traded
component associated with packaging and local distribution, the price
of which is less likely to be equalised. As such services are likely to be
labour-intensive, their prices will mainly reflect local wages, which, in
turn, will partly reflect local living costs. The results of this section
could be interpreted as pointing to a surprising importance of the non-
traded component of marijuana prices.

A final point to note is the role of regional differences in penalties
for possessing marijuana. As discussed in Section 3.5, there seems to
be little, if any, link between penalties and regional price differences.

3.4 Marijuana has become substantially cheaper

Notwithstanding the likely importance of packaging and distribution
costs, marijuana is probably still predominantly an agricultural/
horticultural-based product. The real prices of many primary products

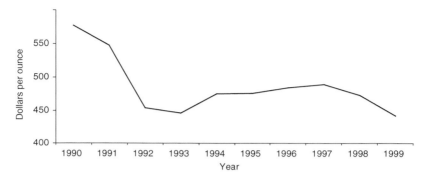

Figure 3.3. Marijuana price index
Source: See Section A3.2 of the Appendix.

exhibit a long-term downward trend of approximately 1–2 per cent per annum (p.a.) due to the workings of Engel's law and productivity growth in agriculture. Are marijuana prices subject to a similar pattern? In this and the next section, we show that, possibly because of a surge in productivity growth due to the adoption of hydroponic techniques of production and a softening of community attitudes to the use of marijuana, prices have fallen by much more than 1–2 per cent, so that the answer to this question is a definitive "No".

Figure 3.3 plots an index of nominal marijuana prices and shows that over the course of the 1990s prices fell from nearly $600 per ounce to approximately $450.[3] Figure 3.4 presents time paths for marijuana prices in terms of the CPI and alcohol prices and it is evident that prices decline in real terms on average by either 4.9 per cent or 5.7 per cent p.a., depending on which deflator is used.

How do marijuana prices compare with those of other commodities? Figure 3.5 presents price changes for 24 internationally traded commodities, as well as marijuana. The striking feature of this graph is that marijuana prices have fallen the most by far. The only commodity to come close is rubber, but its average price decrease is still one percentage point less than that for marijuana (−3.9 versus −4.9 per cent p.a.). After rubber there is a substantial drop-off in the price decreases (palm oil, −2.3 per cent, rice, −2.2 per cent, cotton, −2.0 per cent, etc.). Surprisingly, the price of tobacco, which might be considered to be related to marijuana in terms of both consumption and production, increased by 0.9 per cent p.a. Note also that minerals

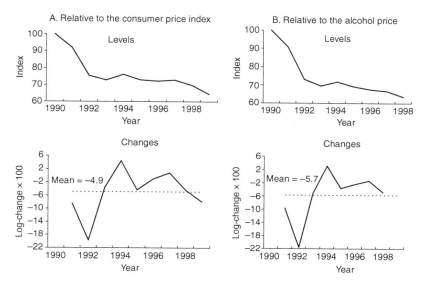

Figure 3.4. Relative prices of marijuana
Source: See Section A3.2 of the Appendix.

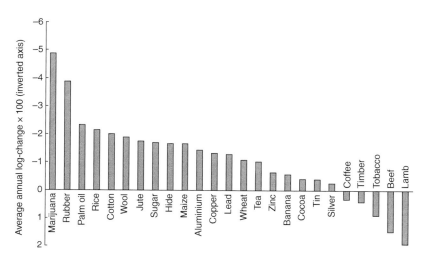

Figure 3.5. Marijuana and commodity relative price changes
Source: *The Economist* (2000); see Section A3.6 of the Appendix for details.

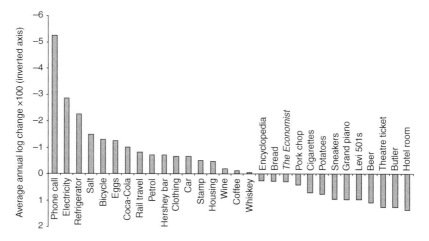

Figure 3.6. Thirty more relative price changes
Source: *The Economist* (2000); see Section A3.6 of the Appendix for details.

(aluminium, copper, lead, zinc, tin and silver) tend to lie in the middle of the spectrum of prices and have agricultural products on either side. The decreases in most of the commodity prices reflect the impact of productivity enhancement coupled with low income elasticity. The mineral prices could also reflect the tendency of GDP to become "lighter" and less metal-intensive over time.

What about the prices of other goods that are not traded commodities? Figure 3.6 presents a selection of relative price changes averaged over the period 1900–2000. As expected, labour-intensive services (such as the cost of a hotel room, a butler and a theatre ticket) increase in relative terms. The prices that fall include those that are: (i) predominantly agricultural or resource-based (coffee, wine, eggs and petrol); and (ii) subject to substantial technological improvements in their manufacture and/or economies of scale (e.g. cars, clothing, refrigerators, electricity). To illustrate, consider the price of cars. According to *The Economist* (2000), "Henry Ford's original Model-T, introduced in 1908, cost $850, but by 1924 only $265: He was using an assembly line, and, in a virtuous circle, was selling far more cars. Over the century the real price of a car fell by 50 per cent". The quality-adjusted price of a car, and some other goods, would have fallen even further, as recognised by *The Economist* (2000). If we omit the cost of phone calls as a possible outlier (as the price falls by 99.5 per cent over the entire century!), the good with the greatest price decrease is electricity. However, even electricity prices fall by only 2.8 per cent p.a., substantially below the decrease for marijuana (4.9 per cent).

In a well-known paper, Nordhaus (1997) analyses the evolution of the price of light over the past 200 years. He uses the service characteristic provided by light, illumination, which is measured in terms of lumens. He notes that a "wax candle emits about 13 lumens [and] a one-hundred-watt filament bulb about 1200 lumens", which shows that the flow of lighting service from different sources of light has increased substantially with the introduction of new products. Nordhaus constructs an index of the true (or quality-adjusted) price of light in real terms. This index falls from a value of 100 in the year 1800 to a mere 0.029 in 1992 (Nordhaus, 1997, Table 1.4, column 3), which represents an average price decline of 4.15 per cent p.a., or a log-change ($\times 100$) of -4.24 p.a. As the real price of marijuana has an annual average log-change ($\times 100$) of -4.87, marijuana relative to light on average falls by $-4.87 - (-4.24) = -0.63$ p.a.. If past trends continue, this implies that the number of years for this relative price to fall by $k \times 100$ per cent is $[\log(1-k)]/-0.0063$, so that it would take approximately 35 years for the price of marijuana relative to light to fall by 20 per cent. In other words, as the price of marijuana relative to light is fairly constant, it can be argued that the production of both goods has been subject to similar degrees of productivity improvement.

A final well-known example of the impact of productivity improvement on prices is the case of personal computers (PCs). Berndt and Rappaport (2001) describe the enhanced capabilities of PCs over the last quarter of a century in the following terms:

When introduced in 1976, personal computers (PCs) had only several kilobytes of random-access memory (RAM) and no hard disk, processed commands at speeds of less than 1 megahertz (MHz), yet typically cost several thousand dollars. Today's PCs have megabytes (MB) of RAM and gigabytes of hard-disk memory, process commands at speeds exceeding 1,000 MHz, and often cost less than $1,000. Ever more powerful PC boxes have been transformed into increasingly smaller and lighter notebooks.

Berndt and Rappaport compute a quality-adjusted price index for PCs, with quality defined in terms of hard-disk memory, processor speed and the amount of RAM. Using more than 9,000 observations on approximately 375 models per year, they find that for desktop PCs, prices declined over the period 1976–1999 at an average rate of 27 per cent p.a. and that the ratio of the price index in 1976 to that in 1999 is 1445:1. For mobile PCs, prices declined by approximately 25 per cent p.a. on average from 1983 to 1999. Although the above-documented decreases in marijuana prices are very substantial among agricultural/horticultural commodities, they are still considerably less than those for PCs, which are nothing less than spectacular. There would seem to be fundamental differences between the limits to productivity enhancement for commodities that are *grown* and those that involve electronics, such as computing, power generation and telecommunications.

3.5 Why did prices fall so much?

One reason for the decline in marijuana prices is that production has been subject to productivity enhancement associated with the adoption of hydroponic growing techniques,[4] leading to a higher-quality product containing higher THC levels.[5] For example, hydroponically grown marijuana from northern Tasmania was analysed as containing 16 per cent THC, while that grown outdoors in the south of the state contained 12.8 per cent (ABCI, 1996). The ease of concealment and the near-ideal growing conditions that produce good-quality plants are the main reasons for the shift to hydroponic systems. According to the ABCI (1996):

Hydroponic systems are being used to grow cannabis on a relatively large scale. Unlike external plantations, hydroponic cultivation can be used in any region and is not regulated by growing seasons. Both residential and industrial areas are used to establish these indoor sites. Cellars and concealed rooms in existing residential and commercial properties are also used... The use of shipping containers to grow cannabis with hydroponic equipment has been seen in many cases. The containers are sometimes buried on rural properties to reduce chances of detection.

Other anecdotal evidence also points to the increase in hydroponic activity over this period. For example, according to the *Yellow Pages* telephone directory, in 1999 Victoria had 149 hydroponics suppliers, NSW 115, SA 69, Queensland 59 and WA 58. We suspect that many of these operations supply marijuana growers. For a further discussion of this anecdotal evidence, see Clements (2002).

Table 3.4: *Infringement notices for minor cannabis offences (Rate per 100,000 population)*

Year	SA	NT	ACT	Australia
1996	1,114	-	96	92
1997	857	124	103	72
1998	725	115	76	60
1999	631	179	49	53
2000	579	401	-	50
2001	580	208	59	48
Mean	748	205	77	63

Source: See Section A3.7 of the Appendix.

A second possible reason for the decline in marijuana prices is that because of changing community attitudes, laws have become softer and penalties reduced. Information on the enforcement of marijuana laws distinguishes between (i) infringement notices issued for minor offences and (ii) arrests. Table 3.4 presents the available Australian data on infringement notices for the three states/territories that use them, SA, NT and ACT. It is evident that per capita infringement notices have declined substantially in SA since 1996, increased in NT, first increased and then declined in ACT, and declined noticeably for Australia as a whole, falling by almost 50 per cent. This information points in the direction of lower policing effort. Data on arrests and prosecution for marijuana offences are presented in Table 3.5. Panel I shows that the arrest rate for NSW was more or less stable over the six-year period, while that for Victoria fell substantially owing to a "redirection of police resources away from minor cannabis offences" (ABCI, 1998). For Queensland, the arrest rate increased by more than 50 per cent in 1997, then fell back to a more or less stable value, but in WA the rate fell markedly in 1999 with the introduction of a trial of cautioning and mandatory education to "reduce the resources previously used to pursue prosecutions for simple cannabis offences" (ABCI, 2000). For Australia, the arrest rate fell from 342 in 1996 to 232 in 2001 (per 100,000 population), a decline of 32 per cent. Data on successful prosecution of marijuana cases for three states are given in Panel II of Table 3.5 (data for the other states/territories are not available). For both NSW and SA, the prosecution rate has fallen

Table 3.5:   *Arrests and prosecutions for marijuana offences*

Year	NSW	VIC	QLD	WA	SA	NT	TAS	ACT	AUST
I. Arrests (Per 100,000 population)									
1996	238	421	286	795	141	210	531	47	342
1997	227	199	441	713	232	245	228	54	304
1998	245	195	380	633	182	222	253	45	287
1999	247	198	385	330	172	183	156	28	256
2000	220	157	386	363	210	62	170	-	242
2001	211	136	366	389	151	224	223	48	232
Mean	231	218	374	537	181	191	260	37	277
II. Successful Prosecutions (Per 100,000 population)									
1991	112	-	-	-	-	-	-	-	-
1992	123	-	-	-	273	-	-	-	-
1993	113	-	-	-	315	-	-	-	-
1994	94	-	-	-	350	-	-	-	-
1995	83	-	-	-	326	-	-	-	-
1996	90	-	-	-	304	-	-	-	-
1997	81	-	-	-	205	-	-	-	-
1998	85	-	-	222	46	-	-	-	-
1999	92	-	-	234	38	-	-	-	-
2000	77	-	-	251	59	-	-	-	-
2001	73	-	-	238	76	-	-	-	-
Mean	93	-	-	236	199	-	-	-	-
III. Prosecutions/Arrests (Percentages)									
1996	38	-	-	-	215	-	-	-	-
1997	36	-	-	-	88	-	-	-	-
1998	35	-	-	35	25	-	-	-	-
1999	37	-	-	71	22	-	-	-	-
2000	35	-	-	69	28	-	-	-	-
2001	35	-	-	61	51	-	-	-	-
Mean	36	-	-	59	72	-	-	-	-

Note: Arrests exclude the issuing of Cannabis Expiation Notices, Simple Cannabis Offence Notices and Infringement Notices, which are used in SA, NT and ACT. For details of these, see Table 3.4.
Source: See Section A3.7 of the Appendix.

substantially. Not only has the prosecution rate decreased, but lighter sentences have also become much more common. Interestingly, in the early 1990s the prosecution rate was much higher in SA than in NSW, but by the end of the decade the rate was approximately the same in the two states. In WA, the prosecution rate is fairly stable, but the period is much shorter. No clear pattern emerges from the information on the percentage of arrests that result in a successful prosecution, as shown in Panel III of Table 3.5.

To understand further the evolution of enforcement of marijuana laws, it is useful to consider a simple model. Let pen_{it}^r be the number of penalties of type i ($i = 1$, 2, for an infringement notice and arrest, respectively) in region r ($r = 1, \ldots, 8$) and year t ($t = 1996, \ldots, 2001$). A simple logarithm decomposition of penalties takes the form $\log(pen_{it}^r) = \alpha_r + \beta_i + \gamma_t + \varepsilon_{it}^r$, where α_r is a regional effect, β_i is a penalty effect, γ_t is a time effect and ε_{it}^r is a disturbance term. If we suppose that the time effect is exponential, so that $\gamma_t = \lambda t$, we can then implement this model as a regression equation,

$$\log(pen_{it}^r) = \delta + \sum_{s=2}^{8} \alpha_s z_{sit}^r + \beta x_{it}^r + \lambda t + \varepsilon_{it}^r \tag{3.1}$$

where $z_{sit}^r = 1$ if $r = s$, 0 otherwise; $x_{it}^r = 1$ if $i =$ an infringement, 0 otherwise; and δ, α_s, β and λ are parameters. The value of the regional parameter α_s indicates the severity of penalties in region s relative to NSW (the base case), the parameter β indicates the infringement rate in comparison to that of arrests and λ is the residual exponential trend for all types of enforcement in all regions.

Table 3.6 provides estimates of model (3.1) obtained with data presented in Tables 3.4 and 3.5. Compared with NSW, Victoria, NT and ACT are all low-penalty regions, while the other four have higher penalties on average. In Section 3.3 we ranked regions in terms of the cost of marijuana, which can be compared with the severity of penalties as follows:

Cost (cheapest to most expensive):	NT	WA	SA	TAS	QLD	VIC	ACT	NSW
Penalties (weakest to most severe):	ACT	NT	VIC	NSW	TAS	SA	QLD	WA

Table 3.6: *Estimates of penalty model* $\log(pen_{it}^r) = \delta + \sum_{s=2}^{8} \alpha_s z_{sit}^r + \beta x_{it}^r + \lambda t$

Parameter	Estimate (standard errors in parentheses)	
Intercept δ	165.36	(60.89)
Regional dummies α_s		
VIC	−0.13	(0.12)
QLD	0.47	(0.11)
WA	0.78	(0.12)
SA	0.09	(0.16)
NT	−0.55	(0.20)
TAS	0.03	(0.15)
ACT	−1.78	(0.13)
Infringement dummy β	0.70	(0.16)
Exponential time trend λ	−0.08	(0.03)
R^2	0.81	
Number of observations	63	

Note: The standard errors are White heteroscedasticity-adjusted.

As the relationship between the two rankings is obviously weak, with major differences for most states, regional disparities in penalties do not seem to be systematically associated with regional price differences.

Controlling for regional and time effects, the estimated coefficient of the infringement dummy, given in Table 3.6, indicates that these are significantly higher than arrests. The estimated trend term shows that all penalties fall on average by approximately 8 per cent p.a., a decrease that is significantly different from zero. Consider the three regions that have infringement notices. To what extent have infringement notices partially displaced arrests? In other words, are the two forms of penalties substitutes for one another? For example, in the NT the infringement rate increased from 179 in 1999 to 401 in 2000, while over the same period the arrest rate fell from 183 to 62. This would seem to support the idea that the two types of penalties are substitutes. However, to proceed more systematically, we need to control for all the effects of factors determining penalties in model (3.1) by using the residuals, and examine the co-movement of residual infringements and arrests in the three regions over the six years. Figure 3.7 is a scatter plot of these residuals and clearly shows that there is a significant negative relationship between arrests and infringements. This means that more

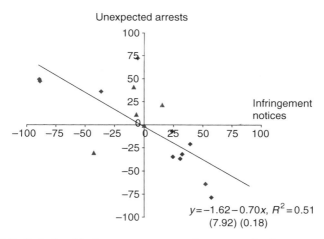

Figure 3.7. Relationship between unexpected arrests and infringement notices (logarithmic ratios of actual to expected × 100)

infringement notices are associated with fewer arrests, other factors remaining unchanged. This, of course, must have been one of the key objectives associated with the introduction of the infringement regime.

Taken as a whole, the above analysis seems to support the idea that participants in the marijuana industry have faced a declining probability of being arrested/successfully prosecuted; even if they are arrested and successfully prosecuted, the expected penalty is now lower. In other words, both the effort devoted to the enforcement of existing laws and penalties imposed seem to have decreased. Accordingly, the expected value of this component of the "full cost" of using marijuana has fallen. During the period considered, NSW, Victoria, WA and Tasmania all introduced marijuana cautioning programmes (ABCI, 2000) and SA, NT and ACT issued marijuana offence notices. This seems to indicate changing community attitudes to marijuana associated with the reduced "policing effort". It is plausible that this has also led to lower marijuana prices. As the risks involved in buying and selling marijuana have fallen, so too may have any risk premium built into prices. This explanation of lower prices has, however, been challenged by Basov *et al.* (2001), who analyse illicit drug prices in the United States. They show that while drug prohibition enforcement costs have substantially increased over the past 25 years, the relative prices of drugs have nonetheless declined. Basov *et al.* suggest four possible reasons for the decrease in prices: (i) production costs of drugs have declined; (ii) tax and regulatory cost increases have raised the prices of legal goods, but not illicit goods such as drugs; (iii) the market power of the illicit drug industry has fallen; and (iv) technologies to evade enforcement have improved. Although hard evidence is necessarily difficult to obtain, Basov *et al.* argue against explanations (i) and (ii) and favour (iii) and (iv) as realistic possibilities. We further address the possible impact of softening attitudes and laws on the workings of drug markets in Chapter 5.

We can summarise the material on marijuana prices from this and the previous section as follows. First, the relative price of marijuana has fallen substantially, by much more than that of many other commodities. Second, two possible explanations for this decline are: (a) productivity improvement in the production of marijuana associated with the adoption of hydroponic growing techniques; and (b) the lower expected penalties for producing, buying and selling marijuana. On the basis of the evidence currently available, both explanations seem to be equally plausible.

3.6 Quantity discounts

In addition to the above two patterns in marijuana prices, there is a third intriguing characteristic of prices, viz. the unit price of marijuana decreases noticeably as the quantity purchased increases. Table 3.2 shows that in Australia in 1999, for example, the average cost of heads purchased in the form of grams is $841 per ounce, while the same quantity purchased in the form of an ounce is $403 per ounce, a discount of more than 50 per cent. Figure 3.8 plots the unit prices of marijuana purchased as an ounce in the eight Australian states and territories over the 1990s against the corresponding gram prices. As all points lie below the 45° line for both heads and leaf, it is evident that unit ounce prices are less than gram prices and quantity discounts pertain. Quantity discounts are quite common in many markets and apply, for instance, to some grocery products, international air fares, where prices for return trips can be substantially less than twice the one-way cost, and private school fees, whereby a discount is given for the second and subsequent children from the same family. In this and the next two sections, we explore quantity discounts in the context of the economics of packaging and show that once these discounts are

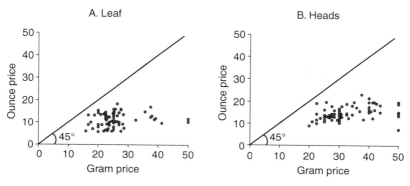

Figure 3.8. Ounce and gram unit prices of marijuana
(Australian dollars per gram)

formulated appropriately, marijuana is priced in a manner not too dissimilar to that of a number of other products, both illicit and licit.

There are several explanations for quantity discounts, the first of which is price discrimination. Here, lower unit prices for large purchases are interpreted as reflecting the fact that large customers have a more elastic demand than smaller ones. Consider the simple case in which there are just two types of customers, large and small. Producers maximise profits by supplying a greater quantity at a lower price to the large-customer market and vice versa for the small-customer market. Of course, producers can only practise price discrimination when competition is lacking and when it is possible to limit resale of the product from one market to another. Such an explanation possibly applies to air fares, where business travellers tend to pay the high-cost fares and tourists the cheaper fares.

A second explanation for quantity discounts is that they reflect cost differences. To illustrate, consider a stylised example presented by Telser (1978, Section 9.4) that focuses on the role of packaging costs in generating quantity discounts. Suppose a certain grocery product of volume s, measured in terms of cubic cm say, is sold in a package in the form of a cube, which has linear dimension $s^{1/3}$, so that its surface area is $6 \times s^{2/3}$ cm^2. If the packaging cost is α dollars per cm^2 and the product cost is β per cm^3, then the total cost of the product, as a function of size s, is $c(s) = \alpha 6 s^{2/3} + \beta s$, so that the elasticity of total cost

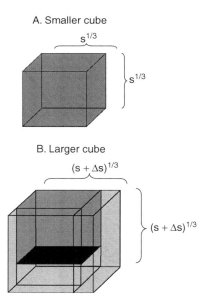

A. Smaller cube

$s^{1/3}$

$s^{1/3}$

B. Larger cube

$(s + \Delta s)^{1/3}$

$(s + \Delta s)^{1/3}$

Figure 3.9. The volumes of two cubes

with respect to size is:

$$\frac{d(\log c)}{d(\log s)} = \gamma \frac{2}{3} + (1 - \gamma),$$

where γ is the share of packaging cost in the total. As γ is a positive fraction, the above equation shows that this elasticity is a weighted average of two thirds and one, which is clearly less than one. Thus, the total cost increases less than proportionally with product size s, so that the unit cost c/s decreases with increasing s. This is clearly evident from the unit cost function, which takes the form $c(s)/s = \alpha 6s^{-1/3} + \beta$. Figure 3.9 illustrates the fundamental non-linear relationship between package size and volume. Another way of describing this result is that packaging is subject to economies of scale.[6] As packaging is a trivial part of the total costs of drugs, if we interpret "packaging" in a narrow sense, this does not explain the large quantity discounts observed for marijuana. However, it may have some explanatory power if we think of packaging as referring to all the "value added" in going from larger to smaller drug packages.

The role of risk in the drug business is another factor that can explain quantity discounts. As each transaction involves exposure to the probability of being apprehended, there are incentives to increase the average size of transactions and reduce their number as a risk-management strategy. This could lead to higher unit prices for smaller lot sizes as a reflection of a risk premium.[7] Additionally, as holding an inventory of drugs is risky, quantity discounts for large transactions could also represent compensation for bearing this risk.

The fourth approach to pricing and packaging is the model proposed by Caulkins and Padman (1993) that explicitly defines the key structural parameters of the packaging industry in the relationship between price and package size.[8] As this model has been applied to illicit drugs, and as we refer back to it subsequently, it is appropriate to provide some details. Suppose there is a log-linear relationship between price of package size s, $p(s)$, and package size,

$$\log p(s) = \alpha + \beta \, \log s, \tag{3.2}$$

where α is an intercept and β is the size elasticity. Thus,

$$p(s) = a \, s^\beta, \tag{3.3}$$

where $a = \exp(\alpha)$. Suppose that initially an ounce of marijuana is purchased and that we measure size in terms of grams, so that $s = 28$ and $p(28)$ is the price of this ounce. If this ounce is then split into 28 one-gram packages, so that $s = 1$ now, the revenue from these 28 packages is $28 \times p(1)$, where $p(1)$ is the price of one gram. We define the ratio of this revenue to the cost of an ounce as the *markup factor*, $\delta = 28 \times p(1)/p(28)$, or $28 \times p(1) = \delta \times p(28)$. More generally, let $\phi > 1$ be the *conversion factor* that transforms the larger quantity s into a smaller one s/ϕ, so that in the previous example $\phi = 28$. Thus, we have the following general relationship between the prices of different package sizes, the markup and conversion factors:

$$\phi \times p \left(\frac{s}{\phi} \right) = \delta \times p(s). \tag{3.4}$$

Our objective is to use equations (3.3) and (3.4) to derive an expression for the size elasticity β that involves the markup and conversion factors δ and ϕ. To do this, we use equation (3.3) in the form $p(s/\phi) = a(s/\phi)^\beta$, so that the left-hand side of equation (3.4) becomes $\phi a(s/\phi)^\beta$. Using equation (3.3) again, we can write the right-hand side of (3.4) as $\delta a s^\beta$. Accordingly, equation (3.4) can be expressed as $\phi(s/\phi)^\beta = \delta s^\beta$, or $\phi^{(1-\beta)} = \delta$, which implies:

$$\beta = 1 - \frac{\log \delta}{\log \phi}. \tag{3.5}$$

As the markup $\delta > 0$ and is presumably less than the conversion factor ϕ, the size elasticity β is a positive fraction. Equation (3.5) also shows that the size elasticity decreases with the markup δ and increases with the conversion factor ϕ. If there is no markup, $\delta = 1$ and the size elasticity $\beta = 1$, so that the price is just proportional to the package size and there is no quantity discount for buying in bulk. When $\delta > 1$, the unit price decreases with the quantity purchased, so that discounts then apply. As the markup increases, so does the quantity discount, and the (proportionate) increase in the total price resulting from a unit increase in package size is lower. In other words, the size elasticity β decreases with the markup. Other things equal, the greater the conversion factor ϕ, the more the product can be "split" or "cut" and the higher is the profit from the operation. The role of the conversion factor in equation (3.5) is then to normalise by deflating the markup by the size of the conversion involved (e.g. in going from ounces to grams), thus making the size elasticity a pure number.

   To illustrate the workings of equation (3.5), suppose that the markup is 100 per cent, so that $\delta = 2$, and we convert from ounces to grams, in which case $\phi = 28$. With these values, $\beta = 1 - \log 2/\log 28 \approx 0.8$, so that a doubling of package size is associated with an 80 per cent increase in price. Equation (3.5) is an elegant result that yields considerable insights into the interactions between price and package size and the role of the structural parameters δ and ϕ.

3.7 The discount elasticity

At the beginning of the previous section, we considered marijuana prices in Australia and compared the price of ounces with that of grams, both expressed in dollars per ounce, to conclude that there was a substantial quantity discount. If we write $p(28)$ and $p(1)$ for the prices of an ounce and gram package, respectively, the corresponding prices per gram are $p(28)/28$ and $p(1)$. The latter prices can be referred to as "unit prices". To compare the price of a package of

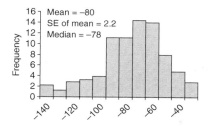

Figure 3.10. Histogram of discount for bulk buying of marijuana (logarithmic ratios of unit ounce to unit gram prices × 100; leaf and heads)

size s to that of a package of size one, define the unit-price ratio as $r = [p(s)/s]/p(1)$.[9] The logarithm of the ratio is

$$d = \log\left[\frac{p(s)/s}{p(1)}\right]. \tag{3.6}$$

For small values of the ratio r, $d \approx r - 1$, which is the proportionate discount for bulk buying. Accordingly, we refer to d as the "logarithmic discount" or the "log discount" for short. The several advantages of using d instead of $r-1$ are discussed in Section A3.8 of the Appendix. Additionally, the log discount is consistent with the log-linear pricing equation (3.2), which is at the root of our subsequent analysis of quantity discounts.

Figure 3.10 presents the log discount (3.6) for marijuana in Australia over the 1990s. It is evident that, on average, the log discount is approximately -0.8, which corresponds to approximately -55 per cent. While this is substantial, it should be remembered that there is also a substantial quantity increase involved in purchasing an ounce of marijuana rather than a gram. In this sense, the measure (3.6) is not really unit-free and thus cannot be compared across products for cases where the discounts involve different units. One way to rectify the problem is to normalise (3.6) by the difference in the two package sizes, s and one. Accordingly, we define

$$d' = \frac{\log\left[\frac{p(s)/s}{p(1)}\right]}{\log\left[\frac{s}{1}\right]} = \frac{\log\left[\frac{p(s)/s}{p(1)}\right]}{\log s}, \tag{3.7}$$

where the second step follows from $\log 1 = 0$. To interpret the measure d', we return to equation (3.2) and subtract $\log s$ from both sides to obtain

$$\log \frac{p(s)}{s} = \alpha + \beta' \log s, \tag{3.8}$$

where $\beta' = \beta - 1$ is the size elasticity of the unit price, or the "discount elasticity" for short. Thus, if there are quantity discounts, the size elasticity β in equation (3.2) is less than unity, the discount elasticity in (3.8) is negative and the unit price $p(s)/s$ decreases with s. Applying equation (3.8) to the unit package size yields $\log p(1) = \alpha$, so that

$$\log \frac{p(s)/s}{p(1)} = \beta' \log s, \quad \text{or} \quad \frac{\log \frac{p(s)/s}{p(1)}}{\log s} = \beta'. \tag{3.9}$$

This establishes that the unit-free measure d' in equation (3.7) is interpreted as the discount elasticity β'. The fact that d' is this elasticity is also evident from the second term of equation (3.7), which is the ratio of the logarithmic change in the unit price to that of the package size:

$$d' = \frac{\log \left[\frac{p(s)/s}{p(1)} \right]}{\log \left[\frac{s}{1} \right]} = \frac{\log \left[\frac{p(s)}{s} \right] - \log \left[\frac{p(1)}{1} \right]}{\log s - \log 1}.$$

For a discussion of the econometric aspects of the price–package size relationship equation (3.8), see Section A3.9 of the Appendix.

3.8 Application to marijuana and other products

To obtain a feel for the order of magnitude of the value of the discount elasticity, we use the mean of the log discount given in Figure 3.10, -0.8. Using this value and $\log 28 \approx 3.33$ in the second term of equation (3.9) yields an estimate of this elasticity of $\hat{\beta}' \approx -0.8/3.33 \approx -0.25$. In words, the discount elasticity is approximately -0.25.[10] Equation (3.5) relates the size elasticity (β) to the markup factor (δ) and the conversion factor in going from a larger package size to a smaller one (ϕ). This equation implies that the discount elasticity is related to these two factors according to $\beta' = -\log \delta / \log \phi$. Thus, $\beta' = -0.25$ and $\phi = 28$ imply a markup factor of $\delta = \exp(0.25 \times \log 28) = 2.30$, or approximately 130 per cent in transforming ounces into grams. This value seems reasonable.

It is remarkable that, in broad terms at least, the above value of the discount elasticity of -0.25 is also obtained using other approaches for the marijuana data, as well as for other illicit drugs and groceries. Full details of this strong claim are provided in Clements (2006), but in what follows we provide some illustrative evidence. Equation (3.8) can be treated as a regression equation and the discount elasticity β estimated as a coefficient. Using the Australian marijuana data over time, products and/or regions yields a number of estimates of this elasticity, a summary of which appears in the form of a histogram in Figure 3.11. It is evident that the centre of gravity of these estimates is clearly very close to -0.25. Next, Figures 3.12 and 3.13 present estimates of the discount elasticity for heroin and other illicit drugs and, on average at least, the values are not too far from -0.25. Finally, Table 3.7 provides estimated discount elasticities for groceries; while there seems to be slightly more dispersion in this case, again the results are clustered around -0.25.[11] The absolute values of β for baked beans and canned vegetables are somewhat higher than those for the other products, which may reflect larger markups and/ or a larger share of packaging costs in the total.

We now introduce another approach for measurement of the discount elasticity that has its roots in index-number theory. In a sense, it is non-parametric in nature as it does not require the discount elasticity to be constant and is thus complementary to the previous approach. As this is a general approach, before considering marijuana, we proceed by considering a number of product sizes (not necessarily restricted to 2), denoted by the set **G**. This approach enables us to consider the nature of the distribution of prices, the size distribution and their relationship to the log discount.

Equation (3.8) is a log-linear relationship between the unit price of package size s, $p(s)/s$, and its size. For convenience, we write p'_s for this unit price, so that

$$\log p'_s = \alpha + \beta' \log s, \qquad (3.10)$$

where β' is the discount elasticity. Let w_s be the market share of the product when sold in the form of size $s \in \mathbf{G}$, with $\sum_{s \in \mathbf{G}} w_s = 1$. We summarise the unit prices and sizes by their weighted geometric means, the logarithms of which are:

$$\log P' = \sum_{s \in \mathbf{G}} w_s \log p'_s, \log S = \sum_{s \in \mathbf{G}} w_s \log s. \qquad (3.11)$$

Table 3.7: *Discount elasticities for groceries (standard errors in parentheses)*

	Discount elasticities	
Product group (1)	With product dummies (2)	Without product dummies (3)
Baked beans	−0.419 (0.020)	−0.383 (0.027)
Cheese	−0.183 (0.016)	−0.176 (0.020)
Flour	−0.259 (0.052)	−0.232 (0.079)
Milk	−0.151 (0.024)	−0.149 (0.040)
Rice	−0.122 (0.012)	−0.140 (0.018)
Sugar	−0.148 (0.033)	−0.296 (0.048)
Canned vegetables	−0.308 (0.019)	−0.388 (0.037)
Mean-unweighted	−0.227	−0.252
Mean-weighted	−0.219	−0.237

Notes:
1. These elasticities are estimated from the equation
   $\log p'_{si} = \alpha + \beta' \log s_i +$ product dummies, where p'_{si} is the unit price of product i sold in the form of package size s.
2. The weights for the weighted means in the last row are proportional to the reciprocals of the standard errors.

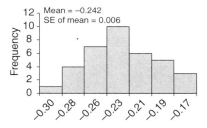

Figure 3.11. Histogram of discount elasticities for marijuana

The use of market shares as weights serves to give more weight to the more popular sizes, which is reasonable. The mean of the prices can be viewed as a stochastic price index with the following interpretation (Theil, 1967, p. 136). Consider the unit prices $\log p'_s$, $s \in \mathbf{G}$, as random variables drawn from a distribution of prices. Suppose we draw prices at random from this distribution such that each dollar of

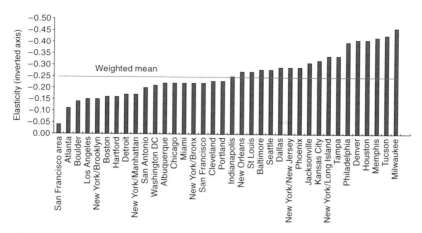

Figure 3.12. Discount elasticities for heroin
Notes:
1. The weights used in the weighted mean are proportional to the reciprocals of the standard errors.
2. Buffalo, Minneapolis, Nashville, Pittsburgh and Honolulu are omitted as outliers.
Source: Derived from Brown and Silverman (1974, Table 2).

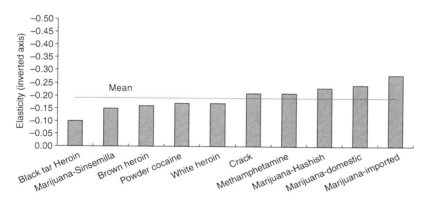

Figure 3.13. Discount elasticities for illicit drugs
Source: Derived from Caulkins and Padman (1993, Tables 3 and 4).

expenditure has an equal chance of being selected. Then, the market share w_s is the probability of drawing $\log p'_s$, so that the expected value of the price is $\sum_{s \in G} w_s \log p'_s$, which is the first term of equation (3.11). A similar interpretation applies to the mean size $\log S$. It follows directly from equation (3.10) that the two means are related according to:

$$\log P' = \alpha + \beta' \log S. \tag{3.12}$$

This shows that the mean unit price is independent of the mean size under the condition that there is no quantity discount, as then the discount elasticity $\beta' = 0$. When there are quantity discounts, $\beta' < 0$ and the mean unit price decreases with increasing mean size.

The means in equation (3.11) can be considered as weighted first-order moments of the price and size distributions. The corresponding second-order moments are:

$$\begin{aligned}
\Pi_p &= \sum_{s \in G} w_s \left(\log p'_s - \log P' \right)^2, \\
\Pi_s &= \sum_{s \in G} w_s \left(\log s - \log S \right)^2.
\end{aligned} \tag{3.13}$$

These measures are unit-free, non-negative, increase with dispersion of the relevant distribution and can be referred to as the *price and size variances*. It follows from equations (3.10) and (3.12) that the deviation of the price of the product of size s from its mean, $\log p'_s - \log p'$, is related to the corresponding size deviation, $\log s - \log S$, that is, $\log p'_s - \log p' = \beta'(\log s - \log S)$. Squaring both sides of this equation, multiplying by the relevant market share w_s and then summing over $s \in G$, we obtain the result $\Pi_p = (\beta')^2 \Pi_s$, or

$$\sqrt{\Pi_p} = |\beta'| \sqrt{\Pi_s}. \tag{3.14}$$

In words, the standard deviation of prices is $|\beta'|$ times the standard deviation of sizes. As $|\beta'|$ is expected to be less than one, result (3.14) implies that the dispersion of prices is less than that of sizes. When the size elasticity is unity, the discount elasticity $\beta' = 0$ and the price distribution is degenerate; this, of course, follows from equation (3.10) with $\beta' = 0$, as then each price takes the same value α.

To apply the above concepts to marijuana with gram and ounce package sizes, we use guesstimates of the two market shares of 20 per cent for grams and 80 per cent for ounces, so that $w_1 = 0.2$ and $w_{28} = 0.8$; see Section A3.2 for a discussion of these weights. Using the price data given in Tables 3.1 and 3.2, we compute the index defined in the first term of equation (3.11) for leaf and heads. Regarding the package size index, this is a constant over time equal

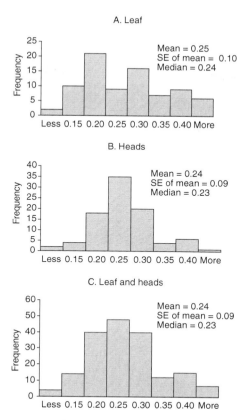

Figure 3.14. Histograms of ratios of standard deviation of prices to standard deviation of size

to $\log S = w_1 \log 1 + w_{28} \log 28 = 0.8 \times 3.33 = 2.67$, or, in terms of grams, $S = \exp(\log S) = 14.4$. Using exactly the same approach, we compute the price and size variances, $\sqrt{\Pi_p}$ and $\sqrt{\Pi_s}$, defined in equation (3.13). It follows from equation (3.14) that the ratio of $\sqrt{\Pi_p}$ to $\sqrt{\Pi_s}$ equals the absolute value of the discount elasticity $|\beta'|$. Figure 3.14 gives histograms of these ratios for the two products in all years and all regions (panels A and B), as well as for the two products combined (panel C).[12] It is evident that the means (and medians) are of the order of 0.25, which reassuringly agrees with the previous estimates of the discount elasticity.

We thus conclude that quantity discounts, as measured by the discount elasticity β', seem to be more or less the same in both licit and illicit markets, at least to a first approximation. In broad terms, the results support the following pricing rule: *The unit price falls by 2.5 per cent when the product size increases by 10 per cent.* While such a rule has much appeal in terms of its elegant simplicity, it is probably somewhat of an exaggeration to claim that it has universal applicability and it would be premature to conclude that the discount elasticity has the status of a "natural constant". Nevertheless, the conclusion to be drawn from this analysis is that the pricing of marijuana seems to be subject to more or less similar principles as other products, both licit and illicit, at least with respect to the price-package size relationship.

3.9 Notes on the literature

Geography, technical change and prices

In Section 3.3, we studied regional differences in marijuana prices in Australia and found them to be substantial. Similar regional differences have been found in the US with respect to prices of other drugs. A prominent paper in this area is that by Caulkins (1995), who analyses the prices of cocaine, LSD and marijuana in a number of locations in the US. He finds that: (i) regional price differences are sustained over time; (ii) prices increase with the distance from the source of the drugs (either the point of import or domestic production); and (iii) prices are lower in larger markets owing to economies of scale.

Regarding the changes in drug prices over time, which was investigated in Section 3.4 for marijuana in Australia, there is some related research also pertaining to the US. Caulkins and Reuter (1998) refer to the US Office of National Drug Control Policy (1997) to show that the gram price of both cocaine and heroin fell by approximately 75 per cent over the 1980s. Since then, these prices have continued to decline, but less rapidly (Office of National Drug Control Policy, 2004). Over shorter periods of time, drug prices can exhibit much volatility. For example, in Australia during late 2000 and early 2001, there was a so-called "heroin shortage" whereby the price of a gram increased by 50 per cent and that of a pure gram increased by more than 400 per cent (Moore, 2006).

Economic historians have long studied the impacts of innovation and how benefits are distributed among various stakeholders such as shareholders, workers and consumers. A leading example of this work relates to textile production in the industrial revolution in Britain, for which it has been estimated that approximately half of the benefits from falling prices went overseas in the form of a worsening of Britain's terms of trade (Crafts, 2001; International Monetary Fund, IMF, 2001, Chapter 3). During the IT boom of the late 1990s, it would also seem that the bulk of the benefits took the form of lower prices rather than higher profits and wages (IMF, 2001, Chapter 3). In related research, Baumol (2002) estimates that on average only 20 per cent of the benefits of innovation are captured by the innovators themselves. Although no data exist on the profitability of marijuana production or on wages paid, the substantial decline in prices would seem to point to the distributional effects of innovation within the marijuana industry as being not very different to those experienced by other sectors at other times.

The rule of six-tenths

The pricing rule of the previous section is not unrelated to what is known as the "rule of six-tenths", according to which the production function exhibits a specific type of scale economy. If Y is the volume of output produced with a piece of capital equipment of size K, then a production function consistent with the rule is $Y = \alpha' K^{1/\beta}$, with $\beta \approx 0.6$, so that the inverse production function, or the "factor demand equation", is $K = \alpha Y^{\beta}$. For example, Whitesides (2005) recommends using this relationship to estimate the cost of equipment of capacity Y_1 on the basis of the known cost of equipment of smaller capacity Y_0 according to $K_1 = K_0 (Y_1/Y_0)^{0.6}$. Whitesides, who attributes the rule to Williams (1947), emphasises its use in the absence of more detailed information. Indeed, he provides specific examples of equipment for which $\beta \neq 0.6$, such as an industrial boiler, where output is measured in terms of lb/hr, and $\beta = 0.50$, a bucket conveyor belt (output in feet), with $\beta = 0.77$, and a stainless steel tank or vessel (gallons), with $\beta = 0.68$. According to this rule, the unit cost function is $K/Y = \alpha Y^{\beta-1}$, so that the elasticity of unit cost with respect to size is $\beta - 1 = -0.4$ when $\beta = 0.6$.

Hence, the unit cost decreases with increasing capacity, so there are scale economies. If it is thought that six-tenths is sufficiently close to three-quarters, then our results are not inconsistent with the rule.

Consider again the expression derived in Section 3.6 for the elasticity of (total) cost c with respect to the package size s: $d(\log c)/d(\log s) = \gamma(2/3)+(1-\gamma)$, where γ is the packaging share of the total cost. This shows that the elasticity lies between two-thirds and unity, a range that excludes 0.6. However, this result depends on the simple stylised case in which the package takes the form of a cube. Although the same result holds in the case of a sphere (as mentioned in Section 3.6), these simple examples should probably not be taken as serious evidence against the rule of six-tenths.[13]

Pricing strategies

A branch of the literature views the price-package relationship as part of the competitive strategy of producers, whereby subtle forms of price discrimination are practised by charging different classes of consumers of a given good a different unit price. Such practices are inconsistent with competitive markets and there must be some form of barrier (real or artificial) preventing arbitrage between the different classes of consumers.

Mills (2002, pp. 121–7) studied approximately 1,750 prices for 149 products sold at Sydney supermarkets. In a number of instances he found *quantity surcharges*, whereby unit prices increase with package size, the opposite to the more familiar case of discounts for larger quantities.[14] Overall, approximately 9 per cent of cases represented quantity surcharges and these were concentrated in five product groups: toothpaste, for which 33 per cent of cases were surcharges, canned meat (33 per cent), flour (23 per cent), snack foods (19 per cent) and paper tissues (19 per cent). To account for the surcharge observed for the largest package size of toothpaste, Mills (p. 122) argues that "... manufacturers probably believe that a significant proportion of customers will nevertheless choose that size – on grounds of convenience, or because the customers think (without checking) that there will be a quantity discount". As prices do not reflect costs in these cases, manufacturers probably practise price discrimination. Moreover, Mills (p. 124) argues that a quantity discount can also be consistent with price discrimination if not all of the cost savings associated with a larger quantity are passed onto consumers.[15]

Others argue that unit price differences may reflect equalising price differences rather than price discrimination. Telser (1978, p. 339), for example, discusses the case of those who buy larger quantities less frequently and pay lower unit prices:

Assume that the retailer has two kinds of customers for some product, customers who buy large amounts for their inventory and customers who buy small amounts more frequently. When there is a large price decrease, there is a large sales increase to those who are willing to store the good. Sales to this group drop sharply after the price reduction and may subsequently return to the normal level. The behaviour of these customers impose a constraint on the retailer, since he cannot expect the same effect on his rates of sale to them for given price reductions without regard to their timing. Those who buy small amounts frequently will not buy much more at temporarily lower prices. Such buyers will have a relatively steady demand over time. Hence sellers hold larger stocks relative to the mean rate of sales for the light buyers than for the heavy buyers. The difference between the regular and the sales price represents the cost of storage to the sellers and is therefore an equalising price difference. It is most emphatically not an example of price discrimination. On the contrary, it is a price pattern consistent with a competitive market.

Hedonics

The hedonic regression model relates the overall price of a product to its basic characteristics and "unbundles" a package of attributes by estimating the marginal cost/valuation of each characteristic in the form of a regression coefficient. The seminal paper on this topic is by Rosen (1974). Equation (3.2) can be thought of as a hedonic regression equation in which the drug in question has one characteristic, package size. Two recent papers by Diewert (2003, 2006) consider some unresolved issues in hedonic regressions that are relevant to the previous discussion, and Section A3.10 of the Appendix contains a simplified summary of some of his results. It is shown there that: (i) the double-log functional form of model (3.2) has some advantages; (ii) an intercept should be included in the model, as it is in (3.2); and (iii) for the results to be representative of the whole spectrum of products available, observations should be weighted to reflect their relative importance. We establish in Section A3.11 that in the context of our application where the products weights are constant over time, weighting has no impact on the results.

APPENDIX

In this appendix, we present details of the more important data used in the chapter. Also included is further analysis of the relative prices of the different varieties of marijuana and the regional price differences, a discussion of the measurement of relative changes, an investigation of the econometric issues associated with the price-package size relationship and a further discussion of the hedonic regression model.

A3.1 The marijuana prices[16]

The data on Australian marijuana prices were generously supplied by Mark Hazell of ABCI. ABCI (1996, pp. 197–8) acknowledges that there are some inconsistencies in the data in the following areas: (i) the lack of uniformity in the way in which different law enforcement agencies (LEAs) record their price data–disparities occur between jurisdictions in terms of recording the type and form of drug; (ii) the recording databases of LEAs vary in design, leading to differences in the way in which information is stored and extracted; (iii) the lack of quality control in data collection in most jurisdictions leads to problems. Some data are missing, incomplete, non-specific or simply cannot be interpreted. In some cases, this leads to distortions in the prices, as it is often difficult to determine the exact weight of small drug seizures in regional areas owing to a lack of precise weighing equipment.

Prices are usually recorded in the form of ranges and the basic data are listed in Clements and Daryal (2001). The data have been edited and "consolidated" by Clements and Daryal by (i) using the mid-point of each price range; (ii) converting all gram prices to ounces by multiplying by 28; and (iii) annualising the data by averaging the quarterly or semi-annual observations. Plotting the data revealed several outliers that probably reflect some of the previously mentioned recording imperfections. Observations are treated as outliers if they are

Table A3.1: *Marijuana prices: leaf, with holes (dollars per ounce)*

Year	NSW	VIC	QLD	WA	SA	NT	TAS	ACT
			Purchased in the form of a gram					
1990	770	735	700	-	700	700	910	630
1991	1,050	770	700	-	700	700	1,050	-
1992	1,060	700	630	700	560	700	700	630
1993	583	-	683	653	630	665	613	595
1994	998	-	648	700	630	665	443	753
1995	1,085	700	560	700	630	735	560	753
1996	1,400	793	665	753	630	788	508	700
1997	1,400	490	560	653	630	718	525	613
1998	1,097	735	630	467	653	683	467	723
1999	1,155	-	700	-	630	700	642	700
			Purchased in the form of an ounce					
1990	438	513	225	210	388	275	313	413
1991	475	450	215	170	400	275	350	325
1992	362	363	188	340	225	300	188	350
1993	383	-	168	200	388	281	175	250
1994	419	394	181	288	325	244	170	400
1995	319	400	400	308	347	294	163	256
1996	325	383	350	283	350	263	200	408
1997	288	285	431	263	350	288	375	386
1998	333	363	375	250	350	300	375	450
1999	275	-	-	250	350	300	-	450

Source: Clements and Daryal (2001).

either less than one half of the mean for the corresponding state or greater than twice the mean. These observations are omitted and replaced with the relevant means, based on the remaining observations. The data, after consolidation and editing, are presented in Tables A3.1 and A3.2 for leaf and heads purchased in the form of grams and ounces. Several "holes" are apparent in these tables owing to missing observations. Tables 3.1 and 3.2 present the same data with the holes "filled in" using estimated values from a regression of the logarithm of the price for the state and product in question on a time trend. The population data used to compute the population-weighted means in Tables 3.1 and 3.2 are presented in Table A3.3.

Table A3.2: *Marijuana prices: heads, with holes (dollars per ounce)*

Year	NSW	VIC	QLD	WA	SA	NT	TAS	ACT
			Purchased in the form of a gram					
1990	1,120	1,050	1,400	1,120	1,400	700	910	840
1991	1,120	1,120	1,400	-	1,400	700	1,120	-
1992	1,400	1,120	910	770	700	700	1,225	770
1993	863	665	858	840	1,173	700	927	747
1994	1,155	770	1,068	840	1,120	770	735	980
1995	1,190	793	-	-	1,138	793	1,155	1,033
1996	1,171	840	-	-	910	840	963	1,400
1997	1,400	858	630	700	840	863	700	793
1998	1,120	840	723	630	840	823	723	840
1999	-	630	-	560	840	840	630	-
			Purchased in the form of an ounce					
1990	600	650	413	600	400	325	525	463
1991	600	550	425	-	200	325	450	375
1992	375	450	388	390	363	450	425	500
1993	500	348	363	431	450	363	344	383
1994	550	367	328	400	425	325	363	550
1995	538	400	320	-	438	358	350	438
1996	550	400	-	-	406	283	388	525
1997	550	400	538	300	400	358	383	442
1998	488	388	550	275	340	325	367	450
1999	-	400	300	-	400	300	325	-

Source: Clements and Daryal (2001).

A3.2 An index of marijuana prices[17]

There are four types of marijuana and we aggregate their prices in the form of a price index. Our starting point is Table A3.4, which reproduces the weighted means of the state prices from Tables 3.1 and 3.2. Let p_{it} be the price of product i ($i = 1, \ldots, 4$) in dollars per ounce in year t, and let w_{it} be a weight that reflects the importance of i in the overall consumption of marijuana in year t. We then take a weighted average of the logarithms of the prices,

$$\log P_t = \sum_{i=1}^{4} w_{it} \log p_{it}, \qquad (A3.1)$$

Table A3.3: *Population data*

	Percentage of Australian population in								Total
Year	NSW	VIC	QLD	WA	SA	NT	TAS	ACT	(Million)
1990	34.1	25.6	17.1	9.5	8.4	1.0	2.7	1.7	17.2
1991	34.1	25.5	17.2	9.5	8.3	1.0	2.7	1.7	17.4
1992	34.0	25.4	17.4	9.5	8.3	1.0	2.7	1.7	17.6
1993	34.0	25.2	17.7	9.5	8.2	1.0	2.7	1.7	17.8
1994	33.9	25.1	18.0	9.6	8.2	1.0	2.6	1.7	18.0
1995	33.9	24.9	18.2	9.6	8.1	1.0	2.6	1.7	18.2
1996	33.9	24.9	18.3	9.7	8.0	1.0	2.6	1.7	18.4
1997	33.8	24.9	18.4	9.7	8.0	1.0	2.5	1.7	18.6
1998	33.8	24.9	18.5	9.8	7.9	1.0	2.5	1.6	18.8
1999	33.8	24.9	18.6	9.8	7.9	1.0	2.5	1.6	19.1

Sources: ABS, *Population by Sex, State and Territories, 31 December, 1788 onwards*. ABS Cat. No. 3105.0.65.001, Australian Historical Population Statistics.

Table A3.4: *Marijuana prices (dollars per ounce)*

	Purchased in the form of a			
	Gram		Ounce	
Year	Leaf	Heads	Leaf	Heads
1990	747	1,159	390	557
1991	852	1,168	381	504
1992	798	1,103	313	401
1993	645	834	326	419
1994	779	992	341	432
1995	797	974	350	430
1996	949	944	339	444
1997	843	977	320	466
1998	798	889	344	437
1999	816	841	322	403
Mean	802	988	343	449

which is the Stone (1953) index. As $\exp\left(\sum_{i=1}^{4} w_{it} \log p_{it}\right) = \Pi_{i=1}^{4} p_{it}^{w_{it}}$, index (A3.1) is the logarithm of a weighted geometric mean of the prices. As there are no data available on consumption of the different products over time, we use constant weights based on the following information: (i) according to the 1998 Australian National Drug Strategy Household Survey (Australian Institute of Health and Welfare, 1999), heads account for 70 per cent of total consumption and leaf the remaining 30 per cent;[18] (ii) regarding the split between grams and ounces, we feel that ounces account for approximately 80 per cent of total consumption. The basis for this is that in Australia marijuana consumption is dominated by heavy users, with estimates indicating that daily and weekly users account for 95 per cent of consumption (Clements and Daryal, 2005). As these are likely to be experienced users, it is reasonable to suspect that they tend to "buy in bulk", i.e. they use ounces rather than grams. As we obviously cannot be certain of this aspect of marijuana consumption, we carry out some sensitivity analysis.

Let π be the share of total consumption accounted for by ounces and $1-\pi$ be the share for grams. Our "best guess" of the value of π is 0.8. In the absence of information to the contrary, we assume that usage by weight is independent of usage by product type (leaf and heads), so that in effect the weights in the individual cells are the products of the corresponding row and column totals. Thus, on the basis of this assumption and the above information, we use the following weighting scheme:

	Product type		
Purchased in the form of	*Leaf*	*Heads*	*Total*
Grams	$0.3 \times (1-\pi)$	$0.7 \times (1-\pi)$	$1-\pi$
Ounces	$0.3 \times \pi$	$0.7 \times \pi$	π
Total	0.3	0.7	1

To illustrate the workings of this idea, suppose the share of ounces is $\pi = 0.8$. Then we have:

	Product type		
Purchased in the form of	*Leaf*	*Heads*	*Total*
Grams	0.06	0.14	0.2
Ounces	0.24	0.56	0.8
Total	0.3	0.7	1

Table A3.5: *Indexes of marijuana prices*

Year				*Weight given to ounces*, π					
	0.1	0.2	0.3	0.4	0.5	0.6	0.7	0.8	0.9
			I. Levels (dollars per ounce)						
1990	946	882	822	765	713	664	619	577	537
1991	978	900	828	762	702	646	594	547	504
1992	907	821	744	674	610	553	501	454	411
1993	721	673	628	587	548	511	477	446	416
1994	849	782	719	662	609	561	516	475	437
1995	845	779	717	661	609	561	517	476	439
1996	870	800	736	677	622	572	526	484	445
1997	862	795	733	676	624	575	531	489	451
1998	799	741	687	638	592	549	509	473	438
1999	770	711	657	607	560	518	478	442	408
Mean	855	788	727	671	619	571	527	486	449
			II. Log-changes (×100)						
1991	3.27	2.05	0.83	−0.39	−1.61	−2.82	−4.04	−5.26	−6.48
1992	−7.57	−9.16	−10.75	−12.34	−13.94	−15.53	−17.12	−18.72	−20.31
1993	−22.93	−19.90	−16.88	−13.85	−10.83	−7.81	−4.78	−1.76	1.27
1994	16.38	14.94	13.51	12.08	10.65	9.22	7.78	6.35	4.92
1995	−0.49	−0.39	−0.28	−0.18	−0.07	0.04	0.14	0.25	0.35
1996	2.87	2.69	2.52	2.34	2.17	1.99	1.81	1.64	1.46
1997	−0.87	−0.59	−0.31	−0.03	0.25	0.53	0.81	1.09	1.37
1998	−7.66	−7.07	−6.48	−5.88	−5.29	−4.70	−4.11	−3.51	−2.92
1999	−3.66	−4.10	−4.55	−4.99	−5.43	−5.88	−6.32	−6.77	−7.21
Mean	−2.30	−2.39	−2.49	−2.58	−2.68	−2.77	−2.87	−2.96	−3.06

This shows that weights accorded to leaf gram, heads gram, leaf ounce and heads ounce are 6, 14, 24 and 56 per cent, respectively.

We evaluate index (A3.1) with $\pi = 0.1, \ldots, 0.9$ and the results are given in Panel I of Table A3.5 in the form of $\exp(\log P_t)$, so that the units are dollars per ounce. It is evident that for each row the value of the index decreases left to right. This is expected, as such a move corresponds to an increase in the weight for ounces (π) and ounces are cheaper than grams. The last three columns indicate that the index is not very sensitive as π changes from 0.7 to 0.8 to

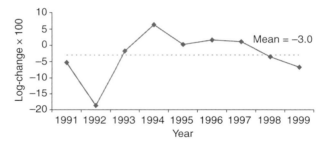

Figure A3.1. Changes in marijuana prices

0.9. Another interesting feature of the table is that for each weight, the price of marijuana has a distinct tendency to decrease over time; for $\pi = 0.8$, for example, the price starts off at $577 per ounce in 1990 and falls by 23 per cent over the ensuing nine years to end at $442 in 1999. Figure 3.3 gives the index for $\pi = 0.8$. One other aspect of the price index should be noted. As mentioned above, the value of the index decreases with increasing ounce weight π, as ounces are cheaper than grams. Although the *level* of the index varies with π, its change over time is less dependent on the weight. This is illustrated in Panel II of Table A3.5, which presents the log-changes of the index $DP_t = \log P_t - \log P_{t-1}$. The last row of the table shows that on average the price index decreases by 2.3–3.1 per cent p.a. for all values of π. Figure A3.1 plots DP_t for $\pi = 0.8$. In what follows, we use the price index based on our best-guess value of $\pi = 0.8$.

Figure 3.4 displays marijuana prices relative to consumer prices and alcohol prices. The marijuana prices are the index given in the second-last column of Table A3.5 (where the weight accorded to ounces is $\pi = 0.8$), with the value in 1990 set to 100. The CPI is from the DX Database, with $1990 = 100$. The Alcohol Price Index is a levels version of the Divisia index of the prices of beer, wine and spirits, with $1990 = 100$, from Clements and Daryal (2005).

A3.3 Relative marijuana prices[19]

As p_{it} is the price of product i in year t and P_t is the overall index of prices given by equation (A3.1), p_{it}/P_t is the relative price of i.

Table A3.6: *Relative prices of marijuana (Logarithms × 100)*

| | Purchased in the form of a | | | | |
| | Gram | | Ounce | | |
Year (1)	Leaf (2)	Heads (3)	Leaf (4)	Heads (5)	Standard deviation of prices (6)
1990	25.88	69.81	−39.11	−3.47	33.11
1991	44.30	75.85	−36.18	−8.20	35.71
1992	56.47	88.83	−37.12	−12.35	41.38
1993	36.94	62.63	−31.30	−6.20	29.79
1994	49.46	73.63	−33.15	−9.50	34.93
1995	51.50	71.55	−30.79	−10.21	34.09
1996	67.32	66.79	−35.62	−8.64	35.25
1997	54.38	69.13	−42.49	−4.90	35.96
1998	52.41	63.20	−31.74	−7.81	31.62
1999	61.40	64.42	−31.59	−9.15	33.07
Mean	50.00	70.58	−34.91	−8.04	34.49

Columns 2–5 of Table A3.6 give these relative prices in logarithmic form, $\log(p_{it}/P_t)$, which satisfy $\sum_{i=1}^{4} w_i \log(p_{it}/P_t) = 0$, where w_i is the (constant) weight for product i. The last entries in these columns indicate that, on average, leaf gram is approximately 50 per cent more expensive than marijuana as a whole, heads gram 71 per cent more expensive, leaf ounce 35 per cent cheaper and heads ounce 8 per cent cheaper. Column 6 of Table A3.6 gives the weighted standard deviation of relative prices across products, which is the square root of $\sum_{i=1}^{4} w_i [\log(p_{it}/P_t)]^2$. This is a measure of the structure of relative prices within a given year, which does not vary too much over time and has a mean of 34 per cent.

Panel I of Table A3.7 presents in columns 2–5 the changes in the four nominal prices $Dp_{it} = \log p_{it} - \log p_{i,t-1}$, while column 6 reproduces from Panel II of Table A3.5 the change in the price index DP_i for $\pi = 0.8$. The means indicate that on average the nominal price of leaf gram increased by approximately 1.0 per cent p.a., heads gram fell by 3.6 per cent, leaf ounce fell by 2.1 per cent and heads ounce decreased by 3.6 per cent. Panel II presents the

Table A3.7:   *Marijuana price log-changes*

Year (1)	Gram Leaf (2)	Gram Heads (3)	Ounce Leaf (4)	Ounce Heads (5)	Price index (6)
		Purchased in the form of a			
	Gram		*Ounce*		
	I. Nominal prices				
1991	13.15	0.77	−2.33	−10.00	−5.26
1992	−6.55	−5.73	−19.66	−22.86	−18.72
1993	−21.29	−27.96	4.07	4.39	−1.76
1994	18.88	17.35	4.50	3.06	6.35
1995	2.28	−1.83	2.61	−0.46	0.25
1996	17.46	−3.13	−3.19	3.20	1.64
1997	−11.84	3.44	−5.77	4.84	1.09
1998	−5.49	−9.44	7.23	−6.43	−3.51
1999	2.23	−5.55	−6.61	−8.10	−6.77
Mean	0.98	−3.56	−2.13	−3.60	−2.96
	II. Relative prices				
1991	18.41	6.04	2.93	−4.74	-
1992	12.17	12.99	−0.94	−4.15	-
1993	−19.53	−26.20	5.82	6.15	-
1994	12.52	11.00	−1.85	−3.30	-
1995	2.04	−2.08	2.36	−0.71	-
1996	15.82	−4.77	−4.83	1.57	-
1997	−12.94	2.34	−6.86	3.74	-
1998	−1.97	−5.93	10.75	−2.91	-
1999	9.00	1.21	0.16	−1.33	-
Mean	3.95	−0.60	0.84	−0.63	-

Note: All entries are to be divided by 100.

associated changes in relative prices, $Dp_{it}-DP_t$. On average, the relative price of leaf gram increased by 4.0 per cent p.a., heads gram fell by 0.6 per cent, leaf ounce increased by 0.8 per cent and heads ounce decreased by 0.6 per cent. The relative prices in Table A3.7 should not be confused with those in Table A3.6: the former deal with changes over time, while the latter refer to levels; the entries in Panel II of Table A3.7 are just first differences of the corresponding entries in columns 2–5 of Table A3.6.

A3.4 More on regional disparities in prices

Thus far, we have considered annual marijuana prices and Section 3.3 used these prices to analyse regional differences. In this section, we explore further the regional price differences, but now using the original data of Clements and Daryal (2001), which are either quarterly or semi-annual. As before, we use the mid-point of each price range. However, as a qualification to what is to follow, owing to the high variability of the original data, it should be noted that these higher-frequency data are likely to contain relatively more noise and be less reliable than the annual data.

Let p_{it}^r be the price of product i ($i = 1, \ldots, 4$) in period t for region r ($r = 1, \ldots, 8$). Using NSW as the base ($r = 1$), the logarithmic ratio $\log(p_{it}^r/p_{it}^1)$, when multiplied by 100, is approximately the percentage difference between the price of marijuana in region r and NSW at time t. The ratios for all regions and products are given in Table A3.8. Several comments are required. First, the number of observations differs across regions and products because of missing observations in the original data. Second, as indicated by the standard deviations, these data exhibit considerable volatility. Third, for a given product and region, in several cases the same value of the regional difference is repeated for consecutive observations. While it is possible that the price difference is constant over time, this phenomenon could also reflect the fact that the data are less than perfect. Fourth, the means for each product and region differ from the estimated price differences given in panel A of Figure 3.1. This is possibly due to the use here of the higher-frequency data, as well as the fact that some of the observations in the data underlying the estimates in Figure 3.1 are based on extrapolation (where the original data are missing).

The major conclusion to be drawn from Table A3.8 is that the vast majority of the entries are negative. Of the 534 individual entries in the table, 395 (or 74 per cent) are negative. This supports the finding of Section 3.3 that marijuana is more expensive in NSW.

Figure A3.2 presents histograms of the price differences (relative to NSW) for each region. Rather than having one histogram for each product (in each region), we now weight the four products according to the relative importance in consumption; see the notes to Table A3.8 for specification of the product weights. In a conventional histogram, each observation has equal weight and the vertical axis records the

Table A3.8: Regional differences in marijuana prices (Logarithmic ratios × 100)

1. Leaf gram

VIC	QLD	WA	SA	NT	TAS	ACT
−7.26	−11.39	22.18	−17.61	−17.61	6.21	0.00
4.58	4.58	9.69	4.58	−17.61	8.72	9.69
−13.47	−17.61	9.69	−17.61	22.18	0.00	9.69
26.32	17.61	−20.41	12.49	9.69	22.18	−5.12
−11.39	9.69	−20.41	0.00	9.69	−20.41	−20.41
−22.18	0.00	4.58	9.69	−5.12	9.69	−20.41
−30.10	12.49	−20.41	4.58	−20.41	4.58	15.97
−69.90	−24.99	−20.41	−30.10	−20.41	−50.52	−20.41
−30.10	−20.41	−30.10	−20.41	4.58	−17.61	−20.41
−30.10	−25.53	−11.39	−24.99	−30.10	−30.10	−30.10
−8.72	−9.02	−11.39	−24.99	−16.27	−16.27	−3.48
	−30.10	−25.96	−34.68	−30.10	−39.79	−7.26
	−21.09	−25.96	−15.97	−11.39	−33.58	−30.10
	−21.09	−25.96	−15.97	−7.26	−11.39	−30.10
	−39.79	−25.96	−34.68	−25.96	−52.29	−30.10
	−30.10	−34.68	−34.68	−22.18	−39.79	−30.10
	−34.68	−39.79	−34.68	−25.96	−39.79	−60.21
	−39.79	−43.93	−34.68	−30.10	−22.18	−30.10
	−39.79	−39.79	−34.68	−30.10	−30.10	−30.10
	−39.79			−30.10	−69.90	−20.41

−30.10	−69.90	−25.96	−4.14	−39.79	
−30.10	−60.21	−16.27	−34.68	−30.10	
−11.39	3.78	−13.83	−34.68	−4.14	
	−69.90	−30.10	−15.97	−30.10	
	−69.90	−30.10			
	−51.19	−11.39			

Mean	−18.48	−16.24	−9.18	−19.52	−19.37	−17.48
S D	17.41	14.44	17.59	16.07	17.98	24.26

II. Leaf ounce

9.69	−13.26	−23.74	−10.27	−32.45	−2.35
−16.48	−16.27	−16.27	0.00	−24.99	15.76
0.00	−13.26	−23.74	−7.46	−34.43	−2.35
−5.80	30.10	51.19	17.61	35.22	54.41
−39.79	−57.40	−13.47	2.80	−27.30	−51.19
0.00	−30.10	−16.27	2.63	−56.07	16.27
0.00	−27.30	−27.30	5.44	−36.99	2.48
9.02	−42.60	−12.49	−12.49	−42.60	3.78
−13.83	−30.78	−35.90	−7.38	−42.60	9.69
−35.22	−43.93	−11.39	−21.21	−11.39	12.49
−43.93	−35.22	−34.24	−10.91	−49.73	−10.91
7.26	−43.93	−21.39	8.89	16.27	
16.27	−43.93	0.00	10.47	10.47	
−2.63	−4.14	10.47	10.47	10.47	
21.39	−13.83	0.00	−8.43	21.39	

Table A3.8: *(continued)*

	VIC	QLD	WA	SA	NT	TAS	ACT
		13.47	−4.14	10.47	−18.91	−13.83	13.47
		17.61	−4.14	10.47	−4.14	13.47	19.92
		17.61	2.31	10.47	−4.14	−13.83	−11.71
		21.39	−7.92	10.47	−4.14	−8.72	17.61
		−17.61	−4.14	6.69	−4.14	−7.92	17.61
			−4.14	10.47	0.00		21.39
				10.47	6.69		7.92
					−16.63		21.39
					10.47		21.39
					−16.63		
					−25.53		
					3.78		
Mean	4.37	−10.61	−10.24	2.26	−9.18	−20.83	1.45
S D	25.07	28.88	23.01	10.36	17.59	21.14	19.70
III. Heads gram							
	0.00	9.69	−22.18	9.69	−20.41	0.00	0.00
	0.00	9.69	0.00	9.69	−20.41	0.00	−11.39
	−9.69	0.00	0.00	−30.10	−30.10	0.00	5.12
	−17.61	0.00	−3.48	12.49	−11.39	−3.78	−20.41
	−3.78	6.69	−12.49	19.96	−20.41	6.69	−20.41
	−20.41	−3.48	−17.61	9.02	−12.49	3.22	−9.69

−17.61	7.46	−12.49	0.00	−17.61	−20.41	−9.02
−20.41	−12.49	−30.10	0.00	−20.41	−20.41	9.69
−12.49	−25.53	−30.10	0.00	−16.27	−25.53	−30.10
−12.49	9.69	0.00	−7.06	−22.18	−12.49	−22.18
−15.49	−27.98		0.00	−16.27	0.00	−22.18
−15.49	2.12		0.00	−52.29	−9.69	−12.49
−12.49	−24.99		−52.29	−15.49	−5.80	
−34.68			−22.18	−18.71	9.69	
				−16.27	−42.60	
				−22.18	−30.10	
					−12.49	
					−20.41	
					−30.10	

Mean −13.76	−3.78	−12.85	−3.63	−20.81	−11.27	−11.92
S D 9.04	14.23	11.97	19.27	9.47	14.37	12.06

IV. Heads ounce

−3.78	−14.98	12.49	−47.71	−26.63	−12.49	−20.41
−3.78	−14.98	−4.14	−47.71	−26.63	−12.49	−20.41
7.92	2.80	−2.48	−6.21	7.92	7.92	−11.20
−26.32	−11.20	−9.69	−6.37	−15.49	−16.63	−13.83
−10.91	−14.13	−13.83	2.35	−26.32	−17.61	0.00
−13.08	−4.58	−13.83	−7.06	−19.63	−15.49	−4.14
−19.63	−26.32	−13.83	−11.20	−26.32	−26.32	3.78
−16.63	−19.63	−13.83	−11.20	−19.63	−19.63	0.00

Table A3.8: *(continued)*

	VIC	QLD	WA	SA	NT	TAS	ACT
	−16.63	−24.90	−19.63	−11.20	−16.63	−19.63	−4.14
	−26.32	−19.63	−8.72	−2.23	−18.71	−8.72	−9.69
	−8.72	−9.69	−19.63	−11.20	−16.63	−13.83	−13.83
	−8.72	−29.32	9.18	−11.20	−34.24	−18.71	−8.72
	−13.83	−29.32	−8.72	−13.83	−26.32	−26.32	−2.02
	−11.20	0.00	−8.72	−13.83	−26.32	−16.63	−2.02
	−16.63	−4.14	−8.72	−13.83	−22.85	−16.63	−2.02
	−2.63	0.00		−13.83	−13.83	−13.83	−11.20
	−13.83	0.00		−13.83	−17.61	−13.83	−8.72
	−13.83	0.00		−13.83	−18.11	−16.63	−8.72
				−28.60	−26.32	−10.35	−8.72
				−4.14	−26.32	−10.35	
				−4.14	−26.32	−11.20	
				−4.14		−3.48	
						−13.83	
						−13.83	
						−13.83	
Mean	−12.24	−12.22	−8.27	−13.41	−21.09	−14.18	−7.68
S D	8.36	10.92	9.14	12.69	8.44	6.74	6.68

V. All four products

Unweighted mean	−10.29	−12.62	−12.58	−9.32	−16.07	−19.17	−8.71
SD	18.21	20.11	17.75	16.73	14.30	20.52	17.22
Weighted mean	−8.73	−11.08	−9.99	−8.64	−17.90	−16.22	−6.73

Notes:

1. The base for all price comparisons is NSW.

2. The weighted mean for region r, given in the last row, is computed as $\sum_{i=1}^{4} w_i x_{ir}^r$, where w_i is the weight for product i and $x_{ir}^r = (1/T^r)\sum_{t=1}^{T^r} \log(p_{it}^r/p_{it}^1)$ is the mean log-ratio for i in r, with T^r the number of observations in that region. The following product weights are used: leaf gram, 0.06; leaf ounce, 0.24; head gram, 0.14; and head ounce, 0.56. These weights reflect the relative importance of the products in consumption; see Section A3.2 for details.

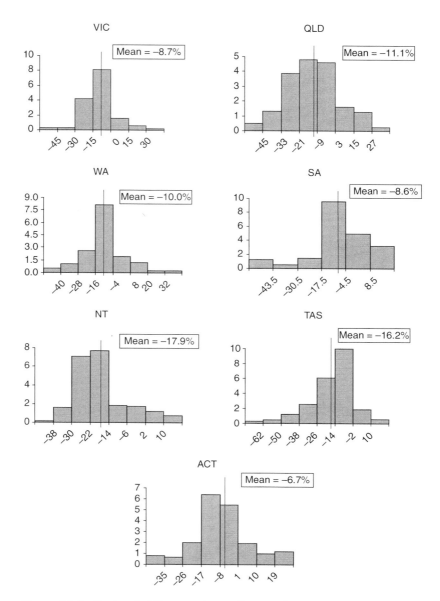

Figure A3.2. Regional differences in marijuana prices
(Product-weighted logarithmic price ratios × 100; base = NSW)

number of observations in each bin. For the weighted version, the observations in a given bin are split into four product groups, weighted accordingly, and then the weighted number of observations is recorded on the vertical axis. The result is that the area of a given column of the histogram is proportional to the weighted importance of the observations that fall within the relevant bin. These histograms also contain the weighted means from the last row of Table A3.8. The histograms seem to have long tails, especially on the left, which in part reflects the high variability of the underlying data.

A3.5 The commodity prices

David Sapsford of Lancaster University kindly provided the unpublished data appendix of Grilli and Yang (1988), which lists the nominal prices of 24 commodities for the period 1901–1986. These data are then deflated by the US CPI to form relative prices, which are listed in log-change form in Clements (2002).[20] Decade averages of these relative price changes are given in Table A3.9, and the averages for the period 1914–1986, given in column 10 of this table, are plotted in Figure 3.5.

A3.6 Prices from *The Economist*

The data underlying Figure 3.6, which gives changes in relative prices, are from *The Economist* magazine. *The Economist* (2000, Chart 1) presents a graph of 30 price changes from 1900 to 2000 and the underlying data, given in Table A3.10, were obtained on request from Carol Howard of *The Economist*. The names of some of the goods/ services are abbreviated in Figure 3.6; where this occurs, the full descriptions are given in Table A3.10. The prices are relative to the CPI in the US. We convert the 101-year price changes to annual average percentage changes and then transform these into log-changes.

There are two minor inconsistencies with these data: (i) the text of the published article states that the price of a phone call fell by 99.9 per cent over the 101 years, while according to the spreadsheet provided to us by *The Economist*, it fell by 99.5 per cent. While the difference may seem trivial, such is not the case when the change is placed on an annual basis. The annualised value of the 99.9 per cent fall over the 101 years is −6.6 per cent, while that of the 99.5 per

Table A3.9: *Changes in relative prices of 24 commodities (Average annual log-changes × 100)*

Commodity	1914–19	1920–29	1930–39	1940–49	1950–59	1960–69	1970–79	1980–86	1914–86
(1)	(2)	(3)	(4)	(5)	(6)	(7)	(8)	(9)	(10)
1. Coffee	0.16	−0.21	−8.88	9.64	−0.14	−3.21	7.54	−3.55	0.32
2. Cocoa	−5.76	−4.87	−5.67	9.82	3.08	−0.27	6.38	−11.43	−0.41
3. Tea	−5.18	2.37	−0.51	2.78	1.12	−6.18	0.86	−6.81	−1.02
4. Rice	−11.82	4.27	−4.50	4.36	−4.24	0.98	−1.38	−11.58	−2.15
5. Wheat	6.10	−3.92	−5.65	6.38	−4.32	−2.42	2.76	−6.28	−1.08
6. Maize	5.34	−4.41	−4.18	5.29	−5.34	−0.92	0.52	−8.94	−1.66
7. Sugar	5.28	−9.85	0.76	4.91	−5.57	−1.22	3.43	−11.49	−1.70
8. Beef	11.57	−6.89	2.92	−1.55	10.27	1.39	5.31	−10.86	1.48
9. Lamb	12.11	−4.89	9.15	−7.98	6.38	1.24	8.16	−7.53	1.92
10. Banana	−6.33	3.42	1.22	0.84	−2.77	−1.62	0.08	−2.18	−0.57
11. Palm Oil	4.21	−6.92	0.48	3.11	−3.18	−4.04	3.99	−18.57	−2.33
12. Cotton	5.57	−5.74	−4.12	6.54	−2.35	−7.09	3.79	−12.88	−2.01
13. Jute	−1.59	−2.61	−0.70	3.57	−3.20	0.50	−2.86	−9.36	−1.75
14. Wool	8.67	−5.03	0.40	1.73	−5.33	−2.44	−1.31	−10.01	−1.89
15. Hide	3.20	−8.33	−0.51	1.96	−2.20	−6.93	9.08	−10.11	−1.66
16. Tobacco	6.95	−1.60	0.95	2.53	1.41	−0.91	1.59	−2.22	0.90
17. Rubber	−18.73	−5.79	0.47	−5.17	5.13	−f5.82	1.92	−11.17	−3.88
18. Timber	9.57	−5.83	1.11	2.13	0.35	−0.25	6.53	−9.72	0.41
19. Copper	−7.24	0.63	−2.96	0.38	2.65	1.73	−0.47	−10.31	−1.32
20. Aluminium	−5.48	−2.01	0.28	−6.85	1.54	−1.52	0.71	1.05	−1.43

21. Tin	−4.63	−2.44	3.14	1.58	−1.93	2.29	7.55	−0.40
22. Silver	−0.28	−6.46	−0.99	0.88	0.18	4.26	11.13	−0.26
23. Lead	−6.01	2.65	−0.96	5.90	−4.49	−0.50	5.52	−1.28
24. Zinc	−6.61	0.23	−0.36	3.43	−2.78	−0.06	2.27	−0.64
25. Mean	−0.04	−3.09	−0.80	2.34	−0.66	−1.38	3.46	−0.93
26. Standard deviation	23.51	20.27	17.78	15.57	18.09	14.60	21.99	18.71

Notes:

1. The relative price of commodity i is the nominal price deflated by the US CPI.

2. The means in row 25 are unweighted.

3. The standard deviations in row 26 are the square roots of $(1/24) \sum_{i=1}^{24} (Dp_{it} - DP_t)^2$, averaged over the period given at the top of the relevant column. Here, Dp_{it} is the log-change from year t−1 to t in the nominal price of commodity i; and $DP_t = (1/24) \sum_{i=1}^{24} (Dp_{it})$ is an index of the 24 prices.

Table A3.10: *Changes in relative prices over the 20th century (Percentage changes from 1900 to 2000)*

1. Phone call – 3 mins, NYC–Chicago	−99.5
2. Electricity	−94.5
3. Refrigerator	−89.8
4. Salt	−77.7
5. Bicycle	−73.4
6. Eggs	−71.9
7. Coca-Cola	−63.7
8. Rail travel	−56.2
9. Petrol	−51.5
10. Hershey bar	−51.4
11. Car, basic Ford	−48.9
12. Clothing	−48.6
13. Stamp – letter NYC–London	−40.7
14. Housing, rent	−38.0
15. Wine	−17.6
16. Coffee	−12.7
17. Whisky	−5.8
18. Encyclopaedia Britannica, hard copy	28.0
19. Bread	30.7
20. *The Economist*	33.8
21. Pork chop	52.0
22. Cigarettes	104.2
23. Potatoes	113.3
24. Sneakers	160.0
25. Grand piano – Steinway NY retail price	163.0
26. Levis 501s	163.8
27. Beer	196.7
28. Theatre ticket	253.6
29. Butler	258.0
30. Hotel room, New York, four-star	295.0

Source: Carol Howard of *The Economist* (personal communication).

cent fall is -5.1 per cent. We base Figure 3.6 on the data contained in the spreadsheet, viz. 99.5 per cent: (ii) in the figure accompanying the article in *The Economist*, clothing experiences a slightly larger price decrease than the car, but in the spreadsheet the reverse is true (but the difference is small). In Figure 3.6 we use the spreadsheet data.

A3.7 Infringement notices, arrests and prosecutions

The data presented on infringement notices in Table 3.4 are from the Australian Bureau of Criminal Intelligence, *Australian Illicit Drug Report 2001–2002*, Australian Bureau of Statistics, *Australian Historical Population Statistics*, 2002, and Australian Bureau of Statistics, *Year Book of Australia* (various issues). The arrests and prosecutions data in Table 3.5 are from the Australian Bureau of Criminal Intelligence, *Australian Illicit Drug Report 2000–2001*, NSW Bureau of Crime Statistics and Research, *NSW Criminal Courts Statistics, 1991–2001*, Office of Crime Statistics and Research, *Crime and Justice in South Australia, 1992–2001*, The University of WA Crime Research Centre, *Crime and Justice Statistics for Western Australia, 1996–2001*, and Australian Bureau of Statistics, *Australian Historical Population Statistics, 2002*.

The arrests data for 1996 for SA seem to be problematic and need to be treated with caution. According to the *Australian Illicit Drug Report 2000–2001*, there were 2,076 arrests, which, when divided by the population of SA of 1,474,253, yields 141 per 100,000, as reported in Panel I of Table 3.5. However, according to the 2001–2002 edition of the above-mentioned publication, arrests for the same state in the same year were 18,477, or 1,253 per 100,000. We used the 141 figure, as it appears to be more consistent with data for adjacent years; however, the use of this figure leads to a prosecutions/arrests rate of 215%, as reported in Panel III of this table.

A3.8 Measuring relative changes

In Section 3.7 we considered a product sold in package size $s > 1$ with unit price $p(s)/s$, and compared that to the unit price of package size $s = 1$, $p(1)$. We used the log discount, defined as $d = \log\left[\frac{p(s)/s}{p(1)}\right]$, as a measure of the quantity discount available for bulk purchase.

In this section, we discuss further this measure and provide some justification.

Suppose the cost of a bale of wool is $500 and the cost of 10 tons of iron ore is $400. How should we measure the cost difference? One way is just their algebraic difference, $x-y = \$100$. The units involve dollars/bale/tons, which is not convenient when comparing differences across different commodities involving different units of measurement and across time, when the real value of a dollar can change from one year to the next due to inflation. One way around this problem is to use the ratio $r = x/y$, which is the relative cost, the relative difference $(x-y)/y = r-1$, or the percentage difference $p = 100 \times (x-y)/y = 100 \times (r-1)$. These three measures have the attraction of being pure numbers, or unit-free.

Although popular, the percentage difference suffers from the problem that it is asymmetric with respect to the base; that is,

$$100 \times \frac{x-y}{y} \neq -100\frac{y-x}{x}.$$

While the cost of wool is $100 \times (500-400)/400 = 25$ per cent more than iron ore, the cost of iron ore is $-100 \times (400-500)/500 = 20$ per cent less than wool, which is counterintuitive and inconvenient. We can avoid this problem by using the mean of the two prices as the base, but this is rather cumbersome. As economic variables are always positive, the percentage difference between two such variables is restricted to the range $[-100, \infty]$, which is a further problem that can give rise to statistical difficulties associated with a tendency to a skewed distribution.

A better approach is to use the logarithmic ratio $\pi = \log(x/y) = \log r$, which is symmetric in the base, as $\log(x/y) = -\log(y/x)$. As $\log(x/y) = \log x - \log y$, the log ratio can also be called the "log difference". Thus, the log difference between the cost of wool and iron ore is $\log(500/400) = 0.2331$, while the reciprocal comparison is just the negative of this value, $\log(400/500) = -0.2331$. Writing $r = \exp\pi$, the relation between the percentage difference, the relative difference and the log ratio is:

$$p = 100 \times (r-1) = 100 \times (\exp\pi - 1).$$

This relationship is illustrated in Figure A3.3. For example, when $r = 1/2$, the percentage difference is $p = -50$ per cent and the

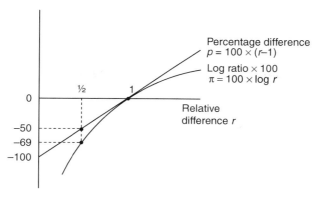

Figure A3.3. Three measures of relative difference

log difference times 100 is $100 \times \pi = -69$. The figure also shows that the percentage difference is never less than the log difference ($\times 100$), and that for $r \approx 1$, these two measures are approximately equal, which follows from $\log z \approx z - 1$ when $z \approx 1$. It should also be noted that the range of π is unrestricted. Another attraction of π is that it has desirable properties when averaged (Clements, 2006).

At a more formal level, Törnqvist *et al.* (1985) establish that within the class of measures of relative changes, the log difference has strong claims to priority. They show that the log difference is the *only* symmetric, additive and normed indicator of relative change. In the context of relative changes, these properties have the following meanings. We define an indicator of the relative difference between the two positive numbers x and y as $H(y/x)$ such that $H(y/x) = 0$ iff $y/x = 1$; $H(y/x) > 0$ iff $y/x > 1$; $H(y/x) < 0$ iff $y/x < 1$; and $H(\bullet)$ is a continuous increasing function in y/x. Then this indicator is *symmetric* iff $H(y/x) = -H(x/y)$. Next, suppose in addition to the change $x \to y$, we have the further change $y \to z$. The indicator $H(\bullet)$ is then said to be *additive* iff it can be expressed as the sum of the indicator of the two intermediate differences; that is, iff $H(z/x) = H(y/x) + H(z/y)$. Finally, $H(\bullet)$ is *normed* iff its derivative at $y/x = 1$ is unity; that is, iff $H'(1) = 1$. The last property rules out the multiplication of the indicator function by a scaling factor. For further details, see Törnqvist *et al.* (1985).

The log discount of Section 3.7 clearly has the form of the log difference.

A3.9 The econometrics of packaging

Equation (7.3) is a log-linear relationship between the unit price of package size s, $p(s)/s$, and its size. For convenience, we write p'_s for this unit price. We apply this equation at time t ($t = 1, \ldots, T$) and add a disturbance term ε_{st}:

$$\log p'_{st} = \alpha + \beta' \log s + \varepsilon_{st}, \tag{A3.2}$$

where α is the intercept and β' is the discount elasticity. In this section, we explore the nature of the least-squares (LS) estimates of this equation.

Suppose we have price data on two package sizes, ounces and grams. If we measure size in terms of grams, we can then write p'_{28} for the per gram price of an ounce purchase and p'_1 for the gram price of a gram purchase. Let $y_{st} = \log p'_{st}$, $\mathbf{y}_s = [y_{s1}, \ldots, y_{sT}]'$ be a vector of T observations on the price of package size s, $s = 1, 28$; ι be a column vector of T unit elements; 0 be a vector of zeros; and $\boldsymbol{\varepsilon} = [\varepsilon'_1, \ldots, \varepsilon_{28}]'$, with $\boldsymbol{\varepsilon}_s = [\varepsilon_{s1}, \ldots, \varepsilon_{sT}]'$. Then, as $\log 1 = 0$, we can write equation (A3.2) for $s = 1, 28$ and $t = 1, \ldots, T$ in vector form as:

$$\begin{bmatrix} \mathbf{y}_1 \\ \hline \mathbf{y}_{28} \end{bmatrix} = \begin{bmatrix} \iota & 0 \\ \hline \iota & \log 28\iota \end{bmatrix} \begin{bmatrix} \alpha \\ \hline \beta' \end{bmatrix} + \begin{bmatrix} \varepsilon_1 \\ \hline \varepsilon_{28} \end{bmatrix},$$

or using an obvious notation, $\mathbf{y} = \mathbf{X}\boldsymbol{\gamma} + \boldsymbol{\varepsilon}$. It follows that

$$\mathbf{X}'\mathbf{X} = T \log 28 \begin{bmatrix} \dfrac{2}{\log 28} & 1 \\ 1 & \log 28 \end{bmatrix},$$

$$(\mathbf{X}'\mathbf{X})^{-1} = \dfrac{1}{T \log 28} \begin{bmatrix} \log 28 & -1 \\ -1 & \dfrac{2}{\log 28} \end{bmatrix} \tag{A3.3}$$

$$\mathbf{X}'\mathbf{y} = \begin{bmatrix} \iota' & \iota' \\ 0' & \log 28 \; \iota' \end{bmatrix} \begin{bmatrix} \mathbf{y}_1 \\ \mathbf{y}_{28} \end{bmatrix} = \begin{bmatrix} \sum_s \sum_t y_{st} \\ \log 28 \sum_t y_{28,t} \end{bmatrix}.$$

The LS estimator of the coefficient vector $\boldsymbol{\gamma}$ is $(\mathbf{X}'\mathbf{X})^{-1} \mathbf{X}\mathbf{y}$. In view of the special structure of model (A3.2) and using the above results, the estimator takes the form

$$\frac{1}{T\log 28}\begin{bmatrix} \log 28 & -1 \\ -1 & \dfrac{2}{\log 28} \end{bmatrix}\begin{bmatrix} \sum_s\sum_t y_{st} \\ \log 28 \sum_t y_{28,t} \end{bmatrix}$$

$$=\frac{1}{T}\begin{bmatrix} \sum_s\sum_t y_{st} - \sum_t y_{28,t} \\ \dfrac{1}{\log 28}\left(-\sum_s\sum_t y_{st} + 2\sum_t y_{28,t}\right) \end{bmatrix}$$

$$=\begin{bmatrix} \bar{y}_1 \\ \dfrac{1}{\log 28}\left(-\bar{y}_1 - \bar{y}_{28} + 2\bar{y}_{28}\right) \end{bmatrix}$$

where $\bar{y}_s = (1/T)\Sigma_t y_{st}$ is the logarithmic mean price of package size s. As $\gamma = [\alpha \;\; \beta']'$,in terms of the parameters of equation (A3.2), we have:

$$\hat{\alpha} = \bar{y}_1, \qquad \hat{\beta}' = \frac{\bar{y}_{28} - \bar{y}_1}{\log 28}. \tag{A3.4}$$

In words, the estimated intercept is the mean of gram prices, while the slope is the excess of the ounce price mean over the gram price mean, normalised by the difference in package size, $\log 28 - \log 1 = \log 28$. Another way to establish result (A3.4) is to note that as equation (A3.2) will pass through the means for both grams and ounces, we have for the two package sizes $\bar{y}_1 = \hat{\alpha}, \bar{y}_{28} = \hat{\alpha} + \hat{\beta}' \log 28$. These two equations then yield result (A3.4). The covariance matrix of the LS estimator is $\hat{\sigma}^2(\mathbf{X'X})^{-1}$, where $\hat{\sigma}^2$ is an estimate of the variance of ε_s, the disturbance in equation (A3.2). It follows from the diagonal elements of the matrix on the far right of equation (A3.3) that var $(\hat{\alpha}) = \hat{\sigma}^2/T$, var $\left(\hat{\beta}'\right) = 2\hat{\sigma}^2/T\,(\log 28)^2$.

The dependent variable in equation (A3.2) is the unit price. Why use this, rather than the total price of package $p_s = s \times p_s'$ and then estimate the size elasticity $\beta = 1+\beta'$, according to equation (3.2), $\log p(s) = \alpha + \beta\log s$? Although either way would yield the same estimates of β' and β, it may appear preferable to use the unit price as the dependent variable because of units of measurement considerations. The units of p_s' are comparable across different package sizes as they are expressed in terms of dollars per gram. By contrast, the units of $p(s)$ differ from dollars per gram, for $s=1$, to dollars per ounce, for $s=28$. We could then argue that as the variance of $p(28)$ would likely be greater than that of $p(1)$, the disturbances could be heteroskedastic. However, such an argument does not apply when we use the logarithms of the prices, as then the factor that converts one price to another becomes an additive constant rather than multiplicative, so that $\operatorname{var}(\log p(s)) = \operatorname{var}(\log p'_s)$.

In the above, the price data are expressed in terms of dollars per gram. It would be equally acceptable, however, to use dollars per ounce as an alternative unit of measurement. How do the estimates (A3.4) change if we were to do this? Intuition suggests that the estimated intercept would become the mean of prices of ounce-sized packets and that the estimated slope would remain unchanged as this is an elasticity, which is a dimensionless concept. We now investigate this issue and show that this intuition is correct.

Recall that p'_s is the price per gram when marijuana is purchased in a package of size s, $s = 1$ (grams), 28 (ounces). These prices can be expressed in terms of ounces simply by multiplying by 28. Thus using a tilde ($\tilde{\;}$) to denote prices and sizes expressed in terms of ounces, we have $\tilde{p}'_{s/28} = 28 \times p'_s$, or $\tilde{p}'_{\tilde{s}} = 28 \times p'_s$, with $\tilde{s} = (1/28) \times s$ for $\tilde{s} = 1/28$ (grams), 1 (ounces). To enhance our understanding of the workings of this notational scheme, it can be enumerated as follows:

	Unit of measurement			
	Grams		Ounces	
Package size	*Size*	*Price*	*Size*	*Price*
	s	p'_s	$\tilde{s}$	$\tilde{p}'_s$
Gram	1	p'_1	1/28	$\tilde{p}'_{1/28}$
Ounce	28	p'_{28}	1	$\tilde{p}'_1$

When using ounces, equation (A3.2) becomes

$$\log \tilde{p}'_{\tilde{s}t} = \tilde{\alpha} + \tilde{\beta}' \log \tilde{s} + \tilde{\varepsilon}_{\tilde{s}t}, \quad \tilde{s} = 1/28, 1; \quad t = 1, \ldots, T. \quad (A3.5)$$

As $\log \tilde{s} = -\log 28$ for $\tilde{s} = 1/28$ and $\log \tilde{s} = 0$ for $\tilde{s} = 1$, proceeding as before, we obtain:

$$\begin{bmatrix} \tilde{y}_{1/28} \\ \tilde{y}_1 \end{bmatrix} = \begin{bmatrix} \iota & -\log 28\,\iota \\ \iota & 0 \end{bmatrix} \begin{bmatrix} \tilde{\alpha} \\ \beta' \end{bmatrix} + \begin{bmatrix} \tilde{\varepsilon}_{1/28} \\ \tilde{\varepsilon}_1 \end{bmatrix}$$

or $\tilde{\mathbf{y}} = \tilde{\mathbf{X}}\tilde{\gamma} + \tilde{\varepsilon}$. Thus[21]

$$\tilde{\mathbf{X}}'\tilde{\mathbf{X}} = T \log 28 \begin{bmatrix} \frac{2}{\log 28} & -1 \\ -1 & \log 28 \end{bmatrix},$$

$$(\tilde{\mathbf{X}}'\tilde{\mathbf{X}})^{-1} = \frac{1}{T \log 28} \begin{bmatrix} \log 28 & 1 \\ 1 & \frac{2}{\log 28} \end{bmatrix}$$

$$\tilde{\mathbf{X}}'\tilde{\mathbf{y}} = \begin{bmatrix} \iota' & \iota' \\ -\log 28\iota & \mathbf{0}' \end{bmatrix} \begin{bmatrix} \tilde{y}_{1/28} \\ \tilde{y}_1 \end{bmatrix} = \begin{bmatrix} \sum_{\tilde{s}}\sum_t \tilde{y}_{\tilde{s}t} \\ -\log 28 \sum_t \tilde{y}_{1/28,t} \end{bmatrix}.$$

The LS estimates now thus take the form

$$\frac{1}{T \log 28} \begin{bmatrix} \log 28 & 1 \\ 1 & \frac{2}{\log 28} \end{bmatrix} \begin{bmatrix} \sum_{\tilde{s}}\sum_t \tilde{y}_{\tilde{s}t} \\ -\log 28 \sum_t \tilde{y}_{1/28,t} \end{bmatrix}$$

$$= \frac{1}{T} \begin{bmatrix} \sum_{\tilde{s}}\sum_t \tilde{y}_{\tilde{s}t} - \sum_t \tilde{y}_{1/28,t} \\ \frac{1}{\log 28}\left(\sum_{\tilde{s}}\sum_t \tilde{y}_{\tilde{s}t} - 2\sum_t \tilde{y}_{1/28,t}\right) \end{bmatrix}$$

$$= \begin{bmatrix} \bar{\tilde{y}}_{1/28} + \bar{\tilde{y}}_1 - \bar{\tilde{y}}_{1/28} \\ \frac{1}{\log 28}\left(\bar{\tilde{y}}_{1/28} + \bar{\tilde{y}}_1 - 2\bar{\tilde{y}}_{1/28}\right) \end{bmatrix}$$

Thus, the estimates of the parameters of equation (A3.5) are:

$$\hat{\tilde{\alpha}} = \bar{\tilde{y}}_1, \qquad \hat{\beta}' = \frac{\bar{\tilde{y}}_1 - \bar{\tilde{y}}_{1/28}}{\log 28}. \tag{A3.6}$$

As $\tilde{p}'_{\tilde{s}} = 28 \times p'_s$, with $\tilde{s} = s/28$, $\tilde{p}_{\tilde{s}} = 28 \times p_{28\tilde{s}}$, in logarithmic terms the two sets of prices are related according to $\tilde{y}_{\tilde{s}} = \log 28 + y_{28\tilde{s}}$, so that $\bar{\tilde{y}}_1 = \log 28 + \bar{y}_{28}$ and $\bar{\tilde{y}}_{1/28} = \log 28 + \bar{y}_1$. It thus follows from equations (A3.4) and (A3.6) that

$$\hat{\tilde{\alpha}} = \log 28 + \bar{y}_{28}, \qquad \hat{\beta}' = \frac{\bar{y}_{28} - \bar{y}_1}{\log 28} = \hat{\beta}'.$$

This establishes that in moving from grams to ounces as the unit of measurement, (i) the estimated intercept becomes the logarithmic mean of the prices of the ounce-sized packages and (ii) the estimated size elasticity remains unchanged. As the diagonal elements of $(\mathbf{X}'\mathbf{X})^{-1}$ and $(\tilde{\mathbf{X}}'\tilde{\mathbf{X}})^{-1}$ coincide, the respective standard errors of $\hat{\alpha}$ and $\hat{\beta}$ are identical to those of $\hat{\alpha}$ and $\hat{\beta}'$.

A3.10 Hedonic regressions

The following is a simplified summary of some results on hedonic regressions from Diewert (2003, 2006).

Consider a cross-section application in which $p_1, \ldots, p_K$ are the prices of K types of a certain product, such as a personal computer, and $z_1, \ldots, z_K$ are the corresponding values of a single characteristic of each type, such as the amount of memory of each of the K computers. Consider further the hedonic regression:

$$f(p_k) = \alpha + g(z_k)\beta + \varepsilon_k, \quad k = 1, \ldots, K, \tag{A3.7}$$

where $f(p_k)$ is either the identity or logarithmic function, so that $f(p_k) = p_k$ or $f(p_k) = \log p_k$; $g(z_k)$ is also either the identity of logarithmic function, α and β are coefficients to be estimated and ε_k is a disturbance term with a zero mean and a constant variance. The question is, what form should the functions $f(s)$ and $g(s)$ take, the identity or logarithmic?

Suppose we use the logarithm of the price on the left on model (A3.7) and the identity function for the characteristic. One advantage of this approach is that the coefficient β is then interpreted as the (approximate) percentage change in the price resulting from a one-unit increase in the characteristic. When we additionally use $\log z_k$ on the right, then β becomes the elasticity of the price with respect to z. Assume we have $\log p_k$ on the left of (A3.7) and we wish to test the benchmark hypothesis that the price increases proportionately with the characteristic z; in other words, that there are constant returns to scale so that the price per unit of the characteristic, p_k/z_k, is constant. With $\log p_k$ on the left of (A3.7), this test can be implemented by setting $g(z_k) = \log z_k$ and testing $\beta = 1$. This convenient property points to the use of logarithms on both sides of model (A3.7).

Now consider the stochastic properties of the disturbance ε_k in equation (A3.7). When $f(p_k) = p_k$ and $f(p_k) = \log p_k$, we have, respectively,

$$\varepsilon_k = p_k - \alpha - \beta g(z_k) \tag{A3.8a}$$

$$\varepsilon_k' = \frac{p_k}{\exp\{\alpha + \beta g(z_k)\}}, \tag{A3.8b}$$

where $\varepsilon_k' = \exp(\varepsilon_k)$. Which disturbance is more likely to have a constant variance? As products with a high value of z_k are likely to be more expensive, and vice versa, the disturbances in equation (A3.8a) would likely take higher values for more expensive products and lower values for cheaper ones. Consequently, these disturbances are likely to be heteroscedastic. This would possibly be less of a problem with the logarithmic formulation, or its transform, the exponential in equation (A3.8b), as this involves the ratio of the price to its conditional mean, which is more likely to have a constant variance. That is, while more expensive products would still tend to have larger disturbances, if these errors are more or less proportional to the corresponding prices, then the variance of the ratio of the price to the conditional mean will be more or less constant. This argument also favours use of the logarithm of the price on the left of equation (A3.7).

Next, consider the implications of ensuring that the hedonic regression model is invariant to a change in the units of measurement of the characteristic z. Suppose that the function $f(s)$ is unspecified, g (t) is logarithmic, and the characteristic is now measured as $z^* = z/c$ with c a positive constant. The hedonic model now takes the form $f(p_k) = \alpha^* + \beta^* \log z_k^*$, where α^* and β^* are new coefficients. Invariance requires that the prices predicted by the two models coincide, so that $\alpha + \beta \log z_k = \alpha^* + \beta^* \log z_k^*$ for all values of z. This implies that the two sets of coefficients are related according to $\beta^* = \beta$ and $\alpha^* = \alpha + \beta^* c$. Note in particular that invariance requires that an intercept be included in the model.

Some types of the product will typically be more economically important than others, which raises the question of weighting. If there are only three types of the product and the sales of the first are twice those of the second and third, for example, it would then seem natural for the first product, relative to the second and third, to receive twice the weight in the hedonic regression. While issues of weighting usually involve questions about how to induce homoscedasticity in the disturbance term, Diewert (2003, 2006) emphasises the idea from index-number theory that the regression should be *representative*. Paraphrasing Diewert (2003, p. 5) slightly to accommodate our terminology and notation, he justifies weighting as follows:

If product type k sold q_k units, then perhaps product type k should be repeated in the hedonic regression q_k times so that the regression is representative of sales that actually occurred.

Diewert argues that an equivalent way of repeating observations is to weight the single observation on product k by $\sqrt{q_k}$; these two approaches yield identical LS estimates.

   Although the (square roots of) quantity weights are preferable to equal weights, value weights are even better. The reason is that quantity weights tend to under- (over-)represent expensive (cheap) products; the value, price $\times$ quantity, strikes a proper balance between the two dimensions of the product. Accordingly, Diewert favours weighting observations in model (A3.7) by the square roots of the corresponding value of sales. This is, of course, equivalent to weighting by the square roots of the market shares, as these differ from sales by a factor proportionality, the reciprocal of the square root of total sales, which drops out in the LS regression.

   To summarise the above discussion, Diewert (2003, 2006) shows: (i) the advantages of using logarithms on both sides of the hedonic model (A3.7); (ii) that an intercept should be included; and (iii) that the model should be estimated by weighted LS, with weights equal to the square roots of the value of sales or, equivalently, market shares. Equation (3.2) satisfies the first two of these three *desiderata*. In the next section we show that if the weights are constant over time, then weighting has no effect on the estimates. Owing to the absence of data, in our context the weights are constant, so that weighting plays no role.

A3.11 Weighted hedonic regressions

Let w_{st} be the market share of marijuana sold in package size s ($s = 1$, 28 for grams and ounces) in year t, with $w_{1,t} + w_{28,t} = 1$. We multiply both sides of equation (A3.2) by the square root of this share to give:

$$\sqrt{w_{st}} \, y_{st} = \alpha \sqrt{w_{st}} + \beta' \sqrt{w_{st}} \log s + \sqrt{w_{st}} \, \varepsilon_{st}, \qquad (A3.9)$$

where $y_{st} = \log p'_{st}$. We write this equation for $s = 1,28$ and $t = 1,\ldots,T$ in vector form as:

$$\begin{bmatrix} \sqrt{\mathbf{W}_1}\mathbf{y}_1 \\ \sqrt{\mathbf{W}_{28}}\mathbf{y}_{28} \end{bmatrix} = \begin{bmatrix} \sqrt{\mathbf{w}_1} & \mathbf{0} \\ \sqrt{\mathbf{w}_{28}} & \log 28 \sqrt{\mathbf{w}_{28}} \end{bmatrix} \begin{bmatrix} \alpha \\ \beta' \end{bmatrix} + \begin{bmatrix} \sqrt{\mathbf{W}_1}\varepsilon_1 \\ \sqrt{\mathbf{W}_{28}}\varepsilon_{28} \end{bmatrix},$$

where $\sqrt{\mathbf{W}_s} = \text{diag}\left[\sqrt{\mathbf{w}_s}\right]$; $\sqrt{\mathbf{w}_s} = \left[\sqrt{w_{s1}},\ldots,\sqrt{w_{sT}}\right]'$; $\mathbf{y}_s = [y_{s1},\ldots,y_{sT}]'$; $\mathbf{0}$ is a vector of zeros; and $\varepsilon_s = [\varepsilon_{s1},\ldots,\varepsilon_{sT}]'$. If we let $w_{s\bullet} = \sum_{t=1}^{T} w_{st}$, it then follows from the constraint $w_{1,t} + w_{28,\,t} = 1$ that $w_{1\bullet} = T - w_{28\bullet}$. Writing the above as $\mathbf{y} = \mathbf{X}\gamma + \varepsilon$, we have:

$$\mathbf{X}'\mathbf{X} = w_{28\bullet}\log 28 \begin{bmatrix} \frac{T}{w_{28\bullet}\log 28} & 1 \\ 1 & \log 28 \end{bmatrix},$$

$$(\mathbf{X}'\mathbf{X})^{-1} = \frac{1}{(T - w_{28\bullet})\log 28} \begin{bmatrix} \log 28 & -1 \\ -1 & \frac{T}{w_{28\bullet}\log 28} \end{bmatrix},$$

$$\mathbf{X}'\mathbf{y} = \begin{bmatrix} \sqrt{\mathbf{w}'}_1 & \sqrt{\mathbf{w}'}_{28} \\ \mathbf{0}' & \log 28 \sqrt{\mathbf{w}'}_{28} \end{bmatrix} \begin{bmatrix} \sqrt{\mathbf{W}_1}\mathbf{y}_1 \\ \sqrt{\mathbf{W}_{28}}\mathbf{y}_{28} \end{bmatrix}$$

$$= \begin{bmatrix} \sum_t w_{1,t}y_{1,t} + \sum_t w_{28,t}y_{28,t} \\ \log 28 \sum_t w_{28,t}y_{28,t} \end{bmatrix}.$$

The LS estimator for the coefficient vector of γ, $(\mathbf{X}'\mathbf{X})^{-1}\mathbf{X}'\mathbf{y}$, thus takes the form:

$$\frac{1}{(T - w_{28\bullet})\log 28} \begin{bmatrix} \log 28 & -1 \\ -1 & \frac{T}{w_{28\bullet}\log 28} \end{bmatrix} \begin{bmatrix} \sum_t w_{1,t}y_{1,t} + \sum_t w_{28,t}y_{28,t} \\ \log 28 \sum_t w_{28,t}y_{28,t} \end{bmatrix}$$

$$= \frac{1}{T - w_{28\bullet}} \begin{bmatrix} \sum_t w_{1,t}y_{1,t} + \sum_t w_{28,t}y_{28,t} - \sum_t w_{28,t}y_{28,t} \\ \frac{1}{\log 28}\left(-\sum_t w_{1,t}y_{1,t} - \sum_t w_{28,t}y_{28,t} + \frac{T}{w_{28\bullet}}\sum_t w_{28,t}y_{28,t}\right) \end{bmatrix}$$

$$= \begin{bmatrix} \sum_t \frac{w_{1,t}}{T - w_{28\bullet}}y_{1,t} \\ \frac{1}{\log 28}\frac{1}{T - w_{28\bullet}}\left\{\left(\frac{T}{w_{28\bullet}} - 1\right)\sum_t w_{28,t}y_{28,t} - \sum_t w_{1,t}y_{1,t}\right\} \end{bmatrix}$$

$$= \begin{bmatrix} \sum_t \frac{w_{1,t}}{T - w_{28\bullet}}y_{1,t} \\ \frac{1}{\log 28}\left(\sum_t \frac{w_{28,t}}{w_{28\bullet}}y_{28,t} - \sum_t \frac{w_{1,t}}{T - w_{28\bullet}}y_{1,t}\right) \end{bmatrix}.$$

As $\sum_t w_{1,t} = T - w_{28\bullet}$ and $\sum_t w_{28,t} = w_{28\bullet}$, the terms $w_{1,t}/(T - w_{28\bullet})$ and $w_{28,t}/w_{28\bullet}$ are both normalised shares, each with a unit sum. We write these as $w'_{st} = w_{st}/w_{s\bullet}$. Thus, the estimates of the parameters of (A3.9) are:

$$\hat{\alpha} = \bar{\bar{y}}_1, \quad \hat{\beta}' = \frac{\bar{\bar{y}}_{28} - \bar{\bar{y}}_1}{\log 28}, \quad \quad (\text{A3.10})$$

where $\bar{\bar{y}}_s = \sum_{t=1}^{T} w'_{st} y_{st}$ is the weighted mean of the (logarithmic) price of package size s. In other words, the estimated intercept is the weighted mean of the gram prices, while the slope coefficient is the difference between the weighted means of the two prices, normalised by the difference in the package size, $\log 28 - \log 1 = \log 28$.

Result (A3.10) should be compared with (A3.4). It is evident that both have exactly the same form and the only difference is that the former involves weighted means of the prices, while the means in the latter are unweighted. It should be noted that the weights in result (A3.10) are with respect to time, not commodities. Accordingly, if the weights are constant over time, $w'_{st} = 1/T, \forall t, \bar{\bar{y}}_s = \bar{y}_s$ and (A3.10) then coincides with (A3.4).

Notes

1. See, for example, Caulkins (1994, 1995, 2007), Caulkins and Pacula (2006), Caulkins and Reuter (1996, 1998), Horowitz (2001), Manski *et al.* (2001), Office of National Drug Control Policy (2004), Moore (2006) and Wendel and Curtis (2000). On the availability of Australian drug data, see Australian Bureau of Statistics (2001), Degenhardt and Dietze (2005) and Moore (2006).

2. While the Australian Bureau of Statistics publishes a Consumer Price Index (CPI) for each of the six capital cities, these indexes are not harmonised. Accordingly, the levels of the CPI cannot be compared across cities to provide information regarding differences in the level of regional living costs.

3. This index is a weighted geometric mean of the four prices for leaf grams, leaf ounces, heads grams and heads ounces. The weights are guestimates of the budget shares. For details, see Section A3.2 of the Appendix.

4. The word *hydroponic* means "water working". For details of hydroponic techniques, see, e.g., Asher and Edwards (1981) and Ashley's Sister (1997).

5. The content of the main psychoactive chemical *Delta-9-tetrahydrocannabinol* (THC) determines the potency and quality of marijuana. This is evidenced by the fact that flowers (so-called "heads"

or "buds"), which contain more THC than leaves, are considerably more expensive.

6. It should be noted that economies of scale in packaging is a general result that does not hinge on the specific assumption that the package takes the form of a cube. To illustrate, consider a sphere of radius r, the surface area and volume of which are $A = 4\pi r^2$, $V = (4/3)\pi r^3$. The area per unit volume is $A/V = 3/r = \alpha V^{-1/3}$, where α is a constant, so that unit packaging costs again decrease with package size.

7. When the penalties increase with volume, this argument for higher unit prices continues to hold as long as penalties increase proportionately less than volume.

8. For further elaboration and application of this model, see Caulkins (1997).

9. In the language of the Caulkins and Padman (1993) model considered above, $r = 1/\delta$. Accordingly, a value of the unit-price ratio of $r \approx 0.5$ implies a markup of approximately 100 per cent in the Australian marijuana industry.

10. Estimating the discount elasticity as the ratio of the mean of the log discount to log 28 is in fact exactly equivalent to the least-squares estimator of the coefficient β' in equation (3.8). For details, see Section A3.9 of the Appendix.

11. The grocery-price data are from Gordon Mills, who generously provided unpublished details from his survey of grocery prices; for details, see Mills (2002, Chapter 7).

12. In panel C of the figure, the ratios for the two products are combined by weighting them according to their relative share in consumption of 0.3 for leaf and 0.7 for heads. See Section A3.2 for a discussion of these weights.

13. We are indebted to Steven Schilizzi, University of Western Australia, and Jean-Baptiste Lesourd, Université de la Méditerranée, for drawing our attention to the rule of six-tenths and its possible relation to our work. In personal communication, Lesourd refers to Arrow and Hahn (1971), Bruni (1965), Gazérian *et al.* (1991) and Park and Lesourd (2000) and describes the rule as " ... not, in fact, anything like a 'universal constant' and, especially with multi-product firms, reality is quite more complex. However, in certain specific areas of production, the rule remains a good approximation."

14. Quantity surcharges have also been identified in several earlier studies (Cude and Walker, 1984; Gerstner and Hess, 1987; Walker and Cude, 1984; Widrick, 1979a, b), as discussed by Mills (2002, pp. 119–20).

15. For further analysis, see Mills (1996).

16. This section draws heavily on Clements and Daryal (2001).

17. This section is based on Clements and Daryal (2001), except that we use population-weighted prices.
18. This survey reports that 29 per cent of respondents consume leaf, 55 per cent heads, 13 per cent skunk, 1 per cent resin (including hash) and oil (including hash oil), and 2 per cent other types of marijuana. For reasons given by Paul Williams, Principal Investigator for the survey, we add skunk to heads (see Clements and Daryal, 2001, for details). We also disregard resin and oil, as well as other types of marijuana, since they constitute an insignificant amount of consumption (3 per cent). This then yields the result that heads account for 70 per cent of consumption and leaf 30 per cent.
19. This section is based on Clements and Daryal (2001), except that we use population-weighted prices.
20. The CPI in the US is from the Bureau of Labor Statistics (www.bls.gov; consulted on 22 November 2000).
21. The relationship between the ounce and gram notation is as follows: $\tilde{\mathbf{y}} = \mathbf{y} + \log 28\iota$ and $\tilde{\mathbf{X}} = \mathbf{X} + [\mathbf{0} : -\log 28\iota]$, where ι is a vector of $2T$ unit elements and $\mathbf{0}$ is a vector of $2T$ zero elements.

References

Arrow, K. J. and Hahn, F. H. (1971). *General competitive analysis*. San Francisco, CA: Holden Day.

Asher, C. J. and Edwards, D. G. (1981). *Hydroponics for beginners*. St Lucia: Department of Agriculture, University of Queensland.

Ashley's Sister (1997). *The marijuana hydroponic handbook*. Carlton South, Melbourne: Waterfall.

Australian Bureau of Criminal Intelligence (1996). *Australian illicit drug report 1995–1996*. Canberra: ABCI.

Australian Bureau of Criminal Intelligence (1998). *Australian illicit drug report 1997–1998*. Canberra: ABCI.

Australian Bureau of Criminal Intelligence (1999). *Australian illicit drug report 1998–1999*. Canberra: ABCI.

Australian Bureau of Criminal Intelligence (2000). *Australian illicit drug report 1999–2000*. Canberra: ABCI.

Australian Bureau of Statistics (2001). *Illicit drug use: sources of Australian data*. Canberra: ABS.

Australian Institute of Health and Welfare (1999). *National Drug Strategy Household Survey, 1998* [computer file]. Canberra: Social Science Data Archives, The Australian National University.

Basov, S., Jacobson, M. and Miron, J. (2001). "Prohibition and the market for illegal drugs: an overview of recent history." *World Economics* 2, 133–57.

Baumol, W. (2002). *The free-market innovation machine: analysing the growth miracle of capitalism.* Princeton, NJ: Princeton University Press.

Berndt, E. R. and Rappaport, N. J. (2001). "Price and quality of desktop and mobile personal computers: a quarter-century historical overview." *American Economic Review* 91, 268–73.

Brown, G. F. and Silverman, L. P. (1974). "The retail price of heroin: estimation and applications." *Journal of the American Statistical Association* 69, 595–606.

Bruni, L. (1965). "Les economies de dimension dans un processus de développement et l'influence de l'intensité de la demande." *Revue d'Economie Politique* March–April, 385–404.

Caulkins, J. P. (1994). *Developing price series for cocaine.* Santa Monica, CA: Drug Policy Research Centre, RAND.

Caulkins, J. P. (1995). "Domestic geographic variation in illicit drug prices." *Journal of Urban Economics* 37, 38–56.

Caulkins, J. P. (1997). "Modelling the domestic distribution network for illicit drugs." *Management Science* 43, 1364–71.

Caulkins, J. P. (2007). "Price and purity analysis for illicit drugs: data and conceptual issues." *Drug and Alcohol Dependence* 90, 561–8.

Caulkins, J. P. and Pacula, R. L. (2006). "Marijuana markets: inferences from reports by the household population." *Journal of Drug Issues* 36, 173–200.

Caulkins, J. P. and Padman, R. (1993). "Quantity discounts and quality premia for illicit drugs." *Journal of the American Statistical Association* 88, 748–57.

Caulkins, J. P. and Reuter, P. (1996). "The meaning and utility of drug prices." *Addiction* 91, 1261–4.

Caulkins, J. P. and Reuter, P. (1998). "What price data tell us about drug markets." *Journal of Drug Issues* 28, 593–612.

Clements, K. W. (2002). "Three facts about marijuana prices." Discussion Paper No. 02.10. Department of Economics, The University of Western Australia.

Clements, K. W. (2004). "Three facts about marijuana prices." *Australian Journal of Agricultural and Resource Economics* 48, 271–300.

Clements, K. W. (2006). "Pricing and packaging: the case of marijuana." *Journal of Business* 79, 2019–44.

Clements, K. W. and Daryal, M. (2001). "Marijuana prices in Australia in the 1990s." Discussion Paper No. 01.01. Department of Economics, The University of Western Australia.

Clements, K. W. and Daryal, M. (2005). "The economics of marijuana consumption." Chapter 10 in S. Selvanathan and E. A. Selvanathan, eds., *The demand for alcohol, tobacco and marijuana: international evidence*. Aldershot: Ashgate, pp. 243–67.

Crafts, N. (2001). "*Historical perspectives on the information technology revolution.*" Washington, DC: International Monetary Fund.

Cude, B. and Walker, R. (1984). "Quantity surcharges: are they important in choosing a shopping strategy?" *Journal of Consumer Affairs* 18, 287–95.

Degenhardt, L. and Dietze, P. (2005). *Data sources on illicit drug use and harm in Australia*. DPMP Monograph Series No. 10. Fitzroy, Melbourne: Turning Point Alcohol and Drug Centre.

Diewert, W. E. (2003). "Hedonic regressions: a review of some unresolved issues." Unpublished paper, Department of Economics, University of British Columbia.

Diewert, W. E. (2006). "Adjacent period dummy variable Hedonic regressions and bilateral index number theory." *Annales d'Economie et de Statistique* 79/80, 1–28.

Gazérian, J., Lesourd, J.-B., Ruiz, J.-M. and Sanfeld, A. (1991). "Engineering foundations of production microeconomics: application to examples concerning the chemical processing industries." *International Journal of Production Economics* 22, 163–8.

Gerstner, E. and Hess, J. D. (1987). "Why do hot dogs come in packs of 10 and buns in 8s or 12s? A demand-side investigation." *Journal of Business* 60, 491–517.

Grilli, E. R. and Yang, M. C. (1988). "Primary commodity prices, manufactured goods prices, and the terms of trade of developing countries: what the long run shows." *World Bank Economic Review* 2, 1–47.

Horowitz, J. L. (2001). "Should the DEA's STRIDE data be used for economic analysis of markets for illegal drugs?" *Journal of the American Statistical Association* 96, 1254–62.

International Monetary Fund (2001). *World economic outlook*. Washington, DC: IMF.

Manski, C. F., Pepper, J. V. and Petrie, C. V., eds. (2001). *Informing America's policy on illegal drugs: what we don't know keeps hurting us*. Washington, DC: National Academy Press.

Mills, G. (1996). "Quantity discounts and quantity surcharges in Australian supermarkets." Working Paper No. 17. Centre for Microeconomic Policy Analysis, University of Sydney.

Mills, G. (2002). *Retail pricing strategies and market power*. Carlton South, Melbourne: Melbourne University Press.

Moore, T. J. (2006). "Australian illicit drug market data: sources and issues." *Australian Economic Review* 39, 442–52.

Nordhaus, W. D. (1997). "Do real-output and real-wage measures capture reality? The history of lighting suggests not." In T. F. Bresnahan and R. J. Gordon, eds., *The economics of new goods*. Chicago, IL: The University of Chicago Press, pp. 29–66.

Office of National Drug Control Policy (1997). *The national drug control strategy, 1997: budget summary*. Washington, DC: Office of National Drug Control Policy.

Office of National Drug Control Policy (2004). *The price and purity of illicit drugs: 1981 through the second quarter of 2003*. Washington, DC: Office of National Drug Control Policy.

Park, S. U. and Lesourd, J.-B. (2000). "The efficiency of conventional fuel power plants in South Korea: a comparison of parametric and non-parametric approaches." *International Journal of Production Economies* 63, 59–67.

Radio National (1999). "Adelaide – cannabis capital." Background briefing 28 November 1999. Transcript available at www.abc.net.au/rn/talks/bbing/stories/s69754.htm. Accessed 7 February 2000.

Rosen, S. (1974). "Hedonic prices and implicit markets, product differentiation in pure competition." *Journal of Political Economy* 82, 34–55.

Stone, R. (1953). *The measurement of consumers' expenditure and behaviour in the United Kingdom, 1920–1938*. Vol. 1., UK: Cambridge University Press.

Telser, L. G. (1978). *Economic theory and the core*. Chicago, IL: The University of Chicago Press.

The Economist (2000). "The price of age", 23 December, 91–94.

Theil, H. (1967). *Economics and information theory*. Amsterdam and Chicago, IL: North-Holland and Rand McNally.

Törnqvist, L., Vartia, P. and Vartia, Y. O. (1985). "How should relative changes be measured?" *The American Statistician* 39, 43–6.

Walker, R. and Cude, B. (1984). "The frequency of quantity surcharge: replication and extension." *Journal of Consumer Studies and Home Economics* 8, 121–8.

Wendel, T. and Curtis, R. (2000). "The heraldry of heroin: 'dope stamps' and the dynamics of drug markets in New York city." *Journal of Drug Issues* 30, 225–60.

Whitesides, R. W. (2005). "Process equipment cost estimation by ratio and proportion." Course notes, PDH Course G127. http://www.pdhonline.org/courses/g127/g127.htm. Accessed 17 March 2009.

Widrick, S. M. (1979a). "Measurement of incidents of quantity surcharge among selected grocery products." *Journal of Consumer Affairs* 13, 99–107.

Widrick, S. M. (1979b). "Quantity surcharge: a pricing practice among grocery store items – validation and extension." *Journal of Retailing* 55, 47–58.

Williams, R. (1947). "Six-tenths factor aids in approximating costs." *Chemical Engineering* 54, 124–5.

4 | More on the economic determinants of consumption

KENNETH W. CLEMENTS

In Chapter 2 we considered probability models for the analysis of the consumption of drugs, both licit and illicit. Those models relate the decision to consume drugs to various socioeconomic factors such as age, sex, income, occupation, as well as to their price. Estimates of those models reveal the impact of changes in the determining factors on the probability of consuming the drug in question. Accordingly, that methodology deals with who does or does not consume drugs, but not how much is consumed; or in other words, the extensive margin of drug consumption is considered by the probability models rather than the intensive margin. The reason for this focus is that most data pertaining to drug consumption deal not with the actual quantity consumed; rather, they are typically surveys of participation, whereby respondents state "yes, I do consume marijuana" or "no, I do not".

The distinction between (i) participation and (ii) how much is consumed is important for the interpretation of the price elasticity of the demand for drugs. The *conventional price elasticity* of demand answers the question: By how much would total consumption of the drug rise following a 1 per cent fall in its price? By contrast, probability models typically deal with a different question: By how much does the *number of users* of marijuana (or "participation") rise following a 1 per cent fall in its price? The latter question relates to the *participation elasticity*, which is not the same as the conventional price elasticity. As the participation elasticity holds constant consumption per user, it ignores what happens to the consumption of pre-existing users when the price falls, thus understating the price sensitivity of total consumption. To understand the size of the marijuana market, its implications for related goods (such as tobacco and alcohol), the likely implications of further deregulation and the potential revenue that could be raised by taxing marijuana, the conventional price elasticity of demand for marijuana is needed. The conventional price elasticity is the main subject of this chapter.

145

As discussed in Chapter 2, there are a number of studies that estimate the participation elasticity of marijuana demand. Estimates of the conventional price elasticity are much rarer and are confined to Clements and Daryal (1999, 2005), Daryal (1999, 2002) and Nisbet and Vakil (1972). At the outset, it is proper to recognise that considerable caution is necessary when dealing with the value of the conventional price elasticity of demand for marijuana. Not only are the number of studies on this topic limited, but even these have their own limitations. Thus, their results have to be qualified and cannot be considered to be definitive. In this chapter, we present results from these previous studies, but do not rely on them exclusively. Additionally, we present theoretical and empirical arguments that point to using the value of minus one-half as a not unreasonable value for the conventional price elasticity of demand for marijuana. We also present some simulation results on the impact on consumption of changes in the marijuana price. While each of these approaches has its weaknesses, taken as a whole they serve to shed considerable light on the important question of the price sensitivity of marijuana consumption. This chapter is based in part on Clements (2004, 2006, 2008) and Clements and Daryal (2005).

4.1 Two types of marijuana demand elasticities

In this section, we first set out the relationship between the participation elasticity and the conventional price elasticity of demand for marijuana. We then present some results from Nisbet and Vakil (1972), the first study of the conventional price elasticity of demand for marijuana.

Let Q be total consumption of marijuana and N be population, so that $q = Q/N$ is per capita consumption. Then if U represents the number of users, these concepts are linked by the identity

$$
\begin{aligned}
Q &= q \times N \\
&= \frac{Q}{U} \times \frac{U}{N} \times N \\
&= (\text{consumption per user}) \times (\text{participation rate}) \times (\text{population}) \\
&= q' \times \pi \times N, \text{ say.}
\end{aligned}
$$

Then if for simplicity of argument the population is constant, $d(\log Q) = d(\log q') + d(\log \pi)$, so that the conventional price elasticity can be decomposed into (i) an intensive margin elasticity and (ii) an extensive margin elasticity:

$$\frac{\partial(\log Q)}{\partial(\log p)} = \frac{\partial(\log q')}{\partial(\log p)}\bigg|_{\pi=\text{constant}} + \frac{\partial(\log \pi)}{\partial(\log p)}\bigg|_{q'=\text{constant}}$$

where p is the price of marijuana. The expression on the left-hand side of the above equation is the *conventional price elasticity of demand* (CED). The right-hand side of this equation reveals that this conventional elasticity is the sum of

- the *elasticity of demand of existing users*, $\partial(\log q')/\partial(\log p)$, and
- the *elasticity of the number of users*, $\partial(\log \pi)/\partial(\log p)$, also known as the *participation elasticity*.

It is reasonable to expect that a fall in the price of marijuana will (i) cause the consumption of existing users to rise, so that $\partial(\log q')/\partial(\log p) < 0$, and (ii) cause the number of users to also rise, so that $\partial(\log \pi)/\partial(\log p) < 0$. Suppose, for example, that each of these elasticities takes the value of $-1/4$, so that the CED is $-1/4 - 1/4 = -1/2$. This shows that the absolute value of the PE underestimates the conventional elasticity. In other words, *as the participation elasticity holds constant the consumption of existing users, it understates the price sensitivity of marijuana consumption.*

Nisbet and Vakil (1972) conducted a survey of university students on their marijuana use. Of the 926 respondents, 47 per cent said they had tried marijuana. The respondents were asked to provide information on what their marijuana consumption would be at various prices, which can be termed a "market survey", as well as their actual consumption corresponding to actual prices paid. The results for the price elasticity of demand are summarised in Table 4.1. As can be seen, although the elasticity varies over a fairly wide range from -1.5 to -0.4, depending on the type of data and the functional form of the demand model used, in all four cases it is significantly negative. The elasticities based on the market survey data are lower (in absolute value) than those based on the actual data. Nisbet and Vakil refer to Stigler (1963, pp. 45–56) in arguing that this is to be expected because:

…when quizzed, individuals tend to see fewer substitution possibilities than when confronted with higher prices. Consequently demand curves

Table 4.1:   *Price elasticities of demand for marijuana*

Type of data	Demand model	
	Double-log	*Linear*
1. Market survey	−0.37 (0.06)	−0.51 (0.04)
2. Actual purchase	−1.01 (0.30)	−1.51 (0.31)

Notes:

1. Standard errors are in parentheses.
2. The elasticities in the last column are evaluated at "the going market price of 10 dollars" per ounce (Nisbet and Vakil, 1972).
Source: Derived from Nisbet and Vakil (1972).

based on market surveys tend to be less elastic than empirically estimated demand curves using market data.

Nisbet and Vakil also estimate income elasticities of demand, but these are insignificantly different from zero. In fact, the point estimates of these elasticities are all negative, which if taken at face value implies that marijuana is an inferior good, which stretches credibility. In fact, Nisbet and Vakil argue that this income response may be picking up part of the "full price" response of consumption. Suppose the cost of getting busted for marijuana use increases with income; this is not unreasonable because the damage done to reputation and other income-earning attributes as a result of a criminal record could well rise with income. Then even if the "cash" price of marijuana is held constant, as income grows, its full price rises. Consequently, there are two effects of higher income that operate in opposite directions: (i) the "pure" income effect could be expected to lead to an increase in consumption; (ii) the rise in the full price causes consumption to fall on account of the conventional substitution effect. In the situation whereby the second effect dominates, there would be a negative correlation between income and marijuana consumption and a negative "measured" income elasticity. This would clearly not be evidence in favour of the hypothesis that marijuana is an inferior good.

4.2 Marijuana consumption

In this section, we provide estimates of marijuana consumption in Australia. Our starting point is the Australian National Drug Strategy

Household Surveys (NDSHS) data. These data were collected in the form of self-reported surveys completed by a random sample of the population. To maintain confidentiality, a sealed section of the questionnaire allowed respondents to indicate their usage of drugs without the interviewer being privy to their answers. The NDSHS data are given in Table 4.2 in the form of percentages of people (aged 14 years and over) who consume marijuana, as well as the frequency of consumption. As can be seen, the number who have ever consumed marijuana increases from 28 per cent in 1988 to 39 per cent in 1998. But this 11 percentage point increase is roughly offset by the growth in those who are no longer users; this category rises from 53 per cent in 1988 to 68 per cent in 1998. These data thus describe a pool of users of roughly the same size (relative to the population), but whose composition is changing with new users constantly replacing old ones. This would seem to be consistent with experimental drug-taking in general.

Next, we use the data in Table 4.2 together with the relevant population figures to estimate the numbers of users, given in Table 4.3. These data reveal the following: (i) the number of daily consumers increases substantially over this period; (ii) on the other hand, the number of weekly and monthly users grows slowly, while the number using every few months declines; (iii) the number who consume once or twice a year increases substantially, from 220,000 to 333,000; (iv) those who have ever used marijuana rises from 3.7 million to 5.9 million, a 59 per cent increase.[1] However, by taking out the number for "no longer a user", the number of current users increases from $3.7 - 1.9 = 1.8$ million to $5.9 - 4.0 = 1.9$ million, which represents a more modest increase of 5 per cent over the 10 years. By comparison, the overall population grows by about 15 per cent over the same period. Table 4.4 presents our guesstimates of consumption per user, by frequency of consumption. As can be seen, we make the realistic assumption that the amount consumed by frequent and regular users is considerably more than that consumed by occasional users. Table 4.5 combines the information in the previous two tables to give estimated total consumption. Our estimate of total consumption in 1998 is about 12 million ounces. The last row of the table shows that per capita (14 years and over) consumption increases from 0.65 ounces per annum (p.a.) in 1988 to 0.79 ounces in 1998.

Table 4.6 gives estimated expenditure on marijuana. In calculating expenditure, the price of marijuana is based on the price index developed in Chapter 3. These prices are given in the last column of

Table 4.2: *Marijuana consumption in Australia (percentages of respondents)*

	1988	1989	1990	1991	1992	1993	1994	1995	1996	1997	1998
Ever used marijuana	28	30	31	33	34	34	33	31	34	36	39
					Frequency of consumption						
Daily	4	4	5	5	5	5	5	5	5	5	5
Once a week or more	11	11	11	11	10	8	9	9	9	8	8
Once a month or more	7	7	8	8	7	6	7	7	6	5	4
Every few months	11	10	9	8	7	6	6	6	6	5	5
Once or twice year	6	6	7	7	11	14	11	8	6	7	6
Less often	8	7	6	5	6	7	7	6	5	5	4
No longer a user	53	54	55	56	55	54	57	59	62	65	68
Total	100	100	100	100	100	100	100	100	100	100	100

Note: Respondents were aged 14 and over.

Sources: Data for 1988, 1991, 1993, 1995 and 1998 are from *National Drug Household Surveys*, Canberra: Social Science Data Archives, The Australian National University. The intermediate years are estimated by linear interpolation. The data in the first row are weighted.

Table 4.3: *Estimated number of marijuana users and total population (thousands of Australians aged 14 and over)*

Frequency of consumption	1988	1989	1990	1991	1992	1993	1994	1995	1996	1997	1998
Daily	147	171	198	227	233	239	235	224	251	272	302
Once a week or more	403	435	467	499	443	383	400	403	438	437	444
Once a month or more	256	290	325	363	327	287	306	313	290	275	262
Every few months	403	396	382	363	327	287	282	269	290	291	297
Once or twice year	220	251	283	318	490	670	517	358	370	350	333
Less often	293	277	255	227	280	335	306	269	273	265	261
No longer a user	1,941	2,136	2,334	2,541	2,566	2,585	2,656	2,641	3,086	3,470	3,986
Total	3,663	3,956	4,243	4,537	4,666	4,787	4,701	4,476	4,998	5,353	5,886
Total population	13,082	13,334	13,541	13,748	13,927	14,079	14,244	14,440	14,660	14,870	15,091

Source: Population data are from ABS, *Population by Age and Sex*, Catalogue No. 3201.0.

Table 4.4: *Estimated marijuana consumption by frequency of consumption*

Frequency of consumption	Consumption per period				
	Weekly	Monthly	Annual		
	Grams	Grams	Grams	Kilos	Ounces
Daily	10	43	520	0.520	18.57
Once a week or more	7	30	364	0.364	13.00
Once a month or more	-	4	48	0.048	1.71
Every few months	-	-	3	0.003	0.11
Once or twice year	-	-	1	0.001	0.04
Less often	-	-	1	0.001	0.04
No longer a user	-	-	0	0	0

Note: An ounce is approximately equal to 28 grams, and a kilogram is 1000 grams or 35.7 ounces.
Source: Personal inquiries and guesstimates.

Panel II of Table 4.7; see Section A4.1 of the Appendix for details. In 1998, for example, we estimate expenditure on marijuana to be $5.6 billion, or $372 per capita. How do our estimates compare with those of others? The Cleeland Report (1989) estimates expenditure on marijuana to be about $1.9 billion in 1988, which is considerably less than our figure for that year of $4.8 billion. Cleeland uses a price of $450 per ounce, which is about 20 per cent less than ours in 1988. Additionally, the quantity consumed is substantially lower in the Cleeland Report. Table 4.2 reveals that in 1988, 28 per cent of people had used marijuana; as 53 per cent are no longer users, $(1 - 0.53) \times$ 28 per cent = 13 per cent are current users. By contrast, Cleeland estimates the user population to be only 6 per cent, which would seem to be too low. Marks (1992) also argues that Cleeland underestimates the number of users. He takes Cleeland's assumed individual usage figures and scales them up by more realistic user numbers to yield estimated expenditure of $4.1 billion, which is about 1 per cent of gross domestic product (GDP) in 1988. Marks' estimate is not too different from ours for that year ($4.8 billion). Interestingly, the United Nations (1997) also estimates that expenditure on all illicit drugs is about equal to 1.4 per cent of world GDP.

Table 4.5: *Estimated marijuana consumption*

Frequency of consumption	1988	1989	1990	1991	1992	1993	1994	1995	1996	1997	1998
					I. Thousands of ounces						
Daily	2,721	3,183	3,677	4,213	4,332	4,445	4,365	4,157	4,668	5,055	5,605
Once a week or more	5,238	5,657	6,067	6,488	5,762	4,978	5,194	5,237	5,691	5,683	5,776
Once a month or more	440	497	558	622	560	492	524	537	497	472	450
Every few months	43	42	41	39	35	31	30	29	31	31	32
Once or twice year	8	9	10	11	17	24	18	13	13	13	12
Less often	10	10	9	8	10	12	11	10	10	9	9
No longer a user	0	0	0	0	0	0	0	0	0	0	0
Total consumption	8,460	9,398	10,362	11,381	10,717	9,983	10,142	9,982	10,910	11,262	11,884
					II. Ounces						
Per capita consumption	0.65	0.70	0.77	0.83	0.77	0.71	0.71	0.69	0.74	0.76	0.79

Notes:
1. Totals may not agree due to rounding.
2. Per capita consumption refers to those aged 14 years and over.

Table 4.6: *Estimated expenditure on marijuana*

Frequency of consumption	1988	1989	1990	1991	1992	1993	1994	1995	1996	1997	1998
					I. Millions of dollars						
Daily	1,559	1,832	2,122	2,305	1,967	1,982	2,073	1,979	2,259	2,472	2,651
Once a week or more	3,002	3,255	3,501	3,549	2,616	2,220	2,467	2,493	2,754	2,779	2,732
Once a month or more	252	286	322	340	254	219	249	256	241	231	213
Every few months	25	24	24	21	16	14	14	14	15	15	15
Once or twice year	5	5	6	6	8	11	9	6	6	6	6
Less often	6	6	5	4	5	5	5	5	5	4	4
No longer a user	0	0	0	0	0	0	0	0	0	0	0
Total expenditure	4,849	5,408	5,979	6,225	4,866	4,452	4,817	4,751	5,280	5,507	5,621
					II. Dollars						
Per capita expenditure	371	406	442	453	349	316	338	329	360	370	372

Note: Per capita expenditure refers to those aged 14 years and over.

Rhodes *et al.* (1997) estimate expenditure on marijuana in the United States by taking the product of the following factors: the estimated number of users in the past month, the average number of joints used, the average weight per joint and the cost per ounce. The number of users (aged 12 and over) was obtained from the US National Household Survey on Drug Abuse and the amount consumed is estimated with an ordered probit model. Using a price of $US269 per ounce, Rhodes *et al.* estimate total expenditure on marijuana to be $US7 billion in 1995. This is equivalent to $US32.5 per capita (12 years and over) or, using a long-term average exchange rate of $A1 = $US0.65, $A50 per capita, much less than our estimate for Australia in 1995 of $A329 per capita. Although the US study considers past-month users only, whereas we consider past-12-month users, this should not lead to substantial differences as Table 4.6 reveals that most marijuana expenditure is accounted for by frequent users. The difference between the two estimates would seem to be due to two factors: (i) the lower relative number of users in the US (8.6 million, or 4 per cent of the population 12 years and over) in comparison with that in Australia (2 million, or 14 per cent of the population 14 years and over);[2] (ii) the average amount of marijuana consumed in the US is estimated to be 3.1 ounces per user p.a., whereas our estimate for Australia is 5.4 ounces.[3] A study using a similar approach is that of the Western Australian Parliament Select Committee (1997), which estimates expenditure on marijuana in Western Australia using the 1995 NDSHS data. It takes into account the number of users in the last year, classified by frequency of use and age, and considers three values of the average number of joints used. Using a price of $A240 per ounce, it estimates total expenditure in Western Australia to lie in the range of $A289–440 million. This implies that per capita expenditure is between $A211 and $A321; our estimate of $A329 lies slightly above this range.[4]

To conclude, the above estimates of marijuana consumption should not be considered hard and fast. As no official data are collected, out of necessity our estimates are based on assumptions that involve judgements. Although we believe these judgements are reasonable, it would still not be unreasonable for others to have different views on some of these matters; see, for example, Jiggens (2005), who challenges our estimates.

4.3 Comparison with alcohol consumption

In this section, we present a comparison of the consumption of marijuana with that of three alcoholic beverages: beer, wine and spirits. Details of the source of the alcohol data are given in Section A4.2 of the Appendix.

The consumption and prices of the three alcoholic beverages and marijuana are presented in Table 4.7, with Figure 4.1 plotting the consumption data. As can be seen, per capita consumption of beer decreases noticeably over this period, from more than 140 litres in 1988 to 117 in 1998. Wine consumption per capita also decreases by almost 1.2 litres to end up at 24.6 litres in 1998. However, in contrast to beer, wine consumption increases in each of the last three years. The time path of spirits is roughly similar to that of wine: it first declines substantially, bottoms out in the early 1990s and then more than recovers to end up at 4.3 litres in 1998. Marijuana consumption starts off at 0.65 ounces in 1988, increases steadily until it reaches a peak of 0.83 ounces in 1991, tends to decrease for the next several years and then increases again to end up at 0.79 ounces in 1998. Retracing our steps, it can be shown that this variability in marijuana consumption is mostly due to weekly and monthly consumers.

Table 4.8 combines the quantity and price data and presents expenditure on and budget shares of the four goods. The budget share is expenditure on the good in question expressed as a fraction

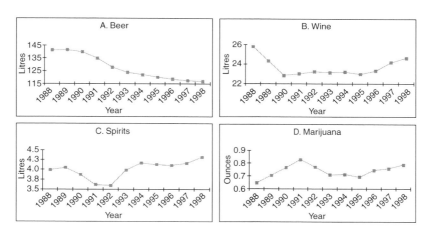

Figure 4.1: Quantities consumed

Table 4.7: *Quantities consumed and prices of alcoholic beverages and marijuana*

Year	Beer	Wine	Spirits	Marijuana
		I. Quantities		
1988	141.4	25.82	3.993	0.6467
1989	141.6	24.32	4.048	0.7049
1990	139.9	22.85	3.870	0.7652
1991	134.9	23.01	3.614	0.8278
1992	127.8	23.23	3.595	0.7695
1993	123.8	23.14	3.982	0.7090
1994	122.1	23.19	4.168	0.7120
1995	120.2	22.96	4.130	0.6913
1996	118.7	23.29	4.106	0.7442
1997	117.6	24.18	4.158	0.7575
1998	116.9	24.63	4.318	0.7875
Mean	127.2	23.69	4.000	0.7378
		II. Prices		
1988	2.819	6.190	30.578	573.12
1989	2.928	6.607	33.315	575.40
1990	3.116	6.801	36.601	577.00
1991	3.271	6.883	39.064	547.00
1992	3.361	7.056	40.532	454.00
1993	3.478	7.271	41.847	446.00
1994	3.583	7.597	43.044	475.00
1995	3.724	7.983	44.254	476.00
1996	3.891	8.306	45.687	484.00
1997	3.981	8.559	46.714	489.00
1998	4.020	8.755	47.088	473.00
Mean	3.470	7.455	40.793	506.32

Notes:

1. Quantities are per capita (14 years and over).

2. Quantities consumed of the alcoholic beverages are in terms of litres; and that of marijuana is in ounces.

3. Prices are in dollars per litre for the alcoholic beverages and per ounce for marijuana.

of total expenditure on the four goods. Several interesting features emerge from this table: (i) marijuana absorbs, on average, a little over 30 per cent of expenditure on the four goods; (ii) expenditure on marijuana is more than that on wine *plus* spirits and is more

Table 4.8: *Expenditure on and budget shares of alcoholic beverages and marijuana*

Year	Beer	Wine	Spirits	Marijuana	Total
I. Expenditures					
1988	398.41	159.84	122.10	370.63	1,050.98
1989	414.80	160.70	134.87	405.55	1,115.92
1990	435.91	155.39	141.67	441.54	1,174.51
1991	441.49	158.52	140.76	452.82	1,193.59
1992	429.43	163.93	145.70	349.36	1,088.42
1993	430.66	168.24	166.62	316.25	1,081.77
1994	437.49	176.17	179.40	338.21	1,131.27
1995	447.64	183.32	182.77	329.05	1,142.78
1996	461.75	193.48	187.60	360.19	1,203.02
1997	468.18	206.96	194.22	370.35	1,239.71
1998	470.11	215.61	203.31	372.48	1,261.51
Mean	439.60	176.55	163.59	373.31	1,153.04
II. Budget shares					
1988	37.91	15.21	11.62	35.27	100
1989	37.17	14.40	12.09	36.34	100
1990	37.11	13.23	12.06	37.59	100
1991	36.99	13.28	11.79	37.94	100
1992	39.45	15.06	13.39	32.10	100
1993	39.81	15.55	15.40	29.23	100
1994	38.67	15.57	15.86	29.90	100
1995	39.17	16.04	15.99	28.79	100
1996	38.38	16.08	15.59	29.94	100
1997	37.77	16.69	15.67	29.87	100
1998	37.27	17.09	16.12	29.53	100
Mean	38.15	15.29	14.14	32.41	100

Notes:
1. Expenditures are in terms of dollars per capita (14 years and over).
2. Budget shares are in percentages.

than three-quarters of beer expenditure; (iii) the budget share of marijuana falls by almost 6 percentage points over the period, while that of spirits rises by more than 4 points. Table 4.9 gives the quantity and price data in terms of log-changes, which when multiplied by 100 are approximate percentage changes. Panel I of

Table 4.9:   *Log-changes in quantities consumed and prices of alcoholic beverages and marijuana*

Year	Beer	Wine	Spirits	Marijuana
		I. Quantities		
1989	0.21	−5.98	1.38	8.61
1990	−1.23	−6.26	−4.49	8.22
1991	−3.65	0.70	−6.85	7.86
1992	−5.43	0.97	−0.55	−7.31
1993	−3.13	−0.40	10.23	−8.18
1994	−1.42	0.22	4.57	0.42
1995	−1.55	−0.97	−0.91	−2.69
1996	−1.29	1.43	−0.57	7.38
1997	−0.89	3.73	1.25	1.76
1998	−0.57	1.83	3.78	3.89
Mean	−1.90	−0.47	0.78	1.97
		II. Prices		
1989	3.83	6.51	8.57	0.40
1990	6.20	2.90	9.41	0.28
1991	4.86	1.19	6.51	−5.34
1992	2.72	2.49	3.69	−18.64
1993	3.41	3.00	3.19	−1.78
1994	3.00	4.38	2.82	6.30
1995	3.85	4.95	2.77	0.21
1996	4.40	3.97	3.19	1.67
1997	2.27	3.00	2.22	1.03
1998	0.98	2.27	0.80	−3.33
Mean	3.55	3.47	4.32	−1.92

Note: All entries are to be divided by 100.

the table shows that, on average, per capita beer consumption decreases by 1.9 per cent p.a., wine decreases by 0.5 per cent, spirits increases by 0.8 per cent and marijuana increases by 2.0 per cent. The growth in consumption of both spirits and marijuana exhibits considerable volatility. For example, while spirits consumption grows at a mean rate of 0.8 per cent p.a., in 1993 consumption of this beverage increases by more than 10 per cent; in the same year, marijuana declines by more than 8 per cent, while its average growth rate is 2.0 per cent.

4.4 The price sensitivity of consumption, Part I: preliminary explorations

In this section, we carry out a preliminary analysis of the price sensitivity of consumption; a more formal approach, based on the utility-maximising theory of the consumer, is used in the next section. As alcohol and marijuana share some important common characteristics, we shall analyse their consumption jointly.

As a way of summarising the data, we start with price and volume indexes of the three alcoholic beverages and marijuana. Let p_{it} be the price of good i in year t and q_{it} be the corresponding quantity consumed per capita. Then, if there are n goods, $M_t = \sum_{i=1}^{n} p_{it}q_{it}$ is total expenditure and $w_{it} = p_{it}q_{it}/M_t$ is the proportion of this total devoted to good i, or the budget share of i. Let $\bar{w}_{it} = \frac{1}{2}\left(w_{it} + w_{i,t-1}\right)$ be the arithmetic average of the budget share over the years $t-1$ and t; and $Dp_{it} = \log p_{it} - \log p_{i,t-1}$ and $Dq_{it} = \log q_{it} - \log q_{i,t-1}$ be the ith price and quantity log-changes. The Divisia price and volume indexes are then defined as

$$DP_t = \sum_{i=1}^{n} \bar{w}_{it}Dp_{it}, \quad DQ_t = \sum_{i=1}^{n} \bar{w}_{it}Dq_{it}. \tag{4.1}$$

The Divisia price index is a budget-share-weighted average of the n price log-changes and thus represents a centre-of-gravity measure of the prices. This index also has an appealing statistical interpretation (Theil, 1967, p. 136): Suppose we draw prices at random such that each dollar of expenditure has an equal chance of being selected. Then, the budget share $\bar{w}_{it}$ is the probability of drawing Dp_{it} for the transition from year $t-1$ to t, so that the expected value of the prices is $\sum_{i=1}^{n} \bar{w}_{it}Dp_{it}$, the Divisia index. The Divisia volume index has a similar interpretation and measures the overall growth in per capita consumption.

Columns 2 and 3 of Table 4.10 contain the price and volume indexes (4.1). Panel I pertains to the three alcoholic beverages plus marijuana (so that $n=4$), while Panel II gives the indexes for alcohol by itself ($n=3$). For the four goods, on average the price

Table 4.10: Divisia moments

Year (1)	Price index (×100) (2)	Quantity index (×100) (3)	Price variance (×10⁴) (4)	Quantity variance (×10⁴) (5)	Price-quantity covariance (×10⁴) (6)	Price-quantity correlation (7)
			I. Alcoholic beverages and marijuana			
1989	3.56	2.44	7.87	26.13	−11.51	−0.80
1990	3.94	1.17	10.61	32.01	−14.22	−0.77
1991	0.72	0.89	24.25	33.13	−28.27	−1.00
1992	−4.67	−4.57	105.28	9.30	20.83	0.67
1993	1.72	−2.34	5.45	34.03	8.78	0.64
1994	4.16	0.32	2.17	4.02	−0.04	−0.01
1995	2.78	−1.69	3.13	0.48	1.06	0.86
1996	3.34	1.81	1.32	13.76	−3.99	−0.94
1997	2.01	0.99	0.48	2.76	0.04	0.04
1998	−0.11	1.85	4.61	4.03	−2.67	−0.62
Mean	1.75	0.09	16.52	15.96	−3.00	−0.19
			II. Alcoholic beverages			
1989	5.32	−1.00	3.57	7.62	−0.99	−0.19
1990	6.09	−2.96	4.35	4.60	1.45	0.32
1991	4.39	−3.34	3.17	5.89	−4.27	−0.99

Table 4.10: *(continued)*

Year (1)	Price index (×100) (2)	Quantity index (×100) (3)	Price variance (×10⁴) (4)	Quantity variance (×10⁴) (5)	Price-quantity covariance (×10⁴) (6)	Price-quantity correlation (7)
1992	2.86	−3.09	0.17	8.07	0.27	0.23
1993	3.27	0.25	0.03	27.30	−0.40	−0.45
1994	3.26	0.27	0.36	5.69	−0.19	−0.13
1995	3.85	−1.28	0.53	0.09	−0.01	−0.06
1996	4.03	−0.51	0.23	1.19	−0.17	−0.33
1997	2.43	0.67	0.10	3.59	0.52	0.86
1998	1.25	0.99	0.33	3.23	0.15	0.14
Mean	3.68	−1.00	1.29	6.73	−0.36	−0.06

index rises by about 1.8 per cent p.a., while the volume index increases by 0.1 per cent p.a. The relationship between the four- and three-good indexes can be illustrated as follows. Write $\bar{W}_{At} = \sum_{i=1}^{3} \bar{w}_{it}$ for the budget share of alcohol as a whole, $DP_{At} = \sum_{i=1}^{3} (\bar{w}_{it}/\bar{W}_{At}) Dp_{it}$ for the price index of alcoholic beverages and $DP_{AM,t} = \sum_{i=1}^{4} \bar{w}_{it} Dp_{it}$ for the index of alcohol and marijuana prices. Then we have:

$$DP_{AM,t} = \bar{W}_{At} DP_{At} + (1 - \bar{W}_{At}) DP_{Mt},$$

where $DP_{Mt} = Dp_{4t}$ is the change in the price of marijuana. Accordingly, the price of alcohol and marijuana as a group is simply a budget-share-weighted average of the price of alcohol and that of marijuana. As the price of marijuana falls on average while the prices of the three beverages rise, the four-good index rises by less than the three-good index.

The indexes defined in equation (4.1) represent weighted first-order moments of n prices $Dp_{1t}, \ldots, Dp_{nt}$ and n quantities $Dq_{1t}, \ldots, Dq_{nt}$. The corresponding second-order moments are the Divisia variances:

$$
\begin{aligned}
\Pi_t &= \sum_{i=1}^{n} \bar{w}_{it}(Dp_{it} - DP_t)^2, \\
K_t &= \sum_{i=1}^{n} \bar{w}_{it}(Dq_{it} - DQ_t)^2.
\end{aligned}
\tag{4.2}
$$

These variances measure the dispersion across commodities of the prices and quantities. Columns 4 and 5 of Table 4.10 give equation (4.2) for $n=4$ and $n=3$. These show that (i) for most years, there is more dispersion in quantities than prices (but note that when marijuana is included, the year 1992 represents a major exception to this tendency), and (ii) including marijuana usually has the effect of increasing both variances.

Finally, the Divisia price-quantity covariance is

$$\Gamma_t = \sum_{i=1}^{n} \bar{w}_{it}(Dp_{it} - DP_t)(Dq_{it} - DQ_t).$$

Given the tendency of consumers to move away from (towards) those goods whose relative prices increase (decrease), we expect Γ_t to be negative. This covariance is given in column 6 of Table 4.10 and, as can be seen, in six out of ten cases is negative (for both $n=4$ and $n=3$).

Column 7 gives the corresponding correlation, $\rho_t = \Gamma_t / \sqrt{\Pi_t K_t}$. When marijuana is included, the mean value of ρ is -0.2; when marijuana is excluded, this mean substantially rises to -0.1, so the relationship is much weaker.

As Dp_{it} is the change in the nominal price of the ith good and DP_t is an index of the change in the prices of all goods (namely, alcoholic beverages and marijuana), $Dp_{it} - DP_t$ is interpreted as the change in the relative price of i. Similarly, as $Dq_{it} - DQ_t$ is the change in the quantity consumed of i relative to the average, this can also be termed the change in the relative quantity of i. The means ($\times 100$) of these relative price and quantity changes are:

Good	Quantity	Price
Beer	−1.8	1.8
Wine	−0.4	1.7
Spirits	0.9	2.6
Marijuana	2.1	−3.7

As in three out of the four cases, the quantity change has the opposite sign to the price change, we see again that there is a tendency for consumption of those goods whose relative prices rise to grow slower than average, and vice versa.

To conclude this section, we use an alternative way of measuring the degree of interrelationship between the consumption of the four goods. Consider, for example, the consumption of beer and marijuana. Suppose that total consumption of the four goods is held constant, as well as relative prices, and that a heat wave causes beer consumption to increase. If at the same time marijuana consumption falls, then, as more of one good compensates for less of the other, it would seem that both goods are capable of satisfying the same type of want of the consumer. In such a case, as these goods are competitive, it would be reasonable to describe beer and marijuana as being substitutes for one another. By a similar argument, goods whose consumption are positively correlated reinforce each other and can be described as complements. This approach to substitutability/complementarity based on residual correlations has a long history, going back to Allen and Bowley (1935).

Table 4.11: *Relative quantity correlation coefficients*

Good	Beer	Wine	Spirits	Marijuana
Beer	1.0	0.32	0.69	−0.79
Wine		1.0	0.48	−0.71
Spirits			1.0	−0.91
Marijuana				1.0

We implement the above idea by computing the correlation coefficients between the relative quantity change in good i, $Dq_{it} - DQ_t$, and that of good j, $Dq_{jt} - DQ_t$; deflating the individual quantity changes by DQ_t serves to hold constant total consumption of the group of four goods. The results, presented in Table 4.11, indicate that the three alcoholic beverages are all negatively correlated with marijuana and are thus substitutes. Interestingly, for each of the beer, wine and spirits rows, the largest (in absolute value) off-diagonal correlation always involves marijuana; these correlations are beer-marijuana -0.8, wine-marijuana -0.7 and spirits-marijuana -0.9. Accordingly, there seems to be some strength in the substitutability relationship between alcohol and marijuana. Note also that the three within-alcohol correlations are positive, indicating complementarity. While this sort of behaviour cannot be ruled out, as these correlations are all lower than the others, possibly less weight should be given to this finding. Two qualifications need to be made regarding these results. First, the number of observations underlying the correlations is small. Second, these correlations ignore changes in relative prices. Consequently, they should be thought of as just preliminary explorations of the consumption interactions among the four goods.

4.5 The price sensitivity of consumption, Part II: a demand system

In this section, we analyse more formally the price sensitivity of consumption of marijuana and its interrelationship with alcohol using a system of demand equations. This material is based on the utility-maximising theory of the consumer and the system-wide approach to demand analysis, details of which are given in Sections A4.3–A4.8 of the Appendix.

The demand system we use is the Rotterdam model, which is due to Barten (1964) and Theil (1965). We choose this model because of its straightforward nature and because it is widely used. The ith equation of this model takes the form

$$\bar{w}_{it} Dq_{it} = \theta_i DQ_t + \sum_{j=1}^{n} \pi_{ij} Dp_{jt} + \varepsilon_{it}, \qquad (4.3)$$

where $\theta_i = \partial(p_i q_i)/\partial M$ is the marginal share of good i; π_{ij} is the $(i, j)^{th}$ Slutsky coefficient; ε_{it} is a disturbance term; and the other notation is as before. The marginal share θ_i answers the question: When total expenditure increases by \$1, what fraction is spent on good i? As the increase has to be spent on something, $\sum_{i=1}^{n} \theta_i = 1$. The Slutsky coefficients deal with the substitution effects of a price change and satisfy demand homogeneity, $\sum_{j=1}^{n} \pi_{ij} = 0$ $(i = 1, \ldots, n)$, and symmetry, $\pi_{ij} = \pi_{ji}(i, j = 1, \ldots, n)$. In words, homogeneity means that an equiproportional change in each of the n prices has no effect on the quantity consumed of any good, when real income remains unchanged (as measured by $DQ_t = 0$). Symmetry means that when real income is constant, the effect on the consumption of good i of a one-dollar increase in the price of good j is exactly the same as the reciprocal effect, viz., the effect on j of a one-dollar increase of i.

By dividing both sides of equation (4.3) by $\bar{w}_{it}$, it can be seen that $\theta_i / \bar{w}_{it}$ is the ith income elasticity and $\pi_{ij} / \bar{w}_{it}$ is the $(i, j)^{th}$ price elasticity. As we shall apply equation (4.3) for $i = 1, \ldots, n$ to a group of goods (alcohol and marijuana), it is to be interpreted as a conditional demand system, which holds constant real total expenditure on the group. As discussed in the Appendix to this chapter, the analysis of demand within the group, independent of the consumption of other goods, is valid under the conditions of separability, whereby consumption of the group of goods forms an independent block in the consumer's utility function. As we have only a limited number of observations, to economise on the number of unknown parameters to be estimated, we make the simplifying assumption that tastes with respect to alcohol and marijuana can be characterised by a utility function of the preference independent form. This means that the utility function is the sum of n sub-utility functions, one for each good, $u(q_1, \ldots, q_n) = \sum_{i=1}^{n} u_i(q_i)$. Preference independence means that the marginal utility of each good is independent of the consumption of all others. The implications of preference independence are that all income elasticities are positive and all pairs of goods are Slutsky substitutes (see Section A4.5 for details). The hypothesis of preference independence has been tested with alcohol data for seven countries by Clements *et al.* (1997) and, using a variety of tests, they find that the hypothesis cannot be rejected.

Under preference independence, the Slutsky coefficients in equation (4.3) takes the form

$$\pi_{ij} = \phi \theta_i (\delta_{ij} - \theta_j), \qquad (4.4)$$

where ϕ is the own-price elasticity of demand for the group of goods as a whole; and δ_{ij} is the Kronecker delta ($\delta_{ij} = 1$ if $i = j$, 0 otherwise). Accordingly, the term involving prices in equation (4.3) becomes $\sum_{j=1}^{n} \pi_{ij} Dp_{jt} = \phi \theta_i (Dp_{it} - DP'_t)$, where $DP'_t = \sum_{i=1}^{n} \theta_i Dp_{it}$ is a marginal-share-weighted average of the prices, known as the Frisch price index. Equation (4.3) thus simplifies to

$$\bar{w}_{it} Dq_{it} = \theta_i DQ_t + \phi \theta_i (Dp_{it} - DP'_t) + \varepsilon_{it}. \qquad (4.5)$$

This equation for $i = 1, \ldots, n$ is the Rotterdam model under preference independence. The disturbance terms ε_{it} are assumed to have zero means and, again to economise on unknown parameters, have variances and covariances of the form

$$\text{cov}(\varepsilon_{it}, \varepsilon_{jt}) = \sigma^2 \bar{w}_i (\delta_{ij} - \bar{w}_j), \qquad (4.6)$$

where σ^2 is a constant; and $\bar{w}_i$ is the sample mean of $\bar{w}_{it}$. This specification, which has been advocated by Selvanathan (1991) and Theil (1987b), implies that (i) the variances of the disturbances increase with the corresponding budget shares for $\bar{w}_i < 0.5$, and (ii) the covariances between disturbances in different equations are all negative. These are plausible implications.[5]

Before applying (4.5) to the alcohol and marijuana data, we make one further simplification. Rather than attempting to estimate the marginal shares, we shall specify their values. Recalling that the income elasticity is the ratio of the marginal share to the corresponding budget share, we proceed by considering the values of the income elasticities and the budget shares. Columns 3–5 of Table 4.12 present estimates of income elasticities for alcohol from Clements *et al.* (1997), and we use them as a broad guide to the likely values to use for the marginal shares. In column 2 of Table 4.13, beer is taken to

Table 4.12:   *Demand elasticities for alcoholic beverages*

Country (1)	Sample period (2)	Income elasticities			Price elasticity of alcohol as a whole (6)
		Beer (3)	Wine (4)	Spirits (5)	
Australia	1955–85	0.81	1.00	1.83	−0.50
Canada	1953–82	0.74	1.05	1.25	−0.42
Finland	1970–83	0.45	1.32	1.32	−1.35
New Zealand	1965–82	0.84	0.88	1.45	−0.44
Norway	1960–86	0.34	1.48	1.55	−0.08
Sweden	1967–84	0.21	0.69	1.52	−1.43
United Kingdom	1955–85	0.82	1.06	1.34	−0.54
Mean		0.60	1.07	1.47	−0.68

Source: Clements *et al.* (1997).

Table 4.13:   *Income elasticities, budget shares and marginal shares*

Good (1)	Income elasticity η_i (2)	Budget share w_i (3)	Marginal share θ_i (4)
Beer	0.5	0.40	0.20
Wine	1.0	0.15	0.15
Spirits	2.0	0.15	0.30
Marijuana	1.2	0.30	0.35
Sum		1.00	1.00

have an income elasticity of 0.5 (so that it is a necessity), wine 1.0 (a borderline case) and spirits 2.0 (a strong luxury); we will come back to the elasticity for marijuana. Column 3 of this table gives the four budget shares, which approximate the sample means given in the last row of Table 4.8, while column 4 presents the implied marginal shares, computed as $\theta_i = \eta_i \times w_i$, where η_i is the income elasticity of i. As the marginal shares have a unit sum, the θ_i for marijuana can be obtained from the other three estimates as $1 - 0.20 - 0.15 - 0.30 = 0.35$. As the budget share of marijuana is 0.30, its income elasticity is 0.35/ 0.30 = 1.2, implying that it is a modest luxury; this value is recorded as the last entry of column 2.

As the values of θ_i are now known, we write equation (4.5) as $y_{it} = \phi x_{it} + \varepsilon_{it}$, where $y_{it} = \bar{w}_{it} Dq_{it} - \theta_i DQ_t$ and $x_{it} = \theta_i (Dp_{it} - DP'_t)$. Since $\sum_{i=1}^{n} \varepsilon_{it} = 0$, one equation is redundant and we write the above for $i = 1, \ldots, n-1$ as $y_t = \phi x_t + \varepsilon_t$, where y_t, x_t and ε_t are all vectors containing the corresponding $n-1$ elements. We estimate the one unknown parameter ϕ by generalised-least-squares, i.e., by minimising the sum over $t = 1, \ldots, T$ observations of the quadratic form $(y_t - \phi x_t)' \Sigma^{-1} (y_t - \phi x_t)$, where Σ is the covariance matrix defined by equation (4.6) for $i, j = 1, \ldots, n-1$, namely, $\sigma^2 (\mathbf{W} - \mathbf{w}\mathbf{w}')$, where $\mathbf{W} = \text{diag}[\mathbf{w}]$ and $\mathbf{w} = [\bar{w}_1, \ldots, \bar{w}_{n-1}]'$. It can be shown (Theil, 1987b, p. 126) that this amounts to minimising $\sum_{t=1}^{T} \sum_{i=1}^{n} (y_{it} - \phi x_{it})^2 / \bar{w}_i$. The alcohol and marijuana data then yield an estimate of ϕ of -0.113, with standard error 0.144. Whilst this estimate of the price elasticity of demand for alcohol and marijuana as a whole is negative, it is low (in absolute value) and insignificantly different from zero. In comparison with the prior estimates of this elasticity for alcohol by itself, given in column 6 of Table 4.12, this estimate also seems to be on the low side.

Moreover, the above estimate is sensitive to the years included in the sample. This can be clearly illustrated by re-estimating ϕ by successively omitting each of the ten years and including the remaining nine:

Year excluded	ϕ-estimate (standard error in parentheses)
None	−0.113 (0.144)
1989	−0.039 (0.147)
1990	−0.026 (0.145)
1991	0.044 (0.150)
1992	−0.675 (0.192)
1993	−0.177 (0.134)
1994	−0.108 (0.152)
1995	−0.119 (0.153)
1996	−0.099 (0.148)
1997	−0.114 (0.152)
1998	−0.107 (0.154)

Table 4.14: *Price elasticities of demand*

Good (1)	Beer (2)	Wine (3)	Spirits (4)	Marijuana (5)
		I. *Compensated*		
Beer	−0.20	0.04	0.08	0.09
Wine	0.10	−0.43	0.15	0.18
Spirits	0.20	0.15	−0.70	0.35
Marijuana	0.12	0.09	0.18	−0.38
		II. *Uncompensated*		
Beer	−0.40	−0.04	0.00	−0.06
Wine	−0.30	−0.58	0.00	−0.13
Spirits	−0.60	−0.15	−1.00	−0.25
Marijuana	−0.36	−0.09	−0.01	−0.74

As can be seen, the estimated value of ϕ ranges from a small positive value that is insignificantly different from zero, to −0.68, which is significant. Evidently, if the estimated price elasticity can change by so much simply by omitting one observation, we cannot place much confidence in the results. To proceed, instead of relying on any of the above estimated price elasticities, we shall use the value of minus one-half for ϕ. The justification for this value is two-fold: (i) it is not inconsistent with the results for marijuana obtained from survey data discussed in the next section; (ii) theoretical and empirical evidence presented in Section 4.8 also points to a price elasticity of minus one-half.

We now have the components needed to construct the 4×4 matrix of own- and cross-price elasticities. To compute the Slutsky coefficient π_{ij}, we use $\phi = -0.5$ in equation (4.4) and the values of the four marginal shares given in column 4 of Table 4.13. As the $(i, j)^{\text{th}}$ price elasticity takes the form $\pi_{ij}/\bar{w}_{it}$, we use the budget shares given in column 3 of Table 4.13 to convert the Slutsky coefficients into elasticities. Panel I of Table 4.14 contains the results. The own-price elasticity of beer is −0.2, wine −0.4, spirits −0.7 and marijuana −0.4. Interestingly, for each alcoholic beverage, the largest cross-price elasticity is for the price of marijuana: the elasticity of beer consumption with respect to the price of marijuana is 0.1, wine-marijuana is 0.2 and spirits-marijuana is 0.4. In comparison with previous studies (Fogarty, 2005, Chapter 2, Selvanathan and Selvanathan, 2005a,

p. 232), the values of the own-price elasticities for the three alcoholic beverages are reasonable.[6] Regarding the own-price elasticity of marijuana, our estimate of -0.4 lies at the bottom end of the range of -0.4 to -1.5 estimated several decades ago by Nisbet and Vakil (1972) with US survey data. However, in view of the conceptual and statistical uncertainties, it would seem appropriate not to make too much of the differences in these estimates. Furthermore, as discussed in the next section, our estimate is not inconsistent with those of Daryal (1999) based on more recent survey-based data.

The above price elasticities are "compensated" as they refer to the substitution effects only – real total expenditure on the four goods is held constant. Alternatively, if we hold nominal total expenditure constant we obtain the corresponding "uncompensated" elasticities; these involve adding back the income effects of the price changes and take the form $\pi_{ij} / \bar{w}_{it} - \bar{w}_{jt} \eta_i$. The uncompensated elasticities, which are computed using the information contained in Table 4.13, are given in Panel II of Table 4.14. The own-price elasticities are now -0.4, -0.6, -1.0 and -0.7 for beer, wine, spirits and marijuana, respectively. An element-by-element comparison of the uncompensated elasticities with their compensated counterparts reveals three major differences: (i) when the income effects are included, the elasticities involving the price of beer (given in column 2) are all (algebraically) much lower; this is due to the high budget share of beer of 40 per cent; (ii) the four uncompensated elasticities of spirits (given in the row for that good) are all much smaller than the compensated versions due to the high income elasticity of spirits of 2; (iii) the three uncompensated cross elasticities involving the price of spirits are all near zero, as the income effect of the price change offsets the substitution effect.

4.6 Evidence from a special survey

Section 4.2 reviewed the study of the price sensitivity of marijuana consumption conducted by Nisbet and Vakil (1972). That study involved a special survey of university students in the US. In this section, we examine in some detail the more recent study by Daryal (1999, 2002) of marijuana consumption patterns of Australian university students. It will become clear from what is to follow that Daryal's work adds substantially to the knowledge of the economic determinants of marijuana consumption.

Table 4.15: *Ever used marijuana? (Number of respondents; percentages are in parenthesis)*

Response	Male	Female	All
Yes	82 (60)	67 (46)	149 (53)
No	54 (40)	78 (54)	132 (47)
Total	136 (100)	145 (100)	281 (100)

Source: Daryal (1999).

Table 4.16: *Frequency of marijuana consumption (Percentages of respondents)*

Frequency of Consumption	Male	Female	All
Daily	9	1	6
Weekly	33	25	30
Monthly	17	25	21
Occasional	21	28	23
No longer	20	21	20
Total	100	100	100

Note: For a given column, the largest entry is shaded.
Source: Daryal (1999).

Daryal surveyed first-year economics students at The University of Western Australia; the mean age of these students is 19 years, while the median is 18. Table 4.15 shows that slightly more than one-half of the respondents use marijuana, with males more intensive users than females. Almost one-third of users consume marijuana on a weekly basis (Table 4.16). The survey investigated the likely impact of legalisation of marijuana on consumption, as well as a fall in the price. Consider first the results for legalisation by itself, contained in Table 4.17. Several comments can be made. First, the largest impact of legalisation is on male daily smokers, whose consumption is estimated to increase by more than 20 per cent, but is not significantly different from zero at the 5 per cent level. Then come female weekly smokers, whose consumption increases by 11 per cent, about half that of the daily males. Second, looking at the last column of the table which

Table 4.17: *Percentage change in consumption of marijuana due to legalisation (Standard errors are in parenthesis)*

Type of consumer	Males		Females		All	
Daily smoker	21.25	(14.8)	0.00	(0.00)	18.89	(13.7)
Weekly smoker	8.15*	(4.07)	11.18*	(5.08)	9.32*	(3.19)
Monthly smoker	6.79*	(3.38)	9.12*	(4.07)	8.06*	(2.79)
Occasional smoker	10.88*	(4.27)	3.89*	(1.96)	7.29*	(2.35)
No longer a smoker	4.69	(4.67)	0.00	(0.00)	2.50	(2.48)
All smokers	9.09*	(2.28)	6.19*	(1.78)	7.79*	(1.49)
Non-smokers	0.19	(0.18)	0.38	(0.24)	0.30*	(0.15)
All types	5.55*	(1.42)	3.07*	(0.86)	4.27*	(0.82)

Notes:
1. The symbol "*" denotes significance at the 5 per cent level.
2. For a given column, the shaded entry represents the maximum consumption increase.
Source: Daryal (1999).

refers to both males and females, the impact of legalisation declines with the frequency of consumption, from 19 per cent for dailies, to 9 per cent for weeklies, 8 per cent for monthlies, 7 per cent for occasionals and 3 per cent for no longer a smoker. Third, for all those who are users, consumption increases by almost 8 per cent (see the third last entry in the last column). Fourth, as the effect on those who have never consumed marijuana (referred to as "non-smokers" in the table) is trivial, and barely significantly different from zero, legalisation has almost no effect on encouraging new users. Finally, including both users and non-users, legalisation increases consumption by about 4 per cent (the last entry of the last column).

Next, consider the effects on consumption of two effects that occur at the same time, (i) legalisation and (ii) a 50 per cent fall in the price. To enhance understanding of this scenario, it is helpful to consider it in two separate steps, as in Figure 4.2, where $D_0 D_0$ is the demand curve for marijuana before legalisation, p_0, q_0 are the initial price and quantity consumed, and E_0 is the associated equilibrium point. Legalisation increases the quantity demanded at each price, so the demand curve shift out to the right to $D_1 D_1$, and at the initial price of p_0 consumption rises to q_1, with E_1 the corresponding equilibrium point. When consumption is legalised and the price falls from p_0 to p',

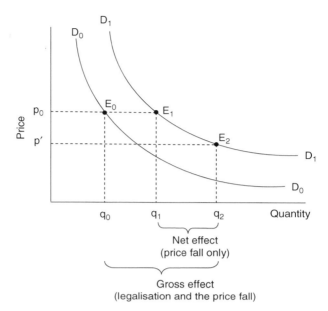

Figure 4.2. Effects of legalisation and a price decrease on marijuana consumption
Source: Daryal (1999).

we move down the new demand curve D_1D_1, from E_1 to E_2, and consumption rises from q_1 to q_2. Thus, this graph shows how the total effect on consumption of legalisation and price fall is q_0q_2, and how this comprises two components:

- a legalisation effect q_0q_1, which holds constant the price, and thus relates solely to the shift in the demand curve;
- a price effect q_1q_2, the movement along the demand curve.

Daryal refers to the total impact q_0q_2 as the "gross effect" and the impact of the price fall q_1q_2 as the "net effect". These concepts will be used in what follows.

Estimates of the gross effect of legalisation and the price fall are contained in Table 4.18. As can be seen, among all groups the consumption of daily males again increases the most and is estimated to rise by 38 per cent. From Table 4.17, we know that consumption of this group grows by 21 per cent on account of legalisation only. The

Table 4.18: *Percentage change in consumption of marijuana due to both legalisation and a 50 per cent price decrease (Standard errors are in parenthesis)*

Type of consumer	Males		Females		All	
Daily smoker	37.50*	(12.5)	25.00	(26.2)	36.11*	(11.1)
Weekly smoker	28.33*	(4.89)	36.46*	(5.69)	31.47*	(3.73)
Monthly smoker	28.92*	(7.11)	26.46*	(6.01)	27.57*	(4.53)
Occasional smoker	18.82*	(5.81)	8.06*	(2.65)	13.29*	(3.22)
No longer a smoker	2.19	(1.64)	0.71	(0.71)	1.50	(0.98)
All smokers	22.25*	(2.87)	18.65*	(2.77)	20.64*	(2.01)
Non-smokers	0.83	(0.59)	0.96	(0.96)	0.91	(0.67)
All types	13.75*	(1.95)	9.14*	(1.55)	11.37*	(1.25)

Notes:
1. The symbol "*" denotes significant at the 5 per cent level.
2. For a given column, the shaded entries represent the maximum consumption increase.
Source: Daryal (1999).

impact of the price decline can thus be isolated by subtracting from the above gross effect (38 per cent) the corresponding legalisation effect (21 per cent) to obtain that the net effect of the price fall of $38 - 21 = 17$ per cent. Dividing this quantity change by the price change (-50 per cent), gives the price elasticity of demand for this group:

$$\text{Price elasticity} = \frac{\text{Percentage change in quantity demanded}}{\text{Percentage change in price}} = \frac{17}{-50} = -0.33.$$

This elasticity, which Daryal calls the "net" price elasticity, is given as the first entry in the "males" column of Panel B of Table 4.19. The elasticities for the other groups are interpreted in a similar manner. Among all groups, the weekly females have the highest absolute elasticity at -0.51.

Panel A of Table 4.19 contains the corresponding "gross" price elasticities, defined as the percentage change in consumption following legalisation and the price fall divided by -50, the amount of the price fall. Figure 4.3 plots all the price elasticities against the frequency of consumption. This shows rather clearly that in broad outline, the price sensitivity of consumption falls with consumption, that is, frequency. This pattern could reflect the higher income effect of the

Table 4.19: *Price elasticities of demand for marijuana (Standard errors are in parenthesis)*

Type of consumer	Males	Females	All
A. Gross price elasticities			
Daily smoker	−0.75* (0.25)	−0.50 (0.53)	−0.72* (0.22)
Weekly smoker	−0.57* (0.10)	−0.73* (0.11)	−0.63* (0.07)
Monthly smoker	−0.58* (0.14)	−0.53* (0.12)	−0.55* (0.09)
Occasional smoker	−0.38* (0.12)	−0.16* (0.05)	−0.27* (0.06)
No longer a smoker	−0.04 (0.03)	−0.02* (0.01)	−0.03 (0.02)
All smokers	−0.45* (0.05)	−0.37* (0.06)	−0.41* (0.04)
Non-smokers	−0.02 (0.02)	−0.02 (0.02)	−0.02 (0.02)
All types	−0.28* (0.04)	−0.18* (0.03)	−0.23* (0.03)
B. Net price elasticities			
Daily smoker	−0.33* (0.16)	−0.50 (0.53)	−0.34* (0.15)
Weekly smoker	−0.40* (0.11)	−0.51* (0.10)	−0.44* (0.08)
Monthly smoker	−0.44* (0.12)	−0.35* (0.11)	−0.39* (0.08)
Occasional smoker	−0.16* (0.07)	−0.08* (0.04)	−0.12* (0.04)
No longer a smoker	0.05 (0.06)	−0.01 (0.01)	0.02 (0.04)
All smokers	−0.26* (0.08)	−0.25* (0.07)	−0.26* (0.05)
Non-smokers	−0.01 (0.01)	−0.01 (0.02)	−0.01 (0.01)
All types	−0.16* (0.05)	−0.12* (0.04)	−0.14* (0.03)

Notes:
1. The symbol "*" denotes significant at the 5 per cent level.
2. For a given column, the shaded entry represents the maximum elasticity.
Source: Daryal (1999).

price change for more frequent users. Finally, as the daily, weekly and monthly users are likely to account for the bulk of total consumption, their price sensitivity as a whole is of particular interest. Daryal is unable to reject the hypothesis that the elasticities for these three groups are identical. Table 4.20 gives the estimated elasticities when the three groups are combined into one ("more frequent users"). As can be seen, the net price elasticity for both sexes is estimated to be −0.41 with a standard error of 0.09.

The above analysis shows that the consumption of marijuana is price inelastic, which is not surprising in view of what is known about alcohol elasticities, but still significantly different from zero.

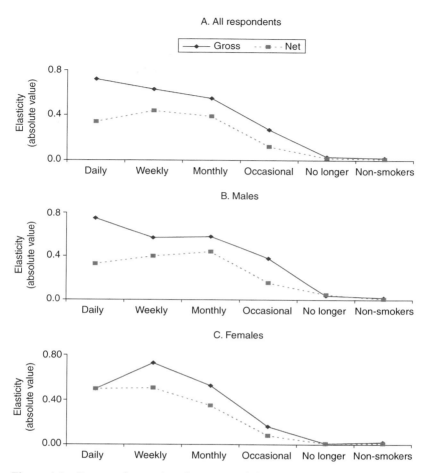

Figure 4.3. Gross and net price elasticities of demand for marijuana
Source: Daryal (1999).

In assessing this degree of price sensitivity of consumption, it should be kept in mind that the above elasticities are associated with a 50 per cent fall in the price, which is large. Suppose there were some upper limit to marijuana consumption because of some physiological (or psychiatric?) reasons. In such a case, a large price fall could take some consumers somewhere near that limit, implying that the absolute value of the elasticity declines with the

Table 4.20: *Price elasticities of demand for marijuana for more frequent users (Standard errors are in parenthesis)*

	Males		Females		All	
			A. *Gross price elasticities*			
	-0.60^*	(0.12)	-0.63^*	(0.12)	-0.61^*	(0.10)
			B. *Net price elasticities*			
	-0.40^*	(0.10)	-0.43^*	(0.10)	-0.41^*	(0.09)

Note: The symbol "*" denotes significant at the 5 per cent level.
Source: Daryal (1999).

size of the price fall; in the limit, when consumption hits its maximum value, the elasticity is zero. This argument means that for a more marginal price change, marijuana consumption could be more price elastic than the above elasticity of -0.4. This elasticity estimate falls at the lower end of Nisbet and Vakil's (1972) range of -0.4 to -1.5, but is consistent with the value discussed in the previous section of -0.4.

4.7 More on marijuana and alcohol

Above, we investigated the link between marijuana usage and drinking in the form of a comparison of consumption patterns, index numbers and their interrelationship in a demand system. This section provides further discussion of this link by briefly reviewing some previous research on the topic and presenting some more results from Daryal (1999).

Prior micro-level studies in Australia seem to point to a substitutability relationship between marijuana and alcohol. Using NDSHS data between 1988 and 1995, Cameron and Williams (2001) find that tobacco is a complement for marijuana and marijuana is a substitute for alcohol. Using a trivariate approach and NDSHS data between 1995 and 2001, Zhao and Harris (2004) find a similar pattern, although the substitutability relationship between marijuana and alcohol is insignificant. On the other hand, in the context of alcohol consumption, there is also evidence of complementarity. Harris *et al.* (2006) investigate alcohol consumption for different types of drinkers using a flexible model.

While there is some indication of a complementary relationship between alcohol participation and marijuana, the response of frequent drinkers to the marijuana price is insignificant. Williams and Mahmoudi (2004) also find marijuana and alcohol to be complements for people who admit to using both at the same time. In a review of the US literature, Cameron and Williams (2001) point out that US studies do not typically use marijuana prices due to their unavailability, instead using proxies such as whether or not a state has decriminalised the use of marijuana. Cameron and Williams also note that the US evidence regarding the relationship between marijuana and alcohol is mixed, with some studies finding them to be substitutes and others complements.

Daryal (1999) sheds further light on the interrelationship between marijuana and alcohol consumption. He included in his survey the following question:

Suppose marijuana were legalised, would your alcohol consumption change?

Respondents were asked to select one response from the following:

a. My alcohol consumption will decrease no matter what the price of marijuana is.
b. My alcohol consumption will increase no matter what the price of marijuana is.
c. My alcohol consumption will decrease only if the price of marijuana decreases.
d. My alcohol consumption will increase only if the price of marijuana decreases.
e. There will be no change in my alcohol consumption.

The answer "yes my alcohol consumption would increase with legalisation" indicates that consumption of the two goods tends to move together. This would imply a tendency of alcohol and marijuana to be consumed together, suggesting they are complements. Conversely, if alcohol consumption falls, the two goods are possibly substitutes.

The first row of Table 4.21 gives the responses to the above question for daily smokers. As can be seen, the modal response for this group is for there to be no change in alcohol consumption, which points to the two commodities being neither substitutes nor complements, but rather independent of each other. On the other hand, 22 per cent say their drinking would increase if marijuana were legalised, and a further 11 per cent say it would increase with

Table 4.21: *The effect of marijuana legalisation and a price fall on alcohol consumption (Percentages of respondents)*

Type of consumer (1)	None (2)	Marijuana is legalised			Marijuana is legalised and its price decreases		
		Increase (3)	Decrease (4)	Increase less decrease (5)	Increase (6)	Decrease (7)	Increase less decrease (8)
Daily smokers	56	22	0	22	11	11	0
Weekly smokers	82	2	5	−3	2	9	−7
Monthly smokers	81	6	6	0	0	7	−7
Occasional smokers	77	3	6	−3	0	14	−14
No longer smokers	97	0	3	−3	0	0	0
All smokers	82	4	5	−1	1	8	−7
Non-smokers	95	3	1	2	1	0	1
All respondents	88	4	3	1	1	4	−3

Notes:

1. For a given row, the sum of columns 2, 3, 4, 6 and 7 equals 100.

2. Column 5 equals the difference between columns 3 and 4; and column 8 equals the difference between columns 6 and 7.

Source: Daryal (1999).

legalisation and a price fall, indicating complementarity. Matters are further complicated by the additional 11 per cent who say that their alcohol consumption would decrease with the legalisation and a fall in the price of marijuana (see the first entry in column 7 of the table). For most other groups of consumers, there are similar conflicting increases and decreases in drinking, as revealed by the subsequent rows of the table. One way to proceed is to summarise the results using the net position of alcohol consumption, defined as the excess of the increases over the decreases, as in columns 5 and 8. As in most cases the net position is negative, indicating a fall in drinking on balance, the results tend to suggest substitutability between marijuana and alcohol. For several reasons, however, we cannot be overly confident of this result. For one thing, daily smokers are a major exception to the general rule of a negative relationship between the two goods. Second, while the signs of the net positions are mostly negative, their magnitudes involved are not too far away from zero. A third reason for caution is that for each type of consumer the majority say that their alcohol consumption would be unchanged, indicating independence.[7]

We can summarise the material of this section as follows. First, the prior literature seems to contain mixed findings regarding the question of whether marijuana and alcohol are substitutes or complements in consumption. Second, while there are indications that marijuana and alcohol are substitutes from Daryal's (1999) survey, that evidence is not completely clear-cut.

4.8 A useful rule of thumb: price elasticities are about minus one-half

The own-price elasticities for alcohol and marijuana discussed in the previous sections are all fractions and tend to be clustered around the value of minus one-half. As this centre-of-gravity value applies in a number of other instances also, we shall consider in this section one theoretical justification lying behind the empirical regularity of price elasticities being approximately equal to minus one-half. We commence the discussion by considering several examples.

Table 4.22 and Figure 4.4 present information from reviews regarding the values of price elasticities that have been estimated for a number of different commodities. It is to be emphasised that underlying each review is a number of individual studies, as recorded in

Table 4.22: *Price elasticities of demand for selected products*

Product (1)	Mean (2)	Median (3)	Number of observations (4)	Length of run (5)	Source (6)
1. Beer	−0.46	−0.35	139		Fogarty (2005, Chapter 2)
	−0.37		10		Selvanathan and Selvanathan (2005a, p. 232)
2. Wine	−0.72	−0.58	141		Fogarty (2005, Chapter 2)
	−0.46		10		Selvanathan and Selvanathan (2005a, p. 232)
3. Spirits	−0.74	−0.68	136		Fogarty (2005, Chapter 2)
	−0.57		10		Selvanathan and Selvanathan (2005a, p. 232)
4. Cigarettes	−0.48		523		Gallet and List (2003)
		−0.40	368	Short run	Gallet and List (2003)
		−0.44	155	Long run	Gallet and List (2003)
5. Residential water	−0.41	−0.35	314		Dalhuisen et al. (2003)
	−0.51		124		Espey et al. (1997)
		−0.38		Short run	Espey et al. (1997)
		−0.64		Long run	Espey et al. (1997)
6. Petrol	−0.26	−0.23	363	Short run	Espey (1998)
	−0.25		46	Short run	Goodwin et al. (2004)
	−0.25	−0.21	387	Short run	Graham and Glaister (2002, p. 48)
	−0.58	−0.43	277	Long run	Espey (1998)
	−0.64		51	Long run	Goodwin et al. (2004)
	−0.53		70		Espey (1996)

	−0.77	−0.55	213	Long run	Graham and Glaister (2002, p. 48)
	−0.35	−0.35	52	Intermediate	Graham and Glaister (2002, p. 54)
7. Residential electricity	−0.35	−0.28	123	Short run	Espey and Espey (2004)
	−0.85	−0.81	125	Long run	Espey and Espey (2004)
8. Branded products	−1.76		337		Tellis (1988)

Notes:

1. The other average elasticities of road traffic and fuel consumption reported in Goodwin *et al.* (2004) and Graham and Glaister (2002) are excluded as they are not confined to the demand by final consumers.

2. Although the elasticities reported by Goodwin *et al.* (2004) and Graham and Glaister (2002) refer to "fuel" used by motor vehicles, which is broader than "petrol" ("gasoline"), for simplicity of presentation of the table we list these under the product "petrol".

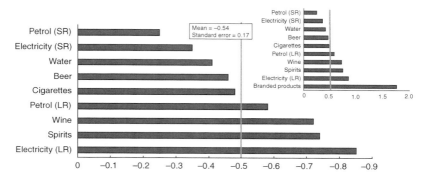

Figure 4.4. Price elasticities of demand

Notes: The elasticity values in this figure are the means from Table 4.22. In cases where there are multiple means for the same product, we use those with the largest number of observations. The elasticity value for petrol (SR) of −0.25 is from the third entry in Panel 6 of the table; electricity (SR) of −0.35 is from the first entry of Panel 7; water of −0.41 is from the first entry of Panel 5; beer of −0.46 is from the first entry of Panel 1; cigarettes of −0.48 is from the first entry of Panel 4; petrol (LR) of −0.58 is from the fourth entry of Panel 6; wine of −0.72 is from the first entry of Panel 2; spirits of −0.74 is from the first entry of Panel 3; electricity (LR) of −0.85 is from the second entry of Panel 7; and branded goods (included only in the "mini version" of the figure in the top right-hand corner) of −1.76 is from Panel 8. SR denotes short run and LR denotes long run.

column 4 of the table. For example, there are as many as 523 studies included in Gallet and List's (2003) review of the price elasticity of demand for cigarettes (row 4). Rows 1–3 of the table show that the major alcoholic beverages have mean/median elasticities not too far away from the value −½. The means from Selvanathan and Selvanathan (2005a) are beer −0.37 (with standard error 0.09), wine −0.46 (0.08) and spirits −0.57 (0.12), the maximum distance from −½ being a mere 1.4 standard errors. The next two rows of the table, rows 4 and 5, show that more or less the same result holds for cigarettes and residential water. For petrol (row 6), the long-run elasticities tend to be closer to −½ than the short-run values. A possible exception to the "rule of minus one-half" is residential electricity (row 7), which has a mean short-run elasticity of demand of −0.35, while the mean long-run value is −0.85.[8] Finally, row 8 of the table shows that the mean price elasticity of "branded products" is −1.76, which is substantially different from −½. However, this is not unexpected as there are many good substitutes for a branded product – other brands of the same basic product. In this sense then, branded products are fundamentally different from the other products in the table: branded products are much more narrowly defined than are products such as alcoholic beverages, cigarettes, water, petrol and electricity. In what follows, we develop a theory that is applicable to broader products only, not more narrowly defined goods like branded products.

We shall present the theory in the context of the Rotterdam model; however, since the arguments that follow are more general, this is only for purposes of convenience. Details of the Rotterdam model and the underlying theory are contained in Sections A4.3–A4.8 of the Appendix. We thus return to demand equation (4.5), which we reproduce here with the disturbance term set at its expected value of zero:

$$\bar{w}_{it} Dq_{it} = \theta_i DQ_t + \phi \theta_i \left(Dp_{it} - DP'_t \right). \tag{4.7}$$

This is the ith demand equation of the Rotterdam model under the assumption of preference independence. Initially, suppose we apply this model to an exhaustive set of n goods, rather than just a subset; we could then describe this as an unconditional application rather than a conditional one.

As equation (4.7) plays an important role in what follows, a brief review of its interpretation is helpful. In equation (4.7), $\bar{w}_{it}$ is the budget share of good i averaged over the two years $t-1$, t; the n budget shares have a unit sum, that is $\Sigma_{i=1}^n \bar{w}_{it} = 1$. The term Dq_{it} is the log-change from $t-1$ to t in the quantity consumed of i, $Dq_{it} = \log q_{it} - \log q_{i,t-1}$, and it can be shown that the left-hand variable of equation (4.7), $\bar{w}_{it} Dq_{it}$, is the quantity component of the change in the budget share of i. The first term on the right of equation (4.7) is $\theta_i DQ_t$, which refers to the effect of a change in real income on the demand for i. In this term, θ_i is the ith marginal share, which answers the question: If income increases by one dollar, what fraction of this increase is spent on i, with $\Sigma_{i=1}^n \theta_i = 1$ (as it is assumed that the increase is spent on something)? The change in real income is measured by the Divisia volume index, $DQ_t = \Sigma_{i=1}^n \bar{w}_{it} Dq_{it}$, which shows that the variable on the left-hand side of equation (4.7) is also interpreted as the contribution of good i to this index. Thus the income term of equation (4.7) is a fraction θ_i of the Divisia volume index.

The second term on the right of equation (4.7), $\phi \theta_i \left(Dp_{it} - DP'_t \right)$, deals with the impact of changes in the relative price of good i. The coefficient ϕ is the income flexibility (the reciprocal of the income elasticity of the marginal utility of income); θ_i is the same marginal share of i; $Dp_{it} = \log p_{it} - \log p_{i,t-1}$ is the log-change in the i_{th} price; and $DP'_t = \sum_{i=1}^n \theta_i Dp_{it}$ is the Frisch price index which uses marginal shares as weights, which has the effect of holding constant the marginal utility of income. Accordingly, in this relative price term the change in the nominal price of good i, Dp_{it}, is deflated by the Frisch index of the change in all n prices, DP'_t. It is to be noted that the right-hand side of equation (4.7) contains only the change in the own-relative price, not those of the others. This is an implication of the assumption of preference independence, whereby tastes can be characterised by a utility function that is additive in the n goods, $u(q_1, \ldots, q_n) = \sum_{i=1}^n u_i(q_i)$, with $u_i(q_i)$ the i_{th} sub-utility function that depends only on the consumption of good i. Preference independence implies that each marginal utility depends only on the consumption of the good in question, not the others, so that all second-order cross derivatives of the utility function vanish. The assumption of preference independence means that as commodities do not interact in the utility function, utility is derived from the consumption of good 1 *and* good 2 *and* good 3, and so on, where the word "and" is italicised to emphasise the additive nature of preferences. Such a hypothesis about tastes is more applicable to broader aggregates than more finely distinguished goods such as "branded products".

To understand further the workings of equation (4.7), we divide both sides by $\bar{w}_{it}$ to yield

$$Dq_{it} = \eta_i DQ_t + \eta'_{ii}(Dp_{it} - DP'_t),$$

where $\eta_i = \theta_i / \bar{w}_{it}$ is the ith income elasticity and $\eta'_{ii} = \phi \theta_i / \bar{w}_{it}$ is the elasticity of demand for good i with respect to its relative price. As this relative price uses the Frisch price index as the deflator, this elasticity holds constant the marginal utility of income and is known as the ith Frisch own-price elasticity. It can be seen that these price elasticities are proportional to the corresponding income elasticities, with factor of proportionality ϕ. That is,

$$\eta'_{ii} = \phi \eta_i, \quad i = 1, \ldots, n. \tag{4.8}$$

Accordingly, luxuries (goods with $\eta_i > 1$) are more price elastic than necessities $\eta_i < 1$. Deaton (1974) refers to a variant of this proportionality relationship as "Pigou's (1910) law". The proportionality relationship (4.8) agrees with the intuitive idea that necessities (luxuries) tend to be essential (discretionary) goods, which have few (many) substitutes.

The budget constraint implies that a budget-share-weighted average of the income elasticities is unity, that is, $\sum_{i=1}^{n} \bar{w}_{it}\eta_i = 1$, so that an "average" commodity has an income elasticity of unity. This means that for such a commodity, the Frisch price elasticity is $\eta'_{ii} = \phi$. An alternative way to establish the same result is to consider an average commodity in Frisch elasticity space; the price elasticity of this good is given by a budget-share-weighted average of the n Frisch elasticities, $\sum_{i=1}^{n} \bar{w}_{it}\eta'_{ii}$. If we multiply both sides of the proportionality relationship (4.8) by $\bar{w}_{it}$, sum over $i = 1, \ldots, n$, and use $\eta_i = \theta_i/\bar{w}_{it}$ and $\sum_{i=1}^{n}\theta_i = 1$, we obtain $\sum_{i=1}^{n} \bar{w}_{it}\eta'_{ii} = \phi$. This reveals that the average Frisch price elasticity is also equal to ϕ. A substantial body of research points to the value of the income flexibility ϕ being approximately minus one-half (see Section A4.8 of the Appendix for details). This means for an average commodity, the Frisch price elasticity will also take the value of minus one-half. As not all goods will coincide with the "average" exactly, we have to modify the above statement to the weaker form that the n Frisch price elasticities will be *approximately* equal to minus one-half. As the more common Slutsky (or "compensated") own-price elasticity is equal to its Frisch counterpart minus a term of order $1/n$, in most cases the differences will be small, so the Slutsky elasticities will also be scattered around $-\frac{1}{2}$.[9]

The above discussion relates to the unconditional case with preference independence. If the assumption of preference independence is given up, the demand equation for good i then becomes more complex with the substitution term on the right-hand side of equation (4.7), $\phi\,\theta_i\,(Dp_{it} - DP'_t)$, replaced by a term involving own- and cross-relative prices, viz., $\sum_{j=1}^{n} v_{ij}(Dp_{jt} - DP'_t)$, where v_{ij} is the new price coefficient. The demand equation thus becomes

$$\bar{w}_{it}Dq_{it} = \theta_i\,DQ_t + \sum_{j=1}^{n} v_{ij}(Dp_{jt} - DP'_t). \tag{4.9}$$

As discussed in Section A4.4 of the Appendix, the price coefficient in this equation v_{ij} is defined as $(\lambda p_i p_j / M)u_{ij}$, where $\lambda > 0$ is the marginal utility of income, p_i is the price of good i, M is nominal income and u_{ij} is the $(i, j)^{th}$ element of the inverse of the Hessian matrix of the utility function. If $v_{ij} > 0 \,(< 0)$, then an increase in the relative price of good j causes consumption of i to increase (decrease), and the two goods are said to be Frisch substitutes (complements). These price coefficients satisfy $\Sigma_{j=1}^n v_{ij} = \phi\theta_i$. As $\eta'_{ij} = v_{ij}/\bar{w}_{it}$ is the $(i, j)^{th}$ Frisch price elasticity (marginal utility of income constant), the constraint of the previous sentence implies $\eta'_{i\bullet} = \phi\eta_i$, where $\eta'_{i\bullet} = \Sigma_{j=1}^n \eta'_{ij}$ is the sum of the own- and cross-price elasticities involving good i, and η_i is the ith income elasticity. Thus, whereas preference independence implies that the Frisch own-price elasticities are proportional to the corresponding income elasticities, when we give up the assumption of preference independence, the sums of own- and cross-price Frisch elasticities are proportional to income elasticities. Application of the argument in the previous paragraph then shows that these sums are approximately equal to minus one-half.[10]

Now consider the conditional case, when we analyse the demand for a group of goods, rather than all goods simultaneously. An example of such a group is "vice" comprising beer, wine, spirits and marijuana, a group analysed earlier in the chapter. Here ϕ is now interpreted as the own-price elasticity of demand for vice as a whole (see Section A4.7 of the Appendix for details). But this version of ϕ is exactly equal to η'_{ii}, the own-price Frisch elasticity that is implied by the unconditional equation when vice is taken to be the ith good among the original n, when preference independence holds. This means that in conditional applications ϕ continues be to approximately equal to minus one-half. Thus, under preference independence, conditional own-price elasticities are approximately minus one-half. When preference independence does not hold, the sums of conditional own- and cross-price elasticities fluctuate around minus one-half.

The assumption of preference independence is a testable hypothesis. As discussed in Section A4.8 of the Appendix, while the matter has not been completely resolved in the prior literature, it seems safe to say that, on the basis of past findings, the assumption of preference independence should not be rejected out of hand. If there were no evidence to the contrary, as would be the case if nothing at all were known about the nature of the demand for a product, and as long as it were a broad aggregate, the assumption of preference independence would seem to be a reasonable starting point. As this assumption is consistent with a demand equation that contains only the own relative price, the simplest possible form, it follows that invoking the assumption of preference independence can be considered as an application of the principle of Occam's Razor.

The results of this section can be summarised as follows:

- The price elasticities for beer, wine, spirits and marijuana tend to be clustered around the value of minus one-half, which can be understood in terms of preference independence.
- Other studies that are not based on preference independence also point to a centre-of-gravity of value of about minus one-half for the price elasticities.
- When nothing else is known about the price sensitivity of a good, a reasonable value of its price elasticity is minus one-half.

4.9 Simulating consumption

A theme of the previous chapter was the substantial fall in marijuana prices over the 1990s. This raises obvious questions such as by how much did this fall stimulate consumption of marijuana, and, since it is reasonable to expect marijuana and alcohol to be substitutes, by how much did the fall inhibit drinking? This section addresses these questions by presenting simulation results showing the likely impact on consumption of two hypothetical trajectories of marijuana prices whereby prices do not fall by as much. These results illustrate the importance of the magnitude of the price elasticities of demand.

Our approach is to first consider the own- and cross-price elasticities and then use these in conjunction with the simulated price changes to derive simulated consumption. For the price elacticities, we use exactly the same procedure as in Section 4.5. That is, under the assumption of preference independence the Slutsky coefficients take the form of equation (4.4), which we then convert to the corresponding elasticities by dividing by the relevant budget share. To evaluate these elasticities, as before, we use the data given in Table 4.13 for the budget and marginal shares. As discussed in Section 4.5, with the Australian data there is considerable uncertainty regarding the value of ϕ, the price elasticity of demand for alcohol and marijuana as a group; and for reasons set out in that section, we use $\phi = -0.5$. To recognise the uncertainty surrounding the value of this parameter, we now undertake sensitivity analysis by considering the implications of alternative values of ϕ. Table 4.23 gives the price elasticities associated with $\phi = -1.0, -0.5, -0.3, -0.1$; note that Panel II of this table, corresponding to $\phi = -0.5$, is identical to Panel I of Table 4.14. As can be seen, the own-price elasticity of marijuana is

Table 4.23: *More price elasticities of demand*

Good	Beer	Wine	Spirits	Marijuana
I. $\phi = -1.0$				
Beer	−0.40	0.08	0.15	0.18
Wine	0.20	−0.85	0.30	0.35
Spirits	0.40	0.30	−1.40	0.70
Marijuana	0.23	0.18	0.35	−0.76
II. $\phi = -0.5$				
Beer	−0.20	0.04	0.08	0.09
Wine	0.10	−0.43	0.15	0.18
Spirits	0.20	0.15	−0.70	0.35
Marijuana	0.12	0.09	0.18	−0.38
III. $\phi = -0.3$				
Beer	−0.12	0.02	0.05	0.05
Wine	0.06	−0.26	0.09	0.11
Spirits	0.12	0.09	−0.42	0.21
Marijuana	0.07	0.05	0.11	−0.23
IV. $\phi = -0.1$				
Beer	−0.04	0.01	0.02	0.02
Wine	0.02	−0.09	0.03	0.04
Spirits	0.04	0.03	−0.14	0.07
Marijuana	0.02	0.02	0.04	−0.08

proportional to the value of ϕ and varies from −0.8 (when $\phi = -1.0$), to −0.4 $(\phi = -0.5)$, to −0.2 ($\phi = -0.3$) and to −0.1 ($\phi = -0.1$). For reasons discussed above, our preferred value of ϕ is still −0.5, so that our preferred value of the own-price elasticity of demand for marijuana is –0.4. We shall return to these elasticity values shortly.

Next, we simulate consumption by replacing the observed fall in marijuana prices with some other counter-factual values. Let p_{it} and q_{it} be the price and per capita consumption of good i ($i = 1, 2, 3, 4$ for beer, wine, spirits and marijuana) in year ($t = 1, \ldots, T$); and let $Dp_i = \log p_{iT} - \log p_{i1}$ and $Dq_i = \log q_{iT} - \log q_{i1}$ be the corresponding log-changes from the first year of the period [$t = 1$ (1988)] to the last [$t = T$ (1998)]. Furthermore, let $\eta_{ij} = \partial(\log q_i)/\partial(\log p_j)$ be the elasticity of consumption of good i with respect to the price of good j. If only the price of good j changes over the ten-year period from 1988 to

1998 by Dp_j, then, as an approximation, the change in consumption of good i over the same period would be $\eta_{ij} \times Dp_j$. As the observed value of Dq_i includes the impact of all factors, including the change in the price of j, it follows that the change in consumption as a result of all factors other than the price of j is

$$Dq_i - \eta_{ij}Dp_j. \qquad (4.10)$$

In the simulation, we suppose that all determinants of consumption over the ten years are unchanged except for the price of marijuana ($j = 4$), which is specified to take the counter-factual value $D\hat{p}_4$. The corresponding change in consumption of good i is then

$$\eta_{i4}D\hat{p}_4. \qquad (4.11)$$

We simulate consumption when (i) the change in the price of marijuana is $D\hat{p}_4$; and (ii) all other determinants take their observed values. The simulated change in consumption from 1988 to 1998, $D\hat{q}_i$, is then the sum of (4.10), for $j = 4$, and (4.11):

$$D\hat{q}_i = Dq_i + \eta_{i4}(D\hat{p}_4 - Dp_4). \qquad (4.12)$$

As $D\hat{q}_i$ and Dq_i are both relative to the same base level consumption (q_{i1}), if we subtract Dq_i from both sides of equation (4.12), on the left we obtain

$$D\hat{q}_i - Dq_i = (\log \hat{q}_{iT} - \log q_{i1}) - (\log q_{iT} - \log q_{i1}) = \log\left(\frac{\hat{q}_{iT}}{q_{iT}}\right),$$

meaning equation (4.12) can be expressed as

$$\log\left(\frac{\hat{q}_{iT}}{q_{iT}}\right) = \eta_{i4}(D\hat{p}_4 - Dp_4). \qquad (4.13)$$

In words, simulated consumption in the last year, relative to observed consumption in that year, equals the relevant price elasticity applied to the difference in the growth of marijuana prices. Similarly, $\eta_{i4}(D\hat{p}_4 - Dp_4) = \eta_{i4}\log(\hat{p}_{4T}/p_{4T})$, so that the term in brackets on the right-hand side of equation (4.13) is also interpreted as the simulated price of marijuana in the last year relative to the corresponding observed value.

From Table 4.24, we see that the observed change in marijuana prices over the ten-year period is $Dp_4 = -19.2 \times 10^{-2}$. We use this value in equation (4.13) for $i = 1, \ldots, 4$ together with the elasticity values given in the last column of Table 4.23. In the first simulation, we take marijuana prices to be constant over the whole period by

Table 4.24:   Data for simulation

| | Logarithmic price change 1988–1998 (×100) | | Quantity |
Good	Average annual	Cumulative, Dp_i	consumed 1998
Beer	3.55	35.5	116.9
Wine	3.47	34.7	24.63
Spirits	4.32	43.2	4.318
Marijuana	−1.92	−19.2	0.7875
Alcohol	3.68	36.8	-

Sources: The average annual log changes are from Tables 4.9 and 4.10. The cumulative changes are 10 times the average annual changes. The quantities consumed are from Table 4.7

Table 4.25:   Counter-factual quantities consumed of alcoholic beverages and marijuana (Logarithmic changes × 100)

Own-price elasticity of demand for alcohol and marijuana as a group, ϕ	Beer	Wine	Spirits	Marijuana
I. Marijuana prices constant ($D\hat{p}_4 = 0$)				
−1.00	3.36	6.72	13.44	−14.56
−0.50	1.68	3.36	6.72	−7.28
−0.30	1.01	2.02	4.03	−4.37
−0.10	0.34	0.67	1.34	−1.46
II. Marijuana prices grow at same rate as alcohol prices ($D\hat{p}_4 = 36.80 \times 10^{-2}$)				
−1.00	9.80	19.60	39.20	−42.47
−0.50	4.90	9.80	19.60	−21.23
−0.30	2.94	5.88	11.76	−12.74
−0.10	0.98	1.96	3.92	−4.25

setting $D\hat{p}_4 = 0$. In comparison with the actual price change, which is negative, in this simulation the price of marijuana in effect increases, so we should expect that marijuana consumption will fall relative to observed consumption. The results of this simulation are contained in Panel I of Table 4.25 for various values of the price elasticity of demand for the group ϕ. Thus when $\phi = -0.5$, we see the impact of marijuana prices being constant, rather than falling by about 20 per cent, is for marijuana consumption to be about 7 per cent less than actual consumption in 1998. It is instructive to examine in detail the computation underlying this result by evaluating equation (4.13) for $i = 4$. From Table 4.23 when $\phi = -0.5$, the own-price elasticity of marijuana is $\eta_{44} = -0.38$, so that

$$\log\left(\frac{\hat{q}_{4T}}{q_{4T}}\right) = \eta_{44}(D\hat{p}_4 - Dp_4) = -0.38(0 - (-19.2)) = -7.3(\text{all} \times 100),$$

which is the second entry in the last column of Table 4.25.

As the three alcoholic beverages are substitutes for marijuana, this counter-factual increase in marijuana prices stimulates drinking. Again focusing on the case in which $\phi = -0.5$, the second row of Panel I of Table 4.25 indicates that beer consumption rises by about 1.7 per cent, wine 3.4 per cent and spirits 6.7 per cent. The differential impact of this price increase in marijuana on the consumption of the three beverages reflects the different values of the cross-price elasticities: from the last column of Panel II of Table 4.23, the beer-marijuana elasticity is 0.09, wine-marijuana 0.18 and spirits-marijuana 0.35. A comparison of the four rows of Panel I of Table 4.25 reveals that changes in the value of the group elasticity ϕ affect the elements proportionally. Thus, for example, if $\phi = -1$ rather than -0.5, the simulated change in consumption of a particular good doubles.

In the second simulation, we assume that marijuana prices increase over the ten years at the same rate as the prices of alcoholic beverages. Using the Divisia index to measure alcohol prices, we see from the last row of Table 4.24 that they increase by about 37 per cent over the period. In the first simulation marijuana prices are held constant, so that effectively prices increase relative to observed prices. As now marijuana prices increase by a substantially larger amount, we expect marijuana consumption to fall relative to observed by more than in the first simulation. For the same reason, drinking will rise by more than before. This is exactly the case, as indicated by a comparison of the corresponding rows of Panels I and II of Table 4.25. Looking at the case in which $\phi = -0.5$ (second row of Panel II), it can be seen that now marijuana consumption falls relative to observed consumption by about 21 per cent, while the consumption of beer, wine and spirits increase by 4.9 per cent, 9.8 per cent and 19.6 per cent, respectively. As before, changes in the value of ϕ lead to equipro-portional changes in the results.

The above results refer to changes in consumption relative to observed in 1998. We can compute the simulated levels of consumption by combining these changes with the observed levels. That is, if we exponentiate both sides of equation (4.13) and rearrange, we then obtain the following expression for the simulated value of consumption of good i in year $[t = T\,(1998)]$:

$$\hat{q}_{iT} = q_{iT}e^{\eta_{i4}(D\hat{p}_4 - Dp_4)}. \tag{4.14}$$

To evaluate equation (4.14), we use the observed quantities consumed given in the last column of Table 4.24, together with the results of Table 4.25 when $\phi = -0.5$ for $\eta_{i4}(D\hat{p}_4 - Dp_4)$. The results are given in graphical form in Figure 4.5. Four comments can be made:

- Over the ten-year period, actual beer consumption falls from about 141 to 117 litres per capita (see Table 4.7). Under the two scenarios of higher marijuana prices, this fall continues, but at a slower rate.

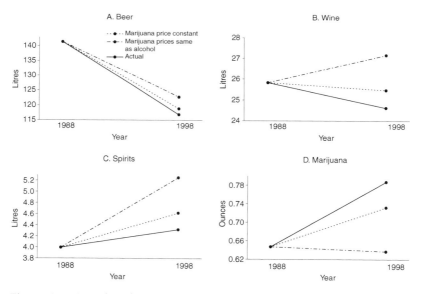

Figure 4.5. Actual and simulated consumption of alcoholic beverages and marijuana

- Actual wine consumption also falls over the period. However, when marijuana prices rise at the same rate as alcohol, this fall is reversed.
- The observed increase in spirits consumption is now amplified in the two scenarios.
- Marijuana consumption rises over the period from about 0.64 to 0.79 ounces per capita. When marijuana prices keep pace with alcohol, marijuana consumption is simulated to fall modestly.

In summary, while the differences between actual and simulated consumption are not huge, they are still not trivial and illustrate the role of the price elasticities of demand. The results also illustrate the interrelationship between drinking and marijuana consumption.

4.10 Concluding comments

A basic economic concern regarding marijuana is its price sensitivity, as measured by the price elasticity of demand. The value of this elasticity reflects the availability of substitutes and has major implications for any proposals to legalise consumption of marijuana and then tax it, as in the case of alcohol and tobacco. The degree of interrelatedness between marijuana and alcohol consumption is also important. For example, if marijuana prices were to rise for some reason or other, the law of demand tells us that marijuana consumption would fall. But if marijuana and alcohol are substitutes in consumption, such a price fall would simultaneously lead to a rise in drinking. In other words, key questions regarding the economic approach to marijuana consumption include:

- What is the price elasticity of demand for marijuana?
- What is the interrelationship between marijuana and alcohol consumption?

With the limited data available it is not easy to definitively answer these questions. Nevertheless, it is still possible to make progress and shed some light on these important issues.

This chapter has investigated the magnitude of the price elasticity of demand for marijuana. In doing so, we reviewed prior studies, drew on our recent work in the area, provided some new theoretical arguments supporting the use of the value of minus one-half for the own-price elasticity of marijuana, and reported simulation results regarding the impact on the consumption of marijuana and alcoholic beverages of changes in the price of marijuana. However, as each approach is subject to its own weaknesses, this chapter is unlikely to constitute the final word on the topic. At the risk of being overcautious, it is appropriate to conclude by mentioning two of the main limitations of our research:

- The marijuana quantity data are based on our own estimates and these involve some subjectivity. Although we believe the estimates can be fully justified and are reasonable, it has to be acknowledged that they do involve opinions, and in view of the controversial nature of the topic of marijuana consumption, it would not be surprising if others held differing views. A related qualification is that where price data were missing, extrapolation was employed.
- With only ten years of data, it was necessary to use a heavily structured demand model. It was assumed that preferences took a very simple form whereby the underlying utility function was additive in the quantities consumed. While on the basis of recent research, we feel this assumption is not as rigid as was once thought to be the case, it should nevertheless be acknowledged that there is still scope for opinions to differ on the applicability of this assumption.

APPENDIX

A4.1 Marijuana prices and usage

In this section, we (i) discuss the marijuana prices used in this chapter and (ii) compare marijuana usage across countries.

Marijuana prices in Australia

Our starting point for the source of Australian marijuana prices is the index developed in Chapter 3. This index, which aggregates prices over regions and product types, is given in Table A3.5. The preferred value of the weight attributed to marijuana purchased in the form of ounces is $\pi = 0.8$, so the index we use is given in the second last column of Panel I of Table A3.5. This index refers to the period 1990–1999. We subsequently use alcohol data that refer to the period 1988–1998. To match the marijuana and alcohol data, we omit the 1999 observation for the marijuana price and backcast observations on this goods price for 1988 and 1989 using the procedures set out below.

Let $Dp_{it} = \log p_{it} - \log p_{i,t-1}$ be the log-change in the price of good i from year $t-1$ to t. Write Dp_{1t}, Dp_{2t} and Dp_{3t} for the log-change in the prices of the three alcoholic beverages for $t = 1989, \ldots, 1998$ (the first observation is lost in forming the changes). A simple decomposition of the alcohol prices into time and commodity effects is

$$Dp_{it} = \alpha_t + \beta_i + \varepsilon_{it} \quad i = 1, 2, 3; \ t = 1989, \ldots, 998, \tag{A4.1}$$

where ε_{it} is a zero-mean disturbance term. The parameter α_t is interpreted as the common trend in the three prices from year $t - 1$ to t; the parameter $\beta_i = E(Dp_{it} - \alpha_t)$ is the expected value of the change in the relative price of i, taken to be constant over the sample period; and the disturbance term ε_{it} represents omitted factors. As model (A4.1) is subject to one additive degree of freedom, to identify the parameters, we set $\beta_1 = 0$.

Next, consider a similar decomposition for the four prices of beer, wine, spirits and marijuana for a shorter period:

$$Dp_{it} = \lambda_t + \gamma_i + \mu_{it} \quad i = 1, \ldots, 4; \ t = 1991, \ldots, 1998, \tag{A4.2}$$

where μ_{it} is a zero-mean disturbance term and $\gamma_1 = 0$. It would seem not unreasonable to assume that:

- the common trend for the three alcoholic beverages in the first two years, α_t, $t = 1989, 1990$, equals the missing trend in those years for the four goods;
- the change in the relative price of marijuana in 1989 and 1990 is the same as that in subsequent years, γ_4.

We use the data given in Panel II of Table 4.7 to estimate models (A4.1) and (A4.2) by least squares and denote the estimated parameters by $\hat{\alpha}_t$, $\hat{\beta}_i$, $\hat{\lambda}_t$ and $\hat{\gamma}_i$. Under the above assumptions, the estimated values of the marijuana price changes for the first two years are thus

$$D\hat{p}_{4t} = \hat{\alpha}_t + \hat{\gamma}_4 \quad t = 1989, 1990.$$

The associated levels are

$$\hat{p}_{4,1989} = \exp\left[\log p_{4,1990} - D\hat{p}_{4,1990}\right],$$
$$\hat{p}_{4,1988} = \exp\left[\log \hat{p}_{4,1989} - D\hat{p}_{4,1989}\right].$$

The values obtained from the above procedure are given as the first two entries of the last column of Panel II of Table 4.7. The remaining entries of this column are from the second last column of Panel I of Table A3.5.

A three-country comparison of usage

In Section 4.2 of the text, we noted the lower usage of marijuana in the US relative to that in Australia. This lower usage rate in the US is a puzzle as it would seem not to agree with other survey evidence such as the following:

Country (1)	Marijuana usage (percentages)	
	Ever (2)	In last 12 months (3)
Australia	34	13
United States	34	9
Amsterdam	27	11

Sources: Australia, 1993 National Drug Household Survey (people aged 14 and over); US, 1994 US National Household Survey on Drug Abuse (people aged 12 and over); and Amsterdam, 1994 survey results reported in Sandwijk *et al.* (1995) (people aged 12 and over). This information is from the Penington Report (1996, p. 17).

Column 2 of the above table shows that "ever" usage rates in Australia and the US are the same and, interestingly, are 7 percentage points above that in Amsterdam which contradicts popular wisdom that the Dutch are one of the biggest users of marijuana in the world. Column 3 shows usage in the last 12 months is a little different as the US is 4 percentage points below Australia and 2 percentage points below Amsterdam. But this 4-point difference is still much less than the 10-point difference reported by Rhodes *et al.* (1997), discussed in the text. Note that the 12-month usage rate for Australia in the above table, 13 per cent, differs from the 14 per cent mentioned in the text as the former refers to 1993, while the latter is for 1995.

A4.2 The alcohol data

In this section, we follow the approach of Clements and Johnson (1983) in deriving the data for alcohol consumption, prices and expenditure for Australia.

Table A4.1 gives per capita consumption and price indexes of beer, wine and spirits. Population (14 years and over), total consumption expenditure and expenditure on alcoholic beverages are contained in Table A4.2. Column 7 of this table contains the alcohol budget share, the proportion of total consumption expenditure absorbed by the three alcoholic beverages.

As no data are directly available for expenditure on the three alcoholic beverages individually, we construct them as follows. According to the information derived from the Australian Bureau of Statistics' *Household Expenditure Survey* (HES), average weekly expenditure in 1991 by all households on beer is $9.52, $3.42 on wine and $3.05 on spirits (see Table A4.3 for details). Hence, the conditional budget shares (the within-alcohol shares) are 0.596 [= 9.52/(9.52 + 3.42 + 3.05)] for beer, 0.214 for wine and 0.190 for spirits. We use these shares to split total alcohol expenditure into the three beverages. From column 6 of Table A4.2, in 1991 expenditure on alcohol is $740.77 per capita per annum. Thus, in 1991 per capita expenditure on beer is 0.596 × 740.77 = $441.49, on wine 0.214 × 740.77 = $158.52 and on spirits 0.190 × 740.77 = $140.76. From Table A4.1, beer consumption in 1991 is 134.9 litres per capita, so that the implied price of a litre of beer is 441.49/134.9 = $3.27. This is to be compared with the value of the beer price index in that year of 109.4 (from column 3 of Table A4.1). It follows that to form a (current-price) expenditure series for beer, we need to multiply the quantity by the price index given in Table A4.1 and then multiply the result by 3.27/109.4 for each year. The resulting expenditure series, given in column 2 of Table A4.4, is then consistent with the HES data.

Using the same procedure for wine and spirits, we multiply the product of the quantity and price indexes for wine and spirits, respectively, by

Table A4.1: *Per capita alcohol consumption and price indexes (Quantities in litres; price indexes have base year 1989/90 = 100)*

Year (1)	Beer		Wine		Spirits	
	Quantity (2)	Price index (3)	Quantity (4)	Price index (5)	Quantity (6)	Price index (7)
1988	141.4	94.2	25.82	91.1	3.993	87.8
1989	141.6	97.9	24.32	97.2	4.048	95.7
1990	139.9	104.2	22.85	100.0	3.870	105.1
1991	134.9	109.4	23.01	101.2	3.614	112.2
1992	127.8	112.4	23.23	103.8	3.595	116.4
1993	123.8	116.3	23.14	107.0	3.982	120.2
1994	122.1	119.8	23.19	111.7	4.168	123.6
1995	120.2	124.5	22.96	117.4	4.130	127.1
1996	118.7	130.1	23.29	122.2	4.106	131.19
1997	117.6	133.1	24.18	125.9	4.158	134.14
1998	116.9	134.4	24.63	128.8	4.318	135.21

Notes:

1. Quantities and price indexes have been converted from financial years into calendar years by averaging adjacent financial years.
2. "Per capita" consumption refers to consumption divided by the number of Australians aged 14 and over.
3. In the original source, per capita spirits consumption is given in terms of litres of alcohol. The estimated volume of consumption of this beverage is calculated by multiplying litres of alcohol by 2.5.

Sources: Consumption data for the years 1988 to 1996 are from ABS, *Apparent Consumption of Foodstuffs*, Catalogue No. 4306.0 (various issues); and for 1997 and 1998 from preliminary unpublished ABS sources (personal communication). Price data are from ABS, *Consumer Price Index*, Catalogue No. 6401.0 (various issues).

$$\frac{158.35/23.01}{101.2} \quad \text{and} \quad \frac{140.76/3.614}{112.2}.$$

Columns 3 and 4 of Table A4.4 contain the results. Total expenditure on the three beverages is given in column 5 of Table A4.4; this is exactly equal to total expenditure given in the last column of Table A4.2 for 1991 and approximately equal for the other years. The price per litre of each beverage is calculated by dividing expenditure by the quantity consumed (given in Table A4.1). The results are contained in Table A4.5. The quantities and prices for the three alcoholic beverages given in Table 4.7 are from Tables A4.1 and A4.5.

Table A4.2: *Population, total consumption expenditure and expenditure on alcoholic beverages*

Year (1)	Population (Millions) (2)	Total consumption expenditure		Expenditure on alcohol		Alcohol budget share (× 100) (7)
		Total ($m) (3)	Per capita ($) (4)	Total ($m) (5)	Per capita ($) (6)	
1988	13.08	185,095	14,148	8,351	638.34	4.51
1989	13.33	206,070	15,454	8,942	670.60	4.34
1990	13.54	223,195	16,483	9,684	715.18	4.34
1991	13.75	235,921	17,160	10,184	740.77	4.32
1992	13.93	248,412	17,836	10,443	749.78	4.20
1993	14.08	260,288	18,487	10,988	780.39	4.22
1994	14.24	274,446	19,267	11,905	835.74	4.34
1995	14.44	292,522	20,258	12,798	886.28	4.38
1996	14.66	307,528	20,978	13,129	895.59	4.27
1997	14.87	323,937	21,785	13,311	895.17	4.11
1998	15.09	342,307	22,682	14,130	936.27	4.13

Notes:
1. Expenditure has been converted from financial years into calendar years by averaging.
2. Population refers to Australians aged 14 and over.
Sources: Population is from ABS, *Population By Age and Sex*, Catalogue
No. 3201.0 (various issues). Total consumption expenditure and expenditure
on alcohol for the years 1988 to 1996 are from ABS, *Australian National Accounts:
National Income, Expenditure and Product*, Catalogue No. 5204.0 (1995–96);
the same data for 1997 and 1998 on a quarterly basis are from unpublished
ABS sources and then converted to a financial-year basis.

Table A4.3: *Average weekly household expenditure on alcoholic beverages (Dollars per household)*

Year	Beer	Wine	Spirits	Total
1988/89	9.74	3.07	2.96	15.77
1993/94	9.29	3.76	3.13	16.18
1991	9.52	3.42	3.05	15.98

Note: The data for 1991 are estimated by averaging the 1988/89
and 1993/94 data.
Source: ABS, *Household Expenditure Survey: Australia*, 1988/89
and 1993/94, Catalogue No. 6535.0.

Table A4.4: *Per capita expenditures on alcoholic beverages (dollars)*

Year (1)	Beer (2)	Wine (3)	Spirits (4)	Total (5)
1988	398.41	159.84	122.10	680.35
1989	414.80	160.70	134.87	710.37
1990	435.91	155.39	141.67	732.96
1991	441.49	158.52	140.76	740.77
1992	429.43	163.93	145.70	739.06
1993	430.66	168.24	166.62	765.52
1994	437.49	176.17	179.40	793.05
1995	447.64	183.32	182.77	813.73
1996	461.75	193.48	187.60	842.84
1997	468.18	206.96	194.22	869.36
1998	470.11	215.61	203.31	889.04

Source: See text.

Table A4.5: *Prices of alcoholic beverages (dollars per litre)*

Year	Beer	Wine	Spirits
1988	2.819	6.190	30.578
1989	2.928	6.607	33.315
1990	3.116	6.801	36.601
1991	3.271	6.883	39.064
1992	3.361	7.056	40.532
1993	3.478	7.271	41.847
1994	3.583	7.597	43.044
1995	3.724	7.983	44.254
1996	3.891	8.306	45.687
1997	3.981	8.559	46.714
1998	4.020	8.755	47.088

Source: See text.

A4.3 Elements of consumption theory

The objective of this section is to briefly set out the utility-maximising theory of the consumer. This involves applying the method for comparative statics to obtain information about the nature of general

Marshallian demand equations. In subsequent sections, we show how this information can be incorporated in differential demand equations, how the nature of preferences translates into observed consumption behaviour and how this general approach can be implemented econometrically. The material of this and the next five sections is mostly based on Theil (1975/76, 1980) and Theil and Clements (1987).

Marshallian demand equations

It is assumed that the consumer chooses the quantities of the n goods, $q_1, \ldots, q_n$ to maximise the utility function $u,(q_1, \ldots, q_n)$, subject to the budget constraint $\sum_{i=1}^{n} p_i q_i = M$, where M is total expenditure ("income" for short). If we write $q = [q_i]$ and $p = [p_i]$ for the vectors of n quantities and prices, the utility function and the budget constraint become $u(q)$ and $p'q = M$. It is assumed that each marginal utility is positive, so that $\partial u / \partial q > 0$ and that there is generalised diminishing marginal utility, so that the Hessian matrix of the utility function $U = \partial^2 u / \partial q \partial q'$ is negative definite. This latter condition is sufficient to ensure an interior maximum.

The first-order conditions for a budget-constrained utility maximum are the budget constraint

$$p'q = M, \tag{A4.3}$$

and the proportionality conditions, $\partial u / \partial q_i = \lambda p_i$, $i = 1, \ldots, n$, where $\lambda > 0$ is the marginal utility of income. We write these as

$$\frac{\partial u}{\partial q} = \lambda p. \tag{A4.4}$$

Equations (A4.3) and (A4.4) are $n + 1$ scalar equations, which can in principle be solved for the $n + 1$ endogenous variables $q_1, \ldots, q_n, \lambda$ in terms of the $n + 1$ exogenous variables $M, p_1, \ldots, p_n$. We write this solution for the quantities consumed as

$$q = q(M, p), \tag{A4.5}$$

which is a system of n Marshallian demand equations.

Comparative statics

We use equations (A4.3) and (A4.4) to ask, How do q and λ respond to changes in M and p? To answer this question, we proceed in three steps.

First, we differentiate (A4.4) with respect to M and p to yield

$$U\frac{\partial q}{\partial M} = \frac{\partial \lambda}{\partial M}p, \quad U\frac{\partial q}{\partial p'} = \lambda I + p\frac{\partial \lambda}{\partial p'}, \quad (A4.6)$$

where U is the Hessian matrix; $\partial q \partial M = [\partial q_i/\partial M]$ is a vector of n income slopes of the demand equations (A4.5); $\partial q \partial p' = [\partial q_i/\partial p_j]$ is the $n \times n$ matrix of price derivatives of the demand functions; I is the $n \times n$ identity matrix; and $\partial \lambda/\partial p\prime = [\partial \lambda/\partial p_i]$. *Second*, we differentiate (A4.3) with respect to M and p:

$$p'\frac{\partial q}{\partial M} = 1, \quad p'\frac{\partial q}{\partial p'} = -q'. \quad (A4.7)$$

Third, to solve (A4.6) and (A4.7) simultaneously, we combine them to yield Barten's (1964) fundamental matrix equation of consumption theory:

$$\begin{bmatrix} U & p \\ p' & 0 \end{bmatrix}\begin{bmatrix} \partial q/\partial M & \partial q/\partial p' \\ -\partial \lambda/\partial M & -\partial \lambda/\partial p' \end{bmatrix} = \begin{bmatrix} 0 & \lambda I \\ 1 & -q' \end{bmatrix}. \quad (A4.8)$$

The second matrix on the left-hand side of equation (A4.8) contains the derivatives of all the endogenous variables with respect to all the exogenous variables. This equation can be solved for the derivatives of the demand equations (see, for example, Theil and Clements, 1987, Sec. 1.11, for details) to yield

$$\frac{\partial q}{\partial M} = \frac{\partial \lambda}{\partial M}U^{-1}p, \quad \frac{\partial q}{\partial p'} = \lambda U^{-1} - \frac{\lambda}{\partial \lambda/\partial M}\frac{\partial q}{\partial M}\frac{\partial q'}{\partial M} - \frac{\partial q}{\partial M}q'.$$

Writing u^{ij} for the $(i, j)^{\text{th}}$ element of U^{-1}, the above two matrix equations can be expressed in scalar form as

$$\frac{\partial q_i}{\partial M} = \frac{\partial \lambda}{\partial M}\sum_{j=1}^{n}u^{ij}p_j, \quad i = 1, ..., n, \quad (A4.9)$$

$$\frac{\partial q_i}{\partial p_j} = \lambda u^{ij} - \frac{\lambda}{\partial \lambda/\partial M}\frac{\partial q_i}{\partial M}\frac{\partial q_j}{\partial M} - \frac{\partial q_i}{\partial M}q_j, \quad i, j = 1, ..., n. \quad (A4.10)$$

Equation (A4.10) shows that the total impact on consumption of good i of a change in the price of good j is made up of three distinct terms:

• First, there is λu^{ij}, which relates to the interaction of goods i and j in the utility function. As this term cannot be decomposed into separate parts involving i and j, it is known as the "specific substitution effect" of a change in the price of j on the consumption of i. As the Hessian matrix of the utility function and its inverse, U and U^{-1} are both symmetric, it follows that the specific substitution effect is symmetric in i and j. The specific substitution effect holds constant the marginal utility of income.

- Second, there is a term that is proportional to the product of the income slopes of the demand functions for the two goods in question, $-(\lambda/\partial\lambda/\partial M)(\partial q_i/\partial M)(\partial q_j/\partial M)$. This term, known as the "general substitution effect", is decomposable and reflects the general competition of all goods for the consumer's income. This general competition operates via the budget constraint and the marginal utility of income. This term is also clearly symmetric in i and j. The sum of the specific and general effects is the "total substitution effect", which is also symmetric.

- Finally, $-(\partial q_i/\partial M)q_j$ is the "income effect" of the price change. If money income is held constant, then an increase in the price of good j lowers real income in proportion to the pre-existing consumption of the good, $-q_j$; and this reduction in real income causes the consumption of i to change according to its income response, $\partial q_i/\partial M$. The income effect is asymmetric in i and j.

It is to be noted that the usual Slutsky equation decomposes the total effect of a price change into two effects, a substitution effect (called the "total substitution effect" in the above) and an income effect. Equation (A4.10) also does this, but additionally splits the substitution effect into its two components, the specific and general effects, so that there is now a three-way decomposition of $\partial q_i/\partial p_j$. This approach will play a prominent role in what follows.

A4.4 A differential demand system

In this section, we use the above results to derive a general differential demand system. Consider the ith equation of the Marshallian demand system (A4.5), $q_i = q_i(M, p_1, \ldots, p_n)$. The total differential of this equation is

$$dq_i = \frac{\partial q_i}{\partial M} \, dM + \sum_{j=1}^{n} \frac{\partial q_i}{\partial p_j} \, dp_j.$$

We transform this into a logarithmic-differential form by multiplying both sides by p_i/M and using the identity $dx/x = d(\log x)$ for any positive variable x:

$$w_i\, d(\log q_i) = \frac{\partial(p_i\, q_i)}{\partial M}\, d(\log M)$$
$$+ \sum_{j=1}^{n} \frac{p_i p_j}{M} \frac{\partial q_i}{\partial p_j}\, d\left(\log p_j\right), \qquad (A4.11)$$

where $w_i = p_i q_i/M$ is the budget share of good i. Using equation (A4.10), the second term on the right-hand side of equation (A4.11) can be expressed as

$$\sum_{j=1}^{n} \frac{p_i p_j}{M} \left(\lambda u^{ij} - \frac{\lambda}{\partial \lambda/\partial M} \frac{\partial q_i}{\partial M} \frac{\partial q_j}{\partial M} - \frac{\partial q_i}{\partial M} q_j \right) d\left(\log p_j\right),$$

so that, after rearrangement, equation (A4.11) becomes

$$w_i\, d(\log q_i) = \frac{\partial(p_i\, q_i)}{\partial M} \left[d(\log M) - \sum_{j=1}^{n} w_j\, d\left(\log p_j\right) \right]$$
$$+ \sum_{j=1}^{n} \left(\frac{\lambda p_i p_j u^{ij}}{M} - \frac{\lambda/M}{\partial \lambda/\partial M} \frac{\partial(p_i\, q_i)}{\partial M} \frac{\partial(p_j\, q_j)}{\partial M} \right) d\left(\log p_j\right).$$

$$(A4.12)$$

Simplifications

Equation (A4.12) can be simplified as follows. The total differential of the budget constraint (A4.3) is $\sum_i p_i dq_i + \sum_i q_i dp_i = dM$, or, if we divide total sides by M, and use $w_i = p_i q_i/M$ and $dx/x = d(\log x)$, $\sum_i w_i d(\log q) + \sum_i w_i d(\log p_i) = d(\log M)$. As $d(\log M) - \sum_i w_i d(\log p_i) = \sum_i w_i d(\log q_i)$, the term in square brackets on the right-hand side of equation (A4.12) is equivalent to a budget-share-weighted average of the growth in the consumption of the n goods. This weighted average is the Divisia volume index which measures the change in the consumer's real income. That is, the Divisia volume index is the excess of the growth in money income, $d(\log M)$, over a budget-share-weighted average of the n price changes, $\sum_i w_i d(\log p_i)$, the corresponding Divisia price index. As a matter of notation, we write $d(\log Q)$ for the Divisia volume index. In equation (A4.12), this $d(\log Q)$ is multiplied by $\partial(p_i q_i)\partial M$, which is the marginal share of good i, denoted by θ_i. The marginal share answers the question: If income increases by one dollar, how much of this is spent on good i? As the additional income is entirely spent, it follows that $\sum_i \theta_i = 1$. This unit-sum constraint is implied by the budget constraint, as indicated by the first member of equation (A4.7) which can be expressed as $\sum_i p_i(\partial q_i/\partial M) = 1$, or as p_i is held constant, $\sum_i(\partial p_i q_i/\partial M) = 1$.

To simplify the price substitution term of (A4.12), we define

$$\phi = \frac{\lambda/M}{\partial\lambda/\partial M} = \left(\frac{\partial\log\lambda}{\partial\log M}\right)^{-1} < 0 \qquad (A4.13)$$

as the reciprocal of the income elasticity of the marginal utility of income, or the income flexibility for short. We also define

$$v_{ij} = \frac{\lambda}{M} p_i p_j u^{ij}, \quad i = 1, \dots, n, \qquad (A4.14)$$

which in view of equation (A4.9) satisfies

$$\sum_{j=1}^{n} v_{ij} = \phi\,\theta_i, \quad i = 1, \dots, n. \qquad (A4.15)$$

With the above definitions, the price substitution term of equation (A4.12) becomes

$$\sum_{j=1}^{n} \left(\frac{\lambda p_i p_j u^{ij}}{M} - \frac{\lambda/M}{\partial\lambda/\partial M}\frac{\partial(p_i q_i)}{\partial M}\frac{\partial(p_j q_j)}{\partial M}\right) d(\log p_j)$$

$$= \sum_{j=1}^{n} \left(v_{ij} - \phi\,\theta_i\,\theta_j\right) d(\log p_j)$$

$$= \sum_{j=1}^{n} v_{ij}\left[d(\log p_j) - \sum_{k=1}^{n} \theta_k\,d(\log p_k)\right]$$

$$= \sum_{j=1}^{n} v_{ij}\left[d(\log p_j) - d(\log P')\right],$$

where the second step is based on constraint (A4.15), while in the third step the Frisch price index, $d(\log P') = \sum_k \theta_k\,d(\log p_k)$, has been introduced. Like its Divisia counterpart, the Frisch price index is a weighted average of prices, but now the weights are marginal shares rather than budget shares.

The distinction between the Frisch and Divisia indexes can be clarified as follows. The income elasticity of demand for good i is defined as the proportionate change in consumption resulting from a unit proportionate change in income $\partial(\log q_i)/\partial(\log M)$. The income elasticity can be expressed as

$$\frac{\partial(\log q_i)}{\partial(\log M)} = \frac{\partial q_i/\partial M}{q_i/M} = \frac{\theta_i}{w_i},$$

which shows that the elasticity is equal to the ratio of the marginal share to the corresponding budget share. Goods with income elasticities greater (less) than unity are said to be luxuries (necessities). It follows from the budget constraint that the average income elasticity is unity: $\sum_{i=1}^{n} w_i(\theta_i/w_i) = 1$. As the marginal share of a luxury (necessity) is greater (less) than its budget share, it can be seen that relative to the Divisia price index, luxuries (necessities) are more (less) heavily weighted in the Frisch index.

Retracing our steps, it can be seen that demand equation (A4.12) can be written as

$$w_i\,d(\log q_i) = \theta_i\,d(\log Q) + \sum_{j=1}^{n} v_{ij}\big[d(\log p_j) - d(\log P')\big]. \qquad \text{(A4.16)}$$

Interpretations

The variable on the left of equation (A4.16), $w_i d(\log q_i)$, has two interpretations:

- Using $w_i = p_i q_i/M$ we have

  $$dw_i = w_i\,d(\log p_i) + w_i\,d(\log q_i) - w_i\,d(\log M).$$

  This shows that $w_i d(\log q_i)$ is the quantity component of the change in w_i.
- The term $w_i d(\log q_i)$ is also the contribution of good i to the Divisia volume index $d(\log Q) = \sum_i w_i\,d(\log q_i)$.

The right-hand side of equation (A4.16) comprises a real income term and a relative price term. The income term is a multiple θ_i of the change in real income as measured by the Divisia volume index $d(\log Q)$. As $d(\log Q) = d(\log M) - d(\log P)$, with $d(\log P) = \sum_i w_i\,d(\log p_i)$, the Divisia price index, it can be seen that this price index transforms the change in money income into the change in real income. Furthermore, as the Divisia price index uses budget shares as weights, this index measures the income effect of the changes in the n prices on the demand for good i.

The relative price term on the right-hand side of equation (A4.16), $\sum_j v_{ij}[d(\log p_j) - d(\log P')]$, deals with the substitution effects of changes in the n prices on the consumption of good i. Here the Frisch price index $d(\log P')$ acts as the deflator of the nominal price change $d(\log p_j)$ to give the change in the relative price of good j. In the demand equation for good i, the jth relative price change is multiplied by v_{ij} which is known as the $(i,j)^{\text{th}}$ Frisch price coefficient. It follows from the definition of v_{ij} given in equation (A4.14) that the price coefficients are symmetric in i and j. That definition also implies that the $n \times n$ matrix of the n^2 price coefficients can be written as $[v_{ij}] = (\lambda/M)PU^{-1}P$, where P is an $n \times n$ diagonal matrix with the elements of the price vector p on the main diagonal. As $(\lambda/M) > 0$ and U^{-1} is negative definite, this latter expression establishes that $[v_{ij}]$ is also negative definite. Note that as $\sum_i \theta_i = 1$, equation (A4.15) implies $\sum_i \sum_j v_{ij} = \phi$; as the left-hand side of this equation is a quadratic form with matrix $[v_{ij}]$ and vector $[1, \dots, 1]'$, the negative definiteness of $[v_{ij}]$ implies $\phi < 0$.

Consider the relative price term of equation (A4.16), $\sum_j v_{ij}[d(\log p_j) - d(\log P')]$, as being made up of two parts, (i) $\sum_j v_{ij} d(\log p_j)$ and (ii) $-\sum_j v_{ij} d(\log P')$. The first term deals with the specific substitution effects, and, as will be shown in the next subsection, this holds constant the marginal utility of income. The second effect, $-\sum_j v_{ij} d(\log P')$, which in view of constraint (A4.15) equals $-\phi\theta_i d(\log P')$, deals with the general substitution effects. To clarify this effect, suppose the price of good j changes by $d(\log p_j)$, and initially all other prices remain unchanged, so that the Frisch price index $d(\log P')$ equals $\theta_j d(\log p_j)$. Then the general substitution effect of this on the consumption of good i, as measured by the left-hand side of equation (A4.16), is $-\phi\theta_i\theta_j d(\log p_j)$. When all n prices change, $-\phi\theta_i \sum_{j=1}^{n} \theta_j d(\log p_j) = -\phi\theta_i d(\log P')$ represents the general substitution effects of these price changes on the consumption of good i. Equation (A4.16) shows that the general substitutions effects act as a deflator to yield the change in the relative price of good i.

The major attractions of demand equation (A4.16) are its generality and its elegant simplicity. As the "coefficients" of this equation, θ_i and v_{ij}, are not necessarily constant, equation (A4.16) is consistent with (almost) any form of the utility function. In contrast to other approaches to generating demand equations, a feature of the differential approach is that it requires no algebraic specification of the utility function, the indirect utility function or the cost function. The elegance of equation (A4.16) revolves around its transparent link to a general utility function, its clean split between the income and substitution effects (of both the specific and general varieties) and the ease of interpretation of its coefficients.

The marginal utility of income

The solution to the fundamental matrix equation (A4.8) yields information on the dependence of consumption on income and prices. It also provides similar information regarding the marginal utility of income λ. To recognise the dependence of λ on income and prices, we write $\lambda = \lambda(M, p)$. It can be shown (see, for example, Theil and Clements, 1987, Section 1.11) that:

$$\frac{\partial \lambda}{\partial p_j} = -\lambda \frac{\partial q_j}{\partial M} - \frac{\partial \lambda}{\partial M} q_j,$$

so that

$$d(\log \lambda) = \left(\frac{\partial \lambda / \partial M}{\lambda / M} \right) d(\log M) + \sum_{j=1}^{n} \left(\frac{\partial \lambda}{\partial p_j} \frac{p_j}{\lambda} \right) d(\log p_j)$$

$$= \frac{1}{\phi} d(\log M) + \sum_{j=1}^{n} \left(-\lambda \frac{\partial q_j}{\partial M} - \frac{\partial \lambda}{\partial M} q_j \right) \frac{p_j}{\lambda} d(\log p_j),$$

where the second step is based on equation (A4.13). Using $\theta_j = \partial(p_j q_j)/\partial M$ and $w_j = p_j q_j / M$, the second term on the right of the above equation can be expressed as

$$\sum_{j=1}^{n} \left(-\lambda \frac{\partial q_j}{\partial M} - \frac{\partial \lambda}{\partial M} q_j \right) \frac{p_j}{\lambda} d(\log p_j) = \sum_{j=1}^{n} \left(-\theta_j - \frac{1}{\phi} w_j \right) d(\log p_j)$$

$$= -d(\log P') - \frac{1}{\phi} d(\log P),$$

where $d(\log P')$ and $d(\log P)$ are the Frisch and Divisia price indexes. Thus as $d(\log Q) = d(\log M) - d(\log P)$, we have the simple result:

$$d(\log \lambda) = \frac{1}{\phi} d(\log Q) - d(\log P'). \qquad (A4.17)$$

Thus, the elasticity of the marginal utility of income with respect to real income is $1/\phi$; and the elasticity with respect to the Frisch price index is minus one.

If we write equation (A4.17) in the form of $d(\log Q) = \phi d(\log \lambda) + \phi d(\log P')$ and then substitute it into equation (A4.16), we obtain

$$
\begin{aligned}
w_i d(\log q_i) &= \theta_i \phi d(\log \lambda) + \sum_{j=1}^{n} v_{ij} d(\log p_j) \\
&= \sum_{j=1}^{n} v_{ij} \left[d(\log p_j) - d(\log \lambda^{-1}) \right]
\end{aligned}
\qquad (A4.18)
$$

where the last step follows from constraint (A4.15) and $d(\log \lambda) = -d(\log \lambda^{-1})$. Equation (A4.18) shows that the logarithmic change in the reciprocal of the marginal utility of income, $d(\log \lambda^{-1})$, plays the role of a price deflator in forming the change in a new form of the relative price of good j, $d(\log p_j) - d(\log \lambda^{-1})$. The final member of equation (A4.18) reveals that the price coefficient v_{ij} measures the impact of a change in the price of good j on the consumption of good i under the condition that the marginal utility of income is held constant, that is, when $d(\log \lambda) = d(\log \lambda^{-1}) = 0$. Note finally that although income does not appear explicitly in demand equation (A4.18), its role is indirectly accounted for via its impact on the value of λ.

An absolute price formulation

Demand equation (A4.16) separates the specific and general substitution effects by employing a relative price formulation. But we could equally well combine these two effects into the total substitution effect as follows. We use constraint (A4.15) to write the second term on the right of equation (A4.16) as

$$\sum_{j=1}^{n} v_{ij}\left[d\left(\log p_j\right) - d\left(\log P'\right)\right] = \sum_{j=1}^{n} \left(v_{ij} - \phi\theta_i\theta_j\right) d\left(\log p_j\right)$$

$$= \sum_{j=1}^{n} \pi_{ij} d\left(\log p_j\right),$$

where

$$\pi_{ij} = v_{ij} - \phi\,\theta_i\theta_j \qquad\qquad (A4.19)$$

is the $(i, j)^{\text{th}}$ Slutsky coefficient. As this coefficient combines the specific and general substitution effects, it refers to the total substitution effect. The Slutsky coefficient π_{ij} for $i, j = 1,\ldots,n$, satisfies three properties. First, demand homogeneity, $\sum_{j=1}^{n} \pi_{ij} = 0, i = 1,\ldots,n$, which implies that an equiproportionate change in all prices has no effect on the quantity consumed of any good, real income remaining unchanged. This property follows from constraint (A4.15) and definition (A4.19). Second, Slutsky symmetry, $\pi_{ij} = \pi_{ji}, i, j = 1,\ldots, n$, which relates to the symmetry of the total substitution effects. This follows from definitions (A4.14) and (A4.19), and the symmetry of the v_{ij}. Third, the $n \times n$ matrix of the Slutsky coefficient $[\pi_{ij}]$ is negative semidefinite with rank $n-1$, which follows from equations (A4.15) and (A4.19), and the negative definiteness of $[v_{ij}]$.

Using definition (A4.19), an equivalent way of writing demand equation (A4.16) is thus

$$w_i\, d(\log q_i) = \theta_i\, d(\log Q) + \sum_{j=1}^{n} \pi_{ij} d\left(\log p_j\right). \qquad\qquad (A4.20)$$

This can be referred to as the absolute price version of the differential demand equation for good i.

A4.5 The structure of preferences

In the above discussion we considered a general utility function that satisfied the minimal requirements of positive marginal utilities and a negative definite Hessian matrix. In this section, we consider the implications for the demand equations of stronger conditions on the utility function which correspond to more specific assumptions about the nature of preferences. We start with the most rigid assumption of preference independence and then consider weaker versions.

Preference independence

Under preference independence, the utility function can be written as the sum of n sub-utility functions, one for each good, that is,

$$u(q_1, ..., q_n) = \sum_{i=1}^{n} u_i(q_i),\tag{A4.21}$$

where $u_i(q_i)$ is the sub-utility function for good i. The additive nature of the utility function means that the marginal utility of good i depends only on the consumption of the good in question, so that all second-order cross derivatives vanish. In other words, the Hessian matrix $U = \partial^2 u / \partial q \, \partial q'$ is diagonal.

The diagonal Hessian means that its inverse is also diagonal, so that $u^{ij} = 0$ for all $i \neq j$, and in view of definition (A4.14), $v_{ij} = 0$ for $i \neq j$. Accordingly, the matrix $[v_{ij}]$ is diagonal with $v_{11}, \ldots, v_{nn}$ on the diagonal; and as this matrix is negative definite, $v_{ii} < 0$, $i = 1, \ldots, n$. This means that for all $i \neq j$, the specific substitution effects are zero under preference independence. Also, preference independence implies that equation (A4.15) takes the form $v_{ii} = \phi \theta_i$, which means that the marginal share θ_i must be positive as $\phi < 0$. This shows that under preference independence inferior goods are ruled out. Demand equation (A4.16) is thus substantially simplified under preference independence:

$$w_i \, d(\log q_i) = \theta_i \, d(\log Q) + \phi \theta_i [d(\log p_i) - d(\log P')],\tag{A4.22}$$

This equation states that under the conditions of preference independence, the consumption of good i depends only on real income and its own relative price $[d(\log p_i) - d(\log P')]$. Under preference independence, the Slutsky coefficient (A4.19) takes the form $\pi_{ij} = \phi \theta_i (\delta_{ij} - \theta_j)$, where δ_{ij} is the Kronecker delta ($\delta_{ij} = 1$ if $i = j$, 0 otherwise). Thus, for $i \neq j$, $\pi_{ij} = -\phi \theta_i \theta_j > 0$, so that an increase in the price of good j leads to a rise in the consumption of i. If we use the sign of the Slutsky coefficient, which refers to the total substitution effect, to measure whether the pair of goods in question are substitutes or complements, we see that preference independence implies that all goods are Slutsky substitutes.

Block structures

Under preference independence, individual goods are independent in the utility function. A weaker condition is that groups of goods are independent, so that there can be interactions between goods belonging to the same group, but more limited interactions between goods from different groups. For example, beer, wine, spirits and marijuana could comprise one group, while food items could form another. Such a specification of preferences would seem not unreasonable when the groups are broad aggregates, as then there would likely be only limited substitutability between them. This subsection sets out the implications of such block structures.

Let the n goods be divided into $G < n$ groups, to be written as $S_1, \ldots, S_G$, such that each good belongs to one group. Consider two goods, i and j, that belong to different groups, g and h, respectively; that is, $i \in S_g$, $j \in S_h$, $g \neq h$. Suppose that the marginal utility of consumption of good i is independent of the consumption of good j, and that this is true for all pairs of goods and all pairs of groups. Write q_i, $i \in S_g$, for the quantities consumed of goods that fall under S_g, and q_g for the corresponding vector. Then, when goods are ordered appropriately, the utility function can be expressed as

$$u(q_1, \ldots, q_n) = \sum_{g=1}^{G} u_g(q_g), \qquad (A4.23)$$

where $u_g(q_g)$ is the sub-utility function for group g. While the preference independence utility function equation (A4.21) is additive in the individual commodities, equation (A4.23) is additive in groups of goods. The Hessian matrix U associated with equation (A4.23) is block diagonal:

$$U = \begin{bmatrix} U_1 & \cdots & 0 \\ \vdots & \ddots & \vdots \\ 0 & \cdots & U_G \end{bmatrix},$$

where U_g is the Hessian matrix of $u_g(\cdot)$. It is for this reason that when preferences can be expressed in the form of equation (A4.23), they are described as being block independent. The term "strong separability" is also used to describe the same thing.

As the inverse of a block-diagonal matrix is also block diagonal, equation (A4.14) implies that the price coefficients pertaining to goods in different groups are zero; that is, $v_{ij} = 0$, $i \in S_g$, $j \in S_h$, $g \neq h$. Equation (A4.16) then becomes for $i \in S_g$:

$$w_i d(\log q_i) = \theta_i d(\log Q)$$
$$+ \sum_{j \in S_g} v_{ij} \left[d\left(\log p_j\right) - d\left(\log P'\right) \right], \qquad (A4.24)$$

so that relative prices of goods outside the group have no effect on the consumption of good i. Block independence also means that constraint (A4.15) takes the form

$$\sum_{j \in S_g} v_{ij} = \phi \theta_i \quad i \in S_g, g = 1, \dots G. \qquad (A4.25)$$

In the next section, we explore further the implications of block independence for consumption behaviour in terms of the demand for groups of goods and the demand for goods within a group.

A4.6 The demand for groups of goods and demand within groups

Under block independence, the consumer can decompose the allocation of expenditure on the n goods into two independent steps. First, there is the allocation to broad groups of goods such as food, clothing, housing etc. Second, given expenditure on a group, the consumer can then allocate expenditure to the items within the group, without any reference to expenditures or prices outside the group. Thus, for example, within the food group, the consumer can take total expenditure on this group as given (as determined by the first step), and then allocate that expenditure to meats, bread, dairy products, etc. on the basis of their relative prices. This section sets out the analytics of the decentralised decision-making process.

Group demand

We write

$$W_g = \sum_{i \in S_g} w_i, \quad \Theta_g = \sum_{i \in S_g} \theta_i \qquad (A4.26)$$

for the budget and marginal shares of group g. We define the group Divisia volume and Frisch price indexes as

$$d\left(\log Q_g\right) = \sum_{i \in S_g} \frac{w_i}{W_g}\, d\left(\log q_i\right),$$

$$d\left(\log P'_g\right) = \sum_{i \in S_g} \frac{\theta_i}{\Theta_g}\, d\left(\log p_i\right). \qquad (A4.27)$$

We obtain the demand equation for group S_g as a whole under block independence by adding over $i \in S_g$ both sides of the demand equation for good i under block independence, equation (A4.24). In view of definitions (A4.26) and (A4.27), this yields

$$W_g\, d\left(\log Q_g\right) = \Theta_g\, d(\log Q) + \sum_{i \in S_g}\sum_{j \in S_g} v_{ij}\left[d\left(\log p_j\right) - d\left(\log P'\right)\right].$$

In the last subsection of this section, it is shown that the second term on the right-hand side of the above equation simplifies and this demand equation takes the form

$$\begin{aligned} W_g\, d\left(\log Q_g\right) = {}&\Theta_g\, d\left(\log Q\right)\\ &+ \phi\,\Theta_g\left[d\left(\log P'_g\right) - d\left(\log P'\right)\right]. \qquad (A4.28) \end{aligned}$$

This is the *composite demand equation* for S_g as a group. This equation reveals that under block independence, the demand for a group of goods as a whole depends on real income and the relative price of the group, $d(\log P'_g) - d(\log P')$. The relative prices of goods outside the group in question play no role in equation (A4.28). By dividing both sides of this equation by W_g, we find that Θ_g/W_g is the income elasticity of demand for the group and that $\phi\Theta_g/W_g$ is the own-price elasticity. A comparison of equation (A4.28) with the demand equation for good i under preference independence, equation (A4.22), reveals that the former is an uppercase version of the latter. This is because under block independence the utility function exhibits preference independence with respect to *groups* of goods, rather than individual commodities, as mentioned before (compare equations (A4.21) and (A4.23)). Note also that if S_g consists of only one good, let it be the ith, then equation (A4.28) for this group coincides with (A4.22).

Conditional demand

Equation (A4.28) describes the allocation of income to group g, $g = 1, \ldots, G$. Given this allocation to the group, conditional demand equations determine the allocation of expenditure to goods within the group.

The demand equation for good i under block independence, equation (A4.24), and the composite demand equation (A4.28) both contain change in real income $d(\log Q)$ on the right-hand side. We can combine these two equations to obtain (see the last subsection of this section for details)

$$
\begin{aligned}
w_i\, d(\log q_i) = {}& \theta'_i\, W_g\, d(\log Q_g) \\
& + \sum_{j \in S_g} v_{ij}\left[d(\log p_j) - d\left(\log P'_g\right) \right],
\end{aligned} \qquad \text{(A4.29)}
$$

where $\theta'_i = \theta_i/\Theta_g$ is the conditional marginal share of good $i \in S_g$, with $\sum_{i \in S_g} \theta'_i = 1$. This share answers the question: If income rises by one dollar, resulting in a certain additional amount spent on group S_g, what is the proportion of this additional amount that is allocated to good i?

Equation (A4.29) is the demand equation for good $i \in S_g$, given the demand for the group as a whole, as measured by $W_g d(\log Q_g)$. It is known as the *conditional demand* equation for $i \in S_g$. This equation shows that the allocation of expenditure to goods within the gth group depends on the total consumption of the group, $W_g\, d(\log Q_g)$ and the relative prices of goods within the group, $\left[d(\log p_j) - d\left(\log P'_g\right)\right]$, $j \in S_g$. As consumption of other goods and the prices of goods outside of S_g do not appear in equation (A4.29), it can be seen that the within-group allocation of expenditure depends only on variables pertaining to the group in question. This underscores the sequential/decentralised nature of the decision-making process that is implied by block independent preferences. Another interesting feature of equation (A4.29) is that the coefficient of the jth relative price is v_{ij}, $i, j \in S_g$. This coefficient is exactly the same price coefficient as in (i) equation (A4.16), the original differential demand equation with no restrictions on preferences, and (ii) equation (A4.24), which can be described as the *un*conditional demand equation for good i under block independence. This shows that the v_{ij} are invariant to the level in which they appear in the consumer's decision-making hierarchy.

Modified conditional demand

This subsection formulates the conditional demand equation in a slightly different format. Write $M_g = \sum_{i \in S_g} p_i q_i$ for total expenditure on the group and $w'_i = p_i q_i / M_g$ for the share of M_g devoted to good i, satisfying $w'_i = w_i / W_g$. This w'_i is referred to as the conditional budget share of i, with $\sum_{i \in S_g} w'_i = 1$. If we divide both sides of conditional demand equation (A4.29) by the group budget share W_g, we obtain

$$
w'_i \, d(\log q_i) = \theta'_i \, d(\log Q_g) \\
+ \sum_{j \in S_g} v'_{ij} \left[d(\log p_j) - d\left(\log P'_g\right) \right] , \qquad \text{(A4.30)}
$$

where $v'_{ij} = v_{ij} / W_g$ is a modified price coefficient. In view of (A4.25), these coefficients for $i, j \in S_g$ satisfy

$$
\sum_{j \in S_g} v'_{ij} = \left(\phi \frac{\Theta_g}{W_g} \right) \theta'_i \quad i \in S_g, g = 1, \dots, G. \qquad \text{(A4.31)}
$$

As $\sum_{i \in S_g} \theta'_i = 1$, the above equation implies $\sum_{i \in S_g} \sum_{j \in S_g} v'_{ij} = \phi \Theta_g / W_g$. In words, the sum of all the modified price coefficients in the group equals the own-price elasticity of demand for the group as a whole. This shows that the term $\phi \Theta_g / W_g$ plays the role in conditional demand that ϕ plays in unconditional demand. Note that this term is the product of the income flexibility ϕ and the income elasticity of demand for the group Θ_g / W_g.

As the budget share on the left-hand side of equation (A4.30), w'_i, is of the conditional variety, all the variables in this equation now refer exclusively to within-group concepts. This characteristic is not shared by the original conditional demand equation (A4.29) as the unconditional budget share w_i is on the left. In this sense, equation (A4.30) could be considered to be slightly preferable to equation (A4.29). But as the two versions are obviously algebraically equivalent, the difference is one of clarity, interpretation and aesthetics.

Suppose that in addition to block independence within group g there is preference independence. Under these conditions, $v'_{ij} = 0$ for $i, j \in S_g$, $i \neq j$ and from equation (A4.31), $v'_{ii} = (\phi \Theta_g / W_g) \theta'_i$. Equation (A4.30) then becomes

$$w_i' \, d(\log q_i) = \theta_i' \, d(\log Q_g)$$
$$+ \left(\phi \frac{\Theta_g}{W_g} \right) \theta_i' \left[d(\log p_i) - d\left(\log P_g' \right) \right]. \qquad (A4.32)$$

This is a conditional version of equation (A4.22). Note again that here the term $\phi \Theta_g / W_g$ plays the same role as ϕ in equation (A4.22). We shall return to equation (A4.32) when we discuss applications in Section A4.7.

Blockwise dependence

Utility function (A4.23) is additive in the sub-utility functions for the G groups of goods. A weaker condition is that rather than a sum, utility is some increasing function, $f(\bullet)$, of the sum of the sub-utility functions:

$$u(q_1, \, \dots, \, q_n) = f\left(\sum_{g=1}^{G} u_g(q_g) \right). \qquad (A4.33)$$

The interactions in the utility function between two goods, i and j, can be conveniently described by the change in the marginal utility of a dollar spent on i when an extra dollar is spent on j, $\partial^2 u / \partial (p_i q_i) \partial (p_j q_j)$. Under (A4.33) for two goods belonging to different groups, these second derivatives of utility take the form

$$\frac{\partial^2 u}{\partial (p_i q_i) \partial (p_j q_j)} = a_{gh}, \quad i \in S_g, \quad j \in S_h, g \neq h.$$

As the coefficient a_{gh} does not have commodity subscripts (i, j), the above states that the change in the marginal utility of a dollar spent on good $i \in S_g$ caused by an additional dollar spent on $j \in S_h$ is independent of i and j. Thus, goods interact in the utility function in a groupwise fashion, and utility function (A4.33) is known as blockwise dependent, or weakly separable.

Although conditional demand equation (A4.29), and the modified version (A4.30), were derived under the assumption of block independence, it can be shown (Theil, 1975/76, Chapter 8) that these equations also hold under the weaker condition of blockwise dependence.

Summary

Table A4.6 provides an analytical summary of the above material. Column 2 describes the results for a general utility function, and the more restricted cases of block independence and preference independence are dealt with in columns 3 and 4, respectively. Thus, the move from left to right in the table corresponds to increasingly more stringent specifications of preferences. As we move down the table, we go from the form of the utility function to the associated demand equations, their coefficients and indexes. Note also that as we move from row 2 to row 3, which involves the transition from unconditional to conditional demand equations, we deal with more detail of the consumption basket. In short, Table A4.6 tells us of the observable implications for consumption behaviour of the nature of preferences.

Derivations

To derive the composite demand equation (A4.28), we need to establish

$$\sum_{i \in S_g} \sum_{j \in S_g} v_{ij} \left[d\left(\log p_j\right) - d\left(\log P'\right)\right]$$
$$= \phi \Theta_g \left[d\left(\log P'_g\right) - d\left(\log P'\right)\right]. \qquad (A4.34)$$

Definition (A4.14) implies that the price coefficients v_{ij} are symmetric in i and j, that is, $v_{ij} = v_{ji}$. This means that constraint (A4.25) can be expressed as $\sum_{i \in S_g} v_{ij} = \phi \theta_j$, so that

$$\sum_{i \in S_g} \sum_{j \in S_g} v_{ij} = \phi \sum_{j \in S_g} \theta_j .$$

Thus we can write the term on the left-hand side of equation (A4.34) as

$$\sum_{i \in S_g} \sum_{j \in S_g} v_{ij} \left[d\left(\log p_j\right) - d\left(\log P'\right)\right]$$
$$= \phi \sum_{j \in S_g} \theta_j \left[d\left(\log p_j\right) - d\left(\log P'\right)\right]$$
$$= \phi \Theta_g \left[d\left(\log P'_g\right) - d\left(\log P'\right)\right],$$

Table A4.6: *Summary of differential approach*

Description (1)	Nature of utility interactions		
	General (2)	Block independence (3)	Preference independence (4)
A. Preferences			
1. Utility function	$u(q_1,\ldots,q_n)$	$\sum_{g=1}^{G} u_g(\mathbf{q}_g)$	$\sum_{i=1}^{n} u_i(q_i)$
B. Demand equations			
2. Unconditional	$w_i d(\log q_i) = \theta_i d(\log Q) +$ $\sum_{j=1}^{n} \nu_{ij}\left[d(\log p_j) - d(\log P')\right]$ $i=1,\ldots,n$	$w_i d(\log q_i) = \theta_i d(\log Q) +$ $\sum_{j\in s_g} \nu_{ij}\left[d(\log p_j) - d(\log P')\right]$ $i\in S_g$	$w_i d(\log q_i) = \theta_i d(\log Q) +$ $\phi\theta_i\left[d(\log p_i) - d(\log P')\right]$ $i=1,\ldots,n$
3. Conditional	—	$w_i' d(\log q_i) = \theta_i' d(\log Q_g) +$ $\sum_{j\in s_g} \nu_{ij}'\left[d(\log p_j) - d(\log P_g')\right]$ $i\in S_g$	$w_i' d(\log q_i) = \theta_i' d(\log Q_g) +$ $\phi\dfrac{\Theta_g}{W_g}\theta_i'\left[d(\log p_i) - d(\log P_g')\right]$ $i\in S_g$
C. Coefficients			
4. Marginal Shares	θ_i, $\sum_{i=1}^{n}\theta_i = 1$	θ_i', $\sum_{i\in S_g}\theta_i' = 1$	

Table A4.6: *(continued)*

Description (1)	Nature of utility interactions		
	General (2)	Block independence (3)	Preference independence (4)
5. Price coefficients / modified price coefficients	$v_{ij},\ \sum_{j=1}^{n} v_{ij} = \phi\theta_i,\ i=1,\ldots,n$	$v'_{ij},\ \sum_{j\in S_g} v'_{ij} = \phi\dfrac{\Theta_g}{W_g}\theta'_i,\ i\in S_g$	$\phi\dfrac{\Theta_g}{W_g}\theta'_i$
6. Income flexibility / own-price elasticity, group g	ϕ	$\phi\dfrac{\Theta_g}{W_g}$	
D. Indexes			
7. Divisia volume	$d(\log Q) = \sum_{i=1}^{n} w_i\, d(\log q_i)$	$d(\log Q_g) = \sum_{i\in S_g} w'_i\, d(\log q_i)$	
8. Frisch price	$d(\log P') = \sum_{i=1}^{n} \theta_i\, d(\log p_i)$	$d(\log P'_g) = \sum_{i\in S_g} \theta'_i\, d(\log p_i)$	

where the second step follows from definitions (A4.26) and (A4.27). This verifies result (A4.34).

Next, we derive conditional demand equation (A4.29). To do this, we rearrange composite demand equation (A4.28) as

$$d\left(\log Q\right) = \frac{W_g}{\Theta_g}\,d\left(\log Q_g\right) - \phi\left[d\left(\log P_g'\right) - d\left(\log P'\right)\right],$$

and then substitute the right-hand side of the above for $d(\log Q)$ in equation (A4.24), thus obtaining:

$$w_i\,d\left(\log q_i\right) = \frac{\theta_i}{\Theta_g}\,W_g\,d\left(\log Q_g\right) - \phi\theta_i\,d\left(\log P_g'\right)$$
$$+ \phi\,\theta_i\,d\left(\log P'\right) + \sum_{j \in S_g} v_{ij}\,d\left(\log p_j\right) - \sum_{j \in S_g} v_{ij}\,d\left(\log P'\right).$$

$$(A4.35)$$

In view of constraint (A4.25), the second term on the right of (A4.35) can be expressed as

$$- \phi\theta_i\,d\left(\log P_g'\right) = - \sum_{j \in S_g} v_{ij}\,d\left(\log P_g'\right),$$

and the third term becomes

$$\phi\,\theta_i\,d\left(\log P'\right) = \sum_{j \in S_g} v_{ij}\,d\left(\log P'\right),$$

which cancels with the last term of (A4.35). Consequently, equation (A4.35) can be written as

$$w_i\,d\left(\log q_i\right) = \frac{\theta_i}{\Theta_g}\,W_g\,d\left(\log Q_g\right) + \sum_{j \in S_g} v_{ij}\,d\left(\log p_j\right) - \sum_{j \in S_g} v_{ij}\,d\left(\log P_g'\right)$$
$$= \theta_i'\,W_g\,d\left(\log Q_g\right) + \sum_{j \in S_g} v_{ij}\left[d\left(\log p_j\right) - d\left(\log P_g'\right)\right],$$

which is conditional demand equation (A4.29).

A4.7 The Rotterdam model

This section discusses the application of differential demand equations. We start with the unconditional case and then turn to conditional demand equations.

Unconditional demand

Equation (A4.16) for $i = 1, \ldots, n$ is a system of general differential demand equations. There are several ways to apply this system to time-series data; for a review, see Clements *et al.* (1995, Sections 1.14–1.17). One popular way is to follow the approach of the Rotterdam model due to Barten (1964) and Theil (1965). This involves making four adjustments to (A4.16). First, the budget share w_i on the left of (A4.16) is replaced with its arithmetic average over the periods t and $t-1$, $\bar{w}_{it} = \frac{1}{2}(w_{it} + w_{i,t-1})$. Second, infinitesimal logarithmic changes are replaced with first differences of the logs; that is, for any positive variable x, $d(\log x)$ is replaced with $Dx_t = \log x_t - \log x_{t-1}$. Third, the coefficients θ_i, v_{ij} and ϕ are all treated as constants. Fourth, to allow for random factors, a disturbance term ε_{it} is added to the equation. Thus, if we let $DP'_t = \sum_{j=1}^{n} \theta_j Dp_{jt}$ denote the Frisch price index in finite-change form, the Rotterdam model is

$$\bar{w}_{it} Dq_{it} = \theta_i DQ_t + \sum_{j=1}^{n} v_{ij}[Dp_{jt} - DP'_t] + \varepsilon_{it} \quad i = 1, \ldots, n. \quad (A4.36)$$

The coefficients of (A4.36) satisfy $\sum_{i=1}^{n} \theta_i = 1$, $\sum_{j=1}^{n} v_{ij} = \phi \theta_i$, $i = 1 \ldots, n$ and $v_{ij} = v_{ji}$, $i, j = 1, \ldots, n$. As the prices in equation (A4.36) are deflated, it is known as the relative price version of the model.

The corresponding absolute price version uses $\sum_{k=1}^{n} \theta_k Dp_{kt}$ to substitute out the Frisch price index DP'_t to express the substitution term as

$$\sum_{j=1}^{n} v_{ij}[Dp_{jt} - DP'_t] = \sum_{j=1}^{n} v_{ij} Dp_{jt} - \sum_{j=1}^{n} v_{ij} \sum_{k=1}^{n} \theta_k Dp_{kt}$$

$$= \sum_{j=1}^{n} (v_{ij} - \phi \theta_i \theta_j) Dp_{jt} = \sum_{j=1}^{n} \pi_{ij} Dp_{jt},$$

where the second step is based on constraint (A4.15) and π_{ij} is the $(i,j)^{\text{th}}$ Slutsky coefficient defined by equation (A4.19). The absolute price version of the Rotterdam model is thus

$$\bar{w}_{it} Dq_{it} = \theta_i DQ_t + \sum_{j=1}^{n} \pi_{ij} Dp_{jt} + \varepsilon_{it} \quad i = 1, \ldots, n,$$

which is a finite-change version of equation (A4.20).

Conditional demand once again

In Section 4.5 of the text, we applied the Rotterdam model to the demand for beer, wine, spirits and marijuana. As it dealt only with those goods, that application is a conditional version of the model. But in order not to overburden the text, in Section 4.5 we did not use the "full-blown" notational system of this Appendix that draws a distinction between conditional and unconditional concepts. To clarify matters, consider equation (A4.32), which we reproduce here:

$$w'_i d(\log q_i) = \theta'_i d(\log Q_g) + \left(\phi \frac{\Theta_g}{W_g}\right) \theta'_i \left[d(\log p_i) - d\left(\log P'_g\right)\right].$$

$$(A4.37)$$

This is the conditional demand equation for $i \in S_g$ under the conditions of (i) block independence and (ii) preference independence within the group.

A finite-change version of equation (A4.37) in the Rotterdam style is

$$\bar{w}'_{it} Dq_{it} = \theta'_i DQ_g + \phi_g \theta'_i \left[Dp_{it} - DP'_g\right] + \varepsilon'_{it}, \qquad (A4.38)$$

where $\bar{w}'_{it} = \frac{1}{2}\left(w'_{it} + w'_{i,t-1}\right)$ is the arithmetic average of the conditional budget share, $DQ_{gt} = \sum_{i \in S_g} \bar{w}'_{it} Dq_{it}$ is the Divisia volume index of group g, $\phi_g = \phi \Theta_g / W_g$ is the own-price elasticity of the demand for group g as a whole, $DP'_g = \sum_{i \in S_g} \theta'_{it} Dp_{it}$ is the Frisch price index of the group and ε'_{it} is a disturbance term. The corresponding demand equation of the text is equation (4.5), reproduced here:

$$\bar{w}_{it} Dq_{it} = \theta_i DQ_t + \phi \theta_i \left(Dp_{it} - DP'_t\right) + \varepsilon_{it}. \qquad (A4.39)$$

Equations (A4.38) and (A4.39) are identical except for the notation. That is, if we interpret appropriately the notation of equation (A4.39), we have equation (A4.38). The exact meaning of the term "interpret appropriately" is made explicit in the following translation table.

A4.8 Some key empirical findings

This section provides a brief review of important findings in applied demand analysis pertaining to the validity of the hypothesis of preference independence and the value of the income flexibility ϕ.

| | Symbol in | |
| | Appendix [equation (A4.38)] | Text [equation (A4.39)] |
Concept		
Conditional budget share of good i	$\bar{w}'_{it}$	$\bar{w}_{it}$
Conditional marginal share of good i	θ'_i	θ_i
Divisia volume index of group g	DQ_{gt}	DQ_t
Own-price elasticity of demand for group g	ϕ_g	ϕ
Frisch price index for group g	DP'_{gt}	DP'_t
Disturbance term for good i within group g	ε'_{it}	ε_{it}

Preference independence

We return to equation (A4.22), the demand equation under preference independence, which we reproduce here:

$$w_i\, d(\log q_i) = \theta_i\, d(\log Q) + \phi\theta_i[d(\log p_i) - d(\log P')].$$

Dividing both sides by w_i, we see that θ_i/w_i is the income elasticity and $\phi\theta_i/w_i$ is the own-price elasticity, the elasticity of consumption of good i with respect to the Frisch-deflated own-price. This shows that preference independence implies own-price elasticities are proportional to income elasticities.

In a widely cited paper, Deaton (1974) examines whether price and income elasticities are proportional, as predicted by preference independence. On the basis of UK data, he finds no such relationship and concludes that

> ...*the assumption of additive preferences* [preference independence] *is almost certain to be invalid in practice and the use of demand models based on such an assumption will lead to severe distortion of measurement.* (Deaton's emphasis)

Deaton's rejection of preference independence on the basis of indirect evidence (the lack of proportionality of price and income elasticities) is consistent with first-generation direct tests that test the implied parametric restrictions on the demand equations; see Barten (1977) for a survey.

The above negative results can be responded to in two ways. First, Selvanathan (1993) examines elasticities from 18 OECD countries and finds the evidence not inconsistent with the proportionality relationship, indicating that Deaton may have been premature in declaring the invalidity of preference independence. Second, as the first-generation tests of the hypothesis of preference independence have only an asymptotic justification, it is appropriate to exercise caution in taking the results at face value when the underlying sample sizes are not large. To avoid potential problems with asymptotics associated with modest sample sizes, Selvanathan (1987, 1993) develops a Monte Carlo test of preference independence, which tends to result in fewer rejections. For example, in applications of the methodology, Selvanathan and Selvanathan (2005b) reject preference independence in only 9 countries out of a total of 45; Clements *et al.* (1997) are unable to reject preference independence for beer, wine and spirits in all of the seven countries they consider; and Selvanathan and Selvanathan (2005a, p. 235) are unable to reject the hypothesis for the three alcoholic beverages in ten countries. While the matter has probably still not been completely resolved and there is still scope for differing views, it now seems safe to conclude that the assumption of preference independence should not be rejected out of hand, or at least not as readily as the older studies tended to do.

The income flexibility

The income flexibility ϕ is defined by equation (A4.13) as the reciprocal of the income elasticity of the marginal utility of income, $(\partial \log \lambda / \partial \log M)^{-1} < 0$. As the income flexibility is the sum of the n^2 price coefficients in the n demand equations, this is a basic parameter related to the overall degree of substitutability among all goods in the consumption basket.

Frisch (1959, p. 189) discussed the possible way in which the income elasticity of the marginal utility of income, the inverse of the income flexibility (that is, ϕ^{-1}), could vary with income. Making the appropriate changes so that the references are to ϕ

rather than ϕ^{-1}, the following passage is known as the "Frisch conjecture":

We may, perhaps, assume that in most cases [ϕ] has values of the order of magnitude given below.

- −0.1 for the extremely poor and apathetic part of the population.
- −0.25 for the slightly better off but still poor part of the population with a fairly pronounced desire to become better off.
- −0.5 for the middle income bracket, "the median part" of the population.
- −1.4 for the better off part of the population.
- −10 for the rich part of the population with ambitions towards "conspicuous consumption".

It would be a very promising research project to determine [ϕ] for different countries and for different types of populations. A universal "atlas" of the values of [ϕ] should be constructed. It would serve an extremely useful purpose in demand analysis.

Thus, Frisch sees the income flexibility increasing in absolute value as the consumer becomes more affluent. This is in contrast to the Rotterdam model in which ϕ is treated as a constant parameter.

The dependence of ϕ on real income has been examined in several studies, and most tests of the Frisch conjecture tend to reject it; see, for example, Clements and Theil (1996), Selvanathan (1993, Sections 4.8 and 6.5), Selvanathan and Selvanathan (2003, Sections 3.6 and 4.6), Theil (1975/76, Section 15.4), Theil (1987a, Section 2.13) and Theil and Brooks (1970/71). Such a finding is not surprising as the Frisch conjecture refers to the third-order derivative of the utility function, and most consumption data could not be expected to be very informative about the nature of this higher-order effect. But the question of the validity of Frisch's conjecture is not completely closed as supporting evidence has been reported by DeJanvry *et al.* (1972) and Lluch *et al.* (1977).

We now turn to a brief review of the available evidence on the estimated values of the income flexibility. Important prior studies for our purpose can be grouped into three categories:

- *A cross-country study.* Selvanathan (1993) uses time-series data to estimate a differential demand system for each of 15 OECD countries. For Australia, the ϕ-estimate is −0.46, with asymptotic standard error 0.08 (Selvanathan, 1993, p. 189). When the data are pooled over the 15 countries, the estimate of ϕ is −0.45, with ASE

0.02 (Selvanathan, 1993, p. 198). Using a related approach, Selvanathan (1993, Section 6.4) obtains 322 estimates of ϕ, one for each year in the sample period for each of 18 OECD countries; the weighted mean of these estimates is very similar to those above at -0.46 (ASE = 0.03).

- *Three other cross-country studies.* Three other sources of cross-country estimates of ϕ are also relevant: (i) using data from the International Comparisons Project for 30 countries from Kravis *et al.* (1982), Theil (1987a, Section 2.8) obtains a ϕ-estimate of -0.53 (0.04); (ii) Chen (1999, p. 171) estimates a demand system for 42 countries and obtains an estimate of ϕ of -0.42 (0.05), when there are intercepts in his differential demand equations which play the role of residual trends in consumption, and -0.29 (0.05) when there are no such intercepts; (iii) Selvanathan and Selvanathan (2003, Tables 3.20 and 4.19) use several approaches to estimate ϕ for 23 OECD countries and 23 developing economies. Averaging over countries, they obtain a ϕ-estimate of about -0.4.

- *An earlier, but still influential, survey.* Brown and Deaton (1972, p. 1206) review earlier findings and conclude that "there would seem to be fair agreement on the use of a value for ϕ around minus one-half".

Taken as a whole, the above suggests that a reasonable value for the income flexibility is about minus one-half. Note also that according to the above passage from Frisch, a ϕ-value of -0.5 would pertain to the "middle income bracket, 'the median part' of the population", which can be taken to mean that this value applies to the centre of gravity of the population.

Notes

1. This intensification of consumption is consistent with opinion polls regarding the social acceptability of marijuana. In the late 1980s, less than a fifth of Australians favoured legalisation (Sullivan, 1993), but by 1995 this had increased to between 40 per cent and 50 per cent, depending on the state (NDSHS, 1993, 1995).
2. For a further discussion of marijuana usage across countries, see Section A4.1 of the Appendix.
3. The figure of 5.4 ounces per user is derived from (i) Table 4.5, where total consumption in 1995 is 9,982 thousand ounces, and (ii) Table 4.3, where

the total number of users in that year is $4,476 - 2,641 = 1,835$ thousand. Accordingly, consumption per user is $9,982/1,835 = 5.4$ ounces.

4. Both Rhodes *et al.* (1997) and the Western Australian Parliament Select Committee (1997) derive their estimates by considering the number of joints consumed. However, it is unlikely that frequent users, especially daily and more than once a week users, smoke joints. It is common knowledge amongst users that while smoking joints is enjoyable, it is not the optimal way of getting high; for example, a better high is obtained with a smaller amount of marijuana using water pipes.

5. Covariance structure (4.6) corresponds to sampling from a multinomial distribution with probabilities equal to budget shares.

6. In Section 4.8, we will have more to say about prior estimates of price elasticities for alcoholic beverages.

7. On the other hand, on the basis of a chi-square test, Daryal (1999, p. 67) rejects the hypothesis of independence between the responses to the two questions: (i) "Suppose marijuana were legalised, would your alcohol consumption change?" and (ii) "Have you ever used marijuana?"

8. In a recent paper, Becker *et al.* (2006, p. 48) seem to endorse the idea that the price elasticity of drugs could also be reasonably taken to be one-half. They write: "There are no reliable estimates of the price elasticity of demand for illegal drugs, mainly because data on prices and quantities consumed of illegal goods are scarce. However, estimates for different drugs generally indicate an elasticity of less than one in absolute value, with a central tendency of about one-half (see Cicala, 2005) …"

9. The relationship between the Slutsky (η_{ii}) and Frisch own-price elasticities is $\eta_{ii} = \eta'_{ii}(1 - \theta_i)$. As $\Sigma_{i=1}^{n} \theta_i = 1$, the order of the marginal shares is $1/n$, as is the difference between η_{ii} and η'_{ii}.

10. Under preference independence, the Hessian matrix of the utility function is diagonal, so that $u^{ij} = 0$ for $i \neq j$. This means that $v_{ij} = 0$ for $i \neq j$, so that constraint $\Sigma_{j=1}^{n} v_{ij} = \phi \theta_i$, becomes $v_{ij} = \phi \theta_i$, and equation (4.9) reduces to equation (4.7).

References

Allen, R. G. D. and Bowley, A. L. (1935). *Family expenditure*. London: P. S. King and Son.

Barten, A. P. (1964). "Consumer demand conditions functions under conditions of almost additive preferences." *Econometrica* 32, 1–38.

Barten, A. P. (1977). "The systems of consumer demand functions approach: a review." *Econometrica* 45, 23–51.

Becker, G. S., Murphy, K. M. and Grossman, M. (2006). "The market for illegal goods: the case of drugs." *Journal of Political Economy* 114, 38–60.

Brown, A. and Deaton, A. S. (1972). "Surveys in applied economics: models of consumer behaviour." *Economic Journal* 82, 1145–236.

Cameron, L. and Williams, J. (2001). "Cannabis, alcohol and cigarettes: substitutes or complements?" *Economic Record* 77, 19–34.

Chen, D. (1999). *World consumption economics.* Singapore: World Scientific.

Cicala, S. J. (2005). "The demand for illicit drugs: a meta-analysis of price elasticities." Working Paper, University of Chicago.

Cleeland Report (1989). Parliamentary Joint Committee on the National Crime Authority. *Drugs, crime and society.* Canberra: Australian Government Publishing Service.

Clements, K. W. (2004). "Three facts about marijuana prices." *Australian Journal of Agricultural and Resource Economics* 48, 271–300.

Clements, K. W. (2006). "Price elasticities of demand are minus one-half." Discussion Paper No. 06.14, Economics Program, The University of Western Australia.

Clements, K. W. (2008). "Price elasticities of demand are minus one-half." *Economics Letters* 99, 490–9.

Clements, K. W. and Daryal, M. (1999). "The economics of marijuana consumption." Paper presented at the 28th Conference of Economists, Economic Society of Australia, La Trobe University, September.

Clements, K. W. and Daryal, M. (2005). "The economics of marijuana consumption." Chapter 10 in S. Selvanathan and E. A. Selvanathan eds., *The demand for alcohol, tobacco and marijuana: international evidence.* Aldershot: Ashgate, pp. 243–67.

Clements, K. W. and Johnson, L. W. (1983). "Unpublished data appendix" to "The demand for beer, wine and spirits: a system-wide analysis." *Journal of Business* 56, 273–304.

Clements, K. W., Selvanathan S. and Selvanathan, E. A. (1995). "The economic theory of the consumer." Chapter 1 in E. A. Selvanathan and K. W. Clements, eds., *Recent developments in applied demand analysis: alcohol, advertising and global consumption.* Berlin: Springer Verlag, pp. 1–72.

Clements, K. W. and Theil, H. (1996). "A cross-country analysis of consumption patterns." Chapter 7 in H. Theil, ed., *Studies in global econometrics.* Boston: Kluwer, pp. 95–108.

Clements, K. W., Yang, W. and Zheng, S. W. (1997). "Is utility additive? The case of alcohol." *Applied Economics* 29, 1163–7.

Dalhuisen, J. M., Florax, R. J. G. M., de Groot, H. L. F. and Nijkamp, P. (2003). "Price and income elasticity of residential water demand: a meta-analysis." *Land Economics* 79, 292–308.

Daryal, M. (1999). *The economics of marijuana*. Unpublished BEc Honours thesis, The University of Western Australia.

Daryal, M. (2002). "Prices, legalisation and marijuana consumption." *University Avenue Undergraduate Journal of Economics*, available at www.econ.ilstu.edu./UAUJA.

Deaton, A. S. (1974). "A reconsideration of the empirical implications of additive preferences." *Economic Journal* 84, 338–48.

DeJanvry, A., Bieri, J. and Nunez, A. (1972). "Estimation of demand parameters under consumer budgeting: an application to Argentina." *American Journal of Agricultural Economics* 54, 422–30.

Espey, J. A. and Espey, M. (2004). "Turning on the lights: a meta-analysis of residential electricity demand elasticities." *Journal of Agricultural and Applied Economics* 36, 65–81.

Espey, M. (1996). "Explaining the variation in elasticity estimates of gasoline demand in the United States: a meta-analysis." *Energy Journal* 17, 49–60.

Espey, M. (1998). "Gasoline demand revisited: an international meta-analysis of elasticities." *Energy Economics* 20, 273–95.

Espey, M., Espey, J. A. and Shaw, W. D. (1997). "Price elasticity of residential demand for water: a meta-analysis." *Water Resources Research* 33, 1369–74.

Fogarty, J. (2005). *Wine investment, pricing and substitutes*. PhD thesis, The University of Western Australia.

Frisch, R. (1959). "A complete scheme for computing all direct and cross demand elasticities in a model with many sectors." *Econometrica* 27, 177–96.

Gallet, C. A. and List, J. A. (2003). "Cigarette demand: a meta-analysis of elasticities." *Health Economics* 12, 821–35.

Goodwin, P., Dargay, J. and Hanly, M. (2004). "Elasticities of road traffic and fuel consumption with respect to price and income: a review." *Transport Reviews* 24, 275–92.

Graham, D. and Glaister, S. (2002). "Review of income and price elasticities of demand for road traffic." Working Paper, Center for Transport Studies, Imperial College of Science, Technology and Medicine, London.

Harris, M., Ramful, P. and Zhao, X. (2006). "An ordered generalised extreme value model with application to alcohol consumption in Australia." *Journal of Health Economics* 25, 782–801.

Jiggens, J. (2005). "The cost of drug prohibition in Australia." Paper presented at the Social Change in the 21st Century Conference, Centre for Social Change Research, Queensland Institute of Technology.

Kravis, I. B., Heston, A. W. and Summers, R. (1982). *World product and income: international comparisons of real gross product*. Baltimore, MD: The Johns Hopkins University Press.

Lluch, C., Powell, A. A. and Williams, R. A. (1977). *Patterns in household demand and savings.* Oxford: Oxford University Press.

Marks, R. E. (1992). "The costs of Australian drug policy." *The Journal of Drug Issues* 22, 535–47.

National Drug Strategy Household Survey (computer file, various issues). Canberra: Social Data Archives, The Australian National University.

Nisbet, C. T. and Vakil, F. (1972). "Some estimates of price and expenditure elasticities of demand for marijuana among UCLA students." *Review of Economics and Statistics* 54, 473–5.

Penington Report (1996). *Drugs and our community: report of the Premier's Advisory Council.* Melbourne: Victorian Government.

Pigou, A. C. (1910). "A method of determining the numerical value of demand elasticities." *Economic Journal* 20, 636–40.

Rhodes, W., Langenbahn, S., Kling, R. and Scheiman, P. (1997). *What America's users spend on illegal drugs, 1988–1995.* Washington, DC: The Office of National Drug Policies, available at www.whitehousedrugpolicy. gov/drugfact/retail/contents.html.

Sanwijk, J. P., Cohen, P. D. A., Musterd, S. and Langmeijer, M. P. S. (1995). *Licit and illicit drugs in Amsterdam II.* Amsterdam: University of Amsterdam Press.

Selvanathan, S. (1987). "A Monte Carlo test of preference independence." *Economics Letters* 25, 259–61.

Selvanathan, S. (1991). "The reliability of ML estimators of systems of demand equations: evidence from 18 countries." *Review of Economics and Statistics* 73, 338–46.

Selvanathan, S. (1993). *A system-wide analysis of international consumption patterns.* Dordrecht: Kluwer Academic Publishers.

Selvanathan, S. and Selvanathan, E. A. (2003). *International consumption patterns: OECD versus LDC.* Singapore: World Scientific.

Selvanathan, S. and Selvanathan, E. A. (2005a). *The demand for alcohol, tobacco and marijuana: international evidence.* Aldershot: Ashgate.

Selvanathan, S. and Selvanathan, E. A. (2005b). "Is utility additive? Further evidence." *Applied Economics* 37, 83–6.

Stigler, G. J. (1963). *The intellectual and the market place and other essays.* New York: Free Press.

Sullivan, L. (1993). "Who says banning marijuana doesn't work?" *News Weekly*, November 20, 12–13.

Tellis, G. J. (1988). "The price elasticity of selected demand: a meta-analysis of econometric models of sales." *Journal of Marketing Research* 25, 331–41.

Theil, H. (1965). "The information approach to demand analysis." *Econometrica* 33, 67–87.

Theil, H. (1967). *Economics and information theory.* Amsterdam and Chicago, IL: North-Holland and Rand McNally.

Theil, H. (1975/76). *Theory and measurement of consumer demand.* Two volumes. Amsterdam: North Holland.

Theil, H. (1980). *The system-wide approach to microeconomics.* Chicago IL: The University of Chicago Press.

Theil, H. (1987a). "Evidence from international consumption comparisons." Chapter 2 in H. Theil and K. W. Clements, eds., *Applied demand analysis: results from system-wide approaches.* Cambridge, MA: Ballinger, pp. 37–100.

Theil, H. (1987b). "The econometrics of demand systems." Chapter 3 in H. Theil and K. W. Clements, eds., *Applied demand analysis: results from system-wide approaches.* Cambridge MA: Ballinger, pp. 101–62.

Theil, H. and Brooks, R. (1970/71). "How does the marginal utility of income change when real income changes?" *European Economic Review* 2, 218–40.

Theil, H. and Clements, K. W. (1987). *Applied demand analysis: results from system-wide approaches.* Cambridge, MA: Ballinger.

United Nations (1997). *United Nations international drug control programme: world drug report.* Oxford: Oxford University Press.

Western Australian Parliament Select Committee (1997). *Taking the profit out of drug trafficking. An agenda for legal and administrative reforms in Western Australia to protect the community from illicit drugs.* Interim Report. Perth: Legislative Assembly.

Williams, J. and Mahmoudi, P. (2004). "Economic relationship between alcohol and cannabis revisited." *Economic Record* 80, 36–48.

Zhao, X. and Harris, M. (2004). "Demand for marijuana, alcohol and tobacco: participation, levels of consumption, and cross-equation correlations." *Economic Record* 80, 394–410.

5 | Decriminalising and legalising marijuana

KENNETH W. CLEMENTS, YIHUI LAN
AND XUEYAN ZHAO

5.1 Introduction

Marijuana-related policies and legislation have long been controversial topics for many countries around the world. The issues involved are complex and have health, social, economic and political dimensions. At the centre of the debate is whether legal sanctions are the best way to reduce use of the drug and the harm associated with this use. Advocates for relaxing marijuana legislation argue that legal sanctions have not been effective in reducing use and the associated harm, and that law enforcement resources are better spent on fighting the use of harder drugs. They also argue that a criminal charge is too severe a penalty for a minor marijuana offender who may otherwise be a law-abiding person. There are also concerns that young marijuana users may be unnecessarily exposed to dealers of harder drugs when marijuana is illegal. Of course, there has also been the ethical argument for individual liberty (Hall, 1997). However, opponents argue that liberalising marijuana laws would send a signal indicating that it is acceptable to use the drug. They are also worried that easier access to marijuana may provide a gateway for users to shift to harder drugs.

Although there is a spectrum of policy options ranging from total prohibition, prohibition with civil penalties for minor offences, partial prohibition and regulation to full legalisation, much of the current debate surrounds legislative details at the prohibition end of the spectrum (Commonwealth of Australia, 1994). Indeed, throughout the past decades, countries such as the Netherlands, the US and Australia have introduced legislative reforms or guidelines reducing penalties for possession of small amounts of marijuana. Empirical evaluations of the experiences in these countries are no doubt valuable for designing effective marijuana policies.

Pacula *et al.* (2003) review the experience regarding marijuana decriminalisation in the US and the associated empirical evaluations, detailing the key dimensions of reduced criminal sanctions for the eleven so-called "decriminalised states". They conclude that although it is impossible to uniquely identify the decriminalised states based on criminal penalties, the association between decriminalisation and increased use is still robust. Adding to the US experience, four of the eight Australian states and territories have also decriminalised marijuana with different regulatory details, thus providing another case study. Although a complete evaluation of marijuana policies would involve careful consideration of all the economic costs and benefits of the policy consequences, as pointed out by Pacula (2005), it is important to empirically test whether liberalisation of marijuana policies results in an increase in consumption of marijuana. Finally, although there is no empirical evidence regarding the impact of complete legalisation and taxation, there are still many interesting questions as to what would happen to the demand for marijuana and related drugs if such legislation were introduced.

As the economic effects of prohibition of the consumption, production and distribution of a commodity are equivalent to the operation of a prohibitive tax, in Section 5.2 we set out the economic principles of taxation. This includes an analysis of who bears the economic burden of a commodity tax (its "incidence") and the role of taxes in dealing with external or "third-party" effects of the use of the commodity. Section 5.3 then contains a discussion of the pros and cons of prohibition and how it has worked in practice, drawing on experience regarding alcohol in the US in the 1920s and 1930s, and other drugs more recently. In Section 5.4 we describe the evolution of marijuana law reform in Australia and examine consumption in the eight states and territories before and after decriminalisation. A brief overview of empirical studies that assess decriminalisation in the US is provided in Section 5.5. In Section 5.6 we present a survey of econometric estimates of decriminalisation on marijuana consumption in Australia.

The remaining sections of the chapter explore the implications of a hypothetical radical change in the legal status of marijuana whereby it is completely legalised and its use is subject to a tax, in the same way as for tobacco and alcohol. To do this, we construct a demand system for the consumption of marijuana, tobacco and alcoholic beverages, which we refer to as "vice". This system allows interaction of the consumption of these products, which reflects the known simultaneous use of several drugs. Owing to a lack of reliable data, we draw on the literature and our own judgement to determine numerical values for demand elasticities. But to acknowledge the genuine uncertainties that surround the workings of drug markets, each basic parameter of the demand system follows a probability distribution and we use a Monte Carlo simulation procedure to derive the corresponding probability distribution of each elasticity. This approach is used to simulate the impacts of a scenario involving legalising and taxing marijuana on vice consumption and tax revenue. Towards the end of the chapter we explore in some depth the role of risk in pricing illicit drugs.

5.2 The economics of taxation

By their very nature, the operation of illicit drug markets is characterised by the prominent role of government. When the use of a drug is declared to be illegal, we expect an underground market to emerge with higher prices than before and a lower quantity transacted. That is, although the intent of the law is to eliminate consumption completely, such an outcome is unlikely as long as the government has finite resources to devote to law enforcement and the commodity is sufficiently highly valued by some consumers. Qualitatively, the higher prices and lower quantity resulting from prohibition are exactly the same outcome that would occur if the government alternatively taxed the commodity. Accordingly, this section draws on the theory of taxation to provide insights into the operation of drug markets when the government intervenes using some instrument that reduces the quantity transacted from what it would otherwise be, and that acts in the same way as a tax would. In what follows, we discuss the theory of tax incidence to show that, from an economic perspective, it is irrelevant whether the authorities enforce the law by prosecuting drug dealers or consumers. We also use a welfare-economics framework to assess the desirability of imposing a tax, prohibitive or otherwise, on drugs. Major references for the economics of taxation include Atkinson and Stiglitz (1980) and Fullerton and Metcalf (2002).

Tax incidence

The key insight from tax incidence theory is that the economic incidence differs from the legal incidence. That is, since both buyers and sellers have economic incentives to avoid paying the tax, their behaviour changes, and changes in exactly the same way regardless of who bears the legal liability for taxation. We establish this fundamental result in a stylised model of a commodity tax.

Consider a commodity whose price to consumers is p^d, whereas p^s is the price received by sellers. Then, if $\eta^d < 0$ and $\eta^s > 0$ are the price elasticity of demand and supply, respectively, the quantities demanded and supplied (q^d, q^s) in change form are:

$$\hat{q}^d = \eta^d \hat{p}^d, \quad \hat{q}^s = \eta^s \hat{p}^s, \tag{5.1}$$

where a circumflex denotes proportional change (so that $\hat{x} = dx/x$). If a tax is levied on consumers at rate $t \times 100$ per cent, then the consumer and producer prices are linked according to $p^d = (1+t)p^s$, so that:

$$\hat{p}^d = \left(\widehat{1+t}\right) + \hat{p}^s. \tag{5.2}$$

Market clearing takes the form $q^d = q^s$, or $\hat{q}^d = \hat{q}^s$. Thus, if we equate the right-hand sides of the two equations in (5.1) and use (5.2), we obtain the equilibrium price changes resulting from a change in the tax:

$$\hat{p}^d = \alpha\left(\widehat{1+t}\right), \quad \hat{p}^s = (\alpha - 1)\left(\widehat{1+t}\right), \tag{5.3}$$

where $\alpha = \eta^s/(\eta^s - \eta^d)$ is a positive fraction. The corresponding change in the equilibrium quantity, $\hat{q} = \hat{q}^d = \hat{q}^s$, is obtained by substituting (5.3) into (5.1):

$$\hat{q} = \eta^d \alpha\left(\widehat{1+t}\right) = \eta^s(\alpha - 1)\left(\widehat{1+t}\right). \tag{5.4}$$

As $0 < \alpha < 1$, $\eta^d < 0$ and $\eta^s > 0$, equation (5.4) shows that application of the tax decreases the quantity of the good transacted.

Equation (5.3) reveals that the tax has a twofold effect, increasing the consumer price and decreasing the producer price. Although consumers are legally obliged to pay all the tax, they can adjust their behaviour so that they end up paying only a fraction of it. As indicated by equation (5.3), the tax causes the consumer price to rise by $\alpha\left(\widehat{1+t}\right) > 0$, which is only a fraction α of the tax increase $\left(\widehat{1+t}\right)$. The remainder of the tax is paid for by producers in the form of a lower price as p^s decreases; from the second term of equation (5.3), the change in this price is $(\alpha - 1)\left(\widehat{1+t}\right) < 0$. If, for example, $\eta^s = 1$ and

$\eta^d = -1$, then $\alpha = 1/2$ and $\alpha - 1 = -1/2$, so that consumers and producers equally share the incidence of the tax. In fact, this "equal sacrifice" result holds more generally whenever $\eta^s = -\eta^d$. Another important special case is when supply is highly sensitive to price, as would be the case when there are no particularly specialised production factors required to manufacture the commodity. Here the fraction α is near its upper limit of unity, so the bulk of the tax burden is borne by consumers; producers bear only a small part of the tax, since they can easily move into other economic pursuits if their returns are squeezed too much by the tax. The key point is that the fraction α is determined by fundamental economic parameters, the price elasticity of demand and the price elasticity of supply, the values of which are unlikely to be affected by the nature of taxation arrangements.

The above case deals with the situation in which the tax is imposed on consumers. Alternatively, suppose the tax is now levied on producers and that for each dollar of revenue received by producers they have to pay a fraction $t/(1 + t) \approx t < 1$ in tax. This means that the link between the producer and consumer prices now becomes $p^s = p^d \left(1 - \frac{t}{1+t}\right) = \frac{p^d}{1+t}$, and equation (5.2) continues to hold. As equation (5.1) remains unchanged, the conclusion is that the equilibrium prices and quantity under this new taxation regime continue to be given by equations (5.3) and (5.4). Accordingly, consumers still bear a fraction α of the tax, whereas producers continue to pay $\alpha - 1$, independent of the institutional arrangements regarding taxation.

The above results are illustrated in Figure 5.1. In Panel A, DD is the demand curve for the commodity, SS is the supply curve and E is the pre-tax equilibrium point. As there is no tax initially, the initial consumer and producer prices coincide at $p_0^d = p_0^s$, with q_0 the corresponding quantity transacted. As the tax incidence is independent of where it is levied, we represent it as a wedge between the demand and supply curves, such as AB in the figure; the length of AB is the difference between the consumer and producer prices and is thus the per-unit tax. The length of AB is given by tax amount and its precise location is uniquely determined by the nature of the demand and supply curves. As evident from the figure, there is only one location to the left of the intersection of the two curves at which the vertical distance between them is equal to AB. The tax causes the consumer price to increase from p_0^d to p_1^d, whereas the producer price decreases

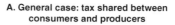

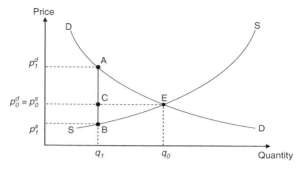

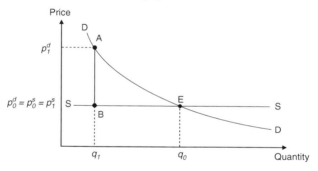

Figure 5.1. Incidence of tax

from p_0^s to p_1^s. The share of the tax paid by consumers is thus the ratio of the price increase, $p_1^d - p_0^d = AC$, to the total tax, $p_1^d - p_1^s = AB$, or AC/AB. This ratio is the above fraction $\alpha = \eta^s/(\eta^s - \eta^d)$. The remaining share, $1 - AC/AB = CB/AB = 1 - \alpha$, is the fraction paid by producers. Panel B of Figure 5.1 shows that when supply is perfectly elastic, all of the tax is paid by consumers.

Welfare economics of tax

Figure 5.2 demonstrates the welfare effects of a commodity tax. Panel A shows the demand for and supply of the commodity; point E is the market equilibrium without a tax and the equilibrium quantity is q_0.

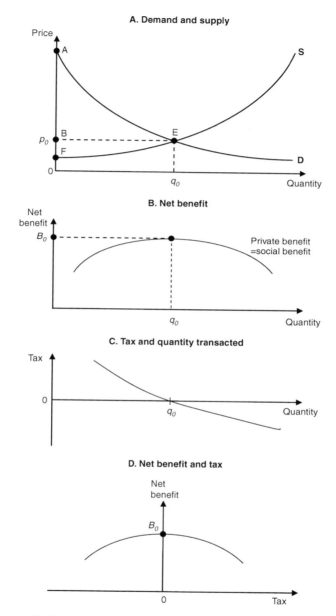

Figure 5.2. Welfare effects of taxation: no externality

The total valuation placed by consumers on these q_0 units of the commodity is the area under the demand curve, viz., AE q_0 O. As the total cost is BEq_0O, the net benefit to consumers is the difference between the two areas, AEq_0O–BEq_0O=AEB, which is the area below the demand curve and above the price line. This area is known as consumer surplus. A similar argument establishes that the area above the supply cure and below the price line, BEF, represents the net benefit to producers. Taking account of both sides of the market, the total net benefit is AEB + BEF = AEF. A fundamental result in welfare economics is that a competitive equilibrium maximises this total net benefit. This result is illustrated in Panel B of Figure 5.2, which plots total net benefit on the vertical axis (abbreviated to "net benefit" for convenience) against the quantity transacted. When the quantity is less than q_0, the net benefit increases with the quantity, reaches a maximum at q_0 and decreases thereafter. The maximum net benefit is denoted by B_0, which is equal to the area AEF in Panel A.

As discussed in the context of Figure 5.1, the effect of a tax is to reduce the quantity transacted, and Panel C of Figure 5.2 shows this tax–quantity relationship. As the impact of the tax is to move the market away from competitive equilibrium, the reduction in the quantity transacted for any positive tax means that the net benefit falls below its maximum.[1] Panel D of Figure 5.2 plots the net benefit against the tax and shows that zero tax is optimal, since this maximises net benefits.[2]

Now consider the case of a negative external effect on consumption. Thus, consumers pay the price of the commodity, but the total cost to the economy as a whole is this price plus an extra cost associated with the externality. An example is tobacco smoking, which generates "second-hand" smoke that imposes health costs and causes inconvenience/annoyance to others. Usually, there are only two parties to a market transaction, the buyer and seller, but here the unwilling recipients of the smoke constitute a third party. It is for this reason that competitive equilibrium results in too large a quantity transacted and a tax is called for as a welfare-enhancing policy.

As the height of the supply curve is the marginal cost of the commodity, the "social supply curve", which includes the external costs of consumption, lies above the one that ignores these factors. The curve labelled S' in Panel A of Figure 5.3 represents this social supply. Panel B shows that the social benefit, which deducts the external cost, is less

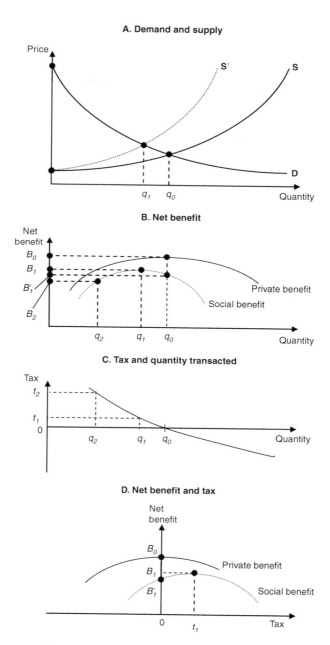

Figure 5.3. Welfare effects of taxation: with externality

than the private benefit. Social net benefits are maximised when the quantity transacted is q_1. When there is no externality, private and social benefits coincide, as in Panel B of Figure 5.2. When there is no tax but there is externality in consumption, the quantity transacted exceeds that which maximises the social benefit, that is, $q_0 > q_1$. Accordingly, the role of public policy is to impose a tax that achieves the social optimum with the quantity q_1. From Panel C, the tax that corrects the distortion is $t_1 > 0$. Panel B illustrates that this tax is welfare-improving, as the social benefit of the commodity with this tax, B_1, exceeds that when it is untaxed, B'_1. Panel D demonstrates that in this case t_1 is indeed the optimal tax.

The above highlights the case of a market failure that can be corrected by a tax. However, it should be acknowledged that the informational requirements for a government to set such a tax at an appropriate rate are onerous. To be able to compute the optimal tax t_1 in Panel C of Figure 5.3, the government needs to know the price responsiveness of demand and supply, as well as the amount of the external cost. These three pieces of information can be estimated, but not with certainty. If any of the three inputs obtained is wrong, it is possible that the resulting tax can make things worse. For example, if in Panels B and C of Figure 5.3 the tax is t_2, this leads to a worse result in terms of welfare than does a zero tax. From Panel C, tax t_2 leads to a quantity transacted of q_2 and Panel B shows that the net social benefit associated with q_2 is B_2, which is below that with no tax, B'_1. This is an example of government failure being worse than market failure.

5.3 Prohibition

In this section, we first discuss the pros and cons of a policy of prohibition. We then briefly review the experience with alcohol prohibition in the US in the 1920s and 1930s and discuss some evidence from outcomes of the more recent "war on drugs".

Pros and cons

In the previous section we demonstrated that in the presence of negative external effects, the appropriate public policy is to impose a tax on the commodity. Thus, when drugs have such third-party effects, they should be subject to a tax, which is the case in many countries for alcohol and tobacco. Governments also need revenue to finance their expenditure and from this perspective such commodities are also good candidates for taxation. As the consumption of alcohol and tobacco is price inelastic, subjecting them to taxation means that the base (the quantity consumed) shrinks only slowly, so that the impact of the tax on resource allocation is modest and the efficiency costs are small. In addition, the nature of the production of alcoholic beverages and tobacco means that the compliance costs (borne by producers and consumers) and the administrative costs (borne by the government) of taxes on these products tend to be low. Accordingly, there are three reasons for the attraction of alcohol and tobacco taxes: negative externalities, low efficiency costs, and low compliance and administrative costs.

A case can be made on the basis of the principles of public finance that drugs that are currently illegal should be treated in the same manner as alcohol and tobacco: they should be legalised, taxed and subject to similar regulations, such as restrictions on the sale to minors. However, this is not the case in most countries, where illegal drugs are just that, *illegal*, which can be thought of as subjecting these goods to a prohibitive tax. It is most unlikely that the negative external effects are so large that prohibitive taxes on drugs are optimal. Why is it that governments resort to prohibiting the consumption, production and distribution of drugs rather than taxing them in the same way as alcohol and tobacco? Drawing on Culyer (1973), Bretteville-Jensen (2006) presents a useful analysis of this issue and discusses six possible reasons for prohibition of drugs, as summarised in Table 5.1. Ostensibly, these all seem satisfactory reasons for banning drugs, but deeper considerations raise substantial doubts, as listed in the last column of the table. Moreover, even when there is a market failure, there is still the question of whether a tax would be a more appropriate policy instrument. As shown in the last column of Table 5.1, and as concluded by Bretteville-Jensen, the case in favour of prohibition is not compelling in all but one instance. The single argument for prohibition is that the young need to be protected from drugs because of their inability to see the full consequences of their actions (row 4 of Table 5.1). But even in this case, libertarians may be inclined to argue that protection of children is the role of parents rather than the government.

Table 5.1: *Possible reasons for prohibition of drugs*

Reason	Explanation	Counter argument
1. Users may physically harm others	Users finance consumption by crime	Illegality of drugs is the problem that causes high prices
2. Drug use causes increased public spending on health	Drug taking is a risky activity that can damage health	Drug-taking is not the only risky activity with adverse health consequences
3. Drug use can upset even those not in contact with users	A type of "informational externality"	Many other items also fall into this category, such as poverty
4. Drug use is contagious, and potential users should be protected from exposure	Young people may not see all consequences of their actions and need to be protected	None
5. Users are less productive	Lost production is a cost to the economy	As the cost is primarily borne by the individual, not entirely an externality
6. Users must be protected against themselves as they are self-destructive	Users not capable of rational choice	Not true in the aggregate; users respond to economic incentives, e.g., higher prices discourage consumption

Source: Derived primarily from Bretteville-Jensen (2006).

In the previous section, we illustrated the case of government failure if the tax rate is set at the wrong level in the presence of a negative externality. If the rate is sufficiently wrong, then the policy can leave society worse off relative to no intervention. The same problem can apply to a policy of prohibition because of its unintended deleterious effects on crime and on the health and stigmatisation of users. Thus, prohibition is unlikely to be the optimal policy for two reasons: (i) the economic case for a prohibitive tax rate is unconvincing and (ii) the side effects of the policy are likely to be substantial. These ideas are summarised by Bretteville-Jensen (2006) as follows:

Prohibition is ... an unusual means of handling externalities, and, as is well known, one unintended effect of this policy has been the development of enormous illegal drug markets. To reduce the problems caused by the drug industry, governments have targeted both the demand and supply sides of the illegal market with an array of interventions. The question being asked by more and more people is whether the costs to society and the individual users are not starting to outweigh the benefits of a prohibitive drug policy. The amount of resources spent by society on drug control (police and customs) and on the legal system (prison administration and administration of justice) and the cost paid by the individual drug user in terms of harassment, stigmatising, imprisonment, increased health risks and so on are substantial. To what extent the prohibitive policy achieves the aims of reduced drug use and the recruitment of drug users is being discussed.

Prohibition in practice

Under the Eighteenth Amendment to its Constitution, the United States prohibited the production, sale and distribution of alcohol for the period 1920–1933. According to Kyvig (1979), although alcohol consumption did decrease, it was not completely eliminated and there is some controversy in the literature regarding the impact of Prohibition on alcohol consumption. Fisher (1926) argues that Prohibition substantially reduced consumption by 80–90 per cent. In contrast, Warburton (1932) estimates that the long-term changes in per capita consumption of beer, wine and spirits during Prohibition were approximately −70 per cent, +65 per cent and +10 per cent, respectively, and that per capita alcohol consumption as a whole fell by approximately 30 per cent. Miron and Zwiebel (1991) estimate alcohol consumption during Prohibition using death rates from liver cirrhosis and alcoholism, hospital admissions for alcoholic psychosis and arrests for drunkenness. Their estimates agree broadly with Warburton's and they emphasise that the decrease in consumption during the later years of Prohibition was quite modest compared to post-Prohibition levels. On this basis, Miron and Zwiebel conclude that the decrease in consumption was not inconsistent with the observed increase in prices during Prohibition, so that there is little role to be played by other factors:

Changes in consumption during Prohibition were modest given the change in price. This suggests that legal deterrents had little effect on limiting consumption outside their effect on price. Social pressure and respect for the law did not go far in reducing consumption during Prohibition. We speculate that this is likely to be true as well with illegal drugs today ...

Miron (1999) also argues that the prices of alcoholic beverages did not increase as much as would be expected during Prohibition and that "Prohibition had virtually no effect on alcohol consumption".

As discussed in Chapter 3, Australian marijuana prices decreased substantially over the 1990s, possibly as a result of two reasons: (i) part of the benefit of significantly enhanced marijuana productivity due to the adoption of hydroponic techniques over this period was passed onto users in the form of lower prices; (ii) owing to more tolerant community attitudes to drug-taking, the "policing effort" decreased, as did the risk premium built into prices. It should be noted that the second explanation does not agree with experience from the US where drug prices have decreased over the last 25 years, whereas policing effort has increased (see Basov et al., 2001, discussed in Section 3.5).

There are several reasons for the apparently perverse impact of regulation on drug prices (Basov et al., 2001), and arguably the most plausible is evasion. The apparent ease with which the restrictions on drinking during Prohibition could be avoided through relabelling of beverages, home production and the underground economy (Kyvig, 1979) meant that its economic impact was more limited than proponents had hoped for. A similar case of widespread evasion can be made for illicit drugs in more recent times. Although this type of regulation seems not to have all of its intended effects, it has several substantial unintended effects, as mentioned in the previous subsection and as discussed in Miron and Zwiebel (1991). The consumption of some illicit drugs poses serious health risks to users owing to the uncertain quality of these drugs. Illicit drugs also stimulate underground markets, leading to associated crime and violence, and clog up the judicial system with drug cases. These are serious social issues with significant economic costs.

5.4 Australian marijuana laws and regulations

Like many other countries, Australia closely follows the development of international drug treaties when considering its drug laws. The first such international convention to cover marijuana was the 1925 Geneva Convention on Opium and Other Drugs. It required that parties limit the availability of marijuana to medical and scientific purposes only, which remains the status of marijuana in the international community (Commonwealth of Australia, 1994). Unlike the opiates, marijuana was little known or used in Australia until the 1960s (Manderson, 1993). The first drug laws introduced in the late nineteenth and early twentieth centuries concerning the Chinese use of opium were racially based, but provided a framework for marijuana prohibition. The first state legislation concerning marijuana use was introduced in Victoria in 1928, penalising the unauthorised use of Indian hemp and resin. This was followed by similar legislation in the other states in the subsequent decades until the late 1950s (Commonwealth of Australia, 1994).

The 1960s saw a dramatic increase in the use of marijuana and other illicit drugs for recreational purposes. Both the Commonwealth and state governments responded by introducing new laws, ratifying conventions, strengthening the law enforcement approach, and increasing penalties. However, from the middle and late 1970s, the debate shifted to distinguishing between drug traffickers and drug users, and between the possession of small amounts of marijuana and other drugs. Numerous Commonwealth and state government inquiries have been conducted over the years into illegal drug use and trafficking, as well as the adequacy of legislation and educational programs. These inquiries generally concluded that penalties should be commensurate with the harm presented by different drugs and that young and first offenders should be treated leniently for marijuana use. The 1980s saw the start of a series of changes in state legislation in relation to the possession of small quantities of marijuana that resulted in the current laws. It should be noted that the Australian

Constitution provides the Commonwealth with no general power to legislate on crime, and criminal laws have largely been the province of the individual states (Commonwealth of Australia, 1994).

The first significant legislative change in relation to marijuana was the introduction of the Cannabis Expiation Notice (CEN) scheme in South Australia (SA) in 1987. Under this scheme, a person found possessing or cultivating small quantities of marijuana for personal use is given an expiation notice. Payment of the expiation fee (between $50 and $150) within 60 days results in avoidance of a court appearance and criminal conviction. If the offender fails to pay the fine, normal court proceedings follow, with a possible jail sentence. Similar expiation schemes have since been introduced to three other Australian states and territories: the Australian Capital Territory (ACT) in 1992, the Northern Territory (NT) in 1996 and Western Australia (WA) in 2004. In other states without such civil penalty schemes, various cautioning and diversion approaches were put in place to divert non-violent, minor and early marijuana offenders from the legal system. These involve issuing caution notices to minor and early offenders rather than immediately initiating criminal proceedings. All cautioning systems also incorporate an educational component on the harm of marijuana (Australian Drug Foundation, 2007). Details of the current laws relating to minor marijuana offences across states and territories are summarised in Table 5.2.

In all states and territories, major marijuana offences still attract a criminal record and penalties remain severe. Convictions for cultivation, trafficking or possession of commercial quantities of marijuana attract significant jail sentences and large fines. In fact, although the penalties for personal consumption have been reduced in many jurisdictions, there have been amendments to legislation to increase the penalties for trafficking offences, shifting the focus from users to suppliers (Manderson, 1993).

Nationally representative data on marijuana consumption were not available to evaluate the effects of decriminalisation until the first wave of the National Drug Strategy Household Survey in 1985 (NDSHS, 2004). Seven large-scale surveys have been conducted since then via the NDSHS, with information collected on the consumption of marijuana and other drugs by individuals. Figure 5.4 shows the participation rates for marijuana consumption for the eight states and

Table 5.2: *Australian laws for minor cannabis offences*

Jurisdiction	Year of legislative change	Amount of cannabis	Penalty
A. Prohibition with civil penalty schemes (infringement notices)			
South Australia	1987	Less than 100 grams and no more than one plant (recently reduced from three)	60 days to pay, adults only. Fines between $50 and $150, where failure to pay usually results in a conviction
Australian Capital Territory	1992	Not more than 25 grams or five plants	60 days to pay, adults and juveniles. $100 fine; failure to pay does not usually lead to a conviction
Northern Territory	1996	Less than 50 grams and no more than two plants	28 days to pay, adults only. $100 fine; failure to pay results in a debt to the state but no conviction
Western Australia	2004	Less than 30 grams and no more than two plants	28 days to pay, adults only. $100–200 fine or attendance at a specified education session

Table 5.2: *(continued)*

Jurisdiction	Year of legislative change	Amount of cannabis	Penalty
B. Prohibition with a caution and diversion to treatment			
Tasmania	1998	Less than 50 grams, plants excluded	Caution for first three offences
Victoria	1998	Less than 50 grams, plants excluded	Up to two formal cautions for those aged over 17 years
New South Wales	2000	Less than 15 grams	State-wide trial extended. Up to two formal cautions
Queensland	2001	Less than 50 grams	Mandatory assessment and brief intervention session

Source: Australian Drug Foundation (2007).

A. Decriminalised states

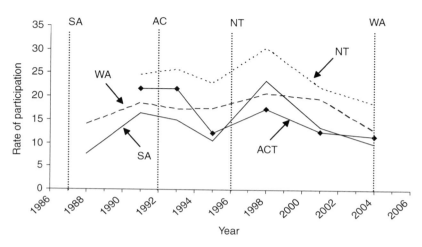

B. Non-decriminalised states

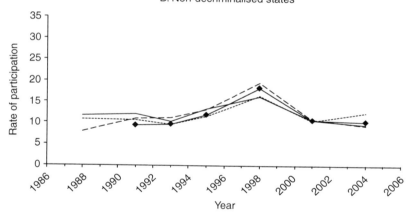

Figure 5.4. Marijuana participation by state

Note: The vertical line in panel A for 1987 represents the year when marijuana was decriminalised in SA. The other three vertical lines (1992, 1996 and 2004) refer to the years of decriminalisation in the other three states.

territories in terms of the proportion of respondents who reported marijuana use in the 12 months prior to the surveys. These are the only data available, but they are not perfect. Unlike later surveys that contain information regarding both lifetime and 12-month use, in

1985 only the lifetime question was asked. In addition, the state codes for Tasmania, NT and ACT were not distinguishable in the 1988 survey data, so only the average participation rate for these states was available.

As shown in Figure 5.4, NT has a persistently higher participation rate than the other states. NT has the highest proportion of indigenous population, and use of marijuana and other substances is a more significant part of the lifestyle and culture of aboriginal communities according to reports by Aagaard *et al.* (2004) and Clough *et al.* (2004). Although it seems that participation increased in NT immediately after decriminalisation in 1996, it decreased in the two subsequent surveys, although still remaining higher than in all other states. Given that the pattern of changes in participation for NT is similar to that for the other states, it is unclear whether the increase after the policy change is due to the influence of other factors common to all states and territories. SA decriminalised marijuana in 1987. Figure 5.4 shows obvious increases in participation in the few years after the legislative change in SA, after which the participation rate appears to have settled to a level comparable to that of other states. The expiation system was introduced in 1992 in the ACT; participation then declined to levels similar to that of other states in subsequent years. Finally, WA has one of the higher participation rates. As marijuana was decriminalised in WA in 2004, it will be interesting to observe whether the 2007 survey reveals any substantial changes in usage. Overall, all states except Queensland have experienced a decrease in marijuana use since 1998.

As a rough way to adjust participation rates for common national and local factors, in Figure 5.5 we use deviations from means. Then in Figure 5.6 we line up these deviations timewise with respect to the year of decimalisation; see the notes to the figure for details. As can be seen from panel C of this figure, once national and regional factors are allowed for, only in the ACT does participation spike around the time of decriminalisation. According to this measure, participation rises in the ACT by approximately six percentage points immediately before and after decriminalisation; but thereafter this effect wears off and participation more or less returns to normal. However, it should be noted that this conclusion is based on a preliminary analysis of the data involving average participation rates; more formal approaches are discussed later in Section 5.6.

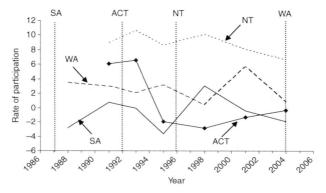

A. Deviations from national trend

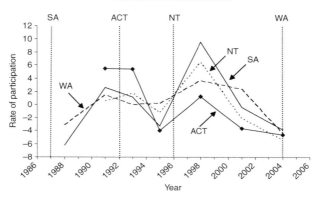

B. Deviations from state trends

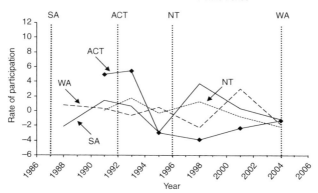

C. Deviations from national and state trends

Figure 5.5. Participation, deviated from trends, by decriminalised state

Notes:

1. The national trend is the unweighted average of participation rates in the eight states.
2. The trend for a given state is the average over time of the participation rates given in panel A Figure 5.4. 3. See notes to Figure 5.4.

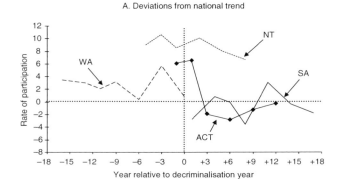

A. Deviations from national trend

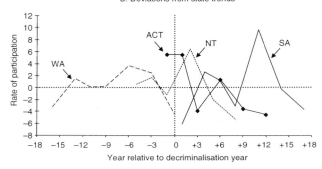

B. Deviations from state trends

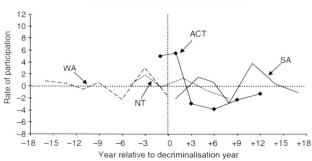

C. Deviations from national and state trends

Figure 5.6. More on participation, deviated from trends, by decriminalised state

Notes:

1. To interpret this figure, take the case of the NT which decriminalised in 1996. For this territory, we label 1996 as "year 0", so that year 3, for example, in the above graph is 1996 + 3 = 1999. Similarly, for each of the three other states, the year zero corresponds to the year in which marijuana was decriminalised.

2. See notes to Figure 5.5.

5.5 Impact of decriminalisation: evidence from the US

During the 1970s, 11 states in the United States enacted legislation removing criminal sanctions for the possession of small amounts of marijuana. However, the campaign for decriminalisation had stalled somewhat by the beginning of the 1980s due to a decrease in user age, the rapid emergence of a paraphernalia industry, a shift in public attitudes from a focus on adult civil liberties to protection of the young, and a broader swing in political ideology to the right (Roffman, 1981). It was not until 1996 that another state, Arizona, also decriminalised first- and second-time marijuana offences, taking the total number of "decriminalised states" to 12 (Pacula *et al.*, 2003).

Empirical evaluation of the effects of decriminalisation on marijuana consumption has generated mixed results. Early studies soon after policy changes in the 1970s compared the number of users before and after the policy change and generally found little or no effect on marijuana use in the short run (Johnston *et al.*, 1981; Maloof, 1981; Single, 1989). In contrast to later studies that pool all states together in the same analysis, these earlier papers consider the experience of individual states. Commentators have argued that the policy changes have been cost-effective, as they resulted in substantial savings in the criminal justice system without significant increases in drug use (Single, 1989). Later studies using more recent data and comparisons with control states have reached mixed conclusions. Thies and Register (1993), DiNardo and Lemieux (2001) and Pacula (1998) found no significant effects of decriminalisation on consumption for adolescents and young adults. On the other hand, Chaloupka *et al.* (1998, 1999) found positive and significant associations between decriminalisation and the probability of marijuana use for high-school students. In addition, Saffer and Chaloupka (1998, 1999) found evidence of a positive decriminalisation effect on consumption for the general population.

Other researchers have found associations between decriminalisation and the adverse effects of drug use such as traffic fatalities and medical emergencies (Model, 1993; Chaloupka and Laixuthai, 1997). In addition, Chaloupka *et al.* (1998, 1999), Farrelly *et al.* (2001) and DeSimone and Farrelly (2003) found some association between higher fines for marijuana possession and police enforcement, as well as a decreased probability of marijuana use among the young population.

However, Pacula *et al.* (2003), Hall and Pacula (2003) and Pacula (2005) have pointed out that there are important differences in the details of the legal penalties for marijuana offences among the 11 original decriminalised states. More importantly, many non-decriminalised states have also introduced reduced penalties for possession of small amounts of marijuana as early as 1989. When the key legal dimensions of marijuana laws in non-decriminalised states are examined along with those in the 11 original decriminalised states, they argue that it is impossible to uniquely identify the so-called decriminalised states. They therefore call for caution in interpretation of the above studies that evaluate decriminalisation policy. Nevertheless, Pacula *et al.* (2003) show that when detailed information on the legal dimensions of these policies is included, the association between decriminalisation and marijuana use is real and there remains clear evidence that demand for marijuana among the youth is responsive to the penalties imposed. Given the association between lower penalties and increased marijuana prevalence, Pacula (2005) points out that the next question is whether the economic value of the consequences of increased consumption exceeds the cost of maintaining the current policies.

5.6 A survey of estimated decriminalisation effects in Australia

Although participation rates such as those shown in Figures 5.4–5.6 provide a comparison of aggregate measures of decriminalisation, econometric models using individual-level data controlling for other factors such as drug prices and other confounding individual characteristics are needed to isolate the partial effect of decriminalisation. A number of papers have examined the effects of decriminalisation on marijuana consumption in Australia using data from the NDSHS. Table 5.3 summarises the estimated marginal effects of decriminalisation on the probability of marijuana use from these studies, together with information on data coverage and econometric models used.

Donnelly *et al.* (1995, 1999) use the 1985–1993 and 1985–1995 NDSHS data, respectively, to evaluate the effect of the CEN scheme introduced in SA in 1987. To do this, they examine whether there has been a greater increase in the prevalence of lifetime and weekly

Table 5.3: *Estimated decriminalisation effects in Australia*

Authors	Marginal effect	Variable of interest	Data	Econometric model
Donnelly *et al.* (1995)	Insignificant	Rate of change in lifetime and weekly use	NDSHS 85–93	Logistic regression (control only for age and gender)
Donnelly *et al.* (1999)	Insignificant	Rate of change in lifetime and weekly uses	NDSHS 85–95	Logistic regression (control only for age and gender)
Cameron and Williams (2001)	2%	12-month use	NDSHS 88–95, excluding ACT and NT	Probit
Williams and Mahmoudi (2004)	1.1%	12-month use	NDSHS 88–98	Probit (including a drinking fine variable)
Zhao and Harris (2004)	(i) 2% (ii) 2% 4%	(i) 12-month use (ii) conditional use given participation: Weekly use Daily use	NDSHS 95–01	(i) Multivariate probit (ii) Two-part (Probit and OP)
Williams (2004)	(i) Insignificant (ii) 5% (iii) Insignificant	(i) 12-month use for full sample (ii) 12-month use for males aged >25 (iii) Conditional use given participation	NDSHS 88–98	Two-part (Probit and OP; including state dummies)

Table 5.3: *(continued)*

Authors	Marginal effect	Variable of interest	Data	Econometric model
Clements and Daryal (2005)	(i) 8% (ii) 4%	Percentage change in consumption quantity (i) current users (ii) whole sample	UWA first-year students 1998	Descriptive statistics
Ramful (2008)	Insignificant	12-month use	NDSHS 98–04	Probit (including an NT state dummy)
Damrongplasit et al. (forthcoming)	(i) 3.7% (ii) 4.0% (iii) 13.7% (iv) 16.2 – 18.3% (v) 5.9 – 11.2%	12-month use	NDSHS 01	(i) Probit Model (ii) Endogenous bivariate probit model (iii) Two-part probit switching model (iv) Endogenous probit switching model (v) Propensity score stratification

marijuana use in SA than in the rest of Australia. They use a logistic regression to test for differences in trends in the prevalence rate, controlling for only age and gender. They find that the increase in prevalence rate in SA was significantly greater than the average increase for the rest of Australia. However, when the trend of prevalence is considered, they find that there is no statistically significant difference in the *rate of increase* in weekly use between SA and the rest of Australia. In fact, they show that Victoria and Tasmania, two non-decriminalised states, have similar rates of increase to SA. Note that these two papers used somewhat different modelling techniques to the subsequent analyses using the same data set. Rather than analysing subsamples of the data set to estimate different rates of change for individual states, later studies have mostly applied a probit model to the whole sample with a dummy variable representing the status of decriminalisation.

Using individual level data from the four waves of 1988, 1991, 1993 and 1995 of the NDSHS, Cameron and Williams (2001) use a probit model to estimate the effects of drug prices, individual characteristics and decriminalisation on marijuana participation probability, in conjunction with models of participation decisions for two other related drugs, tobacco and alcohol. They find a positive 2 per cent effect of decriminalisation on the probability of participation (defined as use in the previous 12 months) when controlling for other factors. They also experiment with eliciting differential decriminalisation effects by individual characteristics, and find that the effect is more likely due to a delay by individuals of 30 years of age or over in giving up marijuana than to an increase in use by young people. They acknowledge that as they omitted both the ACT and NT in their analysis owing to the unavailability of price data, the decriminalisation dummy is in effect equivalent to a SA dummy, and the analysis cannot separately identify the decriminalisation effect from any "SA state effect".

Further exploring the economic relationship between marijuana and alcohol, Williams and Mahmoudi (2004) investigate participation in marijuana by also including as an explanatory variable the fine for a first offence of exceeding the allowable blood alcohol concentration for driving to capture the cost of alcohol consumption. The effect of decriminalisation on the 12-month marijuana participation probability is estimated to be 1.1 per cent.

Zhao and Harris (2004) extend the Cameron and Williams (2001) study by including more recent NDSHS data from 1995, 1998 and 2001 involving over 40,000 individuals. They use a trivariate probit model to jointly estimate the participation decisions for all three drugs, accounting for correlations via unobservable characteristics such as an addictive personality and a difficult family upbringing for the same individual. A two-part model is also estimated that examines separately the binary participation decision and the conditional decision of choosing from five discrete levels of marijuana consumption. Three states were decriminalised by the time of the 2001 survey, and this is modelled by a decriminalisation dummy assuming the appropriate values for each year in the data. Controlling for prices, income and other factors, the marginal effect of decriminalisation on participation in marijuana use is estimated at 2 per cent. In terms of its effect on levels of consumption, they estimated that decriminalisation will increase the probability of daily consumption by 4 per cent and weekly use by 2 per cent, other factors being equal.

Also using a two-part model that considers separately the decisions for 12-month marijuana use and levels of consumption *conditional on participation*, Williams (2004) examines again the impacts of price and decriminalisation using the 1988–1998 NDSHS data, but includes both a decriminalisation dummy and state dummies as explanatory variables. When all seven state dummies are included, decriminalisation only significantly increases marijuana participation for the subsample of males over the age of 25. The decriminalisation effects on both participation and conditional consumption decisions for the full sample or younger subsamples are no longer significant. However, as the author concedes, the decriminalisation effect may have been attributed to state dummies in the model and the data do not contain enough variation to separately identify the policy effect from state fixed effects. Thus, the insignificance of the decriminalisation variable may not be indicative of an insignificant decriminalisation effect.

Clements and Daryal (2005) study marijuana consumption among first-year students enrolled in a large economics class at The University of Western Australia in 1998, with 327 students responding to their survey. The survey asked, "Suppose marijuana is legalised, and suppose there is no price change. How much would your consumption of marijuana change?" Among the current users, the average change in quantity consumed is 7.8 per cent, whereas for all respondents the average consumption change is 4.3 per cent. The data also reveal that males are more responsive to legalisation than females, and the effects are greater for current daily and weekly users than monthly or occasional users. Note that these results are not directly comparable with the other studies in Table 5.3, as the question in this study relates to full legalisation and the survey covers only a young university population. Clements and Daryal (2005) also estimate a demand system for marijuana and three alcoholic drinks using imputed aggregated quantities of marijuana consumed based on consumption frequencies in the NDSHS data. They estimated price and income demand elasticities for marijuana, but not the decriminalisation effect. Versions of this material are presented in Chapter 4.

Ramful (2008) also uses a probit model to study the 12-month participation probability for a pooled sample of the 1998, 2001 and 2004 NDSHS data. She argues that the NT, with its unique ethnic composition and cultural differences relative to other states, has a significant sample selection issue. Although acknowledging the difficulties in separately identifying the state effect from the decriminalisation effect, she included a single dummy variable for the NT. Once the NT dummy is included in the analysis, the decriminalisation variable is positive, but becomes insignificant. She points out that without the NT dummy, the decriminalisation effect becomes positive and statistically significant.

Finally, Damrongplasit *et al.* (forthcoming) use data from the NDSHS and several parametric and non-parametric approaches to highlight potential differences in the estimated decriminalisation effects under alternative behavioural and econometric modelling assumptions. For parametric models, they present an endogenous probit switching model and its four nested models, namely, binary probit, endogenous bivariate probit, a two-part model and a switching model, highlighting the behavioural assumptions underlying each model. As shown in Table 5.3, their estimated average treatment effects (ATEs) differ across models. For a simple binary probit model without accounting for endogeneity of treatment and flexibility in behaviour, the ATE is estimated to be 3.7 per cent. This is similar to the estimates of Cameron and Williams (2001) and Zhao and Harris (2004). When accounting for endogeneity of treatment with an endogenous bivariate probit model, the ATE increases to 4 per cent. However, when allowing for behavioural differences between the treatment and the control groups, but ignoring endogenous treatment as in the two-part model, they obtain an ATE of 13.7 per cent. Lastly, in the two versions of endogenous probit switching models the estimated ATEs are between 16.2 and 18.3 per cent. It is clear that the two-part and the endogenous probit switching models yield substantially larger ATEs than the binary probit and bivariate probit models. These values contrast with the ATE of 5.9–11.2 per cent estimated from the propensity score stratification method, using differing ranges for overlapping regions and ways of partitioning the scores. All of these estimates are statistically significant at the 1 per cent level.

5.7 Modelling the consumption of vice

Empirical studies show that marijuana is closely related in consumption to at least two other goods, tobacco and alcohol.[3] As in many instances marijuana is mixed with tobacco and then smoked, there is a presumption that these goods are complementary. Furthermore, as marijuana and alcoholic beverages contain intoxicating properties that are similar in the minds of many consumers, they both tend to serve the same want, and it is reasonable to suppose that they are substitutes. These considerations imply that consumption of these three goods, which we dub the demand for vice, needs to be modelled jointly as an interrelated system of demand equations. Such interrelations imply cross-commodity impacts of any policy changes, so that changes in one drug market are likely to have spillover effects in related markets. For example, what would be the likely impacts on the markets for tobacco and alcohol, as well as the revenue from taxing these products, if there were further decriminalisation of marijuana? What would be the potential tax revenue from marijuana were it legalised? And how would changes in taxation and regulation arrangements for alcohol and tobacco impact on marijuana consumption?

Answers to these questions depend crucially on unofficial estimates of the price and quantity data for marijuana, as well as on a consistent set of own-and cross-price elasticities characterising interrelationships in the consumption of vice. The problem in constructing such a demand system is that hard data on marijuana consumption are not available. Even the data for alcohol and tobacco consumption are not perfect, as the typically high excise taxes on these goods mean that there are substantial incentives to underreport use, or not report at all, to avoid the tax net.[4] This is an extreme example of the situation faced in modelling exercises such as equilibrium displacement modelling (EDM) (see, e.g., Zhao *et al.*, 2000) and computable general equilibrium (CGE) modelling (see, e.g., Dixon and Rimmer, 2002), for which a large number of base market values and elasticities need to be specified.

Even if CGE modellers do not have the required number of high-quality econometric estimates to draw upon as the basis of their elasticities, they typically have substantial information on consumption and prices to derive base market values. As mentioned above, this is not the case for marijuana, and we have to rely on unofficial data that are subject to more than the usual questions regarding their quality. In what follows, we introduce a simulation procedure in the context of a demand system for vice – marijuana, tobacco and alcohol – to formally account for the inherent uncertainty in the marijuana-related data and demand elasticities. We use separability theory as a basis for organising the fragmentary information that is available on marijuana consumption, and then combine this with econometric estimates and data pertaining to tobacco and alcohol. We then use stochastic simulations as a way to formally recognise the substantial uncertainties inherent in all aspects of the consumption of marijuana, as well as those associated with tobacco and alcohol. Zhao *et al.* (2000) and Griffiths and Zhao (2000) use a similar approach in the context of sensitivity analysis for an EDM of the Australian wool industry. We extend this approach by simulating implied distributions of the demand elasticities through the quantification of uncertainty in the basic demand parameters within a complete demand specification and by allowing for uncertainty in marijuana-related data. These procedures may be of general interest and have applications in EDM and CGE modelling and other areas of applied economics. We apply this approach to the cross-commodity impacts of a decrease in marijuana prices and some changes in taxation arrangements, including a scenario in which marijuana is legalised and then subject to an excise tax.

The next six sections are organised as follows. In Section 5.8, we introduce a demand system for vice using the differential approach to consumption theory as the analytical framework. Section 5.9 presents a set of baseline budget shares using Australian data and the basic parameters that underlie the demand system, from which the income and price elasticities are derived. Section 5.10 introduces uncertainty by specifying subjective probability distributions for the basic preference parameters, allowing for varying degrees of preference structure and deriving implied probability distributions via Monte Carlo simulation for the demand elasticities. In Section 5.11 we simulate the impacts on vice consumption and tax revenue of a reduction in the price of marijuana, possibly resulting from enhanced cultivation productivity and/or lighter regulation, and changes in tobacco and alcohol taxation. Sections 5.12 and 5.13 consider a scenario involving legalisation and taxation of marijuana, which includes the risk premium associated with marijuana and an analysis of how much revenue can be raised. Throughout the analysis, the role of uncertainty surrounding preference interactions, as well as the uncertainties for data pertaining to marijuana consumption, is highlighted by providing the whole probability distributions of all endogenous variables in a consistent multivariate framework. The material in the next six sections is an extended version of Clements *et al.* (2008).

5.8 A demand system

This section sets out the framework for analysis of the demand for vice within a system of demand equations for four goods: marijuana, tobacco, alcohol and "other". We use a differential approach to consumption theory owing to its generality and elegant simplicity, as well as its transparent link between the structure of preferences and the nature of the demand equations. The differential approach, together with some background material, is set out in detail in Sections A4.3–A4.8 of the Appendix to Chapter 4. We start with a brief overview of the relevant parts of that material.

Let p_i be the price of good i ($i = 1, \ldots, n$) and let q_i be the corresponding quantity demanded. Then $M = \sum_{i=1}^{n} p_i q_i$ is total expenditure on the n goods ("income" for short) and $w_i = p_i q_i / M$ is the share of income devoted to good i, also known as the budget share of i. Furthermore, let $d(\log Q) = \sum_{i=1}^{n} w_i d(\log q_i)$ be the Divisia volume index representing the relative change in the consumer's real income. It follows from the budget constraint that $d(\log Q) = d(\log M) - \sum_{i=1}^{n} w_i d(\log p_i)$, so that the change in real income is the change in money income deflated by the Divisia price index $\sum_{i=1}^{n} w_i \, d \, (\log p_i)$. Under standard assumptions, we can express the demand equation for good i in differential form as:

$$w_i \, d \, (\log q_i) = \theta_i \, d \, (\log Q) + \sum_{j=1}^{n} v_{ij} \left[d \, (\log p_j) - d \, (\log P') \right] \quad (5.5)$$

where the parameter $\theta_i = \partial \, (p_i \, q_i) \, / \partial M$ is the marginal share of good i, which answers the question "if income rises by 1 dollar, what proportion of this increase is spent on good i?". It follows from the budget constraint that $\sum_{i=1}^{n} \theta_i = 1$. The term $v_{ij} = (\lambda \, p_i \, p_j / M) \, u^{ij}$ is the (i, j)th Frisch price coefficient, where u^{ij} is the (i, j)th element of U^{-1}, with $U = \partial^2 u / \partial q \, \partial q'$ the Hessian of the utility function $u(q)$ and $q = [q_i]$ the quantity vector, and $\lambda > 0$ is the marginal utility of income. Finally, $d \, (\log P') = \sum_{i=1}^{n} \theta_i \, d \, (\log p_i)$ is the Frisch price index, which uses as weights marginal shares rather than the budget shares in the Divisia price index. If we divide both sides of equation (5.5) by w_i, we find that $\eta_i = \theta_i / w_i$ is the income elasticity of demand for good i, whereas $\eta'_{ij} = v_{ij} / w_i$ is the (i, j)th Frisch price elasticity, which measures the effect of a Frisch-deflated (or relative) price change in the jth good on the consumption of the ith good when holding the marginal utility of income constant.

We define $v = [v_{ij}]$ as the $n \times n$ matrix of Frisch coefficients. For a budget-constrained utility maximum, v is negative definite. Another property of v is that its row sums are proportional to the corresponding marginal shares,

$$\sum_{j=1}^{n} v_{ij} = \phi \, \theta_i, \qquad i = 1, \ldots, n. \quad (5.6)$$

The proportionality factor $\phi = (\partial \log \lambda / \partial \log M)^{-1} < 0$ is the reciprocal of the income elasticity of the marginal utility of income ("income flexibility" for brevity). It can also be shown that $d(\log \lambda) = (1/\phi) d(\log Q) - d(\log P')$. Using this relationship, equation (5.6) and $d(\log \lambda) = -d(\log \lambda^{-1})$, the demand equation (5.5) can be written in terms of the marginal utility of income as:

$$w_i \, d \, (\log q_i) = \sum_{j=1}^{n} v_{ij} \left[d \, (\log p_j) - d \left(\log \lambda^{-1} \right) \right].$$

This confirms the interpretation of the Frisch price elasticity $\eta'_{ij} = v_{ij}/w_i$ as the effect of a change in the price of good j on the consumption of good i with the marginal utility of income held constant. Following Houthakker (1960), goods i and j are called specific substitutes or complements according to the sign of the Frisch price elasticity η'_{ij}.

As demand equation (5.5) is formulated in terms of deflated prices, the substitution term of that equation contains the jth price twice, once explicitly and once within the Frisch price index. We use $d(\log P') = \sum_{i=1}^{n} \theta_i\, d(\log p_i)$ and equation (5.6) to combine these by rewriting (5.5) as:

$$w_i d(\log q_i) = \theta_i d(\log Q) + \sum_{j=1}^{n} \pi_{ij} d(\log p_j)\,, \qquad (5.7)$$

where $\pi_{ij} = v_{ij} - \phi\,\theta_i\,\theta_j$ is the (i,j)th Slutsky price coefficient. The symmetry and homogeneity conditions imply that $\pi_{ij} = \pi_{ji}$ and $\sum_{j=1}^{n} \pi_{ij} = 0$. The Slutsky coefficient and the corresponding elasticity $\eta_{ij} = \pi_{ij}/w_i$ deal with the impact on consumption of good i of a change in the price of j on account of the total substitution effect, with real income remaining unchanged. Goods are called Slutsky (or Hicksian) substitutes or complements according to the sign of the Slutsky price elasticity. Finally, if we substitute $d(\log Q) = d(\log M) - \sum_{i=1}^{n} w_i\, d(\log p_i)$ in (5.7), we obtain a demand equation that holds money income constant:

$$w_i d(\log q_i) = \theta_i d(\log M) + \sum_{j=1}^{n} \pi^*_{ij} d(\log p_j)\,,$$

where $\pi^*_{ij} = \pi_{ij} - \theta_i w_j$ is the Marshallian price coefficient. The corresponding Marshallian (or uncompensated) elasticity is $\eta^*_{ij} = \pi^*_{ij}/w_i = \eta_{ij} - \eta_i w_j$, which gives the percentage change in the consumption of i following a 1 per cent change in the price of j, holding money income constant.

As the Frisch price coefficients deal with the specific substitution effects that directly relate to the interaction of goods in the utility function, these coefficients offer a convenient way to introduce prior notions of the likely structure of preferences. An example is the case of preference independence (PI), whereby goods do not interact with each other, as utility is additive in the n goods, $u(q_1, ..., q_n) = \sum_{i=1}^{n} u_i(q_i)$, with $u_i(q_i)$ a sub-utility function that depends only on the consumption of good i. In this case, $\partial u/\partial q_i = d u_i/d q_i$, so all second-order cross-derivatives vanish and both the Hessian U and its inverse U^{-1} are diagonal. PI thus implies that all Frisch price coefficients v_{ij} for $i \neq j$ are zero and from equation (5.6), $v_{ii} = \phi \theta_i$. Accordingly, under PI, the demand equation (5.5) simplifies to:

$$w_i \, d(\log q_i) = \theta_i \, d(\log Q) + \phi \, \theta_i \, [d(\log p_i) - d(\log P')],$$

so that all cross-price Frisch elasticities, $\eta'_{ij} = v_{ij}/w_i$ for $i \neq j$, are zero. Further implications of PI are that (i) Frisch own-price elasticities are proportional to the corresponding income elasticities and (ii) inferior goods are ruled out. These implications of PI are restrictive and clearly the hypothesis will not hold in all circumstances.

5.9 Data and parameters

In this section, we set out numerical values of the budget shares and parameters of the demand equations of the previous section, as well as the implied elasticities. With these values, the model can be used to simulate the effects of exogenous changes on interrelated vice markets in an internally consistent manner. The demand model refers to $n=4$ goods, marijuana, tobacco, alcohol and other, and the approach to specifying numerical values is similar to that employed in Section 4.5 with one important difference. The model used in Section 4.5 refers to the demand for beer, wine, spirits and marijuana, conditional on the total volume of alcohol and marijuana consumed being held constant. Accordingly, that was a conditional demand model. However, as we now want to determine how consumption of vice responds to changing levels of taxation, for example, it is no longer appropriate to hold total vice constant; we need to use an unconditional demand model with a residual category for non-vice consumption ("other"). Details of the conditional and unconditional approaches, and their differences, are provided in Sections A4.4–A4.7 of the Appendix to Chapter 4.

Table 5.4   *Baseline data for vice demand*

Commodity (1)	Budget share $w_i \times 100$ (2)	Income elasticity η_i (3)	Marginal share $\theta_i \times 100$ (4)
Marijuana	2.0	1.2	2.4
Tobacco	2.0	0.4	0.8
Alcohol	4.0	1.0	4.0
Other	92.0	1.0087	92.8
Total	100.0		100.0
Income flexibility		$\phi = -0.5$	

Budget shares, income elasticities, marginal shares and income flexibility

Column 2 of Table 5.4 gives the baseline budget shares of the four goods based on household expenditure in Australia in the late 1990s; see Appendix A5.1 for details of the data. These data are subject to more than the usual degree of uncertainty, a feature that is taken into account in the analysis in the next section.

Column 3 of Table 5.4 specifies that the income elasticity of marijuana is 1.2, making it a modest luxury; that of tobacco is 0.4, a necessity; and alcohol is 1.0, a borderline case. The basis for choice of these values is as follows. As there are few, if any, reliable published estimates of η_i for marijuana, there are clearly no suitable approaches other than using the similarities between this good and alcohol. Accordingly, there is some presumption that consumers regard the luxuriousness of these two goods to be similar. As discussed below, we use $\eta_i = 1$ for alcohol, but we have a mild preference to regard marijuana as having a slightly higher η_i and set this elasticity at 1.2; see the discussion in Section 4.5. It must be emphasised, however, that the absence of hard evidence means that we cannot have too much confidence in the precision of this estimate. In contrast to marijuana, there have been a large number of studies published on tobacco demand; for reviews of the literature, see Cameron (1998) and Chaloupka and Warner (2000). A recent meta-analysis of 86 different studies of tobacco consumption by Gallet and List (2003) reports a mean income elasticity of 0.42 and a standard deviation of 0.43. We thus set $\eta_i = 0.4$ for tobacco.

The good "alcohol" comprises beer, wine and spirits as a group. As discussed in Chapter 4, prior studies almost invariably find that the income elasticity for beer is less than 1, and not infrequently of the order of 0.5, indicating that this beverage is regarded as a necessity. As wine and spirits are more luxurious than beer, estimates of their η_i value tend to be substantially greater than 1.[5] With these considerations in mind, we use a budget-share-weighted average to estimate the income elasticity for alcohol, with a value of 0.5 for beer and 1.5 for both wine and spirits. Based on data from the Australian Household Expenditure Surveys, we use 0.50, 0.25 and 0.25 as the shares for beer, wine and spirits, respectively, to obtain income elasticity of 1.0 for alcohol as a whole, which agrees well with direct estimates of this elasticity for Australia obtained by Clements and Johnson (1983) and Clements and Selvanathan (1991).[6] On this basis, we set $\eta_i = 1$ for the aggregated good alcohol. Finally, η_i for the remaining good "other" can be obtained using Engel aggregation $\sum_{i=1}^{4} w_i \eta_i = 1$, which implies its income elasticity is 1.0087. The marginal shares of the four commodities are computed as $\theta_i = w_i \eta_i$ and listed in column 4 of Table 5.4.

The final coefficient to be considered is the elasticity of the marginal utility of income, which in reciprocal form is the income flexibility ϕ. The value of ϕ is specified as -0.5, which is based on the prior findings discussed in Section A4.8 of the Appendix of Chapter 4.

What is known about vice interactions?

Previous empirical evidence from Australia seems to indicate that marijuana, tobacco and alcohol are closely related in consumption. Using unit record data from a large-scale Australian survey (NDSHS, 2001), Zhao and Harris (2004) report significant correlation of individual participation across the three goods. Although micro-level demand studies often suffer from a lack of continuous consumption quantity data and individual-level prices, overall the available Australian studies seem to point to a complementary relationship between marijuana and tobacco, and substitutability between marijuana and alcohol. Previous Australian research tends to indicate that tobacco is a complement for marijuana (Cameron and Williams, 2001; Zhao and Harris, 2004) and marijuana is a substitute for alcohol (see Section 4.7). However, as there is some conflicting evidence on the relationship between marijuana and alcohol consumption, guidance from the literature is not completely clear-cut.

Two aspects of the results of Chapter 4, which also uses Australian data, are worth recalling. First, in Section 4.4 we analysed the correlation pattern for consumption of beer, wine, spirits and marijuana and found some evidence indicating that marijuana is a substitute for each of the three alcoholic beverages.[7] Second, as discussed in Section 4.7, on the basis of his survey of first-year students at The University of Western Australia, Daryal (1999) on balance finds a substitutability relationship between marijuana and alcohol, but we cannot be overly confident of this result.

Results from other countries can be summarised as follows. Four other studies deal with the consumption interrelationship between tobacco and alcohol using UK or US data (Decker and Schwartz, 2000; Duffy, 1991; Goel and Morey, 1995; Jones, 1989). The results are mixed in relation to the sign of the cross-price effect. Regarding marijuana and tobacco consumption in the US, Cameron and Williams (2001) note that on the basis of two previous studies (Chaloupka *et al.*, 1999; Farrelly *et al.*, 1999), the evidence can probably be interpreted as indicating that marijuana and tobacco are complements.

Although not completely unambiguous, previous findings regarding vice interactions can possibly be summarised as follows. Marijuana and tobacco are in all probability complements. Although there is no consensus regarding interactions involving alcohol, there seems to be some evidence suggesting it is more likely to be a substitute for marijuana and tobacco than a complement. In what follows, we model demand interactions across drugs to reflect the above considerations in terms of the pattern of the Frisch price coefficients v_{ij}. In Section 5.10, we recognise the uncertainty of the underlying demand responses by specifying probability distributions for the parameters.

To organise the discussion, we start with the restrictive case of preference independence and then move to a more flexible structure that allows for specific substitutability/complementarity relationships.

First-pass price elasticities: preference independence

As a starting point, we assume that the four goods exhibit PI in the consumer's utility function, so that the price coefficients are $v_{ij} = 0 (i \neq j)$

and there is no specific substitution among goods. Using the data in Table 5.4, Table 5.5 presents the Frisch, Slutsky and Marshallian price elasticities under PI. Several comments can be made. First, for each element of vice, the three versions of the own-price elasticities are quite similar, as shown by the following data:

	Frisch η'_{ij}	Slutsky η_{ij}	Marshallian η^*_{ij}
Marijuana	−0.60	−0.59	−0.61
Tobacco	−0.20	−0.20	−0.21
Alcohol	−0.50	−0.48	−0.52

Second, owing to the substantial income effect, the three values of the own-price elasticity for other goods ($\eta'_{44} = -0.50$, $\eta_{44} = -0.04$ and $\eta^*_{44} = -0.96$) differ considerably. Third, the cross-price elasticities involving vice are all quite small, which is due to (i) the assumption of PI and (ii) the small budget shares of these goods. Finally, under PI, all four goods are Slutsky substitutes and Marshallian complements.

Second-pass price elasticities: preference dependence

Under PI, the 4×4 matrix of price coefficients v has the following structure:

$$
\begin{array}{c}
\\
\text{Marijuana} \\
\text{Tobacco} \\
\text{Alcohol} \\
\text{Other}
\end{array}
\begin{array}{cccc}
M & T & A & O \\
\left[\begin{array}{cccc}
\phi\theta_1 & 0 & 0 & 0 \\
0 & \phi\theta_2 & 0 & 0 \\
0 & 0 & \phi\theta_3 & 0 \\
0 & 0 & 0 & \phi\theta_4
\end{array}\right]
\end{array}
\begin{array}{c}
\text{Row sum} \\
\phi\theta_1 \\
\phi\theta_2 \\
\phi\theta_3 \\
\phi\theta_4
\end{array}
$$

We now generalise this structure by allowing marijuana and tobacco to be specific complements, so that v_{12} becomes negative. We thus now set $v_{12} = \alpha < 0$, but additionally, in view of the symmetry of v and the row-sum constraints (5.6), the values of many of the other previously non-zero elements of the matrix must change. In what follows, we discuss in turn each of the four rows of v.

Table 5.5 *First specification of baseline price responsiveness of demand: ρ = 0 (preference independence)*

Good	A. Price coefficient $\mathbf{v}$ ($\times 10^2$)				B. Inverse price coefficient $\mathbf{v}^{-1}$ ($\times 10^{-1}$)				C. Frisch price elasticity $[\eta'_{ij}]$			
	Marijuana	Tobacco	Alcohol	Other	Marijuana	Tobacco	Alcohol	Other	Marijuana	Tobacco	Alcohol	Other
Marijuana	−1.20	0	0	0	−8.33	0	0	0	−0.60	0	0	0
Tobacco	0	−0.40	0	0	0	−2.5	0	0	0	−0.20	0	0
Alcohol	0	0	−2.00	0	0	0	−5	0	0	0	−0.50	0
Other	0	0	0	−46.40	0	0	0	−0.22	0	0	0	−0.50

Good	D. Slutsky coefficient $[\pi_{ij}]$ ($\times 10^2$)				E. Slutsky price elasticity $[\eta_{ij}]$				F. Marshallian price elasticity $[\eta^*_{ij}]$			
	Marijuana	Tobacco	Alcohol	Other	Marijuana	Tobacco	Alcohol	Other	Marijuana	Tobacco	Alcohol	Other
Marijuana	−1.17	0.01	0.05	1.11	−0.586	0.005	0.024	0.557	−0.610	−0.019	−0.024	−0.547
Tobacco	0.01	−0.40	0.02	0.37	0.005	−0.198	0.008	0.186	−0.003	−0.206	−0.008	−0.182
Alcohol	0.05	0.02	−1.92	1.86	0.012	0.004	−0.480	0.464	−0.008	−0.016	−0.520	−0.456
Other	1.11	0.37	1.86	−3.34	0.012	0.004	0.020	−0.036	−0.008	−0.016	−0.020	−0.964

The marijuana row: The elements of the first row of $\mathbf{v}$, v_{11}, v_{12}, v_{13}, v_{14}, refer to the responsiveness of marijuana consumption to changes in the four relative prices. Under (i) PI and (ii) the proposed new preference dependence (PD) structure, this row takes the form:

$$
\begin{array}{ccccccc}
 & \text{M} & \text{T} & \text{A} & \text{O} & \text{Row sum} \\
\text{PI} & [\phi\theta_1 & 0 & 0 & 0] & \phi\theta_1 \\
\text{PD} & [\phi\theta_1 & \alpha & -\alpha & 0] & \phi\theta_1
\end{array}
$$

For PD, we have enforced the row-sum constraint by setting $v_{13} = -\alpha$ and leaving v_{11} and v_{14} unchanged. This means that marijuana and alcohol are taken to be specific substitutes, whereas marijuana and other continue to be independent, which is reasonable considering the aggregated nature of the fourth good.

The tobacco row: Under the two specifications, the second row of $\mathbf{v}$ takes the following form:

$$
\begin{array}{ccccccc}
 & \text{M} & \text{T} & \text{A} & \text{O} & \text{Row sum} \\
\text{PI} & [0 & \phi\theta_2 & 0 & 0] & \phi\theta_2 \\
\text{PD} & [\alpha & \phi\theta_2 & -\alpha & 0] & \phi\theta_2
\end{array}
$$

As $\mathbf{v}$ is a symmetric matrix, $v_{21} = v_{12}$, which implies that under PD $v_{21} = \alpha$. In other words, if marijuana and tobacco are specific substitutes, then so also are tobacco and marijuana. We use the same approach as above in dealing with the row-sum constraint by setting $v_{13} = -\alpha$, so that tobacco and alcohol are specific substitutes. As we have no strong priors, we take tobacco and other to be independent.

The alcohol row: the third row of $\mathbf{v}$ is:

$$
\begin{array}{ccccccc}
 & \text{M} & \text{T} & \text{A} & \text{O} & \text{Row sum} \\
\text{PI} & [0 & 0 & \phi\theta_3 & 0] & \phi\theta_3 \\
\text{PD} & [-\alpha & -\alpha & \phi\theta_3 + 2\alpha & 0] & \phi\theta_3
\end{array}
$$

Under PD, the elements v_{31} and v_{32} are both equal to $-\alpha$ owing to symmetry. As before, we take alcohol and other to be independent, so that $v_{34} = 0$. The constraint on the sum of the elements in the alcohol row under PD then implies that $v_{33} = \phi\theta_3 + 2\alpha$.

The other row: Finally, the fourth row of v is:

	M	T	A	O	Row sum
PI	[0	0	0	$\phi\theta_4$]	$\phi\theta_4$
PD	[0	0	0	$\phi\theta_4$]	$\phi\theta_4$

By symmetry, the first three elements of this row are determined by the last elements in each of the first three rows. Accordingly, these elements are all zero under PI and PD, so that the row for other is the same under the two specifications.

Combining the above four rows, the new v matrix is:

$$
\begin{array}{l}
\text{Marijuana} \\
\text{Tobacco} \\
\text{Alcohol} \\
\text{Other}
\end{array}
\begin{array}{ccccc}
M & T & A & O & \text{Row sum} \\
\phi\theta_1 & \alpha & -\alpha & 0 & \phi\theta_1 \\
\alpha & \phi\theta_2 & -\alpha & 0 & \phi\theta_2 \\
-\alpha & -\alpha & \phi\theta_3 + 2\alpha & 0 & \phi\theta_3 \\
0 & 0 & 0 & \phi\theta_4 & \phi\theta_4
\end{array}
\qquad (5.8)
$$

This matrix is symmetric and satisfies the row-sum constraints. What value should the negative parameter α take? An increase in the tobacco price reduces consumption of tobacco and, as marijuana and tobacco are complements, also reduces marijuana consumption. Similarly, an increase in marijuana prices causes the consumption of both marijuana and tobacco to decrease. As the parameter α represents the degree of complementarity between marijuana and tobacco, it would seem not unreasonable for α to be higher (in absolute value) for higher own-price responsiveness of both marijuana and tobacco, as measured by $\phi\theta_1$ and $\phi\theta_2$. One way to implement this idea is to take α to be some proportion of the mean of $\phi\theta_1$ and $\phi\theta_2$, so that if we use the geometric mean, we have:

$$
\alpha = \rho |\phi| \sqrt{\theta_1 \theta_2}, \qquad -1 < \rho < 0 \qquad (5.9)
$$

Since the price coefficients are $v_{ij} = (\lambda p_i p_j / M) u^{ij}$, the inverse of the 4×4 matrix of all such coefficients, v^{-1}, is proportional to the inverse of the Hessian matrix of the utility function in expenditure terms. Thus, to analyse the implications of matrix (5.8) for the structure of the utility function, we need its inverse. Although this inverse is available, its form is complex. Some insights are available, however, if we follow Barten (1964) and use an approximation to the inverse. We can express $\mathbf{v} = [v_{ij}]$ as $\mathbf{v} = -\mathbf{D}(\mathbf{I} + \mathbf{\Gamma})\mathbf{D}$, where $\mathbf{D} = \mathrm{diag}[-v_{ii}^{1/2}]$, and $\mathbf{\Gamma} = [\gamma_{ij}]$, is a symmetric 4×4 matrix with diagonal elements zero. This means that the (i, j)th off-diagonal element of $\mathbf{v}$ takes the form $v_{ij} = \gamma_{ij}\sqrt{v_{ii}v_{jj}}$. Thus, as $v_{12} = \alpha$, equation (5.9) implies that $\gamma_{12} = \rho$. If the elements of $\mathbf{\Gamma}$ are not "too large", then $\mathbf{v}^{-1} \approx -\mathbf{D}^{-1}(\mathbf{I} - \mathbf{\Gamma})\mathbf{D}^{-1}$, so that $v^{ii} \approx 1/v_{ii}$ and $v^{12} \approx -\rho/|\phi|\sqrt{\theta_1\theta_2} > 0$. As $v^{12} \propto \partial^2 u/\partial(p_1 q_1)\,\partial(p_2 q_2)$, it is evident that additional spending on tobacco $(i = 2)$ increases the marginal utility of expenditure on marijuana $(i = 1)$. Note also that $v^{12} \approx -\rho\sqrt{v^{11} v^{22}} \approx -\rho/\sqrt{v_{11} v_{22}}$. Accordingly, $-\rho \approx v^{12}/\sqrt{v^{11} v^{22}}$ is now interpreted as a type of correlation coefficient for the relevant elements of $\mathbf{v}^{-1}$, so its value determines the degree of complementarity between marijuana and tobacco, where complementarity is understood to refer here to interaction in the utility function.

As it is difficult to obtain a strong prior idea of the precise degree of complementarity, and since $-1 < \rho < 0$, we focus on the case in which $\rho = -0.5$, a value mid-way between the two extremes. Using the data given in Table 5.4, Table 5.6 contains the price elasticities corresponding to $\rho = -0.5$; it is evident that cross-elasticities involving vice are now greater in absolute value than those of Table 5.5. Next, in Figure 5.7 we explore the implication of differing values of ρ for the elasticity of demand for marijuana with respect to the price of tobacco. The Frisch version of this elasticity takes the form $\eta'_{12} = v_{12}/w_1 = \rho|\phi|\sqrt{\theta_1\theta_2}/w_1$. If we invert the scales on both the vertical and horizontal axes, the plot of this elasticity against ρ is a ray emanating from the origin, as shown in Figure 5.7. The corresponding Slutsky elasticity is $\eta_{12} = \eta'_{12} - \phi\,\theta_1\theta_2/w_1$, a plot of which is parallel to the Frisch plot, with vertical intercept equal to the general substitution effect $-\phi\,\theta_1\theta_2/w_1 = 0.5 \times 0.024 \times 0.008/0.02 = 0.0048$, which is very small. Finally, the Marshallian elasticity is $\eta^*_{12} = \eta_{12} - \eta_1 w_2$, which differs from the Slutsky elasticity by the income effect of the price change, $-\eta_1 w_2 = -1.2 \times 0.02 = -0.024$,

Table 5.6: *Second specification of baseline price responsiveness of demand:* $\rho = -0.5$ *(preference dependence)*

Good	Marijuana	Tobacco	Alcohol	Other	Marijuana	Tobacco	Alcohol	Other	Marijuana	Tobacco	Alcohol	Other
	A. Price coefficient ν ($\times 10^2$)				B. Inverse price coefficient ν^{-1} ($\times 10^{-1}$)				C. Frisch price elasticity [$\acute{\eta}_{ij}$]			
Marijuana	−1.20	−0.35	0.35	0	−11.12	9.45	−0.22	0	−0.60	−0.17	0.17	0
Tobacco	−0.35	−0.40	0.35	0	9.45	−36.16	−3.44	0	−0.17	−0.20	0.17	0
Alcohol	0.35	0.35	−2.69	0	−0.22	−3.44	−4.18	0	0.09	0.09	−0.67	0
Other	0	0	0	−46.40	0	0	0	−0.22	0	0	0	−0.50

Good	Marijuana	Tobacco	Alcohol	Other	Marijuana	Tobacco	Alcohol	Other	Marijuana	Tobacco	Alcohol	Other
	D. Slutsky coefficient [π_{ij}] ($\times 10^2$)				E. Slutsky price elasticity [η_{ij}]				F. Marshallian price elasticity [η^*_{ij}]			
Marijuana	−1.17	−0.34	0.39	1.11	−0.586	−0.168	0.197	0.557	−0.610	−0.192	0.149	−0.547
Tobacco	−0.34	−0.40	0.36	0.37	−0.168	−0.198	0.181	0.186	−0.176	−0.206	0.165	−0.182
Alcohol	0.39	0.36	−2.61	1.86	0.099	0.091	−0.653	0.464	−0.079	0.071	−.0693	−0.456
Other	1.11	0.37	1.86	−3.34	0.012	0.004	0.020	−0.036	−0.008	−0.016	−0.020	−0.964

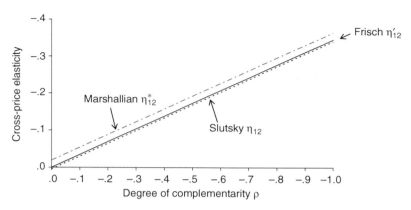

Figure 5.7. Price elasticities of demand for marijuana with respect to the price of tobacco and the degree of complementarity

and is thus the "top" curve in the figure. The main feature of the figure is that the three cross-elasticities all increase in absolute value at approximately half the rate of increase in ρ.

5.10 Stochastic vice

The above price elasticities are consistent with what is known about the demand for vice. Since such knowledge is highly imperfect, in this section we introduce a simulation approach to formally quantify the uncertainty regarding the structure of preferences. This approach involves describing uncertainty with subjective probability distributions of the budget shares and the basic demand parameters based on available prior information such as economic theory, published econometric estimates and our own judgement. The implied probability distributions for the elasticities, which are non-linear functions of the budget shares and parameters, are then obtained through Monte Carlo simulation. These uncertainties in both the data and parameters can then be translated to probability statements regarding the own- and cross-industry impacts in policy analysis. An advantage of the approach is that inequality constraints required by economic theory or subjective beliefs can be imposed easily through simulation.[8]

The basic parameters for the simulation are the four budget and marginal shares (w_i and θ_i), the income flexibility (ϕ) and the correlation ρ. Each of these follows a truncated normal distribution with mode (equivalent to the mean before truncation) given by the base values specified in Section 5.9 and a specified standard deviation. Regarding budget shares, for marijuana the mean of the distribution is 2 per cent and we take the 95 per cent confidence interval to be 1–3 per cent, which, on the basis of normality, implies a standard deviation of 0.5 per cent and coefficient of variation (CV) of $0.5/2 = 25$. Furthermore, we restrict the range of this share by truncation of the normal distribution such that $0 < w_1 < 1$. This information is contained in the first row of Table 5.7. As consumption of tobacco and alcohol is legal, it is reasonable to suppose that there is less uncertainty about their budget shares and we take their CV to be 12.5 per cent, which is half the value for marijuana, as indicated in rows 2 and 3 of column 4 in Table 5.7. We also restrict these shares to the interval $(0, 1)$. As $\sum_{i=1}^{4} w_i = 1$, all the information on distribution of the budget share of the fourth good, "other", can be derived from those pertaining to the first three (row 4 of Table 5.7).

Owing to the unobservable nature of the marginal shares, it is not unreasonable to suppose that their values are more uncertain than those of the budget shares. The CV of θ_i for marijuana is taken to be 50 per cent, whereas that for tobacco and alcohol is taken to be 25 per cent. Here again we use the rule that information for marijuana is twice as uncertain as that for the other two goods. Each θ_i is also constrained to the interval $(0, 1)$ and the four shares have a unit sum. The most likely value for ϕ is -0.5, restricted to the interval $(-\infty, 0)$, and the CV specified as 25 per cent. As there is considerably more uncertainty regarding the value of ρ, we take its CV to be 50 per cent, with a mode of -0.5 and its value restricted to the interval $(-\infty, 0)$. The above information is recorded in rows 5–10 of Table 5.7. Finally, the Frisch matrix $\mathbf{v}$ is restricted to be negative definite, and the distributions for its elements are derived from the above, as indicated in the bottom part of Table 5.7.

To simulate the uncertainty of the data and parameters, we draw 5,000 independent sets of repeated realisations from the eight distributions specified above: three for w_i (the fourth is determined by $\sum_{i=1}^{4} w_i = 1$), three for θ_i (the fourth is again given by $\sum_{i=1}^{4} \theta_i = 1$),

Table 5.7: *Stochastic specification of data and demand coefficients*

Variable/parameter (1)	Mean (2)	Standard deviation (3)	Coefficient of variation (4)	95 percent probability interval (5)	Constraint (6)
Budget share w_i					
1. Marijuana	0.02	0.005	0.25	(0.0114, 0.0283)	$0<w_1<1$
2. Tobacco	0.02	0.0025	0.125	(0.0157, 0.0242)	$0<w_2<1$
3. Alcohol	0.04	0.005	0.125	(0.0316, 0.0483)	$0<w_3<1$
4. Other	0.92	0.0075	0.008	(0.9075, 0.9333)	$0<w_4<1,$ $w_4=1-\sum_{i=1}^3 w_i$
Sum	1.00				
Income flexibility					
5. ϕ	−0.5	0.125	0.25	(−0.7384, −0.2501)	$\phi<0$
Correlation coefficient					
6. ρ	−0.5	0.25	0.50	(−0.9150, −0.0843)	$-1<\rho<0$
Marginal share θ_i					
7. Marijuana	0.024	0.012	0.5	(0.0038, 0.0482)	$0<\theta_1<1$
8. Tobacco	0.008	0.002	0.25	(0.00413, 0.01197)	$0<\theta_2<1$
9. Alcohol	0.04	0.01	0.25	(0.0205, 0.0590)	$0<\theta_3<1$

Table 5.7: *(continued)*

Variable/parameter (1)	Mean (2)	Standard deviation (3)	Coefficient of variation (4)	95 percent probability interval (5)	Constraint (6)
10. Other	0.928	0.016	0.017	(0.8969, 0.9565)	$0 < \theta_4 < 1$, $\theta_4 = 1 - \sum_{i=1}^{3} \theta_i$

Frisch price coefficient matrix v

$$\begin{bmatrix} \phi\theta_1 & \alpha & -\alpha & 0 \\ \alpha & \phi\theta_2 & -\alpha & 0 \\ -\alpha & -\alpha & \phi\theta_3 + 2\alpha & 0 \\ 0 & 0 & 0 & \phi\theta_4 \end{bmatrix}$$

v negative definite

Note: The summary statistics refer to the analytical results for the non-truncated normal distributions.

one for ϕ and one for ρ. If any of the constraints of Table 5.7 are violated, the draw is discarded. The procedure is repeated until there are 5,000 sets that satisfy all the constraints. We then estimate the implied subjective probability distributions for all elasticities using frequency distributions. For example, in Figure 5.8, the estimated probability density functions are plotted for the four Marshallian price elasticities for marijuana, as well as the income elasticity for this good. It is evident that these distributions exhibit varying degrees of asymmetry. The estimated means, standard deviations and 95 per cent probability intervals for all elasticities are given in Table 5.8. In all cases, the dispersion is larger for the marijuana rows, reflecting the greater uncertainties associated with this product.

5.11 Simulating exogenous changes

In this section, we apply the above methodology to two counter-factual changes, (i) a fall in marijuana prices and (ii) an increase in tobacco and alcohol taxation. We abstract from the supply side by assuming infinitely elastic supply schedules, so that all tax changes are fully passed onto consumers.[9] Table 5.9 gives the basic information on pre-existing taxation and consumption in Australia that is used subsequently. It is evident that tax accounts for approximately 54 per cent of the consumer price of tobacco and 41 per cent of that of alcohol.

A decrease in marijuana prices

Suppose marijuana prices were to decrease by 10 per cent due to productivity enhancement and/or a reduced policing effort.[10] When money income remains unchanged, the change in consumption of good i as a result of a change in the price of good j is given by:

$$d(\log q_i) = \eta_{ij}^* \, d(\log p_j), \qquad (5.10)$$

where η_{ij}^* is the (i, j)th Marshallian price elasticity.[11] To implement this for a 10 per cent decrease in marijuana prices, we set $j = 1$ and $d(\log p_1) = -0.1$ on the right-hand side of equation (5.10) to estimate the change in consumption of marijuana, alcohol and tobacco ($i = 1, 2$ and 3). Allowing for the uncertainty involved in η_{i1}^*, we use the previous

Table 5.8: *Summary of demand elasticities*

Good	Price			
	Marijuana	Tobacco	Alcohol	Other
	A. Frisch price elasticity $[\eta'_{ij}]$			
Marijuana	−0.66 (0.41)	−0.18 (0.13)	.18 (0.13)	0 (0)
	[−1.71, −0.09]	[−0.49, −0.01]	[0.01, 0.49]	[0, 0]
Tobacco	−0.17 (0.10)	−0.20 (0.08)	.17 (0.10)	0 (0)
	[−0.42, −0.01]	[−0.38, −0.08]	[0.01, 0.42]	[0, 0]
Alcohol	0.08 (0.05)	.08 (0.05)	−0.68 (0.25)	0 (0)
	[0.01, 0.21]	[0.01, 0.21]	[−1.25, −0.27]	[0, 0]
Other	0 (0)	0 (0)	0 (0)	−0.50 (0.13)
	[0, 0]	[0, 0]	[0, 0]	[−0.75, −0.26]
	B. Slutsky price elasticity $[\eta_{ij}]$			
Marijuana	−0.641 (0.393)	−0.171 (0.125)	0.203 (0.140)	0.609 (0.373)
	[−1.633, −0.089]	[−0.478, −0.012]	[0.024, 0.548]	[0.084, 1.552]
Tobacco	−0.162 (0.102)	−0.201 (0.077)	0.175 (0.106)	0.188 (0.072)
	[−0.408, −0.012]	[−0.377, −0.077]	[0.020, 0.431]	[0.072, 0.355]
Alcohol	0.096 (0.057)	0.088 (0.053)	−0.654 (0.240)	0.470 (0.176)
	[0.013, 0.233]	[0.010, 0.213]	[−1.204, −0.266]	[0.190, 0.875]
Other	0.012 (0.006)	0.004 (0.001)	0.020 (0.007)	−0.037 (0.012)
	[0.002, 0.027]	[0.002, 0.007]	[0.008, 0.035]	[−0.062, −0.017]

C. Marshallian price elasticity $[\eta^*_{ij}]$

Marijuana	-0.648 (0.385)	-0.196 (0.124)	0.150 (0.117)	-0.593 (0.362)
	[-1.570, -0.087]	[-0.502, -0.030]	[-0.007, 0.431]	[-1.472, -0.071]
Tobacco	-0.171 (0.103)	-0.207 (0.076)	0.160 (0.105)	-0.186 (0.072)
	[-0.410, -0.022]	[-0.379, -0.083]	[0.008, 0.405]	[-0.343, -0.068]
Alcohol	0.076 (0.056)	0.068 (0.053)	-0.691 (0.239)	-0.466 (0.181)
	[-0.006, 0.209]	[-0.008, 0.194]	[-1.218, -0.287]	[-0.863, -0.172]
Other	-0.008 (0.008)	-0.016 (0.003)	-0.020 (0.009)	-0.964 (0.012)
	[-0.023, 0.009]	[-0.021, -0.011]	[-0.036, -0.003]	[-0.985, -0.937]

D. Income elasticity $[\eta_i]$

Marijuana	1.286 (0.688)
	[0.186, 2.879]
Tobacco	0.404 (0.112)
	[0.196, 0.628]
Alcohol	1.014 (0.277)
	[0.496, 1.579]
Other	1.008 (0.018)
	[0.973, 1.044]

Note: Results are presented as the mean over 5,000 trials with the standard deviation in parentheses and the 95 per cent probability interval in brackets.

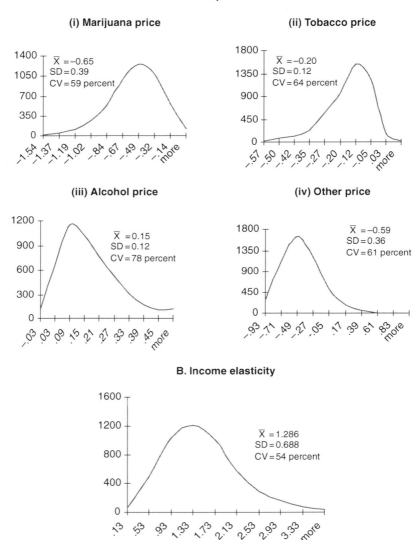

Figure 5.8. Simulated demand elasticities for marijuana
Note: Panel A shows distributions of the price elasticity of demand for marijuana with respect to the price of (i) marijuana, (ii) tobacco, (iii) alcohol and (iv) other.

Table 5.9: *Taxation and consumption of vice*

Variable (1)	Marijuana (2)	Tobacco (3)	Alcohol (4)	Total (5)
Consumption expenditure (dollars per capita)	372	597	879	1848
Tax rate (percent of consumer price)	0	54.3	41.0	—
Tax revenue (dollars per capita)	0	324	360	684

Notes:

1. Consumption expenditure is for 1998. See Appendix A5.1 for details.
2. The tax rate for tobacco is derived from excise and customs revenue published by the Australian Institute of Health and Welfare in Statistics on Drug Use in Australia 2002, Tables 2.5 and 2.6, as well as consumption data from the Australian Bureau of Statistics Cat. No. 5206.0.
3. The tax rate for alcohol is derived from Selvanathan and Selvanathan (2005) as follows. In their Table 11.12 (p. 319), the Selvanathans report for Australia the following taxes (as percentages of consumer prices): beer, 43 percent; wine, 23 percent; and spirits, 55 percent. The corresponding conditional budget shares ($\times 100$), from Clements and Daryal (2005, Panel B of Table A1), are 55, 23 and 22, respectively. Thus a budget-share weighted average tax rate for alcohol as a whole is $0.55 \times 43 + 0.23 \times 23 + 0.22 \times 55 = 41$ percent, as reported in row 2 of column 4 above.
4. Tax revenue is the product of the corresponding tax rate and consumption expenditure.
5. Population, used to convert to per capita, refers to those aged 14 years and over.

5,000 simulated values of this elasticity to generate 5,000 values of $d(\log q_i)$. In column 2 of Panel A in Table 5.10, we present the mean, standard deviation and 95 per cent probability interval for the relative quantity changes for the three goods. As indicated by the 95 per cent probability intervals, there is considerable uncertainty in these quantity changes.

What happens to revenue from taxation as a result of the decrease in the price of marijuana? Although there is no direct effect because marijuana is outside the tax net, there are indirect effects on tobacco and alcohol taxes. Because marijuana and tobacco are complements, the decrease in the price of marijuana stimulates tobacco consumption and thus increases its tax revenue. Offsetting this is the lower

Table 5.10: *Simulations of vice consumption and taxation revenue*

		Exogenous change				
	10 per cent fall in marijuana prices	10 per centage point increase in tax rate		10 percent increase in tax rate		
		Tobacco	Alcohol	Tobacco	Alcohol	
Endogenous variable		$100\times\Delta t'_2 = 10$ $100\times\frac{\Delta t'_2}{t'_2} = 8.4$	$100\times\Delta t'_3 = 10$ $100\times\frac{\Delta t'_3}{t'_3} = 14.4$	$100\times\Delta t'_2 = 11.9$ $100\times\frac{\Delta t'_2}{t'_2} = 10$	$100\times\Delta t'_3 = 7.0$ $100\times\frac{\Delta t'_3}{t'_3} = 10$	
(1)	(2)	(3)	(4)	(5)	(6)	
A. Quantity consumed (logarithmic change ×100)						
1. Marijuana	7.01 (4.11) [1.20, 17.39]	−0.89 (0.57) [−2.30, −0.16]	0.91 (0.82) [−0.14, 2.95]	−1.06 (0.68) [−2.73, −0.19]	0.64 (0.57) [−0.10, 2.07]	
2. Tobacco	1.79 (1.08) [0.20, 4.37]	−0.95 (0.35) [−1.76, −0.39]	0.93 (0.62) [0.02, 2.44]	−1.14 (0.42) [−2.09, −0.47]	0.65 (0.43) [0.02, 1.71]	
3. Alcohol	−0.8 (0.6) [−2.24, 0.09]	0.31 (0.24) [−0.04, 0.88]	−4.08 (1.4) [−7.31, −1.81]	0.37 (0.29) [−0.05, 1.05]	−2.86 (0.98) [−5.12, −1.27]	
B. Taxation revenue (logarithmic change ×100)						
4. Tobacco	1.79 (1.08) [0.20, 4.37]	7.46 (0.35) [6.65, 8.02]	0.93 (0.62) [0.02, 2.44]	8.87 (0.42) [7.91, 9.54]	0.65 (0.43) [0.02, 1.71]	
5. Alcohol	−0.8 (0.6) [−2.24, 0.09]	0.31 (0.24) [−0.04, 0.88]	10.2 (1.4) [6.98, 12.48]	0.37 (0.29) [−0.05, 1.05]	7.14 (0.98) [4.88, 8.73]	
6. Total	0.41 (0.24) [0.07, 1.01]	3.67 (0.16) [3.31, 3.93]	5.85 (0.6) [4.48, 6.79]	4.36 (0.19) [3.93, 4.68]	4.09 (0.42) [3.14, 4.76]	

C. Taxation revenue ($m)

7. Tobacco	87 (52)	362 (17)	45 (30)	431 (20)	32 (21)
	[10, 212]	[323, 390]	[1, 119]	[385, 464]	[1, 83]
8. Alcohol	−43 (32)	17 (13)	551 (76)	20 (16)	386 (53)
	[−121, 5]	[−2, 48]	[377, 674]	[−3, 57]	[264, 472]
9. Total	44 (26)	379 (16)	596 (61)	451 (19)	417 (43)
	[7, 105]	[342, 406]	[458, 693]	[406, 483]	[442, 462]

Note: Results are presented as the mean over 5,000 trials, with the standard deviation in parentheses and the 95 per cent probability interval in brackets.

tax revenue from alcohol, the consumption of which decreases because it is a substitute for marijuana. Assuming that prices and tax rates are unchanged for the two legal goods, the relative change in tax revenue is equal to the relative change in quantity, or $d(\log R_i) = d(\log q_i)$, where R_i denotes the tax revenue for good i ($i = 2,3$). Results for the relative tax revenue changes are given in column 2 of Panel B of Table 5.10. Using the base tax revenues given in Table 5.9 and the Australian population of 15 million (aged 14 years and over), these data translate into an average annual tax revenue change of $87 million for tobacco and $-\$43$ million for alcohol, resulting in a net tax increase of $44 million (column 2 of Panel C, Table 5.10). Accounting for all uncertainty involved in both data and elasticities, the 95 per cent probability interval for the change in total tax revenue is $7–105 million, which is obviously rather wide and reflects the genuine uncertainty surrounding marijuana.

An increase in tobacco and alcohol taxes

Next, consider the effect of a 10 percentage point increase in the taxes on tobacco and alcohol. For tobacco (alcohol), a tax of 54 per cent (41 per cent) on consumer prices implies a tax of 119 per cent (69 per cent) on pre-tax prices, so that a 10 percentage point increase in the latter rate brings the rate to 129 per cent (79 per cent). This increase amounts to a 4.6 per cent (5.9 per cent) relative change in the retail price of tobacco (alcohol).[12] Using equation (5.10) with $d(\log p_2) = 0.046$ and $d(\log p_3) = 0.059$ separately, we can estimate the resulting relative changes in the quantities demanded for all three goods. Again accounting for the uncertainty in the data and the demand parameters, we use the 5,000 sets of elasticities to compute 5,000 sets of relative quantity changes. The mean, standard deviation and 95 per cent probability interval are presented in columns 3 and 4 of Panel A in Table 5.10. For example, a 10 percentage point increase in the alcohol tax rate is estimated to decrease alcohol consumption by 4.1 per cent on average, but to increase marijuana and tobacco consumption by 0.91 and 0.93 per cent, respectively.

The change in taxation revenue from good i is $d(\log R_i) = d(\log t_i') + d(\log q_i)$, where t_i' is tax as a proportion of the pre-tax price. For a 10 percentage point increase in the tobacco tax rate, we have $d(\log t_2') = dt_2'/t_2' \approx 0.1/1.19$, so that $d(\log R_2) = 0.1/1.19 + \eta_{22}^*(0.046)$ is the direct revenue change, and $d(\log R_3) = \eta_{32}^*(0.046)$ is the indirect effect due to the impact of a higher tobacco price on drinking. Similarly, for a 10 percentage point rise in the alcohol tax rate, $d(\log R_2) = \eta_{23}^*(0.059)$ and $d(\log R_3) = 0.1/0.69 + \eta_{33}^*(0.059)$. The mean, standard deviation and 95 per cent probability interval for the annual tax revenue changes (in relative and dollar terms) are given in columns 3 and 4 of Panels B and C of Table 5.10. For example, an increase in alcohol tax causes annual alcohol tax revenue to increase by $551 million on average and tobacco tax revenue to increase by approximately $45 million, resulting in a total annual tax increase of $596 million. The 95 per cent probability interval for this total increase is $458–693 million, which is moderately wide but not huge.

As the base tax rates for tobacco and alcohol differ, a 10 percentage point increase implies a differential change in the tax rates. The two tax increases can be put on a more equal footing by increasing each of the rates by 10 per cent, as shown in columns 5 and 6 of Table 5.10. The major difference is that the mean increase in total tax revenue from tobacco is now approximately the same as that for alcohol, at approximately 4 per cent (row 6, columns 5 and 6).

5.12 Taxing marijuana

If marijuana were legalised and taxed, the new market price would crucially depend on the tax rate the government imposes. If marijuana were legalised and no tax were imposed, its price would fall. This is because producers would no longer have to incur the costs of circumventing the ban, including expenditure to avoid prosecution, the expected cost of being prosecuted and the "inefficiency" cost owing to the difficulty in adopting industrial-scale production techniques. Such "non-production" costs represent the "risk premium" of operating an illegal business. In other words, the supply curve under the current illicit regime is the sum of production costs and the risk premium for dealers. Once marijuana is legal, the risk premium disappears and it is the tax rate that separates producer and consumer prices. To simplify the analysis, we assume that the per unit production cost remains unchanged, so that the marijuana supply curve is perfectly elastic and its price is completely determined by production costs and the tax rate. This permits us to focus on consumer responses in the context of our demand system for marijuana, tobacco and alcohol.

We also assume that the marijuana demand curve will not shift due to legalisation. Although some may increase their consumption once marijuana is legal, others may reduce consumption when it ceases to be a "forbidden fruit", so the demand curve could shift either upwards or downwards. However, as shown in the analysis below, any such shift is likely to be small in magnitude in comparison to the impact of the very high tax rate likely to be imposed, so ignoring the demand shift is not likely to affect the results to any great extent.[13]

We consider two situations denoted by $\tau = 0$ and $\tau = 1$ for before and after the change in taxation arrangements. Total tax revenue from marijuana, tobacco and alcohol in period τ is given by $R^{(\tau)} = \sum_{i=1}^{3} R_i^{(\tau)}$, where $R_i^{(\tau)} = t_i^{\prime(\tau)} p_i^{\prime} q_i^{(\tau)}$ is tax revenue from good i in τ, $t_i^{\prime(\tau)}$ is the tax rate on i in τ, $p_i^{\prime}$ is its pre-tax price determined by production costs (assumed to be constant throughout), and $q_i^{(\tau)}$ is the corresponding quantity consumed. Marijuana is initially not taxed, so that $t_1^{\prime(0)} = 0$, whereas after legalisation it is taxed at rate $t_1^{\prime(1)} > 0$. The taxes on tobacco and alcohol remain unchanged, so that $t_i^{\prime(0)} = t_i^{\prime(1)}$, $i = 2, 3$. In what follows, we discuss how the price of marijuana changes with legalisation and the changes in consumption and tax collections. We then present measures of the degree of uncertainty for the findings and compare our results with those of other studies.

Risk, taxes and marijuana pricing

If marijuana were legalised and nothing else changed it is likely that its price would fall as producers no longer would have to incur the costs of circumventing the ban. In this subsection, we develop this idea by formulating the marijuana "risk premium".

It is assumed that two types of cost are incurred in producing marijuana:

- First, there are costs associated with the basic horticultural nature of the product, together with the distribution costs that would be incurred if marijuana were legal. We denote these costs, on a per unit basis, by p'_1, which is taken to be constant.
- The second type of cost relates to expenditure to avoid prosecution, including concealment activities, the payment of bribes and the costs of violence, both actual and threatened. As there would be some possibility that concealment and bribing would be less than completely successful, the expected cost of being prosecuted is also included in this second type of cost. As the illicit status of marijuana could inhibit the adoption of industrial-scale production techniques, this category of cost could also include an "inefficiency" component that keeps unit costs above what could be achieved on legalisation. These "non-production" costs can be thought of as representing the "risk premium" of operating an illegal business; this risk premium represents the additional cost imposed on the industry by the ban. It is convenient to express the per unit risk premium as $\delta p'_1$, where δ is the proportional premium.

The total cost per unit is thus $(1 + \delta)p'_1$, which, if the market is competitive, will also be the consumer price. We thus write the consumer price as $p_1^{(0)} = (1 + \delta)p'_1$.

To summarise, p'_1 is the equivalent production cost if marijuana were legal and the risk premium $\delta p'_1$ is the additional cost incurred on account of its illicit nature. Thus, if, for example, in the illegal regime the risk premium were 200 per cent, then $\delta = 2$ and the price to consumers would be three times the production costs, that is, $p_1 = 3 \times p'_1$. When marijuana is legalised, the risk premium falls to $\delta = 0$, the production cost p'_1 remains unchanged, the product is taxed at rate $t'^{(1)}_1 > 0$ and the consumer price is $p_1^{(1)} = \left(1 + t'^{(1)}_1\right)p'_1$. Marijuana pricing in the two regimes can be expressed as:

$$\text{Illegal}: p_1^{(0)} = (1 + \delta)p'_1, \quad \text{Legal}: p_1^{(1)} = \left(1 + t_1^{(1)}\right)p'_1. \tag{5.11}$$

The logarithmic change in price in going from the illegal to legal

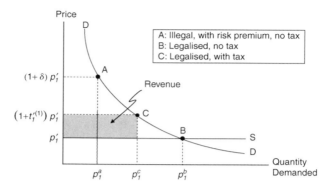

Figure 5.9. The marijuana market

regime is $\log p_1^{(1)} - \log p_1^{(0)}$, which we write as $d (\log p_1)$. It follows from equation (5.11) that:

$$d(\log p_1) = \log(1 + t_1'(1)) - \log(1 + \delta). \qquad (5.12)$$

The consumer price of marijuana remains unchanged when the tax just offsets the impact of disappearance of the risk premium, that is, when

$$t_1'^{(1)} = \delta. \qquad (5.13)$$

Figure 5.9 describes the workings of the marijuana market. The demand curve is labelled DD. Initially, when marijuana is illegal, the price paid by consumers is $(1 + \delta)p_1'$ and the quantity demanded is q_1^a. Thus, point A represents the price/quantity configuration observed. Legalisation leads to vanishing of the risk premium and the equilibrium moves from point A to B, with consumption increasing to q_1^b. Finally, imposition of the tax increases the price from p_1' to $\left(1 + t_1'^{(1)}\right)p_1'$, while consumption falls from q_1^b to q_1^c. Tax revenue collected by the government is given by the product of the per unit tax, $t_1'^{(1)}p_1'$, and the base, q_1^c, which is represented by the area of the shaded rectangle in the figure. It should be noted that in the figure the consumer price decreases with legalisation and consumption increases as the tax rate is set below the risk premium, but there is no reason why this should always be the case.

How does consumption change?

In this sub-section, we merge the marijuana price projections with a demand system to derive estimates of changes in the consumption of marijuana, tobacco and alcohol following legalisation and tax reform.

A Marshallian demand system in relative change form is $d(\log q_i) = \sum_{j=1}^{3} \eta_{ij}^* d(\log p_j)$, $i = 1, 2, 3$, where η_{ij}^* is the elasticity of demand for good i with respect to the price of j. As the prices of tobacco and alcohol are constant, this simplifies to $d(\log q_i) = \eta_{i1}^* d(\log p_1)$, which can be used to estimate the effects of legalisation and the tax change via equation (5.12). Approximating $d(\log q_i)$ with the finite change as $\Delta \log q_i = \log\left(q_i^{(1)} / q_i^{(0)}\right)$, the level of consumption of good i after legalisation and the tax change is:

$$q_i^{(1)} \approx q_i^{(0)} \exp\left\{\eta_{i1}^* \left[\log\left(1 + t_1^{\prime(1)}\right) - \log(1 + \delta)\right]\right\}. \tag{5.14}$$

This equation shows that consumption of each good remains unchanged when the supply curve of marijuana does not shift, that is, when condition (5.13) is satisfied. More generally, (5.13) defines a critical "dividing line" for combinations of the tax and risk premium. That is, when condition (5.13) is satisfied, there is no change in the consumer price of marijuana and no change in the consumption of marijuana, tobacco and alcohol. However, when $t_1^{\prime(1)} > \delta$, the price of marijuana increases, marijuana consumption decreases (the law of demand), tobacco consumption also decreases (as it is a complement for marijuana) and drinking increases (a substitute for marijuana), and vice versa when $t_1^{\prime(1)} < \delta$.[14]

To evaluate equation (5.14), we use various values of the marijuana tax rate and the risk premium, together with the 5,000 sets of elasticities. Table 5.11 gives the results in change form $\log\left(q_i^{(1)} / q_i^{(0)}\right)$. To interpret these results, take the case when the risk premium is 200 per cent and the producer tax t_1' is 100 per cent, which corresponds to the sixth row of panel D of the table. Here, the logarithmic change in the consumer price is:

$$\log\left(1 + t_1^{\prime(1)}\right) - \log(1 + \delta) = \log(1 + 1) - \log(1 + 2) = -0.41,$$

Table 5.11: *Consumption of marijuana, tobacco and alcohol when marijuana is legalised and taxed*

Marijuana tax rate as a percentage of		Change in consumer price (Log-change) $\log\left(\frac{1+t'_1}{1+\delta}\right) \times 100$	Change in consumption (Log-change $\times 100$)			
Producer price $t'_1 \times 100$ (1)	Consumer price $t_1 \times 100$ (2)	(3)	Marijuana (4)	Tobacco (5)	Alcohol (6)	Total (7)
			A. Risk premium $\delta = 0$			
0	0	0	0 (0)	0 (0)	0 (0)	0 (0)
11	10	10	−6.82 (4.05) [−16.55 −0.92]	−1.80 (1.09) [−4.32 −0.23]	0.80 (0.59) [−0.06 2.20]	−1.76 (0.97) [−4.07 −0.35]
25	20	22	−14.45 (8.59) [−35.04 −1.94]	−3.82 (2.31) [−9.14 −0.48]	1.70 (1.26) [−0.12 4.66]	−3.72 (2.05) [−8.62 −0.73]
43	30	36	−23.1 (13.73) [−56.01 −3.10]	−6.11 (3.69) [−14.61 −0.77]	2.71 (2.01) [−0.20 7.45]	−5.95 (3.28) [−13.78 −1.17]
67	40	51	−33.09 (19.66) [−80.22 −4.44]	−8.75 (5.29) [−20.93 −1.11]	3.89 (2.88) [−0.28 10.68]	−8.52 (4.70) [−19.73 −1.68]
100	50	69	−44.90 (26.68) [−108.85 −6.03]	−11.87 (7.17) [−28.40 −1.50]	5.27 (3.91) [−0.38 14.49]	−11.56 (6.38) [−26.77 −2.28]
150	60	92	−59.35 (35.26) [−143.89 −7.97]	−15.69 (9.48) [−37.54 −1.99]	6.97 (5.17) [−0.50 19.15]	−15.28 (8.44) [−35.39 −3.02]
233	70	120	−77.98 (46.33) [−189.07 −10.47]	−20.62 (12.46) [−49.33 −2.61]	9.16 (6.80) [−0.66 25.16]	−20.07 (11.09) [−46.51 −3.96]
400	80	161	−104.25 (61.94)	−27.56 (16.66)	12.24 (9.08)	−26.83 (14.82)

[-252.75   -14.00]   [-65.94   -3.49]   [-0.89   33.64]   [-62.17   -5.30]
-149.14   (88.61)   -39.43   (23.83)   17.51   (13.00)   -38.39   (21.20)
-361.60]   -20.03]   -94.34]   -5.00]   -1.27]   48.12]   -88.94]   -7.58]

900   90   230

B. Risk premium δ = 0.5

			Group 1	Group 2	Group 3	Group 4
0	0	-41	26.26 (15.6) [3.50, 63.51]	6.94 (4.20) [0.88, 16.6]	-3.08 (2.29) [-8.49, 0.22]	6.76 (3.73) [1.33, 15.65]
10	11	-30	19.44 (11.55) [2.59, 47.01]	5.14 (3.11) [0.65, 12.29]	-2.28 (1.69) [-6.29, 0.17]	5.00 (2.76) [0.99, 11.58]
20	25	-18	11.81 (7.02) [1.58, 28.56]	3.12 (1.89) [0.40, 7.46]	-1.39 (1.03) [-3.82, 0.10]	3.04 (1.68) [0.60, 7.04]
30	43	-5	3.16 (1.88) [0.42, 7.64]	0.84 (0.50) [0.11, 2.00]	-0.37 (0.28) [-1.02, 0.03]	0.81 (0.45) [0.16, 1.88]
40	67	11	-6.82 (4.05) [-16.55, -0.92]	-1.80 (1.09) [-4.32, -0.23]	0.80 (0.59) [-0.06, 2.20]	-1.76 (0.97) [-4.07, -0.35]
50	100	29	-18.63 (11.07) [-45.18, -2.50]	-4.93 (2.98) [-11.79, -0.62]	2.19 (1.62) [-0.16, 6.01]	-4.80 (2.65) [-11.11, -0.95]
60	150	51	-33.09 (19.66) [-80.22, -4.44]	-8.75 (5.29) [-20.93, -1.11]	3.89 (2.88) [-0.28, 10.68]	-8.52 (4.70) [-19.73, -1.68]
70	233	80	-51.72 (30.73) [-125.4, -6.95]	-13.67 (8.26) [-32.71, -1.73]	6.07 (4.51) [-0.44, 16.69]	-13.31 (7.35) [-30.84, -2.63]
80	400	120	-77.98 (46.33) [-189.07, -10.47]	-20.62 (12.46) [-49.33, -2.61]	9.16 (6.80) [-0.66, 25.16]	-20.07 (11.09) [-46.51, -3.96]
90	900	190	-122.88 (73.01) [-297.92, -16.5]	-32.49 (19.63) [-77.73, -4.12]	14.43 (10.71) [-1.04, 39.65]	-31.63 (17.47) [-73.28, -6.25]

Table 5.11: (continued)

Marijuana tax rate as a percentage of		Change in consumer price (Log-change) $\log\left(\frac{1+t_1'}{1+\delta}\right)\times 100$ (3)	Change in consumption (Log-change $\times$ 100)			
Producer price $t_1' \times 100$ (1)	Consumer price $t_1 \times 100$ (2)		Marijuana (4)	Tobacco (5)	Alcohol (6)	Total (7)
			C. Risk premium $\delta = 1$			
0	0	−69	44.9 (26.68) [5.99 108.57]	11.87 (7.17) [1.50 28.38]	−5.27 (3.91) [−14.52 0.38]	11.56 (6.38) [2.28 26.75]
11	10	−59	38.07 (22.62) [5.08 92.07]	10.07 (6.08) [1.28 24.06]	−4.47 (3.32) [−12.31 0.32]	9.8 (5.41) [1.94 22.68]
25	20	−47	30.44 (18.09) [4.06 73.62]	8.05 (4.86) [1.02 19.24]	−3.58 (2.65) [−9.85 0.26]	7.84 (4.33) [1.55 18.14]
43	30	−34	21.79 (12.95) [2.91 52.70]	5.76 (3.48) [0.73 13.78]	−2.56 (1.90) [−7.05 0.19]	5.61 (3.10) [1.11 12.98]
67	40	−18	11.81 (7.02) [1.58 28.56]	3.12 (1.89) [0.40 7.46]	−1.39 (1.03) [−3.82 0.10]	3.04 (1.68) [0.60 7.04]
100	50	0	0 (0) [0 0]	0 (0) [0 0]	0 (0) [0 0]	0 (0) [0 0]
150	60	22	−14.45 (8.59) [−35.04 −1.94]	−3.82 (2.31) [−9.14 −0.48]	1.70 (1.26) [−0.12 4.66]	−3.72 (2.05) [−8.62 −0.73]

233	70	51	−33.09 (19.66) [−80.22 −4.44]	−8.75 (5.29) [−20.93 −1.11]	3.89 (2.88) [−0.28 10.68]	−8.52 (4.70) [−19.73 −1.68]
400	80	92	−59.35 (35.26) [−143.89 −7.97]	−15.69 (9.48) [−37.54 −1.99]	6.97 (5.17) [−0.50 19.15]	−15.28 (8.44) [−35.39 −3.02]
900	90	161	−104.25 (61.94) [−252.75 −14.00]	−27.56 (16.66) [−65.94 −3.49]	12.24 (9.08) [−0.89 33.64]	−26.83 (14.82) [−62.17 −5.30]

D. Risk premium $\delta = 2$

0	0	−110	71.16 (42.28) [9.49 172.08]	18.81 (11.37) [2.38 44.98]	−8.36 (6.20) [−23.02 0.60]	18.31 (10.12) [3.62 42.40]
11	10	−99	64.33 (38.22) [8.58 155.57]	17.01 (10.28) [2.16 40.66]	−7.56 (5.61) [−20.81 0.55]	16.56 (9.15) [3.27 38.33]
25	20	−88	56.71 (33.69) [7.56 137.12]	14.99 (9.06) [1.90 35.84]	−6.66 (4.94) [−18.34 0.48]	14.59 (8.06) [2.88 33.78]
43	30	−74	48.06 (28.55) [6.41 116.21]	12.7 (7.68) [1.61 30.37]	−5.64 (4.19) [−15.54 0.41]	12.37 (6.83) [2.44 28.63]
67	40	−59	38.07 (22.62) [5.08 92.07]	10.07 (6.08) [1.28 24.06]	−4.47 (3.32) [−12.31 0.32]	9.8 (5.41) [1.94 22.68]
100	50	−41	26.26 (15.6) [3.5 63.51]	6.94 (4.20) [0.88 16.60]	−3.08 (2.29) [−8.49 0.22]	6.76 (3.73) [1.33 15.65]
150	60	−18	11.81 (7.02) [1.58 28.56]	3.12 (1.89) [0.40 7.46]	−1.39 (1.03) [−3.82 0.10]	3.04 (1.68) [0.60 7.04]
233	70	10	−6.82 (4.05) [−16.55 −0.92]	−1.80 (1.09) [−4.32 −0.23]	0.8 (0.59) [−0.06 2.2]	−1.76 (0.97) [−4.07 −0.35]

Table 5.11: *(continued)*

Marijuana tax rate as a percentage of		Change in consumer price (Log-change) $\log\left(\frac{1+t_1'}{1+\delta}\right) \times 100$ (3)	Change in consumption (Log-change $\times 100$)			
Producer price $t_1' \times 100$ (1)	Consumer price $t_1 \times 100$ (2)		Marijuana (4)	Tobacco (5)	Alcohol (6)	Total (7)
400	80	51	−33.09 (19.66) [−80.22 −4.44]	−8.75 (5.29) [−20.93 −1.11]	3.89 (2.88) [−0.28 10.68]	−8.52 (4.70) [−19.73 −1.68]
900	90	120	−77.98 (46.33) [−189.07 −10.47]	−20.62 (12.46) [−49.33 −2.61]	9.16 (6.80) [−0.66 25.16]	−20.07 (11.09) [−46.51 −3.96]
E. Risk premium $\delta = 3$						
0	0	−139	89.79 (53.35) [11.98 217.14]	23.74 (14.35) [3.01 56.75]	−10.54 (7.82) [−29.04 0.76]	23.11 (12.76) [4.56 53.5]
11	10	−128	82.97 (49.3) [11.07 200.63]	21.93 (13.26) [2.78 52.44]	−9.74 (7.23) [−26.84 0.70]	21.35 (11.79) [4.22 49.43]
25	20	−116	75.34 (44.76) [10.05 182.18]	19.92 (12.04) [2.52 47.62]	−8.85 (6.57) [−24.37 0.64]	19.39 (10.71) [3.83 44.89]
43	30	−103	66.69 (39.62) [8.90 161.27]	17.63 (10.66) [2.23 42.15]	−7.83 (5.81) [−21.57 0.57]	17.16 (9.48) [3.39 39.73]

67	40	56.71 (33.69) [7.56 137.12]	14.99 (9.06) [1.90 35.84]	−6.66 (4.94) [−18.34 0.48]	14.59 (8.06) [2.88 33.78]
100	50	44.90 (26.68) [5.99 108.57]	11.87 (7.17) [1.50 28.38]	−5.27 (3.91) [−14.52 0.38]	11.56 (6.38) [2.28 26.75]
150	60	30.44 (18.09) [4.06 73.62]	8.05 (4.86) [1.02 19.24]	−3.58 (2.65) [−9.85 0.26]	7.84 (4.33) [1.55 18.14]
233	70	11.81 (7.02) [1.58 28.56]	3.12 (1.89) [0.40 7.46]	−1.39 (1.03) [−3.82 0.10]	3.04 (1.68) [0.60 7.04]
400	80	−14.45 (8.59) [−35.04 −1.94]	−3.82 (2.31) [−9.14 −0.48]	1.70 (1.26) [−0.12 4.66]	−3.72 (2.05) [−8.62 −0.73]
900	90	−59.35 (35.26) [−143.89 −7.97]	−15.69 (9.48) [−37.54 −1.99]	6.97 (5.17) [−0.5 19.15]	−15.28 (8.44) [−35.39 −3.02]

Notes:
1. The first entry in each cell is the mean over the 5,000 trials. The second entry, given on the right in parentheses, is the associated standard deviation. The range below the mean and standard deviation is the 95 per cent probability interval.

(notes continued over)

Notes (continued):

2. The change in the total, given in column 7, is a conditional budget-share-weighted average of the logarithmic changes in the consumption of marijuana, tobacco and alcohol. Column 2 of Table 5.4 reports the mean unconditional budget shares of these commodities, which are presented below in column 2. In column 3 below we give the corresponding conditional budget shares, which are normalised versions of their unconditional counterparts. For a given trial, the changes in consumption of the three commodities are weighted by the respective conditional shares and then summed to give the total for that trial. This is repeated for all 5,000 trials and column 7 summarises the results.

| Commodity | Budget share (×100) | |
(1)	Unconditional $\bar{w}_i$ (2)	Conditional $\bar{w}_i$ (3)
Marijuana	2	25
Tobacco	2	25
Alcohol	4	50
Other	92	n/a
Sum	100	100

as indicated by the relevant entry in column 3. This log-change corresponds to $[\exp(-0.41) - 1] \times 100 = -33$ per cent. As the own-price elasticity of demand for marijuana has a mean of -0.65, consumption should increase by approximately $-0.65 \times -0.41 \approx 0.27$ on average, or approximately 27 per cent, which is quite close to the mean for marijuana in column 4 of 26.26 per cent. The standard deviation of the 5,000 values of the change in consumption for this case is approximately 16 per cent and the 95 per cent probability interval is 4–64 per cent, so there is a fair degree of uncertainty in the results.

Equation (5.12) indicates that the price increases when the tax is imposed and decreases as the risk premium vanishes. Thus, for a given tax rate, a higher value of δ implies that consumption of marijuana increases by more, or decreases by less, with the move to legalisation. This pattern is clear from the results in Table 5.11. For example, when $t_1'^{(1)} \times 100 = 100$ per cent, marijuana consumption is constant for a risk premium of $\delta \times 100 = 100$ per cent, but the same tax leads to a 45 per cent increase in consumption when $\delta \times 100 = 300$ per cent (see column 4 and row 6 of panel E of Table 5.11). The role of condition (5.13) is also clear from the results. When $t_1'^{(1)} < \delta$, the consumer price of marijuana decreases falls with legalisation and its consumption increases. In panel C of Table 5.11, for example, column 3 shows that the price switches from decreasing to increasing when $t_1'^{(1)} \times 100 = 100$ per cent, which is the value of the premium for this panel. At this point, marijuana consumption switches from increasing to decreasing.

As tobacco and marijuana are complements, consumption of the former should decrease as the price of the latter increases. For the case when $t_1' = 1$ and $\delta = 2$, the price of marijuana decreases and its consumption increases. Tobacco consumption also increases in this case, by approximately 7 per cent on average (see row 6 and column 5 of Panel D of Table 5.11), thus confirming complementarity. Column 6 shows that alcohol consumption for the same scenario decreases by approximately 3 per cent on average; alcohol consumption decreases with the marijuana price as the two goods are substitutes. For reasons similar to those discussed above for marijuana, a higher risk premium leads to a greater increase (or lesser decrease) in tobacco consumption on legalisation and a greater decrease in drinking.

We can summarise changes in the consumption of marijuana, tobacco and alcohol as a group using a Divisia volume index, defined

as a weighted average of the changes in quantities consumed, with
conditional budget shares as weights. Column 7 of Table 5.11 contains the results for total consumption. From row 6 of Panel D it is
evident that, on average, total consumption increases by approximately 7 per cent when the tax is 100 per cent and the risk premium
is 200 per cent.

Three other comments can be made about the results in
Table 5.11. First, as the marijuana tax increases its price does too
and marijuana consumption decreases on average, as is clear from
equation (5.14), where the own-price elasticity $\eta_{11}^* < 0$. Similarly,
a higher marijuana tax causes the tobacco consumption to decrease
and alcohol consumption to increase by more. Second, marijuana
tends to dominate the vice budget in the sense that on average the
total always moves in the same direction as marijuana consumption. Third, for all three goods (and total vice) and for most values
of the tax and risk premium, the standard deviation of the change
in consumption is slightly more than half of the corresponding
mean.

How much revenue can be generated?

Retracing our steps, revenue from marijuana is:

$$R_1^{(1)} = t_1'^{(1)} \left(\frac{1}{1+\delta} \right) p_1^{(0)} q_1^{(0)} \exp\left\{ \eta_{11}^* \left[\log\left(1 + t_1'^{(1)}\right) - \log(1 + \delta) \right] \right\}.$$

$$(5.15)$$

The components of this equation are the marijuana tax, its price and
consumption, the price elasticity and the risk premium. The role of
each can be explained as follows:

Writing revenue as a function of the tax and the risk premium, $R_1^{(1)} = R_1^{(1)}(t_1'^{(1)}, \delta)$, we have:

$$\frac{\partial \log\left(R_1^{(1)}\right)}{\partial t_1'^{(1)}} = \frac{1}{t_1'^{(1)}}\left[1 + \frac{\eta_{11}^* t_1'^{(1)}}{1 + t_1'^{(1)}}\right]. \tag{5.16}$$

For $t_1'^{(1)} > 0$, the sign of the derivative is determined by that of the term in square brackets. As the consumer price after legalisation is defined as $p_1 = \left(1 + t_1'^{(1)}\right)p'_1$, where p'_1 is the producer price, the per unit tax is $t_1'^{(1)}p'_1$ dollars. This means that the tax as a proportion of the consumer price is $t_1'^{(1)}p'_1 / \left(1 + t_1'^{(1)}\right)p'_1$, or $t_1'^{(1)} / \left(1 + t_1'^{(1)}\right)$, which we write as $t_1^{(1)}$. To illustrate, suppose the pre-tax price of the product is $1 and the tax is $1 per unit, so that $t' = 1$, or 100 per cent. Then the consumer price is $1 + 1 = \$2$ and the tax as a proportion of this price is $t = 1/2$, or 50 per cent. It should be noted that whereas t' can take any positive value, t always lies between 0 and 1. Accordingly, derivative (5.16) is positive if $1 + \eta_{11}^* t_1^{(1)}$ is greater than zero, or if $\left|\eta_{11}^*\right| < 1/t_1^{(1)}$. As consumption is price-inelastic, $\left|\eta_{11}^*\right| < 1$ and as $1/t_1^{(1)}$ is greater than unity, this condition is always satisfied.

The dependence of revenue on the risk premium is given by:

$$\frac{\partial \log\left(R_1^{(1)}\right)}{\partial \delta} = \frac{-(1 + \eta_{11}^*)}{1 + \delta}.$$

This derivative is negative when $(1 + \eta_{11}^*) > 0$, or $\left|\eta_{11}^*\right| < 1$. In other words, revenue decreases with the risk premium when the absolute value of the own-price elasticity of marijuana is less than unity, as it is in our case. The intuition for this decrease in revenue is that legalisation causes the risk premium to disappear, the price to decrease and consumption to increase. However, when demand is price-inelastic, in proportionate terms the increase in the quantity consumed is less than the fall in the price, causing expenditure to decrease on legalisation. A greater value of δ thus implies that expenditure decreases by more following legalisation and as taxation revenue is proportional to expenditure, it also decreases.

Figure 5.10, which plots mean taxation revenue against the marijuana tax rate for various values of the risk premium, illustrates the above results – direct revenue increases with the tax rate and decreases as the risk premium increases. The figure also shows that revenue from tobacco decreases as the marijuana tax increases. This simply reflects the complementarity between the two goods. Conversely, revenue from alcohol always increases with the marijuana tax because the goods are substitutes. Total revenue – from marijuana, tobacco and alcohol – also always increases with the marijuana tax, which reflects the small decrease in tobacco revenue relative to the increases derived from the two other goods.

The detailed results for revenue are given in Table 5.12. It is not easy to make simple summary statements regarding the amount of revenue raised, as this varies with the rate and the risk premium. One way to summarise the results is to consider only mean revenue when marijuana is taxed at a "moderate" rate. An important reason for focusing on the moderate-rate case is that if the tax were too high there would be incentives for a black market to develop to avoid the tax, in which case collections would be substantially less than projected. We could extend the framework to incorporate two sectors supplying the marijuana market, one that is legal and pays the tax and one that does not. As there would be a good substitute for legal marijuana, illegal marijuana, legal demand would thus be more price-elastic than before and projected revenue would be much lower because of "leakage" from the legal market.[15] Although we do not pursue this argument further, it is clear that considerations of tax evasion are of considerable practical importance in setting the appropriate rate of taxation for marijuana.

The moderate tax rate we consider is 50 per cent of the consumer price or 100 per cent of the producer price, which is approximately the same rate as for tobacco (see Table 5.9). Column 2 of Table 5.13 provides the price changes associated with legalisation and taxation for various values of the risk premium. As observed from the first entry in column 3 of this table, when there is no risk premium, mean direct revenue from marijuana is $245 per capita. Pre-existing revenue from tobacco and alcohol is $684 (column 5 of Table 5.9), so this revenue from marijuana represents an increase of approximately 36 per cent (first entry in column 4 of Table 5.13). Revenue decreases noticeably as the risk premium increases and is 22 per cent of existing

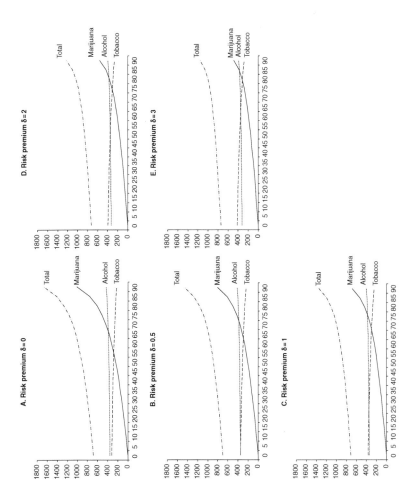

Figure 5.10. Revenue from taxing marijuana

Notes:

1. Revenue (in terms of dollars per capita) is on the vertical axis and the marijuana tax rate (as a percentage of the consumer price) is on the horizontal axis.

2. The lines represent the means over the 5,000 trials for taxation revenue from each commodity.

Table 5.12: *Revenue from legalising and taxing marijuana*

Marijuana tax rate as a percentage of		Change in consumer price (Log-change) $\log\left(\frac{1+t_1'}{1+\delta}\right) \times 100$	Tax revenue (dollars per capita)			
Producer price $t_1' \times 100$	Consumer price $t_1 \times 100$		Marijuana	Tobacco	Alcohol	Total
(1)	(2)	(3)	(4)	(5)	(6)	(7)
A. Risk premium $\delta = 0$						
0	0	0	0 (0)	324 (0)	360 (0)	684 (0)
11	10	10	39 (2)	318 (3)	363 (2)	720 (2)
25	20	22	[35 41]	[310 323]	[360 368]	[715 724]
			81 (7)	312 (7)	367 (5)	759 (8)
43	30	36	[66 91]	[296 323]	[360 378]	[741 772]
			128 (16)	305 (11)	370 (8)	803 (18)
67	40	51	[91 155]	[280 322]	[360 388]	[764 833]
			181 (32)	297 (15)	375 (11)	854 (34)
100	50	69	[111 237]	[263 321]	[359 401]	[781 913]
			245 (58)	289 (20)	380 (15)	914 (59)
150	60	92	[125 350]	[244 319]	[359 417]	[793 1023]
			326 (98)	278 (25)	387 (21)	991 (99)
233	70	120	[132 515]	[223 318]	[359 436]	[799 1184]
			436 (168)	266 (31)	396 (28)	1098 (167)

			[131 782]	[198 316]	[358 464]	[800 1446]
400	80	161	613 (304) [119 1294]	249 (39) [168 313]	409 (39) [357 504]	1271 (301) [791 1949]
900	90	230	1013 (690) [90 2740]	224 (48) [126 308]	433 (60) [356 583]	1671 (680) [781 3379]

B. Risk premium δ = 0.5

0	0	−41	0 (0) [0 0]	348 (15) [327 383]	350 (8) [331 361]	697 (8) [687 718]
11	10	−30	34 (4) [28 44]	341 (11) [326 367]	352 (6) [338 361]	727 (8) [717 747]
25	20	−18	70 (5) [63 82]	335 (6) [325 349]	355 (4) [347 361]	760 (7) [750 776]
43	30	−5	110 (2) [107 115]	327 (2) [325 331]	359 (1) [357 360]	796 (2) [792 802]
67	40	11	155 (6) [140 164]	318 (3) [310 323]	363 (2) [360 368]	836 (7) [821 847]
100	50	29	207 (22) [158 242]	309 (9) [288 322]	368 (6) [360 383]	884 (23) [833 922]
150	60	51	272 (48) [167 356]	297 (15) [263 321]	375 (11) [359 401]	944 (50) [838 1032]
233	70	80	360 (96) [165 540]	284 (23) [234 319]	383 (18) [359 426]	1027 (97) [833 1211]
400	80	120	498 (192) [150 893]	266 (31) [198 316]	396 (28) [358 464]	1160 (191) [818 1557]
900	90	190	805 (462) [113 1892]	239 (43) [149 311]	419 (47) [357 536]	1463 (457) [791 2540]

Table 5.12: (continued)

Marijuana tax rate as a percentage of		Change in consumer price (Log-change) $\log\left(\frac{1+t'_1}{1+\delta}\right) \times 100$	Tax revenue (dollars per capita)			
Producer price $t'_1 \times 100$	Consumer price $t_1 \times 100$		Marijuana	Tobacco	Alcohol	Total
(1)	(2)	(3)	(4)	(5)	(6)	(7)
			C. Risk premium $\delta = 1$			
0	0	−69	0 (0)	366 (27)	342 (13)	708 (16)
			[0 0]	[329 431]	[312 362]	[689 748]
11	10	−59	31 (8)	359 (23)	345 (11)	735 (17)
			[22 52]	[328 412]	[319 362]	[714 778]
25	20	−47	64 (13)	352 (18)	348 (9)	764 (18)
			[48 97]	[327 393]	[327 361]	[740 809]
43	30	−34	100 (14)	344 (12)	351 (7)	795 (17)
			[82 135]	[327 372]	[336 361]	[772 837]
67	40	−18	140 (10)	335 (6)	355 (4)	830 (12)
			[126 165]	[325 349]	[347 361]	[814 858]
100	50	0	186 (0)	324 (0)	360 (0)	871 (0)
			[186 186]	[324 324]	[360 360]	[871 871]
150	60	22	242 (20)	312 (7)	367 (5)	921 (21)
			[197 274]	[296 323]	[360 378]	[874 954]

233	70	51	317 (57) [195 415]	297 (15) [263 321]	375 (11) [359 401]	990 (58) [866 1091]
400	80	92	434 (131) [176 687]	278 (25) [223 318]	387 (21) [359 436]	1099 (132) [845 1356]
900	90	161	690 (343) [134 1455]	249 (39) [168 313]	409 (39) [357 504]	1348 (339) [806 2110]

D. Risk premium δ = 2

0	0	−110	0 (0) [0 0]	394 (48) [332 508]	332 (20) [286 363]	726 (30) [692 802]
11	10	−99	29 (17) [15 65]	386 (42) [331 487]	335 (18) [293 362]	750 (34) [713 836]
25	20	−88	58 (28) [33 122]	378 (36) [330 464]	338 (16) [300 362]	774 (39) [731 872]
43	30	−74	90 (33) [57 170]	369 (30) [329 439]	341 (14) [309 362]	800 (42) [753 902]
67	40	−59	124 (34) [87 208]	359 (23) [328 412]	345 (11) [319 362]	828 (39) [781 925]
100	50	−41	163 (29) [128 234]	348 (15) [327 383]	350 (8) [331 361]	861 (32) [820 938]
150	60	−18	210 (15) [189 247]	335 (6) [325 349]	355 (4) [347 361]	900 (17) [877 939]
233	70	10	270 (11) [245 287]	318 (3) [310 323]	363 (2) [360 368]	952 (11) [926 969]
400	80	51	363 (65) [222 474]	297 (15) [263 321]	375 (11) [359 401]	1035 (66) [894 1150]
900	90	120	560 (216) [168 1005]	266 (31) [198 316]	396 (28) [358 464]	1222 (215) [837 1668]

Table 5.12: *(continued)*

Marijuana tax rate as a percentage of		Change in consumer price (Log-change) $\log\left(\frac{1+t'_1}{1+\delta}\right)\times100$	Tax revenue (dollars per capita)			
Producer price $t'_1\times100$	Consumer price $t_1\times100$		Marijuana	Tobacco	Alcohol	Total
(1)	(2)	(3)	(4)	(5)	(6)	(7)
		E. Risk premium δ = 3				
0	0	−139	0 (0) [0 0]	415 (65) [334 572]	325 (25) [270 363]	741 (43) [694 851]
11	10	−128	28 (27) [12 77]	407 (58) [333 548]	328 (23) [276 363]	763 (51) [712 887]
25	20	−116	56 (44) [26 144]	399 (51) [332 522]	331 (21) [282 363]	785 (61) [727 927]
43	30	−103	85 (53) [44 200]	389 (44) [331 494]	334 (19) [290 362]	808 (66) [744 962]
67	40	−87	117 (55) [67 244]	378 (36) [330 464]	338 (16) [300 362]	833 (65) [766 985]
100	50	−69	152 (51) [99 275]	366 (27) [329 431]	342 (13) [312 362]	860 (58) [795 999]
150	60	−47	193 (40) [145 291]	352 (18) [327 393]	348 (9) [327 361]	892 (44) [838 999]

233	70	−18	245 (18) [220 289]	335 (6) [325 349]	355 (4) [347 361]	935 (19) [908 980]
400	80	22	323 (26) [262 365]	312 (7) [296 323]	367 (5) [360 378]	1002 (27) [940 1046]
900	90	92	488 (148) [199 773]	278 (25) [223 318]	387 (21) [359 436]	1154 (148) [867 1441]

Note: The first entry in each cell is the mean over the 5,000 trials. The second entry, given on the right in parentheses, is the associated standard deviation. The range below the mean and standard deviation is the 95 per cent probability interval.

Table 5.13 Summary of price changes, tax proceeds and consumption changes

		Revenue from						Change in consumption		
		Marijuana		Total vice (marijuana tobacco and alcohol)				(Log-change×100)		
Risk premium $\delta \times 100$	Change in consumer price (Log-change) $log\left(\frac{2}{1+\delta}\right)\times 100$	Dollars per capita	Percent of existing revenue	Dollars per capita	Percent of existing revenue	Marijuana	Tobacco	Alcohol	Total
(1)	(2)	(3)	(4)	(5)	(6)	(7)	(8)	(9)	(10)
0	69	245	36	914	134	−44.90	−11.87	5.27	−11.56
50	29	207	30	884	129	−18.63	−4.93	2.19	−4.80
100	0	186	27	871	127	0	0	0	0
200	−41	163	24	861	126	26.26	6.94	−3.08	6.76
300	−69	152	22	860	126	44.90	11.87	−5.27	11.56

Notes:

1. Entries in columns 3 and 5 are means corresponding to a marijuana tax of 100 per cent of the producer price (i.e. 50 per cent of the consumer price), from Table 5.12.
2. Column 4 is column 3 expressed as a percentage of $684, the observed total revenue from vice (from the last entry in the last row of Table 5.9).
3. Column 6 is column 5 expressed as a percentage of $684.
4. Columns 7–10 are the means corresponding to a marijuana tax of 100 per cent of producer price (i.e. 50 per cent of the consumer price), from Table 5.11.

revenue when $\delta = 3$ (see the last entry in column 4). However, in addition to this direct increase in revenue, there are indirect effects on revenue from tobacco and alcohol. From Table 5.9, pre-existing revenue from tobacco and alcohol is $324 and $360 per capita, respectively. When $\delta = 2$, for example, legalisation and imposition of a 100 per cent tax on marijuana causes its price to decrease by approximately 41 per cent, revenue from tobacco to increase from $324 to $348 (approximately 7 per cent), and revenue from alcohol to decrease from $360 to $350 (3 per cent). The net effect is that total revenue from the three commodities increases from $684 to $861, or by 26 per cent, as indicated by the second-last entry in column 6 of Table 5.13. The last four columns of the table list the corresponding changes in consumption of the three goods and the total. Among the three goods, the largest changes in consumption involve marijuana.

For a sensitivity analysis of the results with respect to the income elasticity of marijuana, see Appendix A5.3.

Uncertainty of the results

Figure 5.10 shows the relationship between mean revenue and the marijuana tax rate for each commodity. We can analyse the uncertainty of these estimates by examining the dispersion among the 5,000 trials. Figures 5.11–5.14 illustrate the underlying uncertainty of tax revenue by presenting a type of fan chart (Britton *et al.*, 1998; Wallis, 1999) in which the darker colours denote values that have a higher probability of occurrence. Figure 5.11 shows that the uncertainty of the results for direct revenue tends to increase with the marijuana tax rate. This result is entirely reasonable: given that marijuana is currently not taxed, as we increase its tax we are in effect moving further and further away from the status quo, and we can have less and less confidence in the projections for revenue.

A closer inspection of Figure 5.11 reveals that in each panel the width of the "uncertainty band" decreases at some tax rate. Take Panel D as an example, which corresponds to a risk premium of 200 per cent. Here the band first increases, decreases to zero at a tax rate of approximately 70 per cent and then increases again. This pattern is even clearer for tobacco revenue for the same risk premium, as shown in Panel D of Figure 5.12. It should be noted that taxes on the horizontal axes of Figures 5.12 and 5.13 are

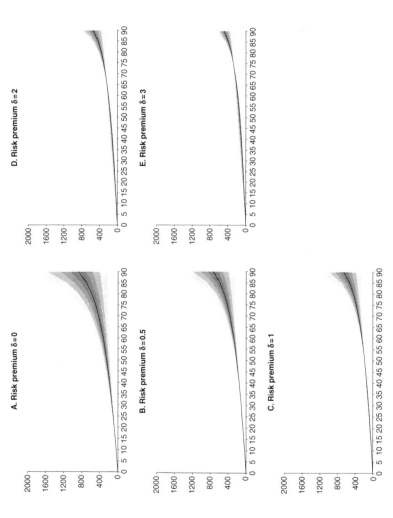

Figure 5.11. Marijuana revenue and the marijuana tax

Notes:

1. Revenue (in terms of dollars per capita) is on the vertical axis and the marijuana tax rate (as a percentage of the consumer price) is on the horizontal axis.

2. The boundaries of the fan charts are the 10, 20, ..., 90 percentiles of the distribution of revenue from the simulation; solid lines are the median values.

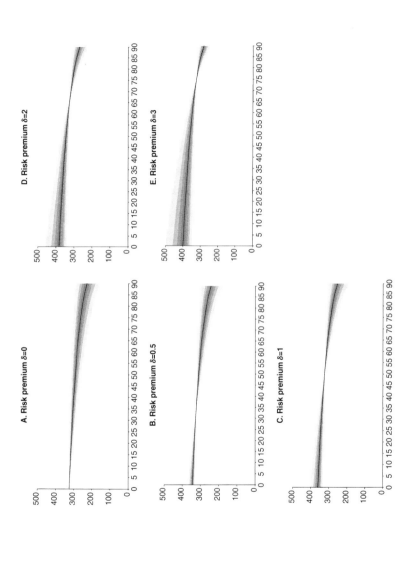

Figure 5.12. Tobacco revenue and the marijuana tax

Notes:

1. Revenue (in terms of dollars per capita) is on the vertical axis and the marijuana tax rate (as a percentage of the consumer price) is on the horizontal axis.

2. The boundaries of the fan charts are the 10, 20, ..., 90 percentiles of the distribution of revenue from the simulation; solid lines are the median values.

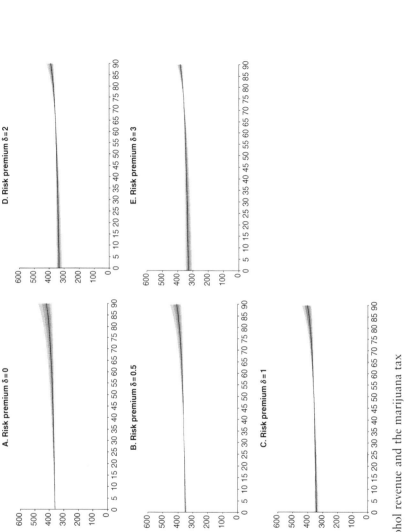

Figure 5.13. Alcohol revenue and the marijuana tax

Notes:

1. Revenue (in terms of dollars per capita) is on the vertical axis and the marijuana tax rate (as a percentage of the consumer price) is on the horizontal axis.

2. The boundaries of the fan charts are the 10, 20, ..., 90 percentiles of the distribution of revenue from the simulation; solid lines are the median values.

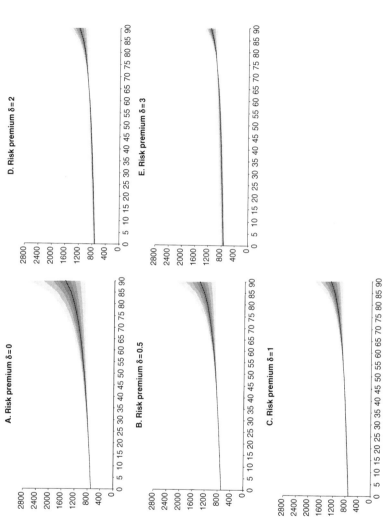

Figure 5.14. Total revenue and the marijuana tax

Notes:

1. Revenue (in terms of dollars per capita) is on the vertical axis and the marijuana tax rate (as a percentage of the consumer price) is on the horizontal axis.

2. The boundaries of the fan charts are the 10, 20, ..., 90 percentiles of the distribution of revenue from the simulation; solid lines are the median values.

expressed as a percentage of the consumer price, that is, $t_1 \times 100$. As discussed above, the link between the producer tax (t_1') and the consumer tax (t_1) is $t_1 = t_1'/(1 + t_1')$, so that $t_1' = t_1/(1 - t_1)$. Thus, the location of the zero "uncertainty band" at a consumer tax of approximately 70 per cent corresponds to a producer tax of approximately 200 per cent. The reason for the zero uncertainty at this tax rate is condition (5.13), which defines the situation in which the tax just offsets the risk premium, leaving the marijuana price unchanged after legalisation. When the price is unchanged, consumption also does not change and the random price elasticity plays no role. As elasticity is the only source of randomness in the analysis, when condition (5.13) holds, given the way the problem is formulated, there is zero uncertainty for the results. This also explains why the point of zero uncertainty occurs at the same rate for each commodity for a given risk premium.

There is a further pattern in the revenue projections of Table 5.12. that is related to uncertainty. In relative terms, the standard deviations for revenue from marijuana are all substantially greater than those for tobacco and alcohol. This reflects the greater uncertainty of the underlying data and parameters pertaining to marijuana compared with those for the other two commodities.

Previous studies

This sub-section compares our revenue projections with those of previous studies.

Several other studies have examined possible revenue from a tax on marijuana in a legalised environment (Bates, 2004; Caputo and Ostrom, 1994; Easton, 2004; Miron, 2005; Schwer *et al.*, 2002). In what seems to be the most widely cited paper in this area, Caputo and Ostrom (1994) estimate that for the US it would have been possible to raise US$3–5 billion from marijuana taxation in 1991. This estimate is based on conservative assumptions regarding the continued existence after legalisation of a black market that evaded the tax. For comparison, tax revenue from tobacco and alcohol combined in the same year was US$22 billion (approximately evenly split between tobacco and alcohol). Using the midpoint of the above range of US$4 billion, the marijuana tax would thus represent an addition of approximately 18 per cent of revenue from vice taxation. In a more recent US study, Miron (2005) estimates that marijuana could generate approximately US$2 billion per annum if taxed at the same rate as other goods, or US$6 billion if taxed at a rate comparable to that for tobacco and alcohol. Miron argues that these figures are similar to the earlier revenue estimates of Caputo and Ostrom (1994).

Comparison of the above results with those in the present study is complicated by the risk premium component of the price. Although we further discuss this premium in the next section, the key problem is that we do not know the value of the premium. One approach is to use the US estimates of revenue to "back out" the implied value of the risk premium. As stated in the previous paragraph, Caputo and Ostrom (1994) estimate that the proceeds from taxing marijuana in the US would increase tax revenue from vice by approximately 18 per cent. Pre-existing revenue from vice (i.e. from tobacco and alcohol before legalisation) in Australia is $684 per capita, so 18 per cent of this is $123. We thus suppose that marijuana is subject to a 50 per cent consumer tax, which is approximately the same as the tobacco tax, set revenue equal to $123, and then solve for the implied value of the risk premium. Extrapolating from column 3 of Table 5.13, the implied risk premium would seem to be something greater than 300 per cent. This means that the costs incurred to avoid prosecution represent something more than three times the production costs of marijuana, which does not seem to be unreasonable.[16]

5.13 More on the risk premium

The risk premium for marijuana represents the costs that producers have to incur to avoid prosecution, that is, costs over and above the basic production costs, as well as what would be the distribution costs in a legal market for marijuana. These "avoidance" costs would not be incurred in a legalised regime, so that if the marijuana industry were competitive, prices could be expected to decrease by the amount of the risk premium. There are, of course, degrees of legalisation, and in Chapter 4 we argued that one of the reasons for the substantial decrease in prices in Australia over the 1990s was the more lenient attitude towards marijuana adopted by society in general, including parliaments, the courts and the police. As mentioned above, although there is no hard evidence on the value of the risk premium for marijuana, the importance of the premium means

Table 5.14: *Tobacco prices*

| Product, packet of (1) | Retail price of product ($A) (2) | Amount of tobacco (grams) (3) | Unit price of tobacco ($A per gram) | |
			Inclusive of tax (4)	Exclusive of tax (5)
Stuyvesant cigarettes	9.60	12.12	0.792	0.362
Marlboro cigarettes	9.70	13.36	0.726	0.332
Champion tobacco	14.50	30.28	0.479	0.219

Notes:

1. The cigarettes and tobacco were purchased by Callum Jones at Campus News and Gifts, The University of Western Australia on April 7, 2008. The tobacco, excluding all packaging and without the filter and cigarette paper (where applicable), was weighed by Callum Jones with the assistance of Allan McKinley in the School of Biomedical, Biomolecular and Chemical Sciences, The University of Western Australia.
2. Column 4 is column 2 divided by column 3.
3. Column 5 is column 4 multiplied by 1–0.543, where 54.3 per cent is the tax rate on tobacco, expressed as a percentage of the consumer price, from the second entry in column 3 of Table 5.9.

that it warrants some further discussion. In this section, we discuss four related pieces of evidence.

Marijuana and tobacco prices

Arguably, marijuana and tobacco are similar products. Both are horticulturally based, subject to some processing and mostly smoked. It may seem plausible to estimate the production costs of marijuana from tobacco prices. As observed from column 5 of Table 5.14, a small sample of products reveals that the retail net-of-tax price of tobacco in Australia in 2008 ranges from 22 cents to 36 cents per gram. We can compare this information with the Australian marijuana prices given in Chapter 3. Table 3.2 shows that for heads the average per ounce cost in 1999 was $841 when purchased

Table 5.15 *Marijuana and tobacco prices*
and the apparent risk premium for marijuana

Marijuana price (dollars per gram)	Tobacco price (dollars per gram)	
	0.22	0.36
	Risk premium (%)	
14.39	6,441	3,897
30.03	13,550	8,242

Note: The premium is computed as $\delta \times 100 =$
$(p_1/p_1'-1) \times 100$, where p_1 is the price of marijuana
and p_1' is the price of tobacco.

in the form of grams and $403 when purchased as an ounce. As there
are approximately 28 grams in an ounce, this implies per gram prices
of $30.03 and $14.39, respectively.

Recall from the previous section that the link between the consumer (or retail) price of marijuana (p_1), production costs (p_1') and
the risk premium (δ) is $p_1 = (1 + \delta)p_1'$. Taking the net-of-tax tobacco
price to represent p_1', we can use the data in Table 5.14 to estimate the
"apparent" risk premium as $\delta = (p_1/p_1' - 1)$, and Table 5.15 contains
the results. Even before any adjustments to make the comparison
between the two sets of prices more precise, such as allowing for the
additional packaging costs of tobacco and changes in marijuana
prices since 1999, at several thousands of percent, it seems that the
estimated risk premia are on the high side. Could it be that the two
products are not similar at all, but fundamentally different? Although
tobacco production and distribution are subject to substantial regulation, such as restriction of sales to adults only and bans on advertising in
some jurisdictions, it is still not an illegal product. The tobacco industry
can take advantage of large-scale production, administration, distribution, research and product innovation, such as selling cigarettes in
vending machines, options that are more difficult or impossible in
marijuana production. However, this difference would mean that if
marijuana were legalised, techniques used for tobacco could be adopted
and marijuana costs would decrease accordingly. Thus, the argument
that tobacco and marijuana are not comparable because of their

differing legal status is not an adequate explanation for the high estimates of the risk premium.

The estimates of the risk premium derived from a comparison of marijuana and tobacco prices are very approximate and appear to be high. Despite this qualification, the order of magnitude of these estimates is still of some interest, and we draw on these below.

Markups illegal and legal

A second source of evidence that relates to the possible value of the risk premium is the markup on drug prices from raw materials to the retail market. This markup reflects the costs of transforming raw materials into the final product purchased by consumers at the retail level. These costs include processing, transportation, distribution, repackaging, and other forms of value added, as well as the incremental costs of avoiding prosecution as the drugs move up the supply chain. Consequently, the markup is not exactly equivalent to our risk premium, which refers to just the costs of avoiding the ban (and the possible inefficiency effect). To clarify this distinction, consider first a production process that takes a legal commodity from the "farm gate" to the final consumer, and write p_f and p_c for the farm-gate and retail prices. If the value added is V dollars per unit, or $v = V/p_f$ as a proportion of the farm-gate price, and the markup is $m = p_c/p_f$, we then have:

$$p_c = (1+t)(1+v)p_f, \quad m = (1+t)(1+v), \qquad (5.17)$$

where t is the tax rate. Thus, if the tax rate is 50 per cent and value added is 100 per cent of the farm-gate price, the markup is $m = (1+t)(1+v) = (1.5)(2) = 3$. If the good is illegal, $t = 0$ and there is now a risk premium $\delta > 0$, so that (5.17) becomes:

$$p_c = (1+\delta)(1+v)p_f, \quad m = (1+\delta)(1+v). \qquad (5.18)$$

For the above tobacco/marijuana contrast, conceptually we compared the consumer price of marijuana with the production costs of tobacco, defined as the consumer price with the tax component stripped out. The estimate of the risk premium is then:

$$\delta = \frac{p_c}{(1+v)p_f} - 1 = \frac{m}{1+v} - 1. \qquad (5.19)$$

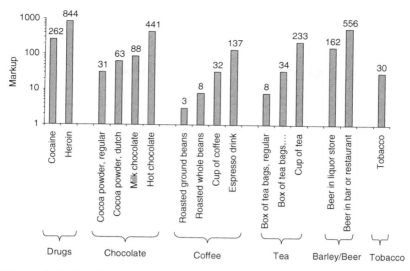

Figure 5.15. Markups for six commodities
Note: Where applicable, the mid-points of ranges have been used.
Source: Derived from Miron (2003).

Equations (5.17)–(5.19) clearly show the relationship between the markup for legal and illegal goods and the risk premium. Thus, if the markup is now 6 and the value added is 100 per cent, then the implied premium is $\delta = m/(1 + v) - 1 = 6/2 - 1 = 2$. In other words, in this example the markup is three times the risk premium.

The size of the markup in drug markets has been studied in the literature as a way to give some indication of the likely impact of prohibition on prices; see Miron (2003) for a brief review. The results indicate that drug markups are typically huge. This finding was further examined by Miron (2003), who compares the markup on cocaine and heroin with that on several legal products. That is, in effect this analysis uses equations (5.17) and (5.18). Figure 5.15, which summarises Miron's findings, shows that although the markup on cocaine is high, with the retail price 262 times the farm-gate price, it is of the same order of magnitude as that on chocolate, coffee, tea and barley/beer, but substantially greater than that on tobacco.[17] At 844, the heroin markup is by far the greatest in Figure 5.15. Miron

(2003, p. 525) argues that the prices of drugs and legal products are comparable:

The transactions used to compute the price of black market cocaine and heroin ... are for small quantities in relatively processed form (e.g., small amounts of crack). Thus, the more appropriate comparison is plausibly with the prices of the relatively processed legal products, such as espresso, implying effects of prohibition at the lower end of the range... This conclusion is not iron-clad; the purchase of an espresso at Starbucks differs in many respects from purchase of cocaine at a crack house. But the fact that substantial retail-to-farm gate ratios exist for legal goods including those with distribution and retailing patterns that are similar to what would plausibly exist for drugs in a legal market, at least raises the possibility that prohibition's effect is far smaller than indicated in previous research.

As indicated above, value added in the production process in part determines the markup. We can reverse engineer and ask what value added would be consistent with the markup observed and the apparent risk premium derived from the marijuana–tobacco comparison. For simplicity, suppose that the markup for cocaine is $m = 250$, which is approximately the value in Figure 5.15, and let the risk premium be $\delta = 80$ (or 8,000 per cent), which is an approximate average of the four estimates of the premium in Table 5.15. From equation (5.19), we have:

$$v = \frac{m}{1+\delta} - 1 = \frac{250}{81} - 1 \approx 2.1. \tag{5.20}$$

Thus, the implied value added is approximately 200 per cent of the farm-gate price. Although somewhat speculative and making no allowance for the differing risks involved with cocaine as opposed to marijuana, this is still not a completely unreasonable result for value added in the production of cocaine. However, it must be admitted that a similar calculation for heroin reveals a much greater value added of almost 1,000 per cent.

Miron's (2003) evidence suggests that illegality *per se* may not increase drug prices as much as some might think. On the basis of this and other evidence, Miron (2003, p. 529) estimates:

... that the black market price of cocaine is 2–4 times the price that would obtain in a legal market, and of heroin 6–19 times. In contrast, prior research has suggested that cocaine sells at 10 to 40 times its legal price and heroin at hundreds of times its legal price.

The smaller markups found by Miron (2003) could be taken to imply that the price effects of legalisation might be more limited than previously thought. Consistent with this line of thinking is research showing that increased enforcement of drug laws does not seem to result in higher prices (DiNardo, 1993; Weatherburn and Lind, 1997; Yuan and Caulkins, 1998).

A decomposition of drug prices

The third source of evidence on the risk premium is from estimates by Caulkins and Reuter (1998) of the components of the cost of cocaine, set out in Table 5.16. In this table, the various cost components are expressed as a percentage of the consumer price, so we can choose units such that the value of this price is $p_c = 100$. In terms of equation (5.18), we interpret the farm-gate price to be the wholesale cost of the drugs, so that $p_f = 1$ percent of the consumer price. Thus, the implied markup is $m = p_c/p_f = 100$, which is substantially less than the above-mentioned estimate of Miron (2003) for cocaine. Value added in Table 5.16 is 29 times the farm-gate price, so that $v = 29$, and the estimated production cost is $(1 + v)p_f = 30$. The risk premium δ then accounts for the difference between the consumer price and the production cost, $p_c = (1 + \delta)(1 + v)p_f$, which implies a premium in this market of:

$$\delta = \frac{p_c}{(1 + v)p_f} - 1 = \frac{100}{30} - 1 \approx 2.3, \qquad (5.21)$$

or 230 per cent. As shown in Table 5.16, the risk premium comprises costs related to money laundering, drug and asset seizures, and compensation for the risk of prison and physical risk. Interestingly, estimate (5.21) is arguably not greatly at odds with our backed-out estimate of the marijuana risk premium of "something greater than 300 per cent" discussed above. However, we should note that as the above estimate of value added of $v = 29$ is more than 10-fold greater than (speculative) estimate (5.20), the two sources of evidence imply markedly different production processes for cocaine.

Table 5.16: *Cost components of retail cocaine, 1990*

Component		Per cent of total
Materials		
Wholesale drugs		1
Value added		
Packaging, processing and inventory	2	
Importing costs	12	
Labour	15	
Sub total		29
Production costs		30
Crime related		
Money laundering	3	
Drug and asset seizures	10	
Risk of prison	24	
Physical risk	33	
Sub total		70
Total		100

Source: Caulkins and Reuter (1998), using the mid-points of ranges.

Distribution of the risk premium

As a final piece of evidence/information on the risk premium, we provide some guidance as to its uncertainty. To do this, we use a stochastic extension of the approach taken at the end of Section 5.12 whereby we attempted to infer the value of the risk premium given values for revenue and the tax rate.

We return to equation (5.15), the expression for revenue from marijuana:

$$R_1^{(1)} = t_1'^{(1)} \left(\frac{1}{1+\delta} \right) p_1^{(0)} q_1^{(0)} \exp\left\{ \eta_{11}^* \left[\log\left(1 + t_1'^{(1)}\right) - \log(1 + \delta) \right] \right\},$$

which can be solved for the risk premium:

$$\delta = {}^{\left(1+\eta_{11}^*\right)}\!\!\sqrt{\frac{t_1'^{(1)} p_1^{(0)} q_1^{(0)} \left(1 + t_1'^{(1)}\right)^{\eta_{11}^*}}{R_1^{(1)}}} - 1. \qquad (5.22)$$

For given values of revenue $R_1^{(1)}$, tax rate $t_1'^{(1)}$, expenditure $p_1^{(0)} q_1^{(0)}$ and price elasticity η_{11}^*, equation (5.22) provides a corresponding value of

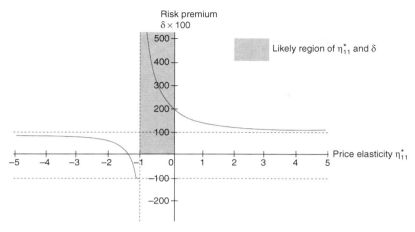

Figure 5.16. Risk premium and price elasticity of demand for marijuana

the risk premium δ. The values of the variables on the right-hand side of equation (5.22) are specified as follows:

- As discussed at the end of Section 5.12, Caputo and Ostrom (1994) estimate that taxation of marijuana in the US could raise approximately 18 per cent of pre-existing revenue from tobacco and alcohol. As before, we suppose that the same relative amount of revenue could be raised in Australia, that is, 18 per cent of \$684 or \$123 per capita.
- As before, we suppose marijuana is taxed at approximately the same rate as tobacco, that is, 50 per cent of the consumer price, or $t_1^{\prime(1)} \times 100 = 100$ percent of the producer price.
- We use observed expenditure on marijuana of $p_1^{(0)} q_1^{(0)} = 372$ from Table 5.9.
- For the price elasticity η_{11}^*, we use the 5,000 values discussed above.

Solution (5.22) does not yield a positive risk premium for all values of the elasticity η_{11}^*, as observed from Figure 5.16, which plots δ against η_{11}^*, with the other variables specified as above. However, for the most likely elasticity range of $-1 \leq \eta_{11}^* \leq 0$ the risk premium is always positive, but the values of $\delta \times 100$ corresponding to this elasticity range always exceed 200 per cent. The figure also reveals that as $\eta_{11}^* \to -1$ from above, the curve becomes very steep. Thus, in this range solution (5.22) is sensitive to variations in the price elasticity. It should also be noted that Figure 5.16 establishes that for negative values of the price elasticity, the risk premium always falls outside the range 100–200 per cent.

The above procedure yields 5,000 values of δ, of which 692 (or 14 per cent) are negative and discarded. The results are summarised in the frequency distributions of Figure 5.17. As there are some large positive values, the distribution is truncated and Panel C, in which truncation occurs at 750 per cent, shows that the mean, median and standard deviation of the premium are approximately 350, 310 and 140 per cent, respectively. The gap in this distribution between 100 and 200 per cent is specific to the data and occurs for the reason discussed in the previous paragraph. Truncation affects the mean and (especially) the standard deviation, whereas the median is relatively insensitive. Column 2 of Table 5.17 shows that there is a 42 per cent chance of the premium lying between 200 and 300 per cent, so there is a fair degree of uncertainty.

Next, to allow for uncertainty of marijuana expenditure, we suppose that it is also random. Recall from Table 5.7 that the budget share of marijuana, $w_1 = p_1 q_1 / M$, follows a normal distribution with mean 0.02 and variance $(0.005)^2$. As expenditure on marijuana is \$372 per capita, implied total expenditure is $M = p_1 q_1 / w_1 = 372/0.02 = \$18,600$ per capita. The normality of the budget share implies that expenditure is also normal, with mean 372 and variance $[18,600 \times 0.005]^2 = 93^2$. We draw 5,000 values from this distribution and discard any falling outside the range [0, 18,600]. In a given trial, we draw the elasticity and expenditure, which, together with the values for revenue and tax rate discussed above, allows us to obtain δ from equation (5.22). The results are summarised in Figure 5.18 and column 3 of Table 5.17. In comparison with the results in Figure 5.17, in all three cases the standard deviation of the distribution is now higher than before, as is to be expected, whereas in Panels A and B the medians are not too different from before. In Panel C of Figure 5.18, some results for the premium now fall within the range 100–200 per cent, which makes the median in this case lower than before. There is now a 23 per cent chance that the premium falls in the range 200–300 per cent (42 per cent chance previously). In short, in the more realistic case in which marijuana expenditure is treated as random, the value of the risk premium seems to be centred around 200–300 per cent, but there is

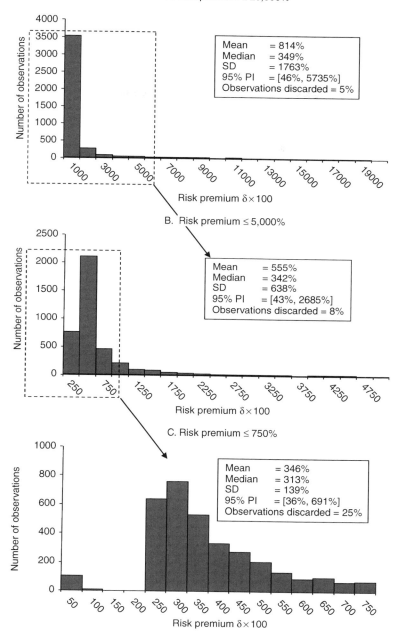

Figure 5.17. Distribution of the risk premium for marijuana: (I) Elasticity random

Notes:

1. Negative values of δ are discarded (14 per cent of the total number of trials).

2. In the boxes in each panel, the term "observations discarded" refers to the per cent of positive values of δ discarded.

Table 5.17: *Probability of the risk premium for marijuana*

Range $\delta \times 100$	What's random?	
	Price elasticity	Price elasticity and expenditure
(1)	(2)	(3)
0–100	0.03	0.14
100–200	0	0.18
200–300	0.42	0.23
300–400	0.26	0.17
>400	0.28	0.28

Note: The probabilities in column 2 (3) are calculated using the distribution of δ in Panel C of Figure 5.17 (5.18).

substantial uncertainty. Note that this range for the premium is somewhat less than that discussed at the end of the previous section of "something greater than 300 per cent", but in view of the underlying uncertainty, we should not be greatly concerned about this difference.

Conclusion

This section can be summarised as follows. The numerical value of the risk premium for the marijuana industry is a key parameter in estimating the likely impact of legalisation on prices and how much revenue could be raised by taxing marijuana. We discussed four sources of evidence, but were not able to make a definitive estimate of the risk premium. However, if we were forced to make a "best guess", we would favour a premium in the range 200–300 per cent. Before the introduction of any taxation, legalisation would cause the consumer price of marijuana to decrease from $(1 + \delta)p'$ to the production cost p'_1, or by $100 \times \delta/(1 + \delta)$ per cent. To illustrate, if the premium were 250 per cent, the price would fall by $100 \times \delta/(1 + \delta) \approx$ 70 per cent. However, as this estimate is subject to considerable uncertainty, further research that sheds more light on the costs of producing marijuana and how these might change in the event of legalisation is desirable.

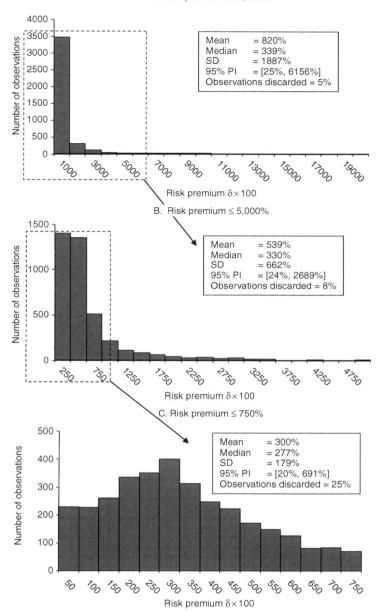

A. Risk premium ≤ 20,000%

Mean	= 820%
Median	= 339%
SD	= 1887%
95% PI	= [25%, 6156%]
Observations discarded = 5%	

Risk premium δ × 100

B. Risk premium ≤ 5,000%

Mean	= 539%
Median	= 330%
SD	= 662%
95% PI	= [24%, 2689%]
Observations discarded = 8%	

Risk premium δ × 100

C. Risk premium ≤ 750%

Mean	= 300%
Median	= 277%
SD	= 179%
95% PI	= [20%, 691%]
Observations discarded = 25%	

Risk premium δ × 100

Figure 5.18. Distribution of the risk premium of marijuana: (II) Elasticity and expenditure random

Notes:

1. Negative values of δ are discarded (13 per cent of the total number of trials).

2. In the boxes in each panel, the term "observations discarded" refers to the per cent of positive values of δ discarded.

5.14 Summary

This chapter has considered the decriminalisation and legalisation of marijuana. This is a complex issue involving aspects of the law, health and economics, as well as community attitudes. Accordingly, it is not very surprising that it is not always possible to provide firm answers. Nevertheless, it is possible to make some progress by providing a deeper understanding of the issues involved. We achieved this by considering the policy of declaring certain drugs to be illegal within an economics-of-taxation framework, and by emphasising the measurement issues involved in estimating the impact of decriminalising marijuana. We now present a brief summary of the major findings on decriminalisation and legalisation.

We reviewed empirical studies on the impact of marijuana decriminalisation policies in Australia and the US, where experiments in relation to legislative arrangements for marijuana consumption have taken place. Eleven US states decriminalised the possession of small amounts of marijuana in the 1970s, followed by a twelfth state in 1996, and four Australian states have done the same since the late 1980s. We examined marijuana usage in the eight Australian states and territories before and after the policy changes, using data from national representative surveys since 1985, and reviewed published econometric studies examining the impact of decriminalisation. Although most published studies indicate a positive effect, it is not clear whether decriminalisation has resulted in a significant increase in marijuana use. This result is similar to findings in the literature on US decriminalisation policies.

We discussed several issues that complicate empirical evaluation of the so-called decriminalisation effect. As in the US (Pacula *et al.*, 2003), a key feature of Australia's decriminalisation laws is that the legislative details are complex and differ across states and territories. Not only are there differences in the penalties for the possession of small quantities of marijuana before a criminal charge is recorded, and in the definition of what constitutes a small quantity, but non-decriminalised states have also introduced a more lenient approach to initial small offences. This calls into question whether the legislative differences across states can be simply represented by a single "decriminalisation status" variable, and how the estimated decriminalisation effect should be interpreted. Another major issue is the availability of sufficient data to be able to confidently identify the policy effect. As there have only been eight national representative surveys of recreational drug use since 1985, there are only a limited number of observations before and after decriminalisation, which is arguably insufficient for proper identification of a statistical "treatment effect". It is thus difficult to separately identify the decriminalisation effect from any "state effect" using the available data.

We explored the possible implications of a radical change involving complete legalisation and taxation of marijuana, so that it was treated in a manner similar to that for tobacco and alcohol. Revenue from vice taxation increases noticeably with the marijuana tax. For example, under the base-case scenario and when the marijuana risk premium is 200 per cent, taxing marijuana at the same rate as tobacco is estimated to yield additional revenue of approximately 26 per cent of the pre-existing proceeds from taxation of tobacco and alcohol. The attractive feature of our approach is that it provides whole distributions of consumption and revenue from taxation corresponding to each rate of marijuana taxation. The dispersion of these distributions, which reflects the underlying uncertainty concerning data and parameters, increases as we move away from the status quo, whereby marijuana escapes the tax net and is subjected to successively higher rates of taxation.

APPENDIX

A5.1 Data

Table A5.1 provides the underlying Australian data. Panel A lists expenditure on marijuana, tobacco and alcohol, as well as total consumption. Panel B converts these data into budget shares. The last column of Panel B presents the budget share of vice – the sum of marijuana, tobacco and alcohol – and, interestingly, this has noticeably decreased over the 1990s. The share was 13.4 per cent in 1988 and decreased by more than 5 percentage points to 7.8 per cent in 1998. The tobacco share, which decreased by almost 4 percentage points, accounts for a large part of the total decrease.

In Table 5.4 we use the following values for the budget shares: marijuana, 2 per cent; tobacco, 2 per cent; alcohol, 4 per cent; and all other goods, 92 per cent. These values approximate the shares given in Panel B of Table A5.1 towards the end of the period.

Table A5.1: *Vice expenditure and total consumption*

Year (1)	Marijuana (2)	Tobacco (3)	Alcohol (4)	Total consumption (5)
A. Expenditure (dollars per capita)				
1988	392	916	703	15,005
1989	417	900	734	16,407
1990	442	873	755	17,068
1991	453	819	754	17,870
1992	349	755	755	18,437
1993	316	692	804	19,005
1994	338	636	810	20,178
1995	329	605	848	21,244
1996	360	597	863	21,802
1997	370	597	895	22,769
1998	372	597	879	23,592
B. Unconditional budget shares for vice (percentage)				
1988	2.6	6.1	4.7	13.4
1989	2.5	5.5	4.5	12.5
1990	2.6	5.1	4.4	12.1
1991	2.5	4.6	4.2	11.3
1992	1.9	4.1	4.1	10.1
1993	1.7	3.6	4.2	9.5
1994	1.7	3.2	4.0	8.8
1995	1.5	2.8	4.0	8.4
1996	1.7	2.7	4.0	8.4
1997	1.6	2.6	3.9	8.2
1998	1.6	2.5	3.7	7.8

Note: In Panel A, the total population aged 14 years and over is used to compute per capita expenditures.

Sources:

1. Marijuana expenditure in column 2 of Panel A is the product of the price per unit and the quantity consumed. The price data are from Clements (2004) and the quantity data from Clements and Daryal (2005). As marijuana prices for 1988 and 1989 are not available, we compute them by backwards extrapolation using the average annual log change in marijuana prices for the period 1990–1998. Except for the first two years, these data are the same as those in Panel I of Table 4.8 in Chapter 4.

2. Column 3 of Panel A is computed as total tobacco expenditure (ABS Cat. No. 5206.0) divided by the population aged 14 and over (ABS Cat. No. 3201).

3. Column 4 of Panel A is from Selvanathan (2003), who provided per capita expenditure on beer, wine and spirits defined for the total population, which we then converted to a 14-year-and-over basis using population data from ABS Catalogue No. 3201.

4. Column 5 of Panel A is conventionally defined total consumption expenditure from Selvanathan (2003), plus marijuana expenditure. The unconditional budget shares in Panel B use this broader measure of total consumption in the denominator.

A5.2 Notes on legalisation, taxes and marijuana prices

In Section 5.12, we considered a scenario involving legalisation of the consumption of marijuana and then subjecting it to varying degrees of taxation. We supposed that legislation would lead to (i) an unchanged demand curve and (ii) a downward shift of the supply curve, as producers no longer incur the costs of avoiding the ban. As this is not the only possibility, in this appendix we explore the issues involved.

Following Miron (2005), we can analyse the price change resulting from legalisation by reference to the relative shifts of the marijuana demand and supply curves. According to the "forbidden fruit" hypothesis, legalisation makes marijuana less attractive and shifts the demand curve down and to the left, as in Panel A of Figure A5.1. Regarding the supply curve, Miron (1998, 2005) argues on *a priori* grounds that legalisation could shift it either up or down, as shown in Panel B of Figure A5.1. On legalisation, producers would no longer be forced to incur costs associated with concealing their activities to avoid prosecution, causing the supply curve to shift down and to the right. On the other hand, legalisation would also mean that producers would have to pay conventional taxes and charges, and comply with all the regulations that legitimate businesses are subject to. In addition, marijuana producers would possibly have to incur advertising expenses if the product were legalised. These effects would cause the supply curve to shift up and to the left.

The net effect of these shifts in the demand and supply curves on prices is ambiguous, as illustrated in Panel C of Figure A5.1 for the simplified case in which the demand curve remains unchanged. This ambiguity can only be resolved with empirical evidence. Although such evidence is not easy to obtain, Miron (2005) argues that on the basis of a comparison of marijuana prices in the US, where restrictions are stronger, and Australia and The Netherlands, where they are weaker, the net effect on prices is likely to be quite small. Another piece of evidence, discussed in Section 5.13, that points in the same direction is Miron's (2003) finding from a detailed analysis that mark-ups from the "farm gate" to consumers of heroin and cocaine are substantially smaller than previously thought.

A5.3 Sensitivity analysis

The results of Section 5.12 are all based on mean values of the underlying parameters that are given in Table 5.4. As one of the key

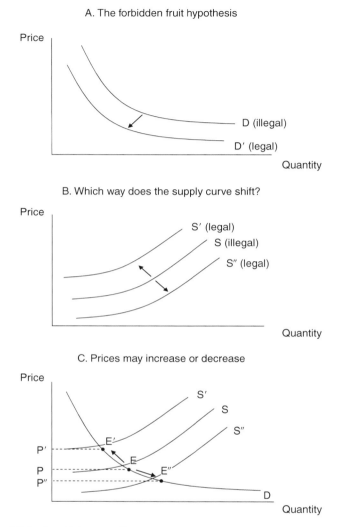

Figure A5.1. Legalising marijuana

parameters is the income elasticity of marijuana η_1, which has a mean of 1.2, in this appendix we investigate the sensitivity of the results to this value.

Table A5.2 contains a summary of the results for consumption and revenue when the income elasticity of marijuana takes values of 0.5,

Table A5.2: *Sensitivity of tax proceeds and consumption changes*

		Revenue from					Change in consumption (log-changes ×100)			
		Marijuana		Total vice (marijuana, tobacco and alcohol)						
Risk premium $\delta \times 100$	Change in consumer price (log-change) $\log\left(\frac{2}{1+\delta}\right) \times 100$	Dollars per capita	Percent of existing revenue	Dollars per capita	Percent of existing revenue	Marijuana	Tobacco	Alcohol	Total
(1)	(2)	(3)	(4)	(5)	(6)	(7)	(8)	(9)	(10)
			A. Income elasticity of marijuana = 0.5						
0	69	309	45	979	143	−19.06	−8.07	2.75	−5.41
50	29	229	34	907	133	−7.91	−3.35	1.14	−2.24
100	0	186	27	871	127	0	0	0	0
200	−41	139	20	834	122	11.15	4.72	−1.61	3.16
300	−69	113	17	816	119	19.06	8.07	−2.75	5.41
			B. Income elasticity of marijuana = 1.0						
0	69	260	38	929	136	−37.98	−10.91	4.65	−9.90
50	29	213	31	890	130	−15.76	−4.53	1.93	−4.11
100	0	186	27	871	127	0	0	0	0
200	−41	156	23	853	125	22.22	6.38	−2.72	5.79
300	−69	140	20	846	124	37.98	10.91	−4.65	9.90

Table A5.2: (continued)

Risk premium $\delta \times 100$ (1)	Change in consumer price (log-change) $\log\left(\frac{2}{1+\delta}\right)\times100$ (2)	Revenue from				Change in consumption (log-changes $\times$ 100)			
		Marijuana		Total vice (marijuana, tobacco and alcohol)		Marijuana (7)	Tobacco (8)	Alcohol (9)	Total (10)
		Dollars per capita (3)	Percent of existing revenue (4)	Dollars per capita (5)	Percent of existing revenue (6)				
			C. Income elasticity of marijuana = 1.2						
0	69	245	36	914	134	−44.90	−11.87	5.27	−11.56
50	29	207	30	884	129	−18.63	−4.93	2.19	−4.80
100	0	186	27	871	127	0	0	0	0
200	−41	163	24	861	126	26.26	6.94	−3.08	6.76
300	−69	152	22	860	126	44.90	11.87	−5.27	11.56
			D. Income elasticity of marijuana = 2.0						
0	69	192	28	861	126	−74.20	−15.43	7.80	−18.51
50	29	185	27	862	126	−30.79	−6.40	3.24	−7.68
100	0	186	27	871	127	0	0	0	0
200	−41	198	29	898	131	43.40	9.03	−4.56	10.83
300	−69	219	32	933	136	74.20	15.43	−7.80	18.51

Notes:
1. The entries in this table are all means over the 5,000 trials corresponding to a marijuana tax of 50 per cent of the consumer price.
2. Panel C is from Table 5.13.
3. The entries of panels A, B and D are computed in exactly the same way as are those of panel C, but now the mean income elasticity of marijuana takes the values of 0.5, 1.0 and 2.0, respectively, rather than 1.2, the base value, as in panel C.

1.0 and 2.0, as well as the base case of 1.2. Here, marijuana is taken to be taxed at 50 per cent of the consumer price, which is equivalent to 100 per cent of the producer price. To interpret these results, start with panel C, which refers to the base case in which $\eta_1 = 1.2$. The results here are reproduced from Table 5.1. The other panels of Table A5.2 refer to alternative values of the income elasticity of marijuana. These reveal two patterns. First, as the income elasticity decreases and the risk premium is held constant, the absolute value of the change in consumption of each good decreases. The explanation for this is that there is a systematic tendency for the price elasticities to decrease (in absolute value) as the income elasticity of marijuana increases. The lower price elasticities then mean that imposition of the marijuana tax brings about a smaller change in consumption of each good. As discussed in Appendix A4.8, under the conditions of preference independence, the own-price elasticity is exactly proportional to the income elasticity. Although in this chapter we did not rely on the assumption of preference independence (marijuana and tobacco are preference-dependent), it seems that there is still a tendency for price elasticities to be related to the income elasticity.

The second pattern in the results of Table A5.2 pertains to taxation revenue. We need to distinguish two cases here:

- *When the tax exceeds the risk premium.* Here, the risk premium is less than 100 per cent, so that the consumer price increases with legalisation and imposition of the tax. Direct revenue from marijuana always increases as the income elasticity decreases and the premium is held constant. The reason is that as its income elasticity decreases, the price elasticity of marijuana also decreases in absolute value. This means that the tax base shrinks by less with the imposition of a given tax rate, so that revenue is higher when the income elasticity is lower. As marijuana dominates, total revenue from vice moves in the same direction as direct revenue from marijuana.
- *When the tax is less than the risk premium.* The consumer price decreases in this case, and revenue decreases as the income elasticity decreases and the premium is held constant. As the price of marijuana decreases, the tax base expands by less when the income (and price) elasticity is lower, in a manner that is exactly the opposite of the above case (in which the price increases).

Notes

1. A negative tax, or a subsidy, has the same welfare-reducing effect, as evident from Panels B and C of Figure 5.2.
2. This result has to be qualified to allow for government revenue requirements.
3. See, for example, Cameron and Williams (2001), Clements and Daryal (2005), Saffer and Chaloupka (1995) and Zhao and Harris (2004).
4. The situation in Russia provides an illuminating example. *The Economist* (September 13, 2003, p. 66) describes it as follows: "The figures prove what everyone knows: Russians drink like mad. In 2001, alcohol overdoses killed 139 people in England and Wales, but more than 40,000 Russians, in a population less than three times the size. But other official figures indicate quite the opposite: the average Briton consumed the equivalent of 8.4 litres of pure alcohol in 2001, the average Russian swallowed a mere 8.1 litres. Why the discrepancy? A mix of understated production by Russian distillers and the Russian taste for industrial alcohol or toxic moonshine could be one explanation."
5. For a brief review of previous studies, see Clements and Selvanathan (1991). More recently, Selvanathan and Selvanathan (2005, pp. 232, 237) use time-series data for ten countries to estimate conditional income elasticities for the three alcoholic beverages. Averaging over countries, they obtain 0.75 for beer, 1.1 for wine and 1.42 for spirits, and 0.75, 0.98 and 1.39, respectively, using a somewhat different approach. In view of sampling variability, these values are unlikely to be significantly different to those described in the text.
6. It should be noted that income elasticity of 1.0 for alcohol also agrees with the evidence of Selvanathan and Selvanathan (2005, p. 195), who estimate this elasticity for 40 countries with time-series data. The average of these 40 estimates is 1.04. Using a somewhat different approach, the mean of another 40 estimates is 0.96 (Selvanathan and Selvanathan, 2005, p. 207).
7. Chapter 4 also presents estimates of a demand model for marijuana, beer, wine and spirits, with preference independence imposed (to keep things manageable). As this rules out complementarity, these estimates cannot shed any light on the issue of substitutes versus complements.
8. Subjective probability distributions and the simulation techniques described above are typically used in modern Bayesian analysis (see, for example, Geweke, 1999). For examples of a similar approach in the context of equilibrium displacement models, see Griffiths and Zhao (2000) and Zhao *et al.* (2000).

9. It is, however, possible to make some approximate adjustments for the supply side along the following lines. Recall from equation (5.3) that within a general demand-and-supply model a fraction α of an increase in a commodity tax is passed onto consumers in the form of higher prices. Accordingly, if we specify directly that consumer prices increase by z percent, then the associated tax increase is z/α per cent. As discussed in Section 5.2, if, for example, the price elasticities of demand and supply are -1 and 1, respectively, then $\alpha = 1/2$, so that a 10-percent increase in consumer prices is associated with a 20 per cent tax increase.

10. Over the 1990s, the relative price of marijuana in Australia decreased by approximately 5 per cent per annum. See Section 3.4.

11. The same analysis could also be carried out using Slutsky price elasticities assuming that real income is constant. However, it is probably more realistic to assume that money income is constant for the scenarios considered in this section.

12. Let p_i, p_i', q_i and t_i' be the retail price, pre-tax price, quantity consumed, and tax as a proportion of the pre-tax price for good i, respectively. The two sets of prices are linked according to $p_i = (1 + t_i')p_i'$, so that $d(\log p_i) = dt_i'/(1 + t_i')$. Thus, with $dt_i' = 0.1$, $t_2' = 1.19$, and $t_3' = 0.69$ and for simplicity holding retail margins and GST unchanged, the relative change in the retail price is $0.1/(1 + 1.19) = 0.046$ for tobacco and $0.1/(1 + 0.69) = 0.059$ for alcohol.

13. In a completely general framework, the change in consumption and the amount of revenue raised depend on a range of factors, including how the demand and supply curves shift, the tax rate, and the price sensitivity of both demand and supply. Legalisation of marijuana could shift its supply and demand curves in either direction and lead to ambiguous effects on the price and quantity consumed; see Appendix A5.2. We focus on what seems to be the most likely case of a stable demand curve and a supply curve that shifts downwards with legalisation.

14. When there is no ambiguity, to simplify the notation we subsequently usually omit superscript (1) from the tax rates $t_1'^{(1)}$ and $t_1^{(1)}$.

15. Similar types of tax-evasion issues are relevant to analysis of the taxation of tobacco and alcohol.

16. The language of this and the previous sentence is deliberately guarded for the following reason. If we evaluate mean revenue for values of the risk premium that are successively greater than 300 per cent, we never actually hit $123.

17. To illustrate the workings of these markup calculations, consider the case of barley/beer. The price of a kilogram of malting barley is $US0.096, whereas this quantity of barley produces beer sold in the

form of a case in a liquor store that costs between $13.32 ...~~~~~~~~~~~~~
⟨Miron, 2003, Table 6⟩. This yields a markup of between 13.32/
0.096 = 139 and 17.78/0.096 = 185. In Figure 5.15, the mid-point of this
range, ½(139+185) = 162, is used in the third-last column from the
right.

References

Aagaard, J., Carter, S., Kiely, L., McAdam, E., Miller, F. and Wood, G.
    (2004). "Petrol sniffing in remote Northern Territory communities."
    Report prepared by the Select Committee on Substance Abuse in the
    Community, Legislative Assembly of the Northern Territory.

Atkinson, A. B. and Stiglitz, J. E. (1980). *Lectures in public economics.*
    New York: McGraw-Hill.

Australian Drug Foundation (2007). *Cannabis law in Australia.* DrugInfo
    Clearing House, Australian Drug Foundation, available at www.
    druginfo.adf.org.au.

Barten, A. P. (1964). "Consumer demand functions under conditions of
    almost additive preferences." *Econometrica* 32, 1–38.

Basov, S., Jacobson, M. and Miron, J. (2001). "Prohibition and the market
    for illegal drugs: an overview of recent history." *World Economics* 2,
    133–57.

Bates, S. W. (2004). "The economic implications of marijuana legalisation in
    Alaska." Report for Alaskans for Rights and Revenues, Fairbanks, Alaska.

Bretteville-Jensen, A. L. (2006). "To legalise or not to legalise? Economic
    approaches to the decriminalisation of drugs." *Substance Use and
    Misuse* 41, 555–65.

Britton, E., Fisher, P. and Whitley, J. (1998). "The inflation report pro-
    jection: understanding the fan chart." *Bank of England Quarterly
    Bulletin* 38, 30–7.

Cameron, L. and Williams, J. (2001). "Cannabis, alcohol and cigarettes:
    substitutes or complements?" *Economic Record* 77, 19–34.

Cameron, S. (1998). "Estimation of the demand for cigarettes: a review of
    the literature." *Economic Issues* 3, 51–70.

Caputo, M. R. and Ostrom, B. J. (1994). "Potential tax revenue from a
    regulated marijuana market: a meaningful revenue source." *American
    Journal of Economics and Sociology* 53, 475–90.

Caulkins, J. P. and Reuter, P. (1998). "What price data tell us about drug
    markets." *Journal of Drug Issues* 28: 593–612.

Chaloupka, F. J. and Laixuthai, A. (1997). "Do youths substitute alcohol
    and marijuana? Some econometric evidence." *Eastern Economic
    Journal* 23, 253–76.

Chaloupka, F. J. and Warner, K. E. (2000). "The economics of smoking." In A. J. Culyer and J. P. Newhouse, eds., *Handbook of health economics.* Vol. 1. Amsterdam: Elsevier, pp. 1539–627.

Chaloupka, F. J., Grossman, M. and Tauras, A. (1998). "The demand for cocaine and marijuana by youth." NBER Working Paper No. 6411. Cambridge, MA: National Bureau of Economic Research.

Chaloupka, F. J., Pacula, R. L., Farrelly, M., Johnston, L. and O'Malley, P. (1999). "Do higher cigarette prices encourage youth to use marijuana?" NBER Working Paper No. 6939, Cambridge, MA: National Bureau of Economic Research.

Clements, K. W. (2004). "Three facts about marijuana prices." *Australian Journal of Agricultural and Resource Economics* 48, 271–300.

Clements, K. W. and Daryal, M. (2005). "The economics of marijuana consumption." Chapter 10 in S. Selvanathan and E. A. Selvanathan, eds., *The demand for alcohol, tobacco and marijuana: international evidence.* Aldershot: Ashgate, pp. 243–67.

Clements, K. W. and Johnson, L. W. (1983). "The demand for beer, wine and spirits: a system-wide analysis." *Journal of Business* 56, 273–304.

Clements, K. W., Lan, Y. and Zhao, X. (2008). "The demand for marijuana, tobacco and alcohol: inter-commodity interactions with uncertainty." Working Paper, Business School, The University of Western Australia and Department of Econometrics and Business Statistics, and Centre for Health Economics, Monash University. Forthcoming in *Empirical Economics*, Springer Publishers.

Clements, K. W. and Selvanathan, S. (1991). "The economic determinants of alcohol consumption." *Australian Journal of Agricultural Economics* 35, 209–31.

Clough, A., Abbs, P. D., Cairney, S., Gray, D., Maruff, P., Parker, R. and O'Reilly, B. (2004). "Emerging patterns of cannabis and other substance use in Aboriginal communities in Arnhem Land, Northern Territory: a study of two communities." *Drug and Alcohol Review* 23(4), 381–90.

Commonwealth of Australia (1994). *Legislative options for cannabis use in Australia.* Monograph No. 26, Department of Health and Ageing, Commonwealth of Australia.

Culyer, A. J. (1973). "Should social policy concern itself with drug 'abuse'?" *Public Finance Quarterly* 1, 449–56.

Damrongplasit, K., Hsiao, C. and Zhao, X. (forthcoming). "Decriminalisation and marijuana smoking prevalence: evidence from Australia." *Journal of Business and Economic Statistics.*

Daryal, M. (1999). *The economics of marijuana.* Unpublished BEc Honours thesis, The University of Western Australia.

Decker, S. L. and Schwartz, A. E. (2000). "Cigarettes and alcohol: substitutes or complements?" NBER Working Paper No. 7535. Cambridge, MA: National Bureau of Economic Research.

DeSimone, J. and Farrelly, M. C. (2003). "Price and enforcement effects on cocaine and marijuana demand." *Economic Inquiry* 41, 98–115.

DiNardo, J. (1993). "Law enforcement, the price of cocaine and cocaine use." *Mathematical and Computer Modeling* 17, 53–64.

DiNardo, J. and Lemieux, T. (2001). "Alcohol, marijuana, and American youth: the unintended consequences of government regulation." *Journal of Health Economics* 20, 991–1010.

Dixon, P. B. and Rimmer, M. T. (2002). *Dynamic general equilibrium modelling for forecasting and policy: a practical guide and documentation of MONASH.* Amsterdam: North-Holland.

Donnelly, N., Hall, W. and Christie, P. (1995). "The effects of decriminalisation on cannabis use in South Australia 1985–1993." *Australian Journal of Public Health* 19, 281–7.

Donnelly, N., Hall, W. and Christie, P. (1999). *Effects of the cannabis expiation notice scheme on levels and patterns of cannabis use in South Australia: evidence from the National Drug Strategy Household Surveys 1985–1995.* National Drug Strategy Monograph Series No. 37, Commonwealth Department of Health and Aged Care, Canberra.

Duffy, M. (1991). "Advertising and the consumption of tobacco and alcoholic drink: a system-wide analysis." *Scottish Journal of Political Economy* 38, 369–85.

Easton, S. T. (2004). "Marijuana growth in British Columbia." Public Policy Sources, Fraser Institute Occasional Paper, Vancouver, BC.

Farrelly, M. C., Bray, J. W., Zarkin, G. A. and Wendling, B. W. (2001). "The joint demand for cigarettes and marijuana: evidence from the National Household Surveys on Drug Abuse." *Journal of Health Economics* 20, 51–68.

Farrelly, M. C., Bray, J., Zarkin, G. A., Wendling, B. W. and Pacula, R. (1999). "The effects of prices and policies on the demand for marijuana: evidence from the National Household Surveys on Drug Abuse." NBER Working Paper No. 6940. Cambridge, MA: National Bureau of Economic Research.

Fisher, I. (1926). *Prohibition at its worst.* New York: Macmillan.

Fullerton, D. and Metcalf, G. E. (2002). "Tax incidence." In A. Auerbach and M. Feldstein, eds., *Handbook of public economics.* Amsterdam: North-Holland.

Gallet, C. A. and List, J. A. (2003). "Cigarette demand: a meta-analysis of elasticities." *Health Economics* 12, 821–35.

Geweke, J. (1999). "Using simulation methods for Bayesian econometric models: inference, development and communication." *Econometric Reviews* 18, 1–126.

Goel, R. K. and Morey, M. J. (1995). "The interdependence of cigarette and liquor demand." *Southern Economic Journal* 62, 451–9.

Griffiths, W. and Zhao, X. (2000). "A unified approach to sensitivity analysis in equilibrium displacement models: comment." *American Journal of Agricultural Economics* 82, 236–40.

Hall, W. (1997). "The recent Australian debate about the prohibition on cannabis use." *Addiction* 92, 1109–15.

Hall, W. and Pacula, R. (2003). *Cannabis use and dependence: public health and public policy.* Cambridge, UK: Cambridge University Press.

Houthakker, H. S. (1960). "Additive preferences." *Econometrica* 28, 247–57.

Hsiao, C., Li, Q. and Racine, J. (2007). "A consistent model specification test with mixed discrete and continuous data." *Journal of Econometrics* 140, 802–26.

Johnston, L. D., O'Malley, P. and Bachman, J. (1981). "Marijuana decriminalisation: the impact on youth, 1975–1980." Monitoring the Future Occasional Paper 13, Institute for Social Research, University of Michigan.

Jones, A. M. (1989). "A systems approach to the demand for alcohol and tobacco." *Bulletin of Economic Research* 41, 85–105.

Kyvig, D. E. (1979). *Repealing national prohibition.* Chicago, IL: The University of Chicago Press.

Maloof, D. (1981). "A review of the effects of the decriminalisation of marijuana." *Contemporary Drug Problems* 10, 307–22.

Manderson, D. (1993). *From Mr Sin to Mr Big: a history of Australian drug laws.* Melbourne: Oxford University Press.

Miron, J. A. (1998). "Drug prohibition." In P. Newman, ed., *The new Palgrave dictionary of economics and the law*, London: Macmillan, pp. 648–52.

Miron, J. A. (1999). "The effect of alcohol prohibition on alcohol consumption." NBER Working Paper No. 7130. Cambridge, MA: National Bureau of Economic Research.

Miron, J. A. (2003). "The effect of drug prohibition on drug prices: evidence from the markets for cocaine and heroin." *Review of Economics and Statistics* 85, 522–30.

Miron, J. A. (2005). "The budgetary implications of marijuana prohibition." Available at www.prohibitioncosts.org/mironreport.html.

Miron, J. A. and Zwiebel, J. (1991). "Alcohol consumption during prohibition." *American Economic Review* 81, 242–7.

Model, K. (1993). "The effect of marijuana decriminalisation on hospital emergency room drug episodes: 1975–1980." *Journal of the American Statistical Association* 88, 737–47.

NDSHS (2001). *Computer files of unit record data, National Drug Strategy Household Surveys 1998 and 2001.* Canberra: Social Science Data Archives, The Australian National University.

NDSHS (2004). National Drug Strategy Household Survey (computer file, various issues). Canberra: Social Science Data Archives, The Australian National University.

Pacula, R. L. (1998). "Does increasing the beer tax reduce marijuana consumption?" *Journal of Health Economics* 17, 557–85.

Pacula, R. L. (2005). "Marijuana use and policy: what we know and have yet to learn." *NBER Reporter,* Winter.

Pacula, R. L., Chriqui, J. F. and King, J. (2003). "Marijuana decriminalisation: what does it mean in the United States?" NBER Working Paper No. 9690. Cambridge, MA: National Bureau of Economic Research.

Ramful, P. (2008). *Recreational Drug Consumption in Australia: An Econometric Analysis.* PhD Thesis, Department of Econometrics and Business Statistics, Monash University, Australia.

Roffman, A. R. (1981). "Editor's page." *Contemporary Drug Problems* 10, 263–4.

Saffer, H. and Chaloupka, F. J. (1995). "The demand for illicit drugs." NBER Working Paper No. 5238. Cambridge, MA: National Bureau of Economic Research.

Saffer, H. and Chaloupka, F. J. (1998). "Demographic differentials in the demand for alcohol and illicit drugs." NBER Working Paper No. 6432. Cambridge, MA: National Bureau of Economic Research.

Saffer, H. and Chaloupka, F. J. (1999). "The demand for illicit drugs." *Economic Inquiry* 37, 401–11.

Schwer, R. K., Riddel, M. and Henderson, J. (2002). "Fiscal impact of Question 9: potential state-revenue implications." Las Vegas, NV: Centre for Business and Economic Research, University of Nevada.

Selvanathan, E. A. (2003). Personal communication, August 18.

Selvanathan, S. and Selvanathan, E. A. (2005). *The demand for alcohol, tobacco and marijuana: international evidence.* Aldershot: Ashgate.

Single, E. (1989). "The impact of marijuana decriminalisation: an update." *Journal of Public Health Policy* 10, 456–66.

Thies, C. and Register, C. (1993). "Decriminalisation of marijuana and the demand for alcohol, marijuana and cocaine." *Social Science Journal* 30, 385–400.

Wallis, K. (1999). "Asymmetric density forecasts of inflation and the Bank of England's fan chart." *National Institute Economic Review* 167, 106–12.

Warburton, C. (1932). "Prohibition and economic welfare." *Annals of the American Academy of Political and Social Science* 163, 89–97.

Weatherburn, D. and Lind, B. (1997). "The impact of law enforcement activity on a heroin market." *Addiction* 92, 557–69.

Williams, J. (2004). "The effects of price and policy on marijuana use: what can be learned from the Australian experience?" *Health Economics* 13, 123–37.

Williams, J. and Mahmoudi, P. (2004). "Economic relationship between alcohol and cannabis revisited." *The Economic Record* 80 (248), 36–48.

Yuan, Y. and Caulkins, J. P. (1998). "The effect of variation in high-level domestic drug enforcement on variation in drug prices." *Socio-Economic Planning Sciences* 32, 265–76.

Zhao, X., Griffiths, W., Griffith, G. and Mullen, J. (2000). "Probability distributions for economic surplus changes: the case of technical change in the Australian wool industry." *Australian Journal of Agricultural and Resource Economics* 44, 83–106.

Zhao, X. and Harris, M. (2004). "Demand for marijuana, alcohol and tobacco: participation, levels of consumption, and cross-equation correlations." *Economic Record* 80, 394–441.

6 | *Are Australians unique?*

KENNETH W. CLEMENTS

6.1 Introduction

The previous chapters have dealt with the workings of the markets for marijuana and related commodities in Australia. Are these results applicable to other countries, or are they specific to Australia? This chapter addresses this question in a number of ways.

A useful starting point is the distinction between the objective and subjective determinants of demand for any product. Real income and relative prices are objective, whereas tastes are subjective. It is usual to take tastes as constant so that they play no role in the economic explanation of consumption. The hard-line interpretation that tastes are an immutable constant is a major tenet of Chicago economics and has long been championed by Chicagoans such as Becker, Friedman and Stigler (Friedman, 1962; Stigler and Becker, 1977). In essence, the proposition that tastes are constant takes the application of the economics of utility maximisation to its logical conclusion, whereby it is only the observable economic variables – income and prices – that determine consumption. To add the unobservable variable "tastes" to this list of determinants is in a sense unscientific, as it can explain any behaviour, no matter how unorthodox. In other words, there is no conceivable evidence that could ever reject the hypothesis that variations in consumption are determined by changes in tastes. To put this in yet another way, to ascribe observed behaviour to variations in tastes really amounts to admitting ignorance as to the fundamental causes. In a highly influential paper, Stigler and Becker (1977) advocate treating tastes as fixed along these lines and they show that a number of examples of apparently capricious behaviour (addiction, custom, tradition, fashion, etc.) can in fact be reconciled with the assumption of stable preferences. Stigler and Becker (p. 89) argue that:

No significant behaviour has been illuminated by the assumption of differences in tastes. Instead, they, along with the assumption of unstable

350

tastes, have been a convenient crutch to lean on when the analysis has bogged down. They give the appearance of considered judgement, yet really have only been ad hoc arguments that disguise analytical failures.

A less controversial attitude is to acknowledge that economic behaviour is complex and models are, at best, approximations to reality. It is inevitable that demand models are stylised abstractions, at least to a certain degree, and necessarily omit some determining factors. Acknowledging the inevitability of the limitations of economic modelling then implies that a hard-edged approach to the constancy of tastes comes with its own problems and should probably be avoided. Nevertheless, the objective/subjective classification of the determinants of consumption, and the associated constancy of tastes proposition, provide a useful organising framework and starting point.

With these considerations in mind, in this chapter we investigate how similar consumers are in different countries. To isolate the possible role of tastes, we adjust observed consumption patterns for differences in income and prices across countries. In broad outline, we find some evidence that tends to support the idea of the similarity of tastes. Although it is not possible to draw hard and fast conclusions, one interpretation of the results of this chapter is that they provide some basis for thinking that at least some of the results of the previous chapters might be applicable elsewhere in the world.

In what follows, we first analyse the determinants in different countries of the consumption of broad commodity groups such as food, clothing, housing, etc. We then turn to a similar analysis regarding the consumption of more narrowly defined commodities that are closer on the scale of substitutability to marijuana, viz., beer, wine and spirits. The literature on international comparisons of consumption patterns dealing with broad groups of commodities includes Clark (1957), Chen (1999), Clements and Chen (1996), Chua (2003), Clements and Qiang (2003), Clements and Selvanathan (1994), Clements and Theil (1979), Clements *et al.* (2006), Houthakker (1957), Kravis *et al.* (1982, Chapter 9), Lluch and Powell (1975), Lluch *et al.* (1977), Selvanathan and Selvanathan (2003), Selvanathan (1993), Theil (1987, 1996), Theil *et al.* (1989), Theil and Suhm (1981), and Yuen (1999). There are fewer studies that compare international consumption patterns of alcoholic beverages; these include Aizenman and Brooks (2007), Clements and Selvanathan (1987), Clements *et al.* (1997), Fogarty (2006), Selvanathan (1991), and Selvanathan and Selvanathan (2005, 2007).

6.2 World food consumption

Food consumption exhibits great diversity across countries. In the poorest countries, food is the most important single item in the consumption basket and can account for more than half of the total budget. However, in the richest countries, food accounts for less than one-tenth of the total. This section, which is based on Clements and Chen (2007), investigates the extent to which income differences account for the diversity of food consumption across countries.

The diversity of food consumption is illustrated in Table 6.1, which contains data on total consumption per capita (denoted by Q) and the food budget share (w), the share of food in total consumption expenditure, for 42 OECD countries in 2002. We interpret Q as a measure of affluence and refer to it as "income" for short. On the basis of the values of Q, Luxembourg is the richest country and Turkey the poorest, with a ratio of incomes of $30,258/4,882 \approx 6$, whereas the food budget share ranges from less than 10 per cent to approximately 30 per cent. Writing the difference between the food shares in countries a and b as $w^a - w^b$, the share for each country can be systematically compared to those of all others via the 42×42 skew-symmetric matrix $\left[w^a - w^b\right]$. The upper triangle of this matrix is given in Table 6.2, where countries are ordered in terms of decreasing affluence in the rows and increasing affluence in the columns. Thus, for example, moving from left to right along the first row, we compare the food budget share of Luxembourg (the richest country) with poorer countries that become successively less poor: the share for Turkey is 17 points above Luxembourg's, Macedonia's is 22 above, etc. As the diagonal elements of this matrix are all zero (the own-country comparisons), these elements are suppressed in the table. However, as we move further away from where the diagonal would be, in a northwesterly direction, countries differ more on the income scale and the budget shares differ by more. With only a few exceptions, for each pairwise comparison, the share in the poorer country is less than that in the richer country, as indicated by the predominance of negative elements in the upper triangle of the matrix, elements that on average become more negative with greater distance from the diagonal. This is a reflection of Engel's law.

Figure 6.1 is a scatter plot of the food share against income, with income measured on a geometric scale. It is evident that points in the figure are scattered reasonably closely around a downward-sloping

Table 6.1: *Affluence and food in 42 countries in 2002*

Country (1)	Consumption per capita (US dollars) (2)	Food budget share (×100) (3)
1. Luxembourg	30,258	7.7
2. USA	24,768	6.4
3. UK	20,899	7.6
4. Switzerland	19,424	9.6
5. Austria	19,161	8.8
6. Norway	18,691	10.6
7. France	18,439	11.4
8. Iceland	18,358	13.9
9. Denmark	18,145	8.8
10. Sweden	17,934	8.7
11. Netherlands	17,871	8.7
12. Canada	17,736	8.0
13. Belgium	17,735	10.4
14. Australia	17,443	9.2
15. Italy	17,403	12.2
16. Germany	16,941	9.8
17. Cyprus	15,969	13.6
18. Ireland	15,965	6.3
19. Japan	15,788	12.3
20. Spain	15,701	13.5
21. Finland	15,596	9.6
22. New Zealand	14,390	11.4
23. Israel	14,358	14.6
24. Greece	13,691	14.5
25. Malta	13,669	16.0
26. Portugal	13,156	15.1
27. Slovenia	11,993	13.9
28. Czech Republic	11,229	14.1
29. Hungary	10,381	15.1
30. Korea	9,717	13.4
31. Slovakia	9,218	19.2
32. Croatia	8,918	22.3
33. Poland	8,729	17.7
34. Lithuania	8,581	23.8
35. Estonia	8,374	18.4

Table 6.1: *(continued)*

Country (1)	Consumption per capita (US dollars) (2)	Food budget share (×100) (3)
36. Latvia	7,330	21.3
37. Mexico	6,756	21.7
38. Bulgaria	5,567	22.9
39. Russia	5,499	27.3
40. Romania	5,336	31.0
41. Macedonia	5,123	29.8
42. Turkey	4,882	24.6

Source: OECD (2004).

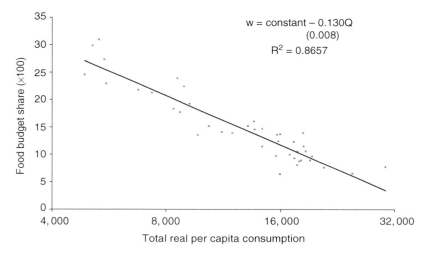

Figure 6.1. Scatter of food budget share against income

straight line, with R^2 equal to 87 per cent. In view of the diversity of countries involved and their food consumption patterns, this is an impressive result that clearly shows that income differences are a key determinant of the differences in the food shares. In other words, the substantial diversity of food budget share across countries can, in large part, be ascribed to differences in an objective economic variable – real income – rather than to differences in tastes. The negative slope of the regression line in the figure indicates the

Table 6.2: *Matrix of differences in food budget shares for 42 countries* $[w^a - w^b] \times 100$

Column order (left → right): Turkey, Macedonia, Romania, Russia, Bulgaria, Mexico, Latvia, Estonia, Lithuania, Poland, Croatia, Slovakia, Korea, Hungary, Czech, Slovenia, Portugal, Malta, Greece, Israel, NZ, Finland, Spain, Japan, Ireland, Cyprus, Germany, Italy, Australia, Belgium, Canada, N'lands, Sweden, Denmark, Iceland, France, Norway, Austria, Switzerland, UK, USA.

	Tur	Mac	Rom	Rus	Bul	Mex	Lat	Est	Lit	Pol	Cro	Slk	Kor	Hun	Cze	Sln	Por	Mal	Gre	Isr	NZ	Fin	Spa	Jap	Ire	Cyp	Ger	Ita	Aus	Bel	Can	Nl	Swe	Den	Ice	Fra	Nor	Aut	Swi	UK	USA
L'bourg	-17	-22	-23	-20	-15	-14	-14	-16	-11	-16	-10	-15	-12	-18	-19	-11	-18	-12	-11	-15	-13	-10	-10	1	-9	-11	-9	-11	-5	-2	-7	-1	-3	-3	-2	-6	-4	-3	-1	-2	-1
USA	-18	-23	-25	-21	-16	-15	-15	-12	-17	-11	-16	-13	-7	-18	-20	-16	-21	-14	-15	-17	-15	-13	-9	2	-9	-13	-9	-13	-5	-2	-8	-2	-2	-2	-2	-6	-5	-4	-2	-3	
UK	-17	-22	-23	-20	-15	-14	-14	-16	-11	-16	-10	-15	-12	-17	-17	-11	-16	-10	-10	-15	-13	-10	-9	0	-7	-10	-7	-9	-4	-2	-6	-1	-2	-2	-1	-5	-3	-2	-3		
Switzerland	-15	-20	-21	-18	-13	-12	-11	-16	-10	-15	-9	-14	-8	-13	-17	-9	-16	-10	-10	-12	-9	-8	-5	3	-5	-8	-5	-8	-3	0	-5	1	0	-1	0	-3	-2	-1			
Austria	-16	-21	-22	-19	-14	-13	-12	-16	-10	-15	-9	-14	-7	-15	-17	-10	-17	-11	-11	-13	-9	-9	-5	3	-5	-9	-5	-9	-3	0	-5	1	0	-1	0	-3	-2				
Norway	-14	-19	-20	-17	-12	-11	-11	-16	-9	-14	-8	-13	-7	-14	-16	-10	-16	-10	-10	-12	-9	-8	-5	4	-4	-7	-4	-7	-2	1	-4	1	1	0	1	-2	-1				
France	-13	-18	-20	-16	-11	-10	-10	-14	-7	-12	-6	-11	-5	-13	-15	-9	-16	-10	-10	-12	-9	-8	-5	4	-4	-7	-4	-7	-2	2	-4	2	1	0	1	-1					
Iceland	-11	-16	-17	-13	-9	-8	-7	-13	-4	-9	-3	-8	-2	-12	-14	-8	-16	-10	-9	-11	-8	-6	-2	5	0	-5	-2	-6	-1	2	-1	3	3	2	2						
Denmark	-16	-21	-22	-19	-14	-13	-12	-17	-10	-15	-9	-14	-6	-15	-17	-10	-17	-11	-10	-13	-9	-9	-5	4	-2	-8	0	-4	0	5	3	6	5	5							
Sweden	-16	-21	-22	-19	-14	-13	-12	-17	-10	-15	-9	-14	-6	-15	-17	-10	-17	-11	-10	-13	-9	-9	-5	4	-2	-8	0	-4	0	5	3	5	0								
N'lands	-16	-21	-22	-19	-14	-13	-11	-15	-9	-15	-9	-14	-6	-14	-17	-9	-17	-11	-9	-13	-9	-8	-4	4	-2	-8	0	-4	0	5	5	0									
Canada	-17	-22	-23	-19	-15	-14	-13	-15	-10	-16	-10	-15	-7	-15	-18	-10	-18	-11	-10	-14	-10	-9	-5	4	-2	-6	2	-2	0	7	6										
Belgium	-14	-19	-21	-17	-12	-11	-10	-16	-8	-13	-7	-12	-4	-16	-19	-10	-21	-12	-9	-13	-8	-8	-4	5	2	-4	2	-2	1	3											
Australia	-15	-21	-22	-18	-14	-13	-12	-18	-10	-16	-10	-16	-7	-18	-21	-14	-20	-13	-12	-14	-9	-8	-4	5	4	-1	5	1	1												
Italy	-12	-18	-19	-15	-11	-10	-9	-12	-6	-12	-8	-14	-2	-15	-20	-11	-18	-12	-10	-10	-7	-7	-3	4	0	-1	4	2													
Germany	-15	-20	-21	-17	-13	-12	-11	-17	-9	-14	-8	-12	-4	-15	-18	-9	-18	-12	-9	-11	-7	-6	-2	5	2	-1	2														
Cyprus	-11	-16	-17	-14	-9	-8	-6	-11	-4	-9	-5	-10	-3	-12	-17	-9	-18	-12	-9	-10	-6	-5	-1	8	4	4															
Ireland	-18	-24	-25	-21	-17	-15	-15	-18	-13	-16	-11	-16	-13	-16	-17	-9	-18	-11	-8	-10	-7	-4	-1	6	7																
Japan	-12	-18	-19	-15	-11	-10	-9	-13	-5	-10	-5	-11	-1	-12	-18	-8	-19	-12	-8	-11	-6	-4	0	6																	
Spain	-11	-16	-17	-13	-9	-8	-8	-11	-5	-10	-6	-13	-3	-12	-18	-9	-18	-12	-9	-10	-7	-6																			
Finland	-15	-20	-21	-18	-13	-12	-12	-16	-9	-14	-8	-13	-10	-13	-15	-5	-15	-9	-6	-8	-4																				
NZ	-13	-18	-20	-16	-11	-10	-9	-14	-7	-12	-6	-11	-8	-13	-16	-5	-14	-8	-5	-7																					
Israel	-10	-15	-16	-13	-8	-7	-6	-12	-4	-9	-3	-8	-5	-11	-13	-3	-12	-7	-4																						
Greece	-10	-15	-16	-13	-8	-7	-7	-12	-4	-9	-3	-8	-7	-11	-13	-3	-12	-7																							
Malta	1	2	2	1	3	3	4	-2	4	-1	5	-2	-6	-3	-3	3	-3																								
Portugal	-9	-15	-16	-12	-8	-7	-6	-11	-4	-9	-3	-8	-7	-11	-13	-2																									
Slovenia	-11	-16	-17	-13	-9	-8	-7	-12	-5	-10	-4	-8	-7	-10	-11																										
Czech	-11	-16	-17	-13	-9	-8	-8	-12	-5	-10	-4	-8	-5	-10																											
Hungary	-9	-15	-16	-12	-8	-7	-6	-12	-3	-9	-3	-7	-6																												
Korea	-11	-16	-18	-14	-9	-8	-8	-13	-5	-10	-4	-8																													
Slovakia	-5	-11	-12	-8	-4	-3	-2	-7	1	-5	1																														
Croatia	-2	-8	-9	-5	-1	1	4	-2	5	-3																															
Poland	-7	-12	-13	-10	-5	-4	-2	-6	-6																																
Lithuania	-1	-6	-7	-4	1	3	5	-6																																	
Estonia	-11	-13	-9	-6	-7	-3	5																																		
Latvia	-3	-9	-10	-6	-2	0																																			
Mexico	-3	-8	-9	-6	-1																																				
Bulgaria	-2	-7	-8	-4																																					
Russia	3	-2	-4																																						
Romania	6	1																																							
Macedonia	5																																								

systematic tendency for the share to decrease with increasing consumer affluence, which also reflects Engel's law.[1]

6.3 Consumption patterns in rich and poor countries

In this and the next two sections, which are based on Clements and Qiang (2003), we consider the differences and similarities in consumption behaviour in rich and poor countries. The data used here, from Clements and Chen (1996), are different to those of the previous section and refer to 31 countries, which are divided into 18 rich countries and 13 poor ones. Brief details of the data are given in Appendix 6.1.

Let p_{it}^c and q_{it}^c be the price and per capita quantity consumed of good i in year t and country c. If there are n goods, then $M_t^c = \sum_{i=1}^n p_{it}^c q_{it}^c$ is total expenditure and $w_{it}^c = p_{it}^c q_{it}^c / M_t^c$ is the budget share of good i. Let $Dp_{it}^c = \log p_{it}^c - \log p_{i,t-1}^c$ be the log-change in the ith price, let $Dq_{it}^c = \log q_{it}^c - \log q_{i,t-1}^c$ be the corresponding quantity log-change, and let $\bar{w}_{it} = \frac{1}{2}(w_{it} + w_{i,t-1})$ be the arithmetic average of the budget share of good i over the years t and $t-1$. If T^c is the sample size for country c, we can then eliminate the time dimension by averaging to define $Dp_i^c = (1/T^c)\Sigma_{t=1}^{T^c} Dp_{it}^c$, $Dq_i^c = (1/T^c)\Sigma_{t=1}^{T^c} Dq_{it}^c$ and $\bar{w}_i^c = (1/T^c)\Sigma_{t=1}^{T^c} \bar{w}_{it}^c$. Column 2 of Table 6.3 presents the budget shares $\bar{w}_i^c$ for $i=1,\ldots,8$ goods, averaged over the 18 rich countries. Column 3 contains the same budget shares averaged over the 13 poor countries. These budget shares reveal the following differences in the structure of consumption patterns for the two groups of countries [(rich–poor)× 100]:

1. Food	−10.85	5. Medicine	1.29
2. Clothing	−0.12	6. Transport	2.65
3. Housing	4.94	7. Recreation	1.56
4. Durables	0.61	8. Other	−0.08

Thus, the major difference is that food is relatively less important in the budget in rich countries, which is a further reflection of Engel's law. Housing and transport in particular absorb most of the "saving" on food. Other than this, the other budget shares are not too different.

Table 6.3: *Consumption data for rich and poor countries*

Commodity (1)	Budget share		Log-change in relative price		Log-change in per capita quantity	
	Rich (2)	Poor (3)	Rich (4)	Poor (5)	Rich (6)	Poor (7)
1. Food	29.59	40.44	−0.28	0.31	1.67	1.69
2. Clothing	9.17	9.29	−1.02	−1.36	2.38	3.45
3. Housing	16.35	11.41	0.64	−0.60	3.30	3.74
4. Durables	9.04	8.43	−0.77	−0.63	3.26	4.01
5. Medicine	5.06	3.77	0.88	−0.12	4.09	4.54
6. Transport	12.37	9.72	0.03	0.58	4.89	5.29
7. Recreation	7.49	5.93	−0.21	−0.43	4.34	4.87
8. Other	10.94	11.02	0.93	0.58	3.17	4.25
9. Divisia index			7.05	13.97	3.05	3.23

Note: All entries to be divided by 100.

The Divisia price and volume indexes are defined as:

$$DP^c_t = \sum_{i=1}^{8} \bar{w}^c_{it} Dp^c_{it}, \quad DQ^c_t = \sum_{i=1}^{8} \bar{w}^c_{it} Dq^c_{it}, \tag{6.1}$$

which measure the overall growth in prices and quantities. Row 9 of Table 6.3 contains (6.1) averaged over time and countries. On average, inflation is approximately twice as high in the poor countries, whereas real income growth (as measured by DQ) is slightly greater than 3 per cent p.a. for both groups. The relative prices given in columns 4 and 5, rows 1–8 are defined as the change in nominal prices deflated by the Divisia index $Dp^c_{it} - DP^c_t$, again averaged over time and countries. It is evident that the relative prices of clothing and durables have decreased in both groups of countries, whereas the prices of medicine and other have increased in the rich countries. The quantities given in columns 6 and 7 are Dq^c_i averaged over countries. The evolution of the quantities consumed is quite similar in the rich and poor countries, with the slowest increase for food and the fastest for transport.

6.4 Explaining the differences

Consider a double-log demand equation for good i in country c:

$$Dq_{it}^c = \alpha_i^c + \eta_i^c DQ_t^c + \gamma_i^c (Dp_{it}^c - DP_t^c) + \varepsilon_{it}^c \qquad (6.2)$$

where α_i^c is the autonomous trend in consumption of i, η_i^c is the ith income elasticity, γ_i^c is the price elasticity of demand for i, and ε_{it}^c is a disturbance term. Selvanathan (1993) estimates equation (6.2) for $i = 1, \ldots, 8$ for each of the rich countries and Chen (1999) estimates the same model for the poor countries; Table 6.4, from Clements and Chen (1996), contains these estimates averaged over countries. The major cross-country differences in the estimates are: (i) the trend terms for clothing and transport are much lower for the rich countries; (ii) transport has a lower income elasticity for the poor countries; and (iii) clothing and transport are both more price-elastic for the rich countries. For a further analysis of the differences in the elasticities, see Clements and Chen (1996).

If we average both sides of demand equation (6.2) over $t = 1, \ldots, T^c$ observations, we obtain:

$$Dq_i^c = \alpha_i^c + \eta_i^c DQ^c + \gamma_i^c (Dp_i^c - DP^c) + \varepsilon_i^c, \qquad (6.3)$$

where the variables are now averages over time. We apply (6.3) to the two groups of countries to decompose observed consumption into components due to income, prices and tastes. First, we use the data in Table 6.3 and the estimates of Table 6.4 to compute $\hat{\varepsilon}_i^c$, the residual from equation (6.3). Columns $11-13$ of row 9 of Table 6.5 give the sum of squared residuals for the two country groups, $SS^c = \Sigma_{i=1}^8 (\hat{\varepsilon}_i^c)^2$, for $c = 1$ (rich), 2 (poor), and for the world as a whole (defined as the 31 rich and poor countries), $SS = \Sigma_{c=1}^2 SS^c$. It is evident that for the rich countries, $SS^c = 0.22 \,(\times 10^4)$, which is approximately one-third of the value for the poor countries $(SS^c = 0.64 \times 10^4)$. Thus, the rich countries account for $0.22/(0.22 + 0.64) \approx 25$ per cent of the lack of fit of the demand model for the whole world, and the poor group accounts for the remaining 75 per cent, as indicated in row 10 of columns 11 and 12. The entries in rows 1–8 of column 11 give the percentage contribution of each commodity to the residual sum of squares, $100 \times (\hat{\varepsilon}_i^c)^2/SS^c$, for the rich countries, and the same rows of columns 12 and 13 give the percentages for the poor group and the

Table 6.4: *Demand elasticities for rich and poor countries*

Commodity (1)	Autonomous trend ×100		Income elasticity		Price elasticity	
	Rich (2)	Poor (3)	Rich (4)	Poor (5)	Rich (6)	Poor (7)
1. Food	−0.24	−0.57	0.59	0.71	−0.37	−0.34
2. Clothing	−2.86	−1.87	1.46	1.33	−0.67	−0.36
3. Housing	2.58	2.30	0.31	0.36	−0.13	−0.15
4. Durables	−2.39	−1.63	1.74	1.77	−0.62	−0.51
5. Medicine	2.61	1.93	0.66	0.81	−0.17	−0.31
6. Transport	−1.22	0.28	2.00	1.55	−0.74	−0.28
7. Recreation	0.64	0.69	1.19	1.13	−0.74	−0.42
8. Other	0.24	0.51	1.05	1.19	−0.37	−0.32

world. Thus, the medicine demand equation exhibits the worst fit for the rich group, with this commodity accounting for 71 per cent of the residual sum of squares, whereas clothing has the worst fit for the poor countries (44 per cent).

Next, we recompute the above measures with the trend terms, income and prices ignored by setting $\alpha_i^c = \eta_i^c = \gamma_i^c = 0$ $i = 1,\ldots,8$, $c = 1, 2$; columns 2–4 of Table 6.5 contain the results. Similarly, columns 5–7 present the sums of squared residuals when all income elasticities are unity $(\alpha_i^c = 0, \ \eta_i^c = 1, \ \gamma_i^c = 0)$ and columns 8–10 are based on unitary income elasticities and price elasticities of minus one $(\alpha_i^c = 0, \ \eta_i^c = 1, \ \gamma_i^c = -1)$. Table 6.6 facilitates comparison of the various columns of Table 6.5. Row 1 of Table 6.6 reproduces the total sums of squares from Table 6.5, whereas in row 3 these are expressed as a percentage of the *SS* when all the coefficients are set equal to zero. Thus, if we ignore the negative signs, these percentage changes in the sums of squares are interpreted as the share of the total variability explained by the elasticities, incomes and prices. Accordingly, row 3 of columns 11–13 shows that the demand equations with the estimated coefficients explain more than 99 per cent of the total variability of consumption. In other words, the observed variation in tastes (i.e. the different elasticities), incomes and prices account for more than 99 per cent of the observed variation in international consumption patterns.

Table 6.5: *Squared residuals from the demand equations*

Commodity (1)	All coefficients zero			Income elasticities unitary			Income elasticities unitary and price elasticities minus unitary			Estimated coefficients for individual country groups		
	Rich (2)	Poor (3)	Rich plus poor (4)	Rich (5)	Poor (6)	Rich plus poor (7)	Rich (8)	Poor (9)	Rich plus poor (10)	Rich (11)	Poor (12)	Rich plus poor (13)
Per cent of total												
1. Food	2.80	2.11	2.41	22.13	18.27	19.81	17.24	9.92	13.67	0.02	0.81	0.61
2. Clothing	5.69	8.80	7.48	5.22	0.37	2.30	17.87	8.52	13.31	4.97	44.44	34.51
3. Housing	10.95	10.35	10.60	0.73	2.00	1.49	4.96	0.05	2.56	9.37	5.45	6.44
4. Durables	10.68	11.89	11.38	0.51	4.69	3.02	1.96	0.15	1.08	8.36	24.69	20.85
5. Medicine	16.81	15.25	15.91	12.57	13.22	12.96	21.88	9.28	15.73	71.09	0.29	18.10
6. Transport	24.03	20.70	22.11	39.34	32.70	35.35	21.88	45.69	33.51	0.48	4.28	3.32
7. Recreation	18.93	17.54	18.13	19.34	20.72	20.17	7.30	9.60	8.42	3.34	19.00	15.06
8. Other	10.10	13.36	11.98	0.17	8.02	4.89	6.90	16.78	11.73	2.37	1.04	1.38
9. Total×10⁴	99.496	135.201	234.697	8.606	12.978	21.584	15.980	15.253	31.233	0.216	0.643	0.859
10. Per cent of total	42.39	57.61	100.00	39.87	60.13	100.00	51.16	48.84	100.00	25.15	74.85	100.00

Table 6.6: *Sum of squared residuals from the demand equations*

Type of residual (1)	All coefficients zero			Income elasticities unitary			Income elasticities unitary and price elasticities minus unitary			Estimated coefficients for individual country groups		
	Rich (2)	Poor (3)	Rich plus poor (4)	Rich (5)	Poor (6)	Rich plus poor (7)	Rich (8)	Poor (9)	Rich plus poor (10)	Rich (11)	Poor (12)	Rich plus Poor (13)
						Total $\times 10^4$						
1. Unweighted	99.496	135.201	234.697	8.606	12.978	21.584	15.980	15.253	31.233	0.216	0.643	0.859
2. Weighted	10.400	12.106	22.506	1.219	1.796	3.014	2.053	1.835	3.888	0.015	0.057	0.072
						Percentage change						
3. Unweighted	0.00	0.00	0.00	−91.35	−90.40	−90.80	−83.94	−88.72	−88.69	−99.78	−99.52	−99.63
4. Weighted	0.00	0.00	0.00	−88.28	−85.17	−86.61	−80.26	−84.84	−82.73	−99.86	−99.53	−99.68

Note: The weights used in rows 2 and 4 are budget shares.

The effect of assuming unitary income elasticities is to reduce the total SS by approximately 90 per cent (row 3, columns 5–7 of Table 6.6). However, the joint assumption of unitary income elasticities and price elasticities of minus one reduces the decrease to between 84 and 89 per cent (row 3, columns 8–10). As it can reasonably be argued that commodities absorbing a larger proportion of expenditure should be more heavily weighted, we repeat the above computations using as weights the budget shares given in Table 6.3. A comparison of rows 3 and 4 of Table 6.6 shows that none of the qualitative results changes due to weighting. For some further explorations, see Appendix A6.1.

6.5 International consumers

In the preceding analysis, the two groups of consumers each had their own sets of demand elasticities; in this sense, the behaviour of consumers in the rich countries is different to that in the poor, or in other words, tastes are permitted to differ. In this section, we analyse the implications of the alternative assumption of identical tastes by examining the corresponding deterioration of the fit of the demand equations.

Consider the following demand equation for good i in country c:

$$Dq_i^c = \alpha_i + \eta_i DQ^c + \gamma_i \left(Dp_i^c - DP^c \right) + \varepsilon_i^c. \tag{6.4}$$

This equation appears similar to (6.2), but is different in that the coefficients do not have country superscripts; that is, since equation (6.4) pertains to both country groups simultaneously ($c = 1, 2$), tastes are now taken to be identical. A simple way of proceeding is to specify the coefficients as weighted averages of their country-group counterparts:

$$\alpha_i = \lambda \alpha_i^1 + (1 - \lambda)\alpha_i^2, \quad \eta_i = \lambda \eta_i^1 + (1 - \lambda)\eta_i^2,$$
$$\gamma_i = \lambda \gamma_i^1 + (1 - \lambda)\gamma_i^2, \tag{6.5}$$

where $0 \leq \lambda \leq 1$ is the weight given to the rich group. It should be noted that (6.5) is a completely symmetric formulation, in that the weight λ is neither commodity- nor elasticity-specific.

We now evaluate the sums of squared residuals from equation (6.4) by specifying various values of λ in (6.5). Table 6.7 contains the results. The unweighted SS values in the upper part of the table are plotted against λ

Table 6.7: *Sum of squared residuals with the same coefficients for both country groups*

	Weight given to rich λ (1)	Rich (2)	Poor (3)	Rich plus poor (4)
		Sums of squared residuals $\times 10^4$		
		Unweighted		
1.	0.0	1.322	0.643	1.965
2.	0.1	1.084	0.612	1.696
3.	0.2	0.875	0.610	1.485
4.	0.3	0.694	0.636	1.330
5.	0.4	0.541	0.691	1.231
6.	0.5	0.416	0.774	1.190
7.	0.6	0.319	0.886	1.206
8.	0.7	0.251	1.027	1.278
9.	0.8	0.211	1.197	1.408
10.	0.9	0.200	1.395	1.594
11.	1.0	0.216	1.621	1.838
12.	Mean	0.558	0.917	1.475
		Weighted		
13.	0.0	0.128	0.057	0.185
14.	0.1	0.105	0.055	0.160
15.	0.2	0.084	0.057	0.141
16.	0.3	0.066	0.061	0.127
17.	0.4	0.050	0.068	0.118
18.	0.5	0.038	0.077	0.115
19.	0.6	0.028	0.090	0.117
20.	0.7	0.021	0.105	0.125
21.	0.8	0.016	0.122	0.138
22.	0.9	0.014	0.143	0.157
23.	1.0	0.015	0.166	0.181
24.	Mean	0.051	0.091	0.142

in Figure 6.2. It is evident from the upper panel of this figure that the sum of squares for the rich group decreases more or less monotonically as its weight rises. Similarly, the middle panel of the figure reveals that the *SS* for the poor group also decreases with its weight $(1 - \lambda)$. Finally, the lower panel shows that the sum of squares for the world as a whole

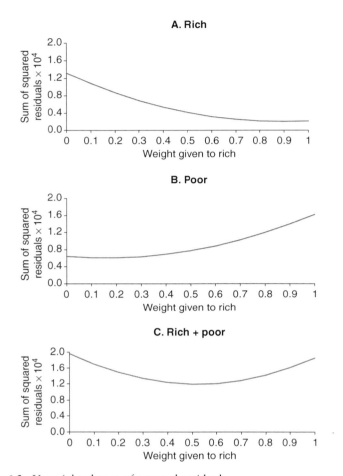

Figure 6.2. Unweighted sum of squared residuals

(rich + poor) has a minimum in the vicinity of $\lambda = 0.5$. As this value of λ involves giving equal weight to both groups of countries, this optimal weighting defines "international consumers" as being located mid-way between the rich and poor countries, which has appealing democratic features. The lower part of Table 6.7 shows that weighting (by budget shares) does not substantially change this conclusion.

Another way of obtaining the optimal value of the weight λ is from the regression $y_i^c = \lambda x_i^c + \varepsilon_i^c$, $i = 1, \ldots, 8$, $c = 1, 2$, where $y_i^c = Dq_i^c - \alpha_i^2 - \eta_i^2 DQ^c - \gamma_i^2 (Dp_i^c - DP^c)$ and $x_i^c = (\alpha_i^1 - \alpha_i^2) + (\eta_i^1 - \eta_i^2)$

$DQ^c + (\gamma_i^1 - \gamma_i^2)(Dp_i^c - DP^c)$. The least-squares estimate of λ yields the same value of λ as before ($\hat{\lambda} = 0.5$), but now we also obtain a standard error of 0.16 for the optimal value of the weight. Accordingly, it is possible to reject the hypothesis that λ takes the extreme values of 0 or 1, so that neither group dominates the world. However, it must be admitted that the two-standard-error band for λ is fairly wide, viz., [0.18, 0.82], which reflects the flatness of the SS function in the bottom panel of Figure 6.2.

Defining international consumers (ICs) in terms of a weighted average of rich and poor consumers means that ICs lie somewhere "between" those in the two groups of countries. It is thus natural to inquire how different are ICs from their rich and poor counterparts, which amounts to asking: how different are tastes? One measure of this difference is the increase in the sum of squared residuals when the individual coefficients in the demand equations are replaced with common values, the weighted averages. This is pursued in Table 6.8, which shows (in row 1, columns 5 and 10) that the SS values for the rich group increases from 0.216 to 0.416 (both $\times 10^4$), or by 93 per cent. The increase in the sum of squares for the poor group is 20 per cent (from 0.643 to 0.774, both $\times 10^4$) and 39 per cent (from 0.859 to 1.190, both $\times 10^4$) for the two groups of countries combined. Although these increases are sub-stantial and point to differences in tastes, it is evident from col-umns 8–10 of row 3 of this table that the demand equations with common coefficients still explain in excess of 99 per cent of the variation in consumption patterns. Moreover, this is true for the rich and the poor groups individually, the world as a whole, and the weighted and unweighted consumption patterns. For some further results, see Appendix A6.1.

The above results can be summarised as follows. Differences in consumption patterns for broad goods internationally are in large part accounted for by differences in incomes and prices. On the basis of the evidence derived from demand elasticities, it does not seem possible to give a completely clear answer to the question as to whether the tastes of different consumers are identical. Although there is some evidence of disparities in tastes across countries, the differences can probably be considered to be at the lower end of the scale. In other

Table 6.8: *Further sums of squared residuals from the demand equations*

Type of residual (1)	All coefficients zero			Estimated coefficients for individual country groups			Same coefficients for both country groups		
	Rich (2)	Poor (3)	Rich plus poor (4)	Rich (5)	Poor (6)	Rich plus poor (7)	Rich (8)	Poor (9)	Rich plus poor (10)
				Total $\times 10^4$					
1. Unweighted	99.496	135.201	234.697	0.216	0.643	0.859	0.416	0.774	1.190
2. Weighted	10.400	12.106	22.506	0.015	0.057	0.072	0.038	0.077	0.115
				Percentage change					
3. Unweighted	0.00	0.00	0.00	−99.78	−99.52	−99.63	−99.58	−99.43	−99.49
4. Weighted	0.00	0.00	0.00	−99.86	−99.53	−99.68	−99.64	−99.36	−99.49

Note: The weights in rows 2 and 4 are budget shares.

words, whatever differences in tastes there are, we can probably safely conclude that these differences are not huge.

6.6 Tastes and geography

In an ambitious study, Selvanathan (1988, 1993) compares tastes internationally with time-series data on the consumption of 10 commodity groups in 15 OECD countries. She estimates a system of demand equations (i) for each country (whereby tastes differ internationally) and (ii) for all 15 countries combined (identical tastes). A test of the extent to which tastes are identical then involves the deterioration in fit of the demand equations in going from (i) to (ii). This approach is basically the same as that employed in the previous section, but its implementation is now more elaborate, as it involves estimation of a system-wide demand model with time-series data for each country. This section describes Selvanathan's results.

Panel A of Table 6.9 summarises Selvanathan's results. On the basis of the root-mean-squared (RMS) percentage prediction error, it can be seen that the country-specific and the pooled models are similar. As the difference in the weighted mean RMS errors is 1.95–1.87=0.08 percentage points (row 17), the conclusion is that tastes are not too dissimilar across countries.

There are many non-economic differences between the 15 OECD countries of Table 6.9 that could not be reasonably ascribed to tastes. For example, there are substantial climatic differences between Norway and Australia (that can be summarised as "cold versus hot"), cultural practices are often thought to be different in the US and France (Big Macs versus croissants?), and the dominant language differs among many of these countries (English versus all others). To control for some of these non-economic factors, Selvanathan (1988, Chapter 8) conducts a similar analysis with data from different regions of the same country, namely the six states of Australia (see also Selvanathan and Selvanathan, 1994). Panel B of Table 6.9 shows that the differences are smaller than those above, so tastes are even more similar within a country, as expected. However, this result cannot be taken to be conclusive due to the small sample sizes.

Table 6.9:   *Quality of budget share predictions in OECD countries and Australian states*

Country/state	RMS percentage prediction error Individual country/ state model	Pooled country/ state model
A. OECD countries		
1. US	1.65	1.72
2. Canada	3.16	3.32
3. Sweden	1.88	1.91
4. Denmark	2.16	2.16
5. Australia	2.41	2.46
6. France	1.39	1.39
7. Belgium	2.59	2.74
8. Norway	2.07	2.35
9. Netherlands	3.20	3.58
10. Iceland	4.70	4.99
11. Finland	3.68	3.67
12. Austria	2.34	2.50
13. UK	1.77	1.79
14. Spain	2.33	2.29
15. Italy	1.88	2.13
16. Unweighted mean	2.48	2.60
17. Weighted mean	1.87	1.95
B. Australian states		
18. NSW	2.16	2.14
19. Victoria	2.49	2.59
20. Queensland	3.07	2.97
21. SA	2.47	2.51
22. WA	2.54	2.46
23. Tasmania	3.42	3.56
24. Unweighted mean	2.69	2.70
25. Weighted mean	2.47	2.48

6.7 Alcohol idiosyncrasies?

In this and the next two sections, we move from broad commodity groups and consider one that is closer to marijuana, alcoholic beverages. We start by considering the extent to which the price responsiveness of the demand for alcohol is similar across countries.

Suppose there are n goods; we denote by p_{it} the price of good i in year t and by q_{it} the corresponding quantity consumed per capita. Let $w_{it} = p_{it}q_{it}/M_t$ be the budget share of i, where $M_t = \sum_{i=1}^{n} p_{it}q_{it}$ is total expenditure. Let $\bar{w}_{it} = \frac{1}{2}(w_{it} + w_{i,t-1})$ be the arithmetic average of the budget share over the years $t - 1$ and t, and $Dp_{it} = \log p_{it} - \log p_{i,t-1}$ and $Dq_{it} = \log q_{it} - \log q_{i,t-1}$ be the ith price and quantity log-changes. The Divisia price and volume indexes are then defined as:

$$DP_t = \sum_{i=1}^{n} \bar{w}_{it} Dp_{it}, \quad DQ_t = \sum_{i=1}^{n} \bar{w}_{it} Dq_{it}. \tag{6.6}$$

These are weighted means of the n price and quantity log-changes, where the weights are the budget shares; these indexes were previously encountered in equation (6.1). In Section 4.5 we introduced the preference independence version of the Rotterdam model, the ith equation of which takes the form:

$$\bar{w}_{it} Dq_{it} = \theta_i DQ_t + \phi\theta_i (Dp_{it} - DP_t') + \varepsilon_{it}. \tag{6.7}$$

This expresses the change in consumption of good i, weighted by its share $\bar{w}_{it} Dq_{it}$, as the sum of three terms, each of which is explained below.

For convenience, we give a brief description of the above demand model. The first term on the right-hand side of equation (6.7) is an income term, $\theta_i DQ_i$, which is a proportion θ_i of the change in the Divisia volume index defined in equation (6.6). The proportion θ_i is the marginal share of good i defined as $\theta_i = \partial(p_i q_i)/\partial M$; this share answers the question: if income rises by one dollar, what fraction of this increase is spent on i? As the additional income is taken to be spent on something, the marginal shares have a unit sum. Under preference independence, each θ_i is a positive fraction. The second term in equation (6.7) is $\phi\theta_i (Dp_{it} - DP_t')$, which deals with the substitution effect of a change in the relative price of the good, $Dp_{it} - DP_t'$. This relative price is the change in nominal price of good i,

Dp_{it}, deflated by the change in Frisch price index, defined as $DP'_t = \sum_{i=1}^n \theta_i Dp_{it}$. Like the Divisia price index in equation (6.6), Frisch is also a weighted average of the change in prices of the n goods, but now the weights are the marginal shares θ_i, not the budget shares $\bar{w}_{it}$. The term $\phi\theta_i$ in equation (6.7) measures the impact on consumption of good i of a change in its relative price on account of the substitution effect. This term is the product of the good's marginal share θ_i and $\phi<0$, which is the income flexibility, the reciprocal of the income elasticity of the marginal utility of income. Note that the changes in the relative prices of other goods are excluded from (6.7), which is an implication of the assumption of preference independence. The third and final term on the right of equation (6.7) is a zero-mean random disturbance, ε_{it}, that accounts for all other factors.

If we divide both sides of equation (6.7) by $\bar{w}_{it}$, we obtain:

$$Dq_{it} = \eta_i DQ_t + \phi\eta_i\left(Dp_{it} - DP'_t\right) + \varepsilon^*_{it}, \qquad (6.8)$$

where $\eta_i = \theta_i/\bar{w}_{it}$ is the income elasticity of demand for good i, $\phi\eta_i$ is the own-price elasticity and $\varepsilon^*_{it} = \varepsilon_{it}/\bar{w}_{it}$. Equation (6.8) applies to each of the $i=1,\ldots,n$ goods in the budget, so that the own-price elasticities, $\phi\eta_i$, $i=1,\ldots,n$ are proportional to the corresponding income elasticities, η_i, $i=1,\ldots n$, with factor of proportionality ϕ. This proportionality relationship is also an implication of the assumption of preference independence. To simplify further, suppose all income elasticities are unity, so that consumption of each good is proportional to income when the other determinants remain unchanged. As the income elasticity is the ratio of the marginal to the budget share, a unitary income elasticity implies that these two shares coincide, that is, $\theta_i = \bar{w}_{it}$. This means that the Frisch price index, DP'_t, is then equal to its Divisia counterpart, DP_t, so that demand equation (6.8) becomes:

$$Dq_{it} - DQ_t = \phi(Dp_{it} - DP_t) + \varepsilon^*_{it}. \qquad (6.9)$$

This equation states that aside from random factors (which have a zero expectation), the change in consumption of good i relative to the change in income, $Dq_{it} - DQ_t$ is a multiple ϕ of the change in its relative price, $Dp_{it} - DP_t$. It should be noted that the multiple ϕ is the same for each of the n goods.

Selvanathan and Selvanathan (2007) use equation (6.9) in a preliminary analysis of the consumption of three alcoholic beverages, beer, wine and spirits. As this relates to consumption within the group of alcoholic beverages, it is a conditional analysis. As discussed in Section A4.6, conditional demand analysis is based on the assumption that the group in question is blockwise independent in the consumer's utility function. The conditional nature of the analysis means that equation (6.9) has to be reinterpreted appropriately. As discussed in Section A4.7, this requires four adjustments:

- The Divisia volume index DQ_t becomes the conditional counterpart, defined as $DQ_{gt} = \sum_{i \in S_g} \bar{w}'_{it} Dq_{it}$, where S_g is the set of alcoholic beverages and $\bar{w}'_{it}$ is the arithmetic average of the conditional budget share of $i \in S_g$. This conditional budget share is the proportion of expenditure on the group that is devoted to i.
- The income flexibility ϕ becomes the own-price elasticity of demand for the group as a whole, $\phi_g = \phi N_g$, where N_g is the income elasticity of demand for the group as a whole. The assumption of blockwise independence means that $N_g > 0$.
- The Divisia price index DP_t becomes $DP_{gt} = \sum_{i \in S_g} \bar{w}'_{it} Dp_{it}$ the conditional Divisia price index.
- The unconditional disturbance term ε^*_{it} becomes the conditional version ε'^*_{it}.

Accordingly, the conditional version of demand equation (6.9) for $i \in S_g$ is:

$$Dq_{it} - DQ_{gt} = \phi_g \left(Dp_{it} - DP_{gt} \right) + \varepsilon'^*_{it}. \tag{6.10}$$

On the basis of equation (6.10), Selvanathan and Selvanathan (2007) plot $Dq_{it} - DQ_{gt}$ against $Dp_{it} - DP_{gt}$ for $i \in S_g$ and $t = 1, \ldots, T$ (the number of annual observations). They construct one such plot for each of the 10 countries listed in the first column of Table 6.10 over the periods listed in the second column. For each country, the points are scattered around a line of negative slope, which seems to provide some visual support for equation (6.10). The slope of the regression line in this plot is interpreted as an estimate of the own-price elasticity of demand for alcohol as a whole. These estimates for the 10 countries are contained in the last column of Table 6.10. These are all negative and significantly different from zero for all countries except Finland and France. In most cases, the estimated elasticity is not too far away

Table 6.10: *Own-price elasticity of demand for
alcoholic beverages in ten countries (Standard errors in
parentheses)*

Country	Sample period	Own-price elasticity
Australia	1955–98	−0.65 (0.11)
Canada	1955–99	−0.33 (0.09)
Finland	1969–85	−0.67 (0.41)
France	1971–95	−0.06 (0.09)
Japan	1963–02	−0.44 (0.15)
New Zealand	1965–82	−0.60 (0.19)
Norway	1962–96	−0.43 (0.16)
Sweden	1961–99	−0.66 (0.13)
UK	1955–02	−0.65 (0.08)
US	1950–00	−0.33 (0.05)
Mean		
Unweighted		−0.48
Weighted		−0.44 (0.03)

Note: The weights in the weighted mean are proportional to the
reciprocals of the squared standard errors, s_c^{-2}/S, where s_c is the
standard error for country c and $S = \sum_c s_c^{-2}$. The SE of this
weighted mean is $S^{-1/2}$.

from −0.5, whereas the unweighted and weighted means are −0.48
and −0.44, respectively.

Although the above results of the Selvanathans are based on a
preliminary analysis of the data that involves the major simplifying
assumption of unitary conditional income elasticities, they still reveal
three substantial conclusions:

- Demand curves for alcoholic beverages slope downwards. In other
  words, alcohol satisfies the law of demand.
- There seem to be substantial similarities across countries of the
  price sensitivity of alcohol consumption.
- The estimated price elasticities of demand for alcoholic beverages
  as a whole are clustered around the value −0.5. This is another
  piece of evidence in favour of the "rule of minus one half", which
  states that the price elasticity of demand for broad aggregates

is −0.5; see the discussion in Section 4.8. Additionally, in broad outline these price elasticities are not too different from the earlier set of cross-country estimates of Clements *et al.* (1997), mentioned in Section 4.5.

Selvanathan and Selvanathan (2007) go further than this preliminary analysis and use the Rotterdam model for each country for testing and estimation. They find that for the three alcoholic beverages beer, wine and spirits, the hypotheses of homogeneity and symmetry are acceptable in most countries, and that the pattern of income elasticities is similar across countries. These findings point towards international similarities among consumers. The Selvanathans also formally test the hypothesis that the coefficients of the Rotterdam model are identical across countries. On the basis of a likelihood ratio test, the hypothesis is rejected, which the authors interpret as indicating that tastes with respect to alcohol differ internationally. Such a finding differs from the results of their preliminary analysis discussed above, as well as from the results discussed in early sections of this chapter regarding broad aggregates. It is conceivable that tastes become more disparate as commodities are more finely disaggregated, i.e. as we move from food, clothing, housing, etc., to beer, wine and spirits. It is equally conceivable that allowing for differing country intercepts in the alcohol demand equations and then testing for equality of the income and price coefficients across countries would lead to an acceptance of the hypothesis. Such a formulation allows consumption to differ across countries according to a "levels effect", via the country intercepts, which could possibly capture some of the non-economic determinants mentioned in the last paragraph of the preceding section, but tastes are taken to be the same by specifying the income and price slopes of the demand equations to be identical internationally.

6.8 International drinking patterns I: budget shares

In this and the next section, we examine patterns in the consumption of beer, wine and spirits in 44 countries. Among other things, we analyse cross-country dispersion, whether or not consumers are becoming more similar over time and how Australians compare with drinkers in other countries. The data used in this and the next section are from Euromonitor International's Global Market Information Database (GMID).[2]

One way of comparing consumption patterns in different countries is in terms of budget shares, the proportions of total expenditure devoted to each good. These shares are positive fractions with a unit sum; as they are unit-free and independent of currency units in particular, they can be directly compared across countries without the need to convert to a common currency. For the three alcoholic beverages, we use the conditional budget shares, which are the within-group expenditure proportions. Table 6.11 contains these shares for the 44 countries, averaged over the period 1997–2006.

There are several intriguing features of the alcohol budget shares of Table 6.11. Beer is the dominant beverage in 26 of the 44 countries, while wine and spirits are dominant in 10 and 8 countries, respectively. Beer consumption seems to be the most "global", without any obvious geographic pattern to the locations where this beverage dominates. Eight of the ten wine-drinking countries are in Western Europe and most of these are substantial wine producers, such as France, Italy and Portugal. The remaining two wine-drinking countries are Argentina and Chile, both of which have cultural roots in Western Europe. The eight spirit-drinking countries are Ireland, Spain, Hungary, Poland, Russia, Ukraine, China and Thailand. It is sometimes argued that the length of winter nights in countries occupying the northern latitudes is associated with heavy drinking of spirits. This could be consistent with the predominance of spirit-drinking in Russia, but not in Thailand.

The cross-country dispersion of consumption across countries can be measured by the standard deviation (SD) of the budget shares. The SDs for the three beverages in each of the ten years are contained in columns 2–4 of Table 6.12. These are of the same order of magnitude for each beverage in the earlier years of the period; for example, in 1997 the SDs are 17.9 per cent, 19.1 per cent and 16.1 per cent for beer, wine and spirits, respectively. Over time, there is a clear tendency for the SDs to decrease, ending in 2006 at 14.6 per cent, 18.0 per cent and 10.6 per cent, respectively. Thus, there is a tendency for countries to move towards the world mean, so that in this sense drinkers are becoming more similar.[3] The same is true if we use Australian drinkers as the reference point and recompute the SDs around that country's shares, rather than the world means

Table 6.11: *Alcohol budget shares, average 1997–2006 ($\times 100$)*

Country	Beer	Wine	Spirits	Country	Beer	Wine	Spirits
Western Europe				North America			
Austria	46.8	39.1	14.1	Canada	49.0	25.7	25.3
Belgium	32.8	47.2	20.0	USA	54.7	18.6	26.8
Denmark	44.1	42.1	13.8	Latin America			
Finland	50.7	19.4	29.9				
France	14.5	59.9	25.6	Argentina	37.6	55.6	6.8
Germany	38.6	36.5	24.9	Brazil	51.1	25.4	23.5
Greece	20.5	53.9	25.6	Chile	38.2	38.5	23.2
Ireland	30.2	32.1	37.7	Colombia	70.0	5.0	25.1
Italy	17.9	70.5	11.6	Mexico	78.1	1.4	20.5
Netherlands	38.8	37.9	23.3	Venezuela	73.1	1.5	25.4
Norway	45.3	30.5	24.1	Asia Pacific			
Portugal	21.8	64.9	13.2				
Spain	31.5	31.2	37.4	China	37.1	8.4	54.4
Sweden	30.9	39.8	29.3	Hong Kong	61.0	24.3	14.7
Switzerland	12.6	76.5	10.9	Japan	62.6	19.5	17.9
UK	33.2	43.8	23.1	Philippines	50.1	2.2	47.7
				Singapore	57.8	29.1	13.1
				South Korea	62.4	11.1	26.5

Table 6.11: *(continued)*

Country	Beer	Wine	Spirits	Country	Beer	Wine	Spirits
Eastern Europe				Taiwan	**44.7**	25.1	30.2
Bulgaria	**45.7**	18.0	36.2	Thailand	39.1	2.1	**58.8**
Czech	**45.7**	16.4	37.9	Australasia			
Hungary	30.8	33.0	**36.2**	Australia	**55.7**	30.5	13.8
Poland	39.1	10.4	**50.5**	NZ	**46.6**	38.7	14.7
Romania	**54.0**	24.3	21.7	Africa, Middle East			
Russia	28.9	18.5	**52.7**	Israel	**61.9**	29.4	8.7
Slovakia	**38.4**	30.1	31.5	South Africa	**66.0**	17.5	16.5
Ukraine	38.9	18.1	**43.0**				

Note: The budget share of the dominant beverage for each country is shown in bold.

Table 6.12: *Dispersion of budget shares (× 100)*

Year	Standard deviation around mean			Standard deviation around Australia		
	Beer	Wine	Spirits	Beer	Wine	Spirits
(1)	(2)	(3)	(4)	(5)	(6)	(7)
1997	17.9	19.1	16.1	22.3	18.9	21.0
1998	17.4	18.8	15.1	21.3	18.6	19.7
1999	16.3	18.7	14.6	20.5	18.5	19.2
2000	15.6	18.6	13.7	19.4	18.4	18.3
2001	15.4	18.6	13.2	18.8	18.5	17.9
2002	15.1	18.5	12.5	18.6	18.4	17.3
2003	15.3	18.3	11.9	18.7	18.2	17.0
2004	15.0	18.3	11.3	18.6	18.1	16.5
2005	14.6	18.1	10.8	18.6	17.9	16.3
2006	14.6	18.0	10.6	18.7	17.8	16.1
Average	15.7	18.5	13.0	19.6	18.3	17.9

(columns 5–7 of Table 6.12). Thus, a homogenisation is evident whereby Australian and non-Australian drinkers are becoming more alike over time.

As the three shares have a unit sum, they have a revealing geometric representation.[4] Consider Australia in 1997, when the shares for beer, wine and spirits were 57 per cent, 29 per cent and 14 per cent, respectively. These are plotted in Panel A of Figure 6.3. Here, the ray for beer AB is parallel to the spirits axis OC, that for spirits BC is parallel to the beer axis OA, and the wine ray ED is parallel to OB (the beer–spirits ray coming from the origin). The three rays intersect at D, which represents the budget point for Australia in 1997. Consider the structure that has as boundaries (i) the three axes and (ii) the triangle with vertices corresponding to each share taking the value of 100 per cent. This is a 3-simplex or a tetrahedron. In the above discussion, the budget point D was located by working *inside* this tetrahedron. An alternative journey that arrives at the same budget point is via the surface of, or *outside*, the tetrahedron, as shown in Panel B of the figure. Yet another way of visualising the geometry is to consider the wine share as a function of the other two, $w_w = 100 - w_b - w_s$. Given the values of the beer and

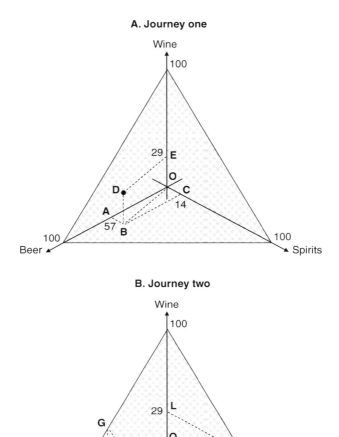

Figure 6.3. The geometry of drinking: two journeys

spirits shares, which can be plotted on the two horizontal axes, we know the wine share, which is plotted on the vertical axis; the budget point is then the intersection of the three shares. This perspective corresponds to the first journey described above.

Anywhere along the boundaries of the triangular surface ABC in Panel A of Figure 6.4, one of the three shares is zero and the other

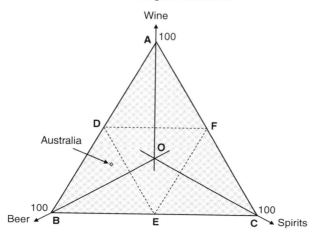

A. Two triangular measures

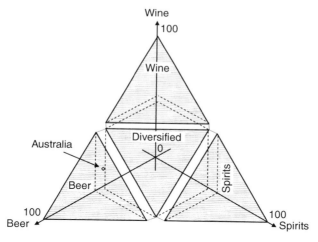

B. Regions of specialisation and diversification

Figure 6.4. Drinking regions

two shares sum to 100. It follows that any budget point must lie somewhere on this surface, such as the diamond that represents the budget point for Australia in 1997. This panel also contains a smaller (inverted) triangular surface that is indicated by the broken lines and labelled DEF. As point D is mid way between A and B, and similarly for the other two vertices, the boundaries of the triangle DEF correspond to one share being 50 per cent. Accordingly, a point lying anywhere within DEF means that no single beverage dominates the budget in the sense of its share exceeding 50 per cent. The region DEF thus represents diversified drinking patterns and can be used as a benchmark. When the budget point lies in the area DBE, for example, such as the diamond for Australia, beer consumption absorbs more than 50 per cent of the drinking budget. Similarly, the area FEC corresponds to spirits dominating and in ADF wine dominates. More generally, as the budget point moves away from any of the three vertices A, B, C towards the centre of the surface ABC (or DEF), consumption patterns become less intensive in one beverage and more diversified. The geometry of beverage intensity is further elaborated in Panel B of Figure 6.4. It is evident that each of the three specialisation structures is itself a tetrahedron, whereas diversified budgets are associated with a truncated cube – a cube with a tetrahedron "sliced" off it.

Figure 6.5 gives the budget points for each of the 44 countries at the beginning and end of the period. The overall pattern is a movement away from the specialisation corners towards the centre. In 1997, spirits dominated in four countries, but by 2006 this role of spirits disappeared in all cases. The dominant roles of the other two beverages also decreased over the period, but more modestly. The dominant role of wine decreased from 6 to 5 countries and that of beer from 16 to 15, again reflecting an international homogenisation of drinking patterns.

The standard deviation was used above as a measure of dispersion of consumption across countries. Now we consider dispersion in a different dimension, viz. across beverages, and use the entropy, which is a natural measure of the diversity of consumption patterns (Theil, 1967, Chapter 4; Theil and Finke, 1983). If there are n goods in the consumption basket with budget shares $w_1, \ldots, w_n$, their entropy is then:

$$H = \sum_{i=1}^{n} w_i \log \frac{1}{w_i}$$

This H takes a minimum of 0 when consumption is specialised in one good, so that $w_i = 1$ for some i and all other shares vanish. When each w_i equals $1/n$, then H takes its maximum value of $\log n$. It is

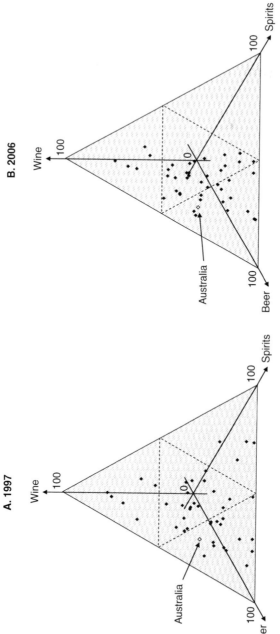

Figure 6.5. Drinking patterns in 44 countries

Table 6.13: *Alcohol entropies, 1997–2006 (×100)*

Country	1997	1998	1999	2000	2001	2002	2003	2004	2005	2006	Average
Western Europe											
Austria	10.28	9.97	10.20	10.27	9.97	10.12	10.18	9.81	9.74	9.80	10.03
Belgium	4.47	5.02	5.69	5.57	5.62	5.76	6.14	6.14	6.24	6.30	5.69
Denmark	10.23	10.08	10.25	10.20	10.01	10.47	10.30	9.63	9.54	9.61	10.03
Finland	10.01	9.11	8.53	8.29	7.21	6.66	5.73	6.87	6.77	6.97	7.61
France	15.90	16.03	17.31	16.88	16.21	16.50	15.94	16.29	15.99	15.56	16.26
Germany	1.64	1.48	1.73	1.83	2.00	1.96	1.90	1.90	1.75	1.57	1.78
Greece	7.79	7.48	7.42	7.40	9.10	9.43	10.50	11.38	11.17	11.23	9.29
Ireland	2.01	1.82	1.42	1.13	0.91	0.74	0.49	0.27	0.17	0.23	0.92
Italy	35.72	33.83	32.97	31.29	30.56	28.56	27.05	25.16	25.07	25.11	29.53
Netherlands	1.27	1.52	1.80	2.12	2.40	2.74	2.70	3.45	3.94	4.64	2.66
Norway	7.67	6.67	5.80	4.91	4.78	4.68	2.14	1.53	1.27	1.32	4.08
Portugal	26.96	26.36	22.81	21.70	20.79	21.06	20.11	20.30	19.92	19.39	21.94
Spain	0.90	0.88	0.55	0.41	0.45	0.60	0.67	0.73	0.70	0.65	0.65
Sweden	0.07	0.13	0.33	0.48	0.58	0.79	1.70	2.24	2.66	3.04	1.20
Switzerland	39.23	38.82	39.19	41.23	41.29	40.95	40.62	39.52	35.97	35.60	39.24
UK	29.95	29.30	31.85	33.55	30.88	30.03	30.41	32.19	32.48	33.98	31.46
Eastern Europe											
Bulgaria	7.98	7.01	5.88	5.91	7.15	6.23	6.00	5.91	6.40	6.55	6.50
Czech	10.65	10.17	9.78	8.91	8.23	7.33	6.43	5.98	5.65	5.22	7.84

Hungary	1.02	0.94	0.85	0.43	0.28	0.20	0.14	0.00	0.00	0.01	0.39
Poland	20.57	17.87	16.70	15.18	15.12	14.49	14.55	14.72	14.70	14.73	15.86
Romania	4.63	7.48	9.28	15.28	14.75	12.82	11.48	10.77	8.51	5.54	10.05
Russia	20.32	13.12	15.60	12.51	10.11	8.24	6.95	5.83	5.06	6.18	10.39
Slovakia	3.31	2.36	0.88	0.51	0.37	0.82	0.98	1.12	1.57	1.91	1.38
Ukraine	4.17	4.96	8.61	8.07	6.98	5.74	6.94	7.77	9.61	10.31	7.32
North America											
Canada	7.27	7.20	6.56	5.65	5.20	4.81	5.07	4.74	3.89	3.41	5.38
USA	11.00	11.06	10.29	10.64	10.79	10.52	10.01	10.04	9.38	9.41	10.31
Latin America											
Argentina	24.46	23.37	22.98	24.71	23.96	24.43	21.35	20.69	19.71	19.19	22.49
Brazil	8.70	7.98	3.76	4.48	6.98	7.95	6.92	8.08	8.07	8.35	7.13
Chile	0.69	1.14	2.53	3.23	3.95	2.92	3.39	3.93	2.85	2.65	2.73
Colombia	51.48	46.99	40.20	33.95	28.57	30.04	30.18	30.99	34.08	35.63	36.21
Mexico	49.04	50.25	52.76	53.81	57.02	54.49	53.61	52.24	48.36	49.13	52.07
Venezuela	43.07	43.98	44.18	42.20	45.54	44.46	56.80	48.08	45.02	47.72	46.10
Asia Pacific											
China	36.45	28.75	23.84	20.17	17.74	16.16	15.20	15.33	15.60	15.59	20.48
Hong Kong	26.04	35.88	23.67	17.13	14.23	14.39	13.90	14.30	12.22	10.44	18.22
Japan	19.38	19.93	19.02	18.57	19.37	17.52	16.51	17.50	16.65	15.18	17.96
Philippines	34.28	32.41	31.98	32.18	32.26	31.17	30.41	31.06	30.73	30.51	31.70
Singapore	17.17	15.68	12.37	11.43	16.56	16.36	14.38	18.27	19.43	19.07	16.07

Table 6.13: (continued)

Country	1997	1998	1999	2000	2001	2002	2003	2004	2005	2006	Average
South Korea	27.56	23.20	22.34	24.74	21.83	19.56	19.28	18.00	17.65	16.87	21.10
Taiwan	1.37	5.51	6.31	4.80	4.04	1.88	1.86	1.91	2.25	2.52	3.25
Thailand	46.93	43.23	37.30	35.81	34.42	32.23	31.88	31.13	29.85	29.85	35.26
Australasia											
Australia	13.80	13.45	13.38	12.93	12.87	13.06	13.64	14.31	14.97	15.48	13.79
New Zealand	8.62	8.52	8.79	8.81	9.11	9.49	10.02	10.37	10.36	10.42	9.45
Africa, Middle East											
Israel	27.14	25.17	24.38	23.60	22.54	21.74	21.68	20.56	21.12	22.18	23.01
South Africa	23.11	22.80	22.41	19.63	19.62	24.20	24.73	24.44	21.33	21.49	22.37
Average	17.14	16.57	15.78	15.28	15.05	14.64	14.57	14.44	14.05	14.10	15.16

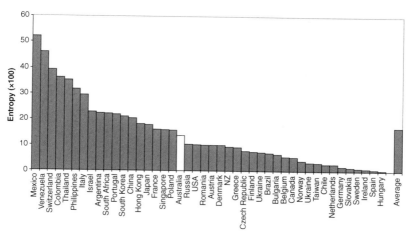

Figure 6.6. Alcohol entropies in 44 countries, average 1997–2006 (× 100)

convenient to express the entropy as a deviation from its maximum, $H' = \log n - H$, so that:

$$H' = \sum_{i=1}^{n} w_i \left(\log w_i - \log \frac{1}{n} \right). \qquad (6.11)$$

This measure is a weighted average of the logarithmic deviations of the budget shares from their mean, $1/n$, where the weights are the budget shares. Accordingly, $H' \times 100$ is approximately the average percentage distance of the n budget shares from their mean and thus is a measure of dispersion of the shares across commodities. The value of H' varies between 0, when each w_i equals $1/n$, and $\log n$, when $w_i = 1$ for some i. Thus, when the shares are more equal, total expenditure is more widely distributed over goods, there is more diversity in the consumption basket and H' takes lower values. Conversely, H' is higher when there is more specialisation in consumption.

Table 6.13 applies the entropy (6.11) to the alcohol budget shares in each country in each year, so that $n = 3$. In the majority of countries, H' decreases over time, indicating that drinking patterns become more diversified. The last column of the table, which refers to the averages over the 10-year period, shows that Mexico has the largest value at approximately 52 per cent, reflecting the large diversity of its budget shares; on average, these are beer 78 per cent, wine 1 per cent and spirits 21 per cent (Table 6.11). The smallest average entropy is for

Hungary (0.4 per cent). In Figure 6.6 we plot the average entropy, which reveals that Australia occupies a middle-ranking position, indicating that the behaviour of its drinkers is unexceptional.

6.9 International drinking patterns II: quantities and prices

This section examines the international differences and similarities of the volume and price components of the alcohol budget shares. The link between budget shares, prices, quantities and income is discussed in Appendix A6.2.

Table 6.14 shows the quantities consumed per capita of the three beverages, averaged over the 10-year period (columns 2–4). These quantities are plotted in Figure 6.7 and it is evident that for each beverage there is substantial variability across countries. Australia, which is highlighted in each panel, is one of the larger beer-drinking countries, and the same is true for wine. However, consumption of spirits is substantially lower in Australia than in many other countries. Columns 5–7 of Table 6.14 contain the log-changes in quantities, again averaged over time. These log-changes are plotted in Panels A–C of Figure 6.8, from which it can be seen that the values for Australia are not at either the high or low ends of the growth spectrum. The overall growth in the volume of consumption of the beverages can be measured by the conditional Divisia volume index mentioned in Section 6.7. This volume index, averaged over 1997–2006, is given in column 8 of Table 6.14 and is plotted in Panel D of Figure 6.8. Again, in comparison with other countries, Australian drinkers do not really distinguish themselves by having a particularly large or small growth in overall consumption.

Next, we consider parallel information on prices. The prices in columns 2–4 of Table 6.15 are nominal, so their differences across countries reflect in part differences in overall price levels. To eliminate the impact of these nominal differences, we use the changes in relative prices $Dp_{it} - DP_t$, where $Dp_{it} = \log p_{it} - \log p_{i,t-1}$ is the log-change in the price of good i and $DP_t = \sum_{i=1}^{3} \bar{w}'_{it} Dp_{it}$ is the Divisia price index of alcohol, with $\bar{w}'_{it}$ the conditional budget share of beverage i. These relative price changes for alcohol, averaged over the 10-year period, are given in columns 5–7 of Table 6.15 and plotted in Figure 6.9. The evolution of prices in Australia is again towards the centre of the cross-country distributions.

Table 6.14: *Quantity of alcoholic beverages consumed, average 1997–2006*

| Country | Level (Litres per capita) | | | Log-change (×100) | | | Divisia index (×100) |
(1)	Beer (2)	Wine (3)	Spirits (4)	Beer (5)	Wine (6)	Spirits (7)	(8)
Western Europe							
Austria	67.19	16.04	2.02	-0.735	1.721	-1.023	0.175
Belgium	40.68	18.31	2.52	1.236	1.818	0.347	1.324
Denmark	69.44	26.81	1.90	-3.255	-0.068	2.109	-1.182
Finland	59.07	8.60	4.81	1.982	4.010	4.165	2.991
France	22.52	30.11	4.55	-0.977	-2.642	-0.509	-1.859
Germany	71.80	20.26	4.47	-1.037	1.325	-1.256	-0.231
Greece	12.98	11.50	1.96	1.743	0.809	0.567	0.933
Ireland	24.39	10.95	3.54	2.955	8.554	-2.921	2.547
Italy	16.67	31.86	1.33	1.968	-3.220	0.903	-1.862
Netherlands	54.48	18.54	3.06	-0.164	5.002	-4.615	0.787
Norway	39.92	9.94	2.22	-0.156	5.213	2.425	2.051
Portugal	30.45	32.39	1.84	1.234	-0.206	3.579	0.589
Spain	22.58	13.81	2.66	3.630	-1.989	-0.499	0.327
Sweden	44.02	14.15	2.41	-1.688	4.251	-2.070	0.562
Switzerland	26.89	30.02	2.15	0.589	-0.448	1.747	-0.060
UK	33.87	15.25	3.16	2.318	3.901	2.108	2.942

Table 6.14: (continued)

Country	Level (Litres per capita)				Log-change (×100)			Divisia index (×100)
	Beer	Wine	Spirits		Beer	Wine	Spirits	
(1)	(2)	(3)	(4)		(5)	(6)	(7)	(8)
Eastern Europe								
Bulgaria	36.50	4.07	4.92		5.953	4.827	0.706	3.856
Czech	84.02	8.55	5.82		−0.326	4.335	−1.302	0.092
Hungary	55.39	23.99	4.25		1.116	−0.061	−1.141	−0.063
Poland	41.66	6.43	5.71		6.941	−0.821	−0.915	1.918
Romania	37.62	9.97	3.42		8.103	−10.329	−5.235	0.147
Russia	40.50	5.83	14.37		15.159	1.864	−0.907	3.798
Slovakia	58.34	8.24	3.34		−0.073	2.645	−1.793	0.204
Ukraine	23.46	3.17	5.44		17.895	2.634	6.017	9.775
North America								
Canada	49.76	8.21	3.50		1.462	4.106	1.492	2.153
USA	63.26	6.10	3.63		−0.232	2.055	1.065	0.539
Latin America								
Argentina	30.90	28.47	0.71		2.620	−3.605	−0.844	−1.050
Brazil	16.70	1.45	2.21		2.458	3.751	1.531	2.650
Chile	22.16	12.97	2.65		2.847	3.845	2.252	2.975
Colombia	25.18	0.39	1.64		−0.924	3.114	−1.194	−1.030
Mexico	39.52	0.12	1.20		3.127	4.163	1.171	2.804
Venezuela	70.92	0.23	2.98		0.789	2.743	2.218	1.217
Asia Pacific								
China	12.84	0.69	3.19		5.628	6.434	−9.900	−3.080

Hong Kong	12.98	0.72	0.26	−7.005	1.484	−6.578	−5.077
Japan	38.52	5.67	5.74	0.477	−3.526	3.114	0.213
Philippines	10.24	0.05	5.30	2.368	10.898	0.742	1.794
Singapore	7.59	0.87	0.44	1.708	7.229	−9.214	1.901
South Korea	18.91	4.75	12.49	0.617	1.858	2.069	1.167
Taiwan	14.70	2.50	1.46	−0.212	−3.183	−6.293	−2.958
Thailand	14.00	0.06	8.46	14.446	10.898	1.001	6.141
Australasia							
Australia	68.97	16.60	2.09	−0.372	1.395	−2.154	−0.074
New Zealand	55.37	16.48	1.62	−0.579	1.663	−2.945	−0.064
Africa, Middle East							
Israel	5.30	1.48	0.26	0.326	3.515	0.000	1.236
South Africa	35.01	5.28	1.80	1.781	−1.628	−1.842	0.626
Average	36.98	11.18	3.49	2.176	2.053	−0.541	0.951

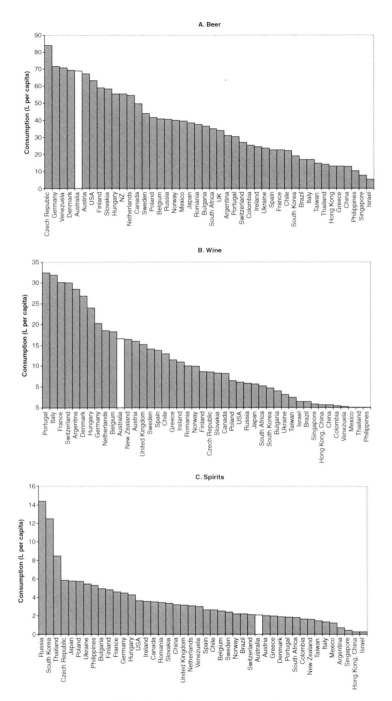

Figure 6.7. Quantity of alcoholic beverages consumed, average 1997–2006

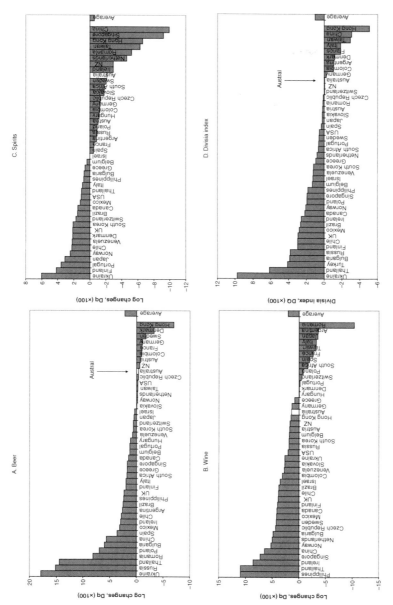

Figure 6.8. Changes in the quantity of alcoholic beverages consumed, average 1997–2006 (log-change × 100)

Table 6.15: *Price of alcoholic beverages, average 1997–2006*

Country	Level (domestic currency units per litre)			Deflated log-change (× 100)		
	Beer	Wine	Spirits	Beer	Wine	Spirits
(1)	(2)	(3)	(4)	(5)	(6)	(7)
Western Europe						
Austria	1.31	4.59	13.15	−0.007	−0.352	0.982
Belgium	1.52	4.85	14.90	0.738	−0.245	−0.662
Denmark	17.96	44.14	205.32	1.590	−0.723	−2.929
Finland	3.61	9.53	26.61	0.540	1.421	−1.928
France	1.54	4.76	13.37	−0.428	0.787	−1.606
Germany	0.92	3.09	9.54	−0.031	−0.489	0.802
Greece	1.84	5.50	15.19	−1.124	1.026	−1.302
Ireland	3.15	7.61	27.05	0.542	−2.642	1.733
Italy	1.35	2.82	10.94	−0.810	0.282	−0.659
Nether-lands	1.40	4.05	15.10	0.130	−1.422	2.154
Norway	41.81	114.02	404.95	−1.379	1.726	0.323
Portugal	1.34	3.73	13.41	0.494	−0.104	−0.247
Spain	1.23	1.98	12.40	−0.344	−0.433	0.704
Sweden	19.26	77.30	331.82	1.466	−1.000	−0.248
Switzerland	3.10	16.91	33.86	0.920	0.089	−1.583
UK	2.00	5.90	14.94	−1.221	1.401	−0.745
Eastern Europe						
Bulgaria	1.03	3.66	6.16	−3.137	−0.577	4.269
Czech Republic	22.33	78.86	267.48	0.179	0.005	−0.135
Hungary	206.91	509.20	3129.30	1.097	0.124	−0.986
Poland	4.52	7.76	42.39	−0.217	3.024	−0.634
Romania	1.83	3.80	9.88	−6.419	6.682	7.566
Russia	25.94	113.33	128.62	−2.064	1.352	0.379
Slovakia	28.93	161.27	408.15	0.592	3.276	−3.504
Ukraine	4.80	14.95	20.80	−0.902	1.347	−0.170
North America						
Canada	4.32	13.79	31.69	−0.740	0.938	0.428

Table 6.15: *(continued)*

Country (1)	Level (domestic currency units per litre)			Deflated log-change ($\times$ 100)		
	Beer (2)	Wine (3)	Spirits (4)	Beer (5)	Wine (6)	Spirits (7)
USA	1.90	6.69	16.19	0.463	−0.671	−0.487
Latin America						
Argentina	1.46	2.36	11.70	−0.237	0.120	0.467
Brazil	1.63	9.44	5.52	−0.096	3.268	−2.954
Chile	673.43	1167.20	3409.80	0.461	0.895	−2.098
Colombia	3373.70	15333.00	18469.00	−1.610	−1.274	5.458
Mexico	15.02	91.46	130.40	−0.245	0.172	1.256
Venezuela	1241.92	8683.70	9326.80	1.307	2.061	−3.805
Asia Pacific						
China	4.93	20.79	30.76	−2.219	−2.613	2.500
Hong Kong	25.94	177.49	306.72	−0.888	1.169	1.661
Japan	516.23	1093.70	987.86	−0.843	2.087	0.888
Philippines	53.65	479.54	98.16	0.186	−1.358	−0.174
Singapore	8.79	38.73	36.57	−0.640	−0.631	4.921
South Korea	3804.90	2728.50	2444.40	−0.551	5.335	−0.764
Taiwan	81.48	278.42	593.21	−2.021	−0.965	3.441
Thailand	62.47	749.45	145.07	−1.168	5.099	0.521
Australasia						
Australia	5.86	13.33	48.00	0.232	−0.467	0.122
New Zealand	4.70	13.13	50.79	−0.219	−0.029	0.886
Africa, Middle East						
Israel	21.57	36.83	62.28	−0.209	0.059	1.430
South Africa	11.17	19.71	55.72	−1.370	1.912	3.570
Average				−0.459	0.674	0.428

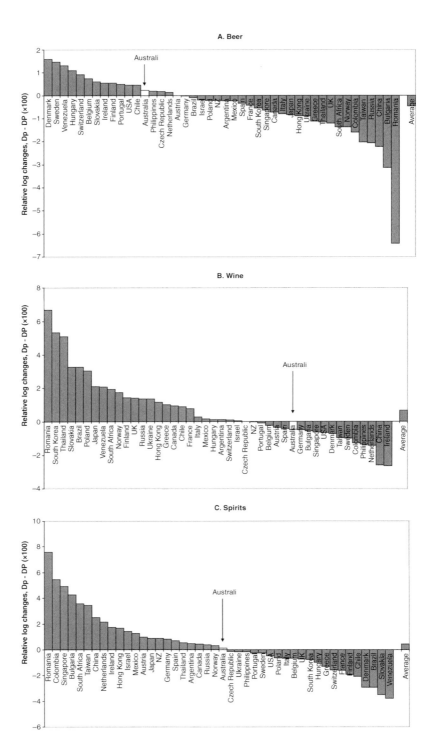

Figure 6.9 Relative price change in alcoholic beverages, average 1997–2006

6.10 Summary

Homo sapiens is a diverse species physically, culturally and behaviourally. Human beings are large and small, black and white, smart and dull, strong and weak; some believe in God and others in the market, whereas still others place their faith in government. There are meat-eaters and vegetarians, rice-eaters and bread-eaters, smokers and non-smokers, drinkers and abstainers, and so on. As such differences are so profound, at a basic level it is difficult to come to grips with even the concept of human diversity, let alone its measurement. It is thus clear that it is not easy to provide an unambiguous and complete answer to the question "Are Australians unique?".

In this chapter, we used the economic perspective to address this question and examined the substantial diversity of consumption patterns across countries. We showed that much of the variation in consumption of broad aggregates such as food, clothing, housing, etc. is accounted for by differences in incomes and prices across countries. At a broad level, this means that consumption is mostly driven by variation in observable economic variables. We also investigated patterns in income and price elasticities and found that, by and large, these were similar, if not identical, across countries. The conclusion is that although differences in tastes cannot be completely ruled out, they seem to be of minor importance. An analysis of alcohol consumption patterns revealed that the price responsiveness of consumption is very similar across countries and that Australia's drinking patterns are not substantially different to global norms. On this basis, we conclude that Australians are (probably) not unique, and there is some basis for thinking that many of the earlier results on the operation of markets for marijuana and related products in Australia are probably applicable to other countries.

APPENDIX

A6.1 The data and some further explorations

Table A6.1 lists the 31 countries used in Sections 6.3–6.5. The first 18 countries (USA–Spain) were members of the OECD in 1985 and are ranked in terms of GDP per capita in that year. The remaining

Table A6.1: *Alternative definitions of rich and poor countries*

Country	Mean per capita GDP in international dollars in 1985 prices	Definition of country groups					
		1	2	3	4	5	6
1. USA	13,012						
2. Switzerland	12,224						
3. Canada	10,879						
4. Australia	9,659						
5. Sweden	9,538						
6. Denmark	9,109						
7. France	9,086						
8. Norway	8,898						
9. Germany	8,548	Rich					
10. UK	8,466		Rich	Rich			
11. Japan	8,237				Rich	Rich	
12. Belgium	7,925						Rich
13. Austria	7,520						
14. Italy	7,512						
15. Netherlands	6,881						
16. Finland	6,702						
17. Iceland	6,673						
18. Spain	5,381						
19. Israel	8,077						
20. Hong Kong	7,035						
21. Singapore	6,420						
22. Puerto Rico	5,831						
23. Mexico	4,939						
24. Malta	4,398						
25. Columbia	3,053	Poor	Poor				
26. Ecuador	2,809			Poor	Poor		
27. Taiwan	2,677					Poor	Poor
28. Korea	2,271						
29. Thailand	1,795						
30. Sri Lanka	1,469						
31. Zimbabwe	1,290						

13 countries (Israel–Zimbabwe) are also ranked according to GDP per capita in 1985. The table also contains six alternative groupings of countries into "rich" and "poor". According to the first definition, the countries listed from the USA to Iceland are classified as rich and the

remaining countries as poor. In definition two, Spain is moved from poor to rich, and so on.

All computations in Sections 6.3–6.5 are based on definition two of the country groups given in Table A6.1. Clements and Chen (1994) use the other five definitions to recompute the budget shares and elasticities and find only minor changes. We also used these alternative groups to repeat the calculations of Sections 6.3–6.5 and found that, in the main, they were not particularly sensitive to alternative country groupings. Furthermore, we analysed the impact of individual commodities by re-doing the computations underlying Table 6.8 by successively omitting each commodity; again, the results were not overly sensitive to the inclusion/exclusion of any one good.

Recall from the last row of Table 6.5 (columns 11–12) that rich countries account for 25 per cent of the residual sum of squares for the world, with poor countries accounting for the remaining 75 per cent. This may suggest a three-fold higher weight for the rich group than for the poor, so that $\lambda = 0.75$. If we define international consumers in this alternative way, then, interpolating linearly from Table 6.7, the (unweighted) sums of squared residuals $(\times 10^4)$ are:

Rich	0.231
Poor	1.112
Rich + poor	1.343

Comparing these figures with the sums of squares from the demand equations with the individual-country coefficients (0.216, 0.643 and 0.859 for the rich, poor and the world, respectively, all $\times 10^4$; from row 9, columns 11–13 of Table 6.5) yields the following percentage increases:

Rich	7
Poor	73
Rich + poor	56

Relative to the results with $\lambda = 0.5$ discussed in Section 6.5, using $\lambda = 0.75$ improves the situation for the rich group and worsens it for the poor group and the world.

A6.2 Budget shares, prices and income

This appendix sets out the algebraic links between budget shares, prices and income. Although this analysis refers to the unconditional case of the overall budget with n goods, with appropriate reinterpretations it is equally applicable to a group of goods such as alcoholic beverages when the group is separable in the utility function.

A decomposition of the change in the budget share

The budget share of good i is $w_i = p_i q_i / M$, so its total differential is:

$$dw_i = w_i d(\log p_i) + w_i d(\log q_i) - w_i d(\log M) \qquad (A6.1)$$

where we have used the identity $d(\log x) = dx/x$. This shows the dependence of the budget share on the nominal price of the commodity, its quantity consumed and nominal income (strictly speaking, nominal total expenditure). It is convenient to formulate equation (A6.1) in terms of the relative price and real income using the Divisia index of the prices of the n goods, $d(\log P) = \sum_{i=1}^{n} w_i d(\log p_i)$. Adding and subtracting $w_i d(\log P)$ to and from the right-hand side of equation (A6.1) yields:

$$dw_i = w_i[d(\log p_i) - d(\log P)] + w_i d(\log q_i) - w_i d(\log Q), \qquad (A6.2)$$

where $d(\log Q) = d(\log M) - d(\log P) = \sum_{i=1}^{n} w_i d(\log q_i)$ is the Divisia volume index of the change in real income. The relative price and real income changes are given to the consumer; by contrast, the quantity change is determined by the consumer on the basis of prices and income. As the quantity depends on relative prices and real income, the relative price has two effects on the budget share, viz.:

- a direct effect, $w_i[d(\log p_i) - d(\log P)]$
- an indirect effect via the dependence of the quantity consumed on the price, $w_i d(\log q_i)$. This is the substitution effect of the price change.

Preference independence

To analyse further the indirect effect and its relation to the direct effect, we follow Theil (1975/76, pp. 31–2) and consider the simplified case of preference independence. As discussed in Appendix 4.5, the demand equation for good i under this condition is:

$$w_i \, d(\log q_i) = \theta_i \, d(\log Q) + \phi\theta_i[d(\log p_i) - d(\log P')] \qquad \text{(A6.3)}$$

where $\theta_i = \partial(p_i q_i)/\partial M$ is the marginal share of i, $\phi < 0$ is the income flexibility (the reciprocal of the income elasticity of the marginal utility of income) and $d(\log P') = \sum_k \theta_k \, d(\log p_k)$ is the Frisch price index. Equation (A6.3) is an infinitesimal-change version of equation (6.7) in this chapter. Substituting the right-hand side of equation (A6.3) for $w_i d(\log q_i)$ in (A6.2), we obtain:

$$\begin{aligned} dw_i = {} & (\theta_i - w_i) d(\log Q) + (\phi\theta_i + w_i)[d(\log p_i) - d(\log P')] \\ & + w_i[d(\log P') - d(\log P)]. \end{aligned} \qquad \text{(A6.4)}$$

This equation has three terms on the right involving changes in real income, the own-relative price and the difference between the Frisch and Divisia price indexes. We consider each in turn.

The income term is $(\theta_i - w_i)d(\log Q)$. To determine the impact of growth in real income $[d(\log Q) > 0]$ on the budget share, we need to know the sign of $\theta_i - w_i$, the excess of the marginal share over its budget share. As the income elasticity is $\eta_i = \theta_i/w_i$, this excess is positive for luxuries ($\eta_i > 1$) and negative for necessities ($\eta_i < 1$). Accordingly, when relative prices remain constant, the budget share increases (decreases) with income if the good is a luxury (necessity).

The relative price term in equation (A6.4) is $(\phi\theta_i + w_i)[d(\log p_i) - d(\log P')]$. The impact of an increase in the relative price of good $i\,[d(\log p_i) - d(\log P') > 0]$ is given by the term $\phi\theta_i + w_i$, which has two components. The first component is $\phi\theta_i$, which refers to the substitution effect of the price change. As the income flexibility $\phi < 0$ and each marginal share $\theta_i > 0$ under preference independence, the effect of an increase in the relative price of i is to lower its budget share on account of the substitution effect. The second component of the term $\phi\theta_i + w_i$ is w_i, which relates to the direct effect. As $w_i > 0$, the budget share increases with its relative price according to this direct effect. As the two effects move in opposite directions, the sign of the change in the budget share depends on the relative magnitudes of the indirect and direct effects, or on the sign of the term $\phi\theta_i + w_i$. Using $\eta_i = \theta_i/w_i$, the term $\phi\theta_i + w_i$ is positive when

$\phi\eta_i + 1 > 0$, or equivalently when

$$\eta_i < \frac{1}{|\phi|}. \tag{A6.5}$$

In words, the budget share of a good increases with its relative price when its income elasticity is less than the absolute value of the income elasticity of the marginal utility of income. This statement holds when (i) real income remains unchanged and (ii) the Frisch and Divisia price indexes coincide, so that $[d(\log P') - d(\log P)] = 0$. Condition (A6.5) restricts the own-price elasticity of demand $\phi\eta_i$ such that the direct effect of the price change dominates the substitution effect.

As discussed in Appendix A4.8, many estimates of ϕ are centred around the value -0.5, so $|\phi|^{-1}$ is likely to be of the order of 2, whereas the income elasticity η_i is of the order of one (since the Engel aggregation condition is $\sum_{i=1}^{n} w_i\eta_i = 1$). Accordingly, condition (A6.5) will be met in most cases; it will not be satisfied only when the commodity is a strong luxury. It is thus likely that the direct effect will dominate the indirect effect, which means that the budget share will increase with its relative price.

The final term on the right of equation (A6.4) is $w_i[d(\log P') - d(\log P)]$, which is a multiple w_i of the difference between the Frisch price index $d(\log P')$ and its Divisia counterpart $d(\log P)$. As the Frisch index is marginally weighted and the Divisia index is budget share-weighted, and since the income elasticity is the ratio of the marginal share to the corresponding budget share, it is clear that the difference between the two price indexes is related to the manner in which the relative prices of luxuries and necessities change. To clarify this, consider the n income elasticities $\eta_1, \dots, \eta_n$ which have a budget-share-weighted mean of unity, $\sum_{i=1}^{n} w_i\eta_i = 1$. Consider also the n price changes $d(\log p_1), \dots, d(\log p_n)$, which have a budget-share-weighted mean of $d(\log P)$. The budget-share-weighted covariance between the income elasticities and the price changes is:

$$C = \sum_{i=1}^{n} w_i(\eta_i - 1)[d(\log p_i) - d(\log P)]$$

This covariance is positive when, on average, the relative prices of luxuries increase and those of necessities decrease; it is negative in the converse situation and zero when relative price changes are independent of the nature of the goods. Note that as a budget-share-weighted average of relative price changes is zero, that is, $\sum_{i=1}^{n} w_i[d(\log p_i) - d(\log P)] = 0$, it is impossible for the relative prices of both luxuries and necessities to move in the same direction. In this sense then, the value of the covariance C measures the nature of the change in the structure of relative prices. It can easily be shown that the difference between the two prices indexes $d(\log P') - d(\log P)$ is equal to C. As the budget share is positive, the sign of the last term of equation (A6.4) is the same as that of the covariance C.

Combining the price terms
The relative price term in equation (A6.4) contains direct and indirect components, and condition (A6.5) reveals when the former dominates the latter. As discussed above, that condition holds when real income is constant and the Frisch and Divisia price indexes coincide. Although this is a perfectly acceptable formulation of the problem, as $d(\log P')$ and $d(\log P)$ both contain the individual price changes $d(\log p_i)$, we could still inquire if it is possible to combine all the price terms to go somewhat further. Of course, if all the prices change equipro-portionally, so that $d(\log p_i) = k$, then $d(\log P') = d(\log P) = k$ and this problem "disappears". But this is not a particularly interesting case, as it means that all relative prices remain constant. Alternatively, Theil (1975/76, pp. 31–2) assumes that prices change such that the numerical values of the Frisch and Divisia indexes coincide, thereby again causing the problem to vanish. This also occurs when all income elasticities are unity, so that $\theta_i = w_i$, $i = 1, \ldots, n$.

We investigate the above issue in the simplified case when only the price of good i increases by $d(\log p_i) > 0$ and all other prices remain constant. Then the relative price of i and the difference between the two indexes become:

$$d(\log p_i) - d(\log P') = (1 - \theta_i)d(\log p_i),$$
$$d(\log P') - d(\log P) = (\theta_i - w_i)d(\log p_i).$$

In this case, the sum of the second and third terms on the right of equation (A6.4) takes the form:

$$[(\phi\theta_i + w_i)(1 - \theta_i) + w_i(\theta_i - w_i)]d(\log p_i)$$
$$= [\phi\theta_i(1 - \theta_i) + w_i(1 - w_i)]d(\log p_i) \qquad \text{(A6.6)}$$

The sign of (A6.6) is determined by that of the term in square brackets in the second line, $[\phi\theta_i(1 - \theta_i) + w_i(1 - w_i)]$. On dividing by w_i this term is positive when $[\phi\eta_i(1 - \theta_i) + (1 - w_i)] > 0$, or when

$$\eta_i < \frac{1}{|\phi|}\left(\frac{1 - w_i}{1 - \theta_i}\right) \tag{A6.7}$$

Condition (A6.7) differs from (A6.5) by the multiplicative ratio

$$\frac{1 - w_i}{1 - \theta_i} \tag{A6.8}$$

When good i has a unitary income elasticity, this ratio is unity and conditions (A6.5) and (A6.7) coincide. Ratio (A6.8) is greater than unity for luxuries, so that, relative to condition (A6.5), the upper bound for the income elasticity in (A6.7) is now higher than before, and conversely for necessities. Inequality (A6.7) is the condition under which an increase in the nominal price of good i, p_i, leads to an increase in its budget share. Condition (A6.7) applies when (i) real income and the prices of all goods other than i remain unchanged and (ii) all three price terms in equation (A6.4) are combined.

A simple "linearised" version of condition (A6.7) can be obtained as follows. When θ_i is "small", $1/(1 - \theta_i) \approx 1 + \theta_i$, so that the ratio (A6.8) can be expressed as:

$$\frac{1 - w_i}{1 - \theta_i} \approx (1 - w_i)(1 + \theta_i) \approx 1 + \theta_i - w_i,$$

where in the second step the cross product $w_i\theta_i$ has been ignored as w_i and θ_i are both positive fractions. Thus, the approximate version of condition (A6.7) is:

$$\eta_i < \frac{1}{|\phi|} + \frac{\theta_i - w_i}{|\phi|} \tag{A6.7$'$}$$

The second term on the right is positive for a luxury, negative for a necessity and zero for the borderline case of a unitary income elasticity. As expected, the approximate condition (A6.7$'$) leads to the same qualitative conclusions regarding the range of the income elasticity as does (A6.7).

Notes

1. It is worth noting that Figure 6.1 is consistent with the Working (1943)–Leser (1963) Engel curve, $w = \alpha + \beta \log Q$, where α and β are constants.

2. The data are described by GMID as "off-trade", which excludes alcohol consumed on licensed premises. For details of GMID, see www. euromonitor.com/gmid. As they have relatively low (reported) per capita alcohol consumption, we exclude the following countries: Indonesia, Malaysia, Morocco, Turkey and Vietnam.

3. Using cross-country consumption patterns of beer and wine, Aizenman and Brooks (2007) reach a similar conclusion.

4. For related work, see Clements and Lan (2000) and Fogarty (2005, Appendix 2.2).

References

Aizenman, J. and Brooks, E. L. (2007). "Globalisation and taste convergence: the case of wine and beer." *Review of International Economics* **16**, 217–33.

Chen, D. (1999). *World consumption economics*. Singapore: World Scientific Publishing.

Chua, G. (2003). "Food and cross-country income comparisons." Discussion Paper No. 03.14, Economics Program, The University of Western Australia.

Clark, C. (1957). *The conditions of economic progress*, 3rd edition. London: Macmillan.

Clements, K. W. and Chen, D. (1994). "Fundamental similarities in consumer behaviour." Discussion Paper No. 94.03, Economics Program, The University of Western Australia.

Clements, K. W. and Chen, D. (1996). "Fundamental similarities in consumer behaviour." *Applied Economics* **28**, 747–57.

Clements, K. W. and Chen, D. (2007). "Food and affluence." Unpublished paper. UWA Business School, The University of Western Australia.

Clements, K. W. and Lan, Y. (2000). "World fibres demand." Discussion Paper No. 00.07, Economics Department, The University of Western Australia.

Clements, K. W. and Theil, H. (1979). "A cross-country analysis of consumption patterns." Report of the Centre for Mathematical Studies in Business and Economics, The University of Chicago (published in H. Theil, ed., (1996). *Studies in global econometrics*, Dordrecht: Kluwer, pp. 95–108.

Clements, K. W. and Qiang, Y. (2003). "The economics of global consumption patterns." *Journal of Agricultural and Applied Economics Supplement* **35**, 21–37.

Clements, K. W. and Selvanathan, E. A. (1987). "Alcohol consumption." In H. Theil and K. W. Clements, eds., *Applied demand analysis: results from system-wide approaches*, Cambridge, MA: Ballinger, pp. 185–264.

Clements, K. W. and Selvanathan, S. (1994). "Understanding consumption patterns." *Empirical Economics* 19, 69–110.

Clements, K. W., Wu, Y. and Zhang, J. (2006). "Comparing international consumption patterns." *Empirical Economics* 31, 1–30.

Clements, K. W., Yang, W. and Zheng, S. W. (1997). "Is utility additive? The case of alcoholic beverages." *Applied Economics* 29, 1163–7.

Fogarty, J. (2006). "The nature of the demand for alcohol: understanding elasticity." *British Food Journal* 108, 316–32.

Fogarty, J. (2005). *Wine investment, pricing and substitutes.* Unpublished PhD thesis, Economics Program, The University of Western Australia.

Friedman, M. (1962). *Price theory: a provisional text.* Chicago, IL: Aldine.

Houthakker, H. S. (1957). "An international comparison of household expenditure patterns, commemorating the centenary of Engel's Law." *Econometrica* 25, 532–51.

Kravis, I. B., Heston, A. W. and Summers, R. (1982). *World product and income: international comparisons of real gross product.* Baltimore, MD: Johns Hopkins University Press.

Leser, C. E. V. (1963). "Forms of Engel functions." *Econometrica* 31, 694–703.

Lluch, C. and Powell, A. A. (1975). "International comparison of expenditure patterns." *European Economic Review* 5, 275–303.

Lluch, C., Powell, A. A. and Williams, R. A. (1977). *Patterns in household demand and saving.* Oxford: Oxford University Press.

OECD (2004). *Purchasing power parities and real expenditures: 2002 benchmark year.* Paris: Eurostat and OECD.

Selvanathan, E. A. (1991). "Cross-country alcohol consumption comparisons: an application of the Rotterdam demand system." *Applied Economics* 23, 1613–22.

Selvanathan, E. A. and Selvanathan, S. (2003). *International consumption comparisons: OECD versus LDC.* Singapore: World Scientific.

Selvanathan, S. (1988). *A system-wide analysis of international and inter-regional consumption patterns.* PhD thesis, Economic Research Centre, Department of Economics, The University of Western Australia.

Selvanathan, S. (1993). *A system-wide analysis of international consumption patterns.* Boston, Dordrecht and London: Kluwer.

Selvanathan, S. and Selvanathan, E. A. (1994). *Regional consumption patterns: a system-wide approach.* London: Avebury Publishers.

Selvanathan, S. and Selvanathan, E. A. (2005). *The demand for alcohol, tobacco and marijuana: international evidence.* Aldershot: Ashgate.

Selvanathan, S. and Selvanathan, E. A. (2007). "Another look at the identical tastes hypothesis on the analysis of cross-country alcohol data." *Empirical Economics* 32, 185–215.

Stigler, G. J. and Becker, G. S. (1977). "De gustibus non est disputandum." *American Economic Review* **67**, 79–90.

Theil, H. (1967). *Economics and information theory*. Amsterdam: North-Holland.

Theil, H. (1975/76). *Theory and measurement of consumer demand*. Two volumes. Amsterdam: North-Holland.

Theil, H. (1987). "Evidence from international consumption comparison." In H. Theil and K. W. Clements, eds., *Applied demand analysis: results from system-wide approaches*, Cambridge, MA: Ballinger, pp. 37–100.

Theil, H. (1996). *Studies in global economics*. Dordrecht: Kluwer.

Theil, H., Chung, C.-F. and Seale, J. L. Jr. (1989). *International evidence on consumption patterns*. Greenwich and London: JAI Press.

Theil, H. and Finke, R. (1983). "The consumer's demand for diversity." *European Economic Review* **23**, 395–400.

Theil, H. and Suhm, F. E. (1981). *International consumption comparisons: a system-wide approach*. Amsterdam: North Holland.

Yuen, W.-C. (1999). "Food consumption in rich countries." In D. Chen, *World consumption economics*. Singapore: World Scientific. pp. 137–52.

Working, H. (1943). "Statistical laws of family expenditure." *Journal of the American Statistical Association* **38**, 43–56.

7 | *Perspectives*

KENNETH W. CLEMENTS

This book has dealt with the economic approach to drugs, that is, the application of economic principles to clarify the workings of drug markets. Three important aspects of this approach are as follows:

1. *The analytical framework of rational addiction provided by Stigler and Becker (1977) and Becker and Murphy (1988).* According to rational addiction, consumers exhibit forward-looking behaviour and trade off current benefits of using the addictive good today against its future costs. This framework clearly shows how conventional economic concepts apply to an addictive commodity.

2. *Micro data on the usage of drugs by individuals.* Large cross-sectional databases are increasingly used to study the determinants of individuals' drug consumption.

3. *Current experiments with decriminalising marijuana.* The unintended consequences of prohibition of drugs, such as criminality, corruption, violence, disrespect for the law and uncertain product quality associated with underground markets, are now recognised as representing substantial costs. Are these costs more than those associated with the likely increased consumption that would accompany the legalisation of drugs? Although it is difficult to give a precise answer to this question, some countries (such as the US and Australia) are now trialling policies of reduced penalties for the possession of small amounts of marijuana.

This book has dealt with all three aspects. For example, in Chapter 1 we gave considerable prominence to the theory of rational addiction. In Australia, the Commonwealth government has carried out a number of waves of a large-scale, national survey of the usage of illicit drugs known as the National Drug Strategy Household Survey since the mid-1980s. This survey was used extensively in Chapter 2 to investigate the nature of those who consume marijuana. In Chapter 5 we also conducted an analysis of the possible impact of complete

406

legalisation of marijuana and then subjecting it to taxation, so it would be treated like tobacco and alcohol. This analysis included projections of the consequential changes in the consumption of marijuana and the related goods tobacco and alcohol, as well as the amount of taxation revenue that the government could derive from marijuana.

In addition, we have presented research results on two other related topics. First, the patterns of marijuana prices in Australia were explored in Chapter 3. This included an investigation of the quantity discounts available when marijuana is purchased in bulk, the identification of regional disparities in prices and the substantial fall in prices. Second, in Chapter 6 we analysed differences in consumption patterns across countries. Using both broad commodity groups and alcoholic beverages (beer, wine and spirits), we found a tendency for consumers in different countries to be more similar than different. With respect to drinking patterns, we found that (i) there is a tendency for greater international homogeneity and (ii) despite popular perceptions to the contrary, Australians are unexceptional with respect to alcohol consumption. We interpret these findings as indicating that the results in the book pertaining to Australia are likely to have at least some applicability and implications for other countries.

A theme throughout the book is the uncertainties surrounding the workings of the market for marijuana. The importance of this theme makes it worthwhile to emphasise it once more. Due to its illicit status, there are no official data on marijuana prices and consumption, and we are aware that the measures used in this book are highly imperfect – though the best we could obtain or develop – and subject to more than the usual qualifications associated with economic data. Our approach to this issue has been twofold. First, throughout the book we have freely acknowledged the qualifications to data such as the prices we obtained from the police and the assumptions underlying our own estimates of marijuana consumption. Similarly, we have attempted to provide an awareness of the "reliability" or "robustness" of our estimates of key parameters such as the price elasticity of demand for marijuana. Second, to explicitly recognise the uncertainties underlying marijuana data and parameters, we introduced the idea of "stochastic vice", whereby a Monte Carlo approach is used to quantify uncertainty in the form of probability distributions of key variables such as consumption and the possible revenue from taxation.

Rather than reiterate the findings of the book in further detail, we confine the remainder of the chapter to a discussion of two issues that deserve further attention in subsequent research, namely, the supply side of the marijuana market and the implications of globalisation for illicit drugs.

7.1 The supply of marijuana

There has been considerable research into patterns in drug prices, including quantity and quality discounts, regional disparities, price trends over time and markups from the farm gate to final consumers. Chapters 3 and 5 provide references to and discuss key studies in this area. Although this research gives some indication of the nature of the supply side of drugs, the supply side per se has been a neglected topic.

A recent paper by Pacula *et al.* (2008) does, however, deal with the supply of marijuana, at least indirectly. As this seems to be the first paper in this area, it is useful to discuss it in some detail to highlight the importance of the supply side. The paper presents evidence that marijuana prices are higher in those states of the US that have decriminalised marijuana usage. This evidence is used to draw inferences about the nature of the supply curve in three steps:

1. A decrease in penalties for using marijuana is taken to shift the demand curve upwards and to the right.
2. This rightward shift of the demand curve is associated with an increase in prices.
3. The inference is then that the supply curve must be upward sloping, rather than horizontal or perfectly elastic.

This is illustrated in Figure 7.1, where DD is the initial demand curve, D'D' is the demand curve after decriminalisation, SS is the supply curve, point A is the initial equilibrium and B is the point of equilibrium after decriminalisation. It is evident that decriminalisation has the effect of increasing both the price and the quantity transacted from p_A, q_A to p_B, q_B. Thus, the price increase following decriminalisation is consistent with a rising supply curve.

Pacula *et al.* (2008) draw a sharp distinction between transactions risks on the buyer side and those on the seller side of the market. Risks on the buyer side shift the demand curve, whereas those on the seller

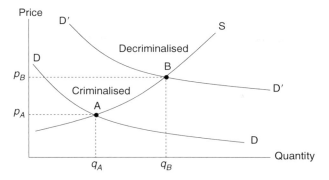

Figure 7.1. Decriminalisation and the marijuana market

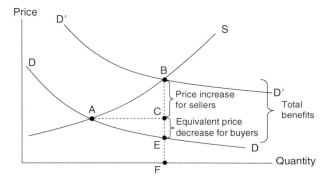

Figure 7.2. The incidence of decriminalisation

side shift the supply curve. Although this distinction is true, the workings of the market result in spillover effects from one side to the other, as illustrated in Figure 7.2. Here, the price received by sellers increases, whereas the "equivalent" price paid by buyers decreases. This equivalent price decrease for buyers is how much the price would have to decrease to generate the same increase in consumption using the original demand curve.[1] Thus, the "benefits" of the reduction in buyer transaction risk are shared between buyers and sellers, and this sharing of benefits is determined by the magnitude of the supply and demand elasticities. As revealed by Figure 7.3, as supply becomes less elastic, sellers capture a greater share of the total benefits.[2]

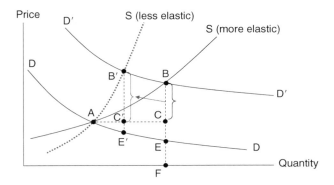

Figure 7.3. Sellers gain more when supply is less elastic

Studies of the impact of decriminalisation on consumption tend to find a small positive effect. However, as these studies typically omit the price, the two effects – decriminalisation and prices – are confounded in the coefficient of the decriminalisation dummy variable. The results of Pacula *et al.* (2008) can be used to isolate the "pure demand shift" from the composite effect as follows. Suppose decriminalisation leads to an increase in the quantity consumed of $\alpha \times 100$ per cent. Then, with q the quantity and p the price, the quantity demanded (q^d) can be expressed as $\hat{q}^d = \eta^d \hat{p} + \alpha$, where a circumflex denotes a proportional change (so that $\hat{x} = dx/x$) and $\eta^d < 0$ is the price elasticity of demand. We can write the quantity supplied (q^s) as $\hat{q}^s = \eta^s \hat{p}$, where $\eta^s > 0$ is the supply elasticity. The equilibrium price change resulting from decriminalisation is then:

$$\hat{p} = \frac{\alpha}{\eta^s - \eta^d} > 0. \tag{7.1}$$

It follows that when Pacula *et al.* regress prices on a dummy variable that takes a value of 1 if the state in question has decriminalised marijuana (plus other control variables), the coefficient for this dummy can be interpreted as the right-hand side of equation (7.1).

For example, in their Table 4 (column 5), Pacula *et al.* (2008) estimate this coefficient to be 26 per cent, indicating that prices are on average 26 per cent higher in decriminalised states. This value also has implications for the magnitude of the pure demand shift α.

Below we use equation (7.1) to solve for α conditional on various values of the demand and supply elasticity:

Supply elasticity η^s	Demand elasticity η^d		
	-1	$-1/2$	0
0	26	13	0
1	52	39	26
2	78	67	52

Using $\eta^s = 1$ and $\eta^d = -1/2$, for example, we see that the pure demand shift due to decriminalisation is as much as 39 per cent. This demonstrates that legal sanctions could possibly have a substantially greater impact on consumption than previously thought.

The supply elasticity plays another role within the above framework. As the change in the quantity supplied is $\hat{q}^s = \eta^s \hat{p}$, it follows from equation (7.1) that the change in the equilibrium quantity transacted following the demand shift is $\hat{q} = \eta^s \alpha / (\eta^s - \eta^d) > 0$ and the equivalent price change for consumers is this quantity change divided by the price elasticity of demand $\hat{q}/\eta^d$, or:

$$\text{Equivalent price change} = \frac{1}{\eta^d} \cdot \frac{\eta^s \alpha}{\eta^s - \eta^d} < 0. \qquad (7.2)$$

Whether or not consumers benefit from decriminalisation then depends on the net effect of the actual price increase and the decrease in the equivalent price. Adding the right-hand sides of equations (7.1) and (7.2), we see that:

$$\text{Net impact of decriminalisation on consumers} = \frac{\alpha}{\eta^s - \eta^d}\left(1 + \frac{\eta^s}{\eta^d}\right).$$

$$(7.3)$$

When expression (7.3) is positive, consumers lose from decriminalisation, as in this case the actual price increase (measured as a proportion of its initial value) exceeds the decrease in the equivalent price (measured the same way). As $\eta^d < 0$, expression (7.3) reveals that consumers lose when $\eta^s < |\eta^d|$, that is, when supply is less elastic than demand. Clearly, the magnitude of the supply elasticity is of considerable importance in evaluating the impact of decriminalisation in this way.

The above result can also be formulated geometrically. In terms of Figure 7.2, the proportionate increase in the actual price is BC/CF, whereas the decrease in the equivalent price is CE/CF. Consumers lose if BC > CE, that is, if point C lies more than halfway down the line BE. Visually, it is clear that the distance BC increases relative to CE as supply becomes less elastic (as in Figure 7.3) and as demand becomes more elastic.

Before concluding this discussion, two other points need to be made. First, Pacula *et al.* (2008) attribute the rising supply curve to risk aversion. They argue that expansion of the production of marijuana draws in new suppliers who are more risk averse and demand higher compensation for bearing the risk, leading to an increasing supply price. It is, however, also possible to explain the rising supply curve in terms of a constant degree of risk aversion. It could be that greater marijuana production increases the probability of detection and prosecution, so that the expected value of the per unit penalty increases with the scale of the industry. The rising supply curve then reflects this increasing expected penalty, even with constant risk aversion.

The second point to note is that the above formulation is slightly different to our treatment of the legalisation of marijuana. In Chapter 5, the impact of legalisation was to shift the supply curve down and to the right because producers no longer had to incur costs to avoid the ban; the demand curve remained unchanged. The quantity transacted increases with reduced penalties in both approaches, but the price of marijuana moves in opposite directions: up with decriminalisation according to Pacula *et al.* (2008) and down with legalisation according to us. The reason for this apparently contradictory result is the key difference in the two approaches. In the approach used by Pacula *et al.*, only the possession of small amounts of marijuana is decriminalised, so the objective of the policy is to reduce penalties faced by consumers. As the production and sale of the drug remain illegal, the increased quantity transacted entails more risk for producers, a risk that is priced via the rising supply curve. By contrast, when we suppose marijuana is legalised, there is no risk of prosecution for either buyers or sellers. This is why legalisation causes the risk premium to disappear and the price to decrease (before any tax is imposed) in our approach. Aside from this difference, the two approaches are similar as they both emphasise the role of risk as a significant influence on behaviour on the supply side.

7.2 Globalisation

Over the last several decades, transport costs have decreased, communication technology has improved and barriers to the movement of goods, people and capital across national boundaries have fallen noticeably. This has led to a substantial expansion of international trade, migration and capital flows, a phenomenon known as globalisation. Globalisation has led to lower prices of many consumer goods in Western countries, thus increasing real incomes. At the same time, however, it has had disruptive effects by putting substantial pressures on many domestic manufacturing and service industries in the West due to import competition and outsourcing. Thus, as a policy issue, globalisation generates considerable controversy. Although it seems entirely reasonable that the forces of globalisation would have important implications for the workings of drug markets, this is an under-researched area that should be the focus of more attention in the future. To give an indication of the issues involved, in what follows we provide a brief summary of Costa Storti and De Grauwe (2008a), one of the few papers on this topic.

The starting point is the decomposition of the retail price of drugs (p_r) into the price at the farm gate (p_f) and the margin (m), $p_r = p_f + m$, so that in terms of proportionate changes

$$\hat{p}_r = \varphi\hat{p}_f + (1 - \varphi)\hat{m}, \qquad \varphi = p_f/p_r. \qquad (7.4)$$

This equation states that the change in the retail price is a weighted average of that at the farm gate and the change in the margin, where the weight φ is the share of the retail price accounted for by the cost of the "raw" product, the farm-gate price. This share is small, of the order of 1 per cent. The margin is to be interpreted as inclusive of the value added in transforming the product from the bottom to the top of the supply chain. If, for simplicity, the margin is constant, then $\hat{m} = 0$ and equation (7.4) becomes $\hat{p}_r = \varphi\hat{p}_f$, which shows that as the weight φ is small, the retail price is relatively unresponsive to changes in the farm-gate price. Dividing both sides of the previous equation by the change in the quantity of drugs supplied ($\hat{q}^s$) and then inverting, we obtain the following expression for the price elasticity of supply at the retail level:

$$\eta^{sr} = \frac{1}{\varphi}\eta^{sf}, \qquad (7.5)$$

where $\eta^{sr} = \hat{q}^s/\hat{p}^r > 0$ and $\eta^{sf} = \hat{q}^s/\hat{p}^f > 0$ are the supply elasticities at the retail and farm-gate levels. Equation (7.5) shows that the small share φ "magnifies" the size of the farm-gate elasticity into that at the retail level. For example, if the farm-gate price is 1 per cent of the retail price, so that $1/\varphi = 100$, the retail elasticity is 100 times that at the farm gate.

The above supply-chain framework is shown in Figure 7.4, where S_rS_r and S_fS_f are the supply curves at the retail and farm gate levels, the margin is the (constant) difference between them and DD is the retail demand curve. Thus, the market-clearing prices, quantity and margin are p_r^0 and p_f^0, q^0 and m = p_r^0–p_f^0, respectively.

Over the past two decades the retail prices of cocaine and heroin have decreased substantially – to the order of 50 per cent or more – and Costa Storti and De Grauwe (2008a) use their framework to interpret this development. Increased production has the effect of shifting the farm-gate supply curve downwards and to the right, but because the margin is so high, this would have only a minimal impact on the retail supply curve. That is, from equation (7.4), because the weight φ is small, changes in the farm-gate supply price have a small impact on retail prices. Thus, increased production can probably be ruled out as a major cause of the price decreases. Similarly, a decrease in demand is also unlikely to be the source of the price decrease. The reason is that in view of the high elasticity of the retail supply curve S_rS_r in Figure 7.4, this would require an implausibly large shift downwards and to the left of the demand curve DD.

Costa Storti and De Grauwe (2008a) conclude that the most likely cause of the decrease in prices at the retail level is a squeeze in margins brought about by globalisation. Thus, in Figure 7.5 the decrease in the margin means that the retail supply curve shifts downwards and to the right to $S'_r S'_r$, with the retail price substantially decreasing to $p^1{}_r$. The quantity increases to q^1, whereas the farm-gate price increases to $p_f{}^1$; these changes agree with developments in cocaine and heroin markets over the last two decades. Costa Storti and De Grauwe argue that

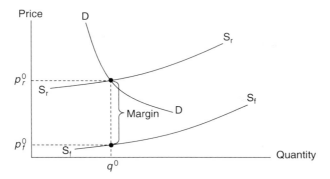

Figure 7.4. Supply chain for drugs

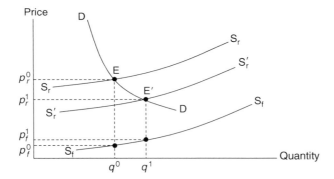

Figure 7.5. Globalisation and drugs

there are three mechanisms by which globalisation squeezes margins. First, there is a market-structure effect. Because of reduced trade barriers and transport costs, globalisation facilitates the entry of new firms into existing industries, thus promoting competition and destroying monopolistic practices. Second, the decrease in transport costs, the use of new information technologies and the increased sophistication of financial systems lead to an efficiency effect. Part of this effect includes the expansion of international trade, which makes it easier to conceal drugs. As Costa Storti and De Grauwe (2008a) put it, "The 'haystack' has become bigger each year making it more difficult to find the 'needle'".

Finally, the greater mobility of labour from low-wage to high-wage countries generates a larger pool of low-cost workers. These three effects of globalisation all lead to lower costs, prices and margins. Costa Storti and De Grauwe (2008a) argue that these effects are at work in the drugs industry, causing the decrease in margins. In the case of the third effect, the larger pool of low-cost workers, they interpret this to mean that globalisation has led to greater availability of workers willing to bear risk in return for the substantial rewards offered in the drugs industry, and refer to this as a risk premium effect.

It is clear from this discussion that globalisation can have profound effects on the way in which drug markets operate, effects that have substantial implications for public policy. In a related paper, Costa Storti and De Grauwe (2008b) summarise their argument as follows:

Globalisation has forceful effects in the drug market. The force of these effects can be gauged by the fact that as globalisation unfolded, governments of major drug consuming countries significantly tightened policies aimed at reducing supply. These policies in isolation should have increased retail prices, reduced consumption and production. We observe that exactly the opposite occurred: retail prices declined significantly, and consumption and production continued to increase. This suggests that the forces of globalisation more than offset the effects of supply containment policies. In this sense it can be concluded that these policies are waging a losing battle against the forces of globalisation.

Although the analysis by Costa Storti and De Grauwe (2008a, b) relates to cocaine and heroin, it probably also has implications for marijuana. If the process of globalisation continues, this could mean that more marijuana would be traded internationally, so that the physical and economic distance between producers and consumers would increase. There would be greater competition in the production and distribution of marijuana, which would put further downward pressures on retail prices and could lead to increased consumption.

Notes

1. This formulation uses the initial demand DD curve to define the equivalent price decrease. Alternatively, we could use the new demand curve D'D' to give an equivalent price increase to sellers. This results in exactly the same decomposition of the total benefits.

2. Let $\lambda = BC/BE$ be the share of the total benefits captured by sellers and $1 - \lambda$ be the share going to buyers. Then, $\lambda = \frac{1/\eta^s}{1/\eta^s - 1/\eta^d}$ and $1 - \lambda = \frac{-1/\eta^d}{1/\eta^s - 1/\eta^d}$, where $\eta^s > 0$ and $\eta^d > 0$ are the price elasticities of supply and demand.

References

Becker, G. S. and Murphy, K. M. (1988). "A theory of rational addiction." *Journal of Political Economy* 96, 675–700.

Costa Storti, C. and De Grauwe, P. (2008a). "Globalisation and the price decline of illicit drugs." *International Journal of Drug Policy* 20, 48–61.

Costa Storti, C. and De Grauwe, P. (2008b). "Modelling the cocaine and heroin markets in the era of globalisation and drug reduction policies." Paper presented at CESifo Venice Summer Institute 2008, Venice International University.

Pacula, R. L., Kilmer, B., Grossman, M. and Chaloupka, F. J. (2008). "Risks and prices: The role of user sanctions in marijuana markets." Paper presented at CESifo Venice Summer Institute 2008, Venice International University.

Stigler, G. J. and Becker, G. S. (1977). "De gustibus non est disputandum." *American Economic Review* 67, 79–90.

Index

1925 Geneva Convention on Opium
  and Other Drugs, 249

Aagaard, J., 254
AIHW, 19, 21, 23
Aizenman, J., 351, 403n
Alcohol consumption, 156
  international drinking patterns
    budget shares, 373
    quantities and prices, 386
Allen, R. G. D., 164
Arrow, K. J., 139n
Asher, C. J., 138n
Atkinson, A. B., 237
Australian Bureau of Criminal
    Intelligence, 70, 84, 127
Australian Bureau of Statistics, 56, 76,
    127, 151, 187, 199–201
Australian Drug Foundation, 250, 252
Australian Institute of Health and
    Welfare, 287
Australian marijuana laws and
    regulations, 249
Australian National Drug Strategy
    Household Survey, 1, 9, 16,
    18, 19, 24, 33, 46, 53, 110,
    149, 150, 198, 250

Barten, A. P., 166, 204, 224, 227
Basov, S., 89, 248
Bates, S. W., 320
Baumol, W., 103
Becker, G. S., 5, 6, 7, 8, 16, 230n, 350,
    406
Berndt, E. R., 83
Bowley, A. L., 164
Bretteville-Jenson, A. L., 245–47
Britton, E., 315
Brooks, E. L. 351, 403n
Brooks, R., 228

Brown, A., 229
Brown, G. F., 99
Bruni, L., 139n
Buiter, W., 8

Cameron, L., 6, 16, 17, 36, 178, 259,
    261, 262, 271, 272, 342n
Cameron, S., 270
Cannabis Expiation Notice Scheme, 250
Caputo, M. R., 320, 321, 329
Caulkins, J. P., 68, 69, 70, 93, 99, 102,
    138n, 139n, 327, 328
Chaloupka, F. J., 11, 16, 36, 257, 270,
    272, 342n
Chen, D., 229, 351, 352, 356, 358, 397
Chua, G., 351
Cicala, S. J., 230n
Clark, C., 351
Cleeland Report, 152
Clements, K. W., 5, 17, 68, 70, 84, 97,
    106–08, 110n, 112n, 115, 129,
    139n, 140n, 146, 167, 168, 199,
    203, 210, 224, 227, 228, 260, 262,
    263, 266, 271, 336, 342n, 351,
    352, 356, 358, 373, 397, 403n
Clough, A., 254
Cocaine and heroin, 21, 33, 414
Collins, D. J., 15
Commonwealth of Australia, 235, 249,
    250
Consumption models
  demand equations. See Demand
    equations
  multivariate probit models, 35
    cocaine and heroin, 36, 37
    marginal effects, 41
    tobacco and alcohol, 36
    unconditional versus conditional
      probabilities, 43
    unobservable factors, 36

418

ordered probit model, 52
probit model, 29, 52
  marginal effects, 30
Rotterdam model, 166, 167, 185,
  223, 369, 373
sequential model, 49
simulating consumption, 189
zero-inflated ordered probit model, 54
Cooney, A., 3, 8
Costa Storti, C., 413, 414, 416
Crafts, N., 103
Cude, B., 139n
Culyer, A. J., 245
Curtis, R., 69, 138n

Dalhuisen, J. M., 182
Damrongplasit, K., 260
Daryal, M., 17, 70, 106, 107, 108,
  110n, 112n, 115, 139n, 140n,
  146, 171–81, 230n, 262, 263,
  272, 336, 342n
De Grauwe, P., 413, 414, 416
Deaton, A. S., 186, 226, 229
Decker, S. L., 272
Decriminalisation
  Australia, 258
  impact on consumers, 411
  USA, 257
Degenhardt, L., 138n
DeJanvry, A., 228
Demand equations
  budget shares, prices and income, 398
  consumption theory, 202
  demand for groups of goods and
    demand within groups, 215
  differential demand system, 205
  Marshallian demand equations, 203
  price sensitivity of consumption,
    160, 165
  pure demand shift, 410
  Rotterdam model. See Consumption
    models
DeSimone, J., 36, 257
Dietze, P., 138n
Diewert, W. E., 105, 134, 135, 136
DiNardo, J., 17, 36, 257, 327
Divisia indexes
  price, 160, 357, 369
  price-quantity covariance, 163
  size variances, 100

variances, 163
volume, 160, 185, 206, 357, 369
Dixon, P. B., 265
Donnelly, N., 252, 258, 259
Duffy, M., 272

Easton, S. T., 320
Economic approach to drugs, 4
Economics of taxation, 237
  tax incidence, 237
  welfare economics of tax, 240
Ecstasy (designer drugs), 20
Edwards, D. G., 138n
Engel's law, 352, 356
Entropy, 380
Espey, J. A., 182–183
Espey, M., 182–183
Euromonitor International's Global
  Market Information Database,
  374

Farrelly, M. C., 16, 36, 257, 272
Finke, R., 380
Fisher, I., 247
Fogarty, J., 170, 351, 403n
Food consumption, 352
Friedman, M., 7, 350
Frisch, R., 227
Fullerton, D., 237

Gallet, C. A., 184, 270
Gateway theory, 17
Gazérian, J., 139n
Gerstner, E., 139n
Geweke, J., 342n
Glaister, S., 182
Globalisation, 413
Goel, R. K., 272
Goodwin, P., 182
Graham, D., 182
Griffiths, W., 265, 342n
Grilli, E. R., 123
Grossman, M., 16
Gruber, J., 12

Hahn, F. H., 139n
Hall, W., 12, 235, 258
Harris, M., 16, 17, 34, 37, 40, 46, 51,
  52, 54, 55, 57, 64n, 178, 262,
  271, 342n

Hazell, M., 106
Hedonic regressions, 105, 134
Hess, J. D., 139n
Horowitz, J. L., 138n
Houthakker, H. S., 268, 351
Howard, C., 123, 126

Index-numbers
    Divisia indexes. See Divisia indexes
    Frisch price index, 186
    stochastic price index, 98
    theory, 97, 136
Infringement notices, arrests and
    prosecutions, 127
International consumers, 362
International Monetary Fund, 103

Jiggens, J., 155
Johnson, L. W., 5, 199, 271
Johnston, L. D., 257
Jones, A. M., 272, 322
Jones, C., 322

Kravis, I. B., 229, 351
Kyvig, D. E., 247, 248

Laixuthai, A., 36, 257
Lan, Y., 403n
Lapsley, H. M., 15
Lemieux, T., 17, 36, 257
Leser, C. E. V., 402n
Lesourd, J.-B., 139n
Lind, B., 327
List, J. A., 184, 270
Lluch, C., 228, 351

MacCoun, R. J., 11, 12
Mahmoudi, P., 6, 179, 261
Maloof, D., 257
Manderson, D., 249, 250
Manski, C. F., 138n
Marijuana
    consumption, 148
    legalisation, 20, 235, 291
    prices. See Prices
    supply, 408
    taxing marijuana, 291, 337
    trends for consumption, 20
Marks, R. E., 152
McKinley, A., 322
Metcalf, G. E., 237

Mills, G., 104n, 139n
Miron, J. A., 8, 247, 248, 320, 325,
    326, 327, 337, 344n
Model, K., 257
Moore, T. J., 102, 138n
Morey, M. J., 272
Murphy, K. M., 5, 6, 16, 406

Nadelmann, E., 8
New Zealand House of Representatives
    Health Committee, 12
Nisbet, C. T., 146, 148, 171, 178
Nordhaus, W. D., 83
NSW Bureau of Crime Statistics and
    Research, 127

OECD, 354
Office of Crime Statistics and
    Research, 127
Office of National Drug Control
    Policy, 102, 138n
Ostrom, B. J., 320, 321, 329

Pacula, R. L., 6, 12, 17, 36, 138n, 235,
    236, 257, 258, 334, 408, 410, 412
Padman, R., 93, 99, 139n
Park, S. U., 139n
Penington Report, 198
Pigou, A. C., 186
Powell, A. A., 351
Preference independence, 166, 213,
    226, 369
    block structures, 213
    Pigou's law, 186
    structure of preferences, 212
Price elasticities
    conventional price elasticity, 145, 147
    participation elasticity, 145, 147
    Rule of minus one-half, 184, 372
Prices
    commodity prices, 123
    conventional pricing, 69
    equalising price differences, 105
    experience good, 69
    geography, 78
    index of marijuana prices, 108
    location, 68
    marijuana prices, 106, 112
    packaging, 96, 130
    pricing rule, 102

pricing strategies, 104
purity, 68
regional disparities, 73, 115
technical change, 102
The Economist, 81, 82, 123, 126
transaction size, 68
Productivity enhancement, 84
Prohibition, 244
in practice, 247
pros and cons, 244
Pudney, S., 12, 17, 18

Qiang, Y., 351, 356
Quantity discounts, 72, 90
cost differences, 91
discount elasticity, 94
logarithmic discount, 95
price discrimination, 91
risk, 92
surcharges, 104

Radio National, 73
Ramful, P., 6, 16, 17, 30–32, 35, 37, 38, 40, 42, 44, 46, 64n, 259, 263
Rappaport, N. J., 83
Register, C., 257
Reuter, P., 12, 69, 102, 138n, 327, 328
Rhodes, W., 155, 198, 230n
Rimmer, M. T., 265
Risk premium, 321
decomposition of drug prices, 327
distribution of the risk premium, 328
marijuana and tobacco price, 322
markups, illegal and legal, 324
Roffman, A. R., 257
Rosen, S., 105
Rule of six-tenths, 103

Saffer, H., 16, 257, 342n
Sandwijk, 198
Sapsford, D., 123
Schilizzi, S., 139n
Schwartz, A. E., 272
Schwer, R. K., 320
Selvanathan, E. A., 5, 170, 184, 227, 228, 229, 336, 342n, 351, 367, 370, 371, 373
Selvanathan, S., 5, 167, 170, 184, 227, 228, 229, 271, 342n, 351, 358, 367, 370, 371, 373

Sickels, R., 16
Silverman, L. P., 99
Single, E., 257
Skeels, C., 6
Socioeconomic characteristics of users, 23
Aboriginal, 26
age, 27
cocaine and heroin, 27
education, 23
education level, 26
gender, 23
heavy users, 45
income, 23, 26
married, 26
single, 26
Torres Strait Islander, 26
unemployed, 26
Speed (meth/amphetamine), 20
Stigler, G. J., 5, 147, 350, 406
Stiglitz, J. E., 237
Stone, R., 109
Suhm, F. E., 351
Sullivan, L., 229n
Supply elasticities at the retail and farm gate levels, 414

Tastes and geography, 367
Taubman, P., 16
Tellis, G. J., 183
Telser, L. G., 91, 105
The Economist Magazine, 8, 82, 123, 342n
Theil, H., 98, 160, 166, 167, 203, 210, 219, 224, 228, 229, 351, 380, 398, 401
Thies, C., 257
Tobacco and alcohol, 21, 33
Törnqvist, L., 129

United Kingdom House of Commons Science and Technology Committee, 12
United Nations, 152
University of Western Australia, 172
Crime Research Centre, 127
US National Household Survey on Drug Abuse, 198

Vakil, F., 146, 148, 171, 178
van Ours, J. C., 6, 12, 18

Vice
  consumption, 264
  interactions, 271
  stochastic, 279

Walker, R., 139n
Wallis, K., 315
Warburton, C., 247
Warner, K. E., 270
Weatherburn, D., 327
Wendel, T., 69, 138n
Wesney, D., 76
Western Australian Drug and Alcohol
  Office, 12
Western Australian Parliament Select
  Committee, 155, 230n
Whitesides, R. W., 103

Widrick, S. M., 139n
Williams, J., 6, 16, 17, 36, 178, 179,
  259, 261, 262, 271, 272, 342n
Williams, P., 103n
Williams, R., 103
Wodak, A., 3, 8
Working, H., 402n

Yang, M. C., 123
Yuan, Y., 327
Yuen, W.-C., 351

Zhao, X., 16, 17, 30–32, 34, 35, 37,
  38, 40, 42, 44, 50, 52, 54,
  55, 57, 178, 259, 262, 265,
  271, 342n
Zwiebel, J., 8, 247, 248